PROSPERITY VERSUS PLANNING

PROSPERITY VERSUS PLANNING

*How Government Stifles
Economic Growth*

DAVID OSTERFELD

T-154

New York   Oxford
OXFORD UNIVERSITY PRESS
1992

Oxford University Press

Oxford   New York   Toronto
Delhi   Bombay   Calcutta   Madras   Karachi
Petaling Jaya   Singapore   Hong Kong   Tokyo
Nairobi   Dar es Salaam   Cape Town
Melbourne   Auckland

and associated companies in
Berlin   Ibadan

Copyright © 1992 by Oxford University Press, Inc.

Published by Oxford University Press, Inc.,
200 Madison Avenue, New York, New York 10016

Oxford is a registered trademark of Oxford University Press

Permission has been received from the following publishers to quote from copyrighted works:
Hancock, Graham (1989), *Lords of Poverty*, New York: Atlantic Monthly Press;
de Soto, Hernando (1988), "Constraints on People: The Origins of Underground Economies and
Limits to Their Growth," in Jerry Jenkins (ed.), *Beyond the Informal Sector*,
San Francisco: ICS Press; Copyright 1966 by von Mises, Ludwig,
Human Action, Washington, DC: Regnery Gateway, Inc.
Reprinted by special permission from Regnery Gateway, Inc.

Library of Congress Cataloging-in-Publication Data
Osterfeld, David.
Prosperity versus planning : how government stifles
economic growth / by David Osterfeld.
p. cm.   Includes bibliographical references and index.
ISBN 0-19-507353-3 — ISBN 0-19-507614-1 (pbk.)
1. Developing countries—Economic policy.   2. Free enterprise—
Developing countries.   3. Economic assistance—Developing
countries.   4. Capitalism—Developing countries.   5. International
business enterprises—Developing countries.   I. Title.
HC59.7.O835   1992   338.9′009172′4—dc20   91-33042

1 3 5 7 9 8 6 4 2

Printed in the United States of America
on acid-free paper

For Emmy, Michael, and Sarah

PREFACE

This book has been several years in the making. When it was begun the Berlin Wall was intact; countries in the Warsaw Pact were armed, if not exactly dangerous; and the idea that communism or socialism was about to collapse was unthinkable. Those advocating a free-market approach were generally dismissed as reactionaries and ideologues.

The dominant development model, for both the development experts outside the Third World and the development practitioners inside it, was that of interventionism if not outright socialism.

Government, it was believed, was necessary to ensure that enough of what was earned was being saved, that investment was occurring in the right places, that the country was industrializing rapidly enough, that farmers were planting the right crops in the right amount, that families were having the correct number of children, that foreign investors were investing in the right places, using the right equipment, and paying the right wages, neither too high nor too low. No matter what the problem, government, it seemed, was the solution. That the government could be the problem rather than the solution to Third World economic lethargy was regarded as an idea bordering on lunacy. There were, of course, those intrepid few, Lord Peter Bauer in particular, who raised their voices in dissent. They pointed out that the king had no clothes; that far too often the results of the interventionist model were counterproductive to the point of tragedy. Few listened. The tragedies continued.

But in light of the African famine of the mid-1980s and the so-called collapse of '89 in Eastern Europe and the Soviet Union, the gap between interventionist promise and interventionist performance simply became too glaring to ignore. As events put the interventionist model on the defensive, it suddenly became permissible to question government's role in the economy.

This book is an attempt to present an alternative development model that is 180 degrees removed from the interventionist paradigm. Arguing on both theoretical and empirical grounds that the most effective means to promote economic growth is to establish a wall of separation between government and the economy, it proposes maximizing the role of the market while minimizing that of the government. While this may not guarantee economic growth, at least it does not preclude it at the outset. To put it in social science terms, the wall of separation is a necessary but not a sufficient condition for economic growth and development.

In the absence of government control, however, how can one be sure that resources will not be wasted or consumed too rapidly, that families will not have too many children, that enough of what is earned will be invested and that investment will go where it is most needed, and that multinational corporations will not take advantage of economically backward countries and their citizens?

These are some of the questions that I try to answer in this book. They necessitated that I go far beyond the bounds of traditional economics. Economic incentives are affected by the political framework within which they operate. Changing the political framework may change the incentives. Thus this book is, in some sense, an attempt to transcend today's highly artificial placement of economics and politics into hermetically sealed containers, acting as if one realm had no effect on the other. It is an attempt to return to the traditional approach of frankly recognizing the interrelationships between the two fields, to return to the study of what was once recognized as the field of "political economy."

Part I, comprising Chapters 1 and 2, presents my theoretical outlook, the way I see and interpret the world. Part II, containing Chapters 3, 4, and 5, demonstrates that much of the commonly held alarmist views regarding food production, resource availability, and population growth are myths flatly contradicted by the data. It also advances theoretical explanations to show why the alarmist views are fundamentally flawed. Chapters 6, 7, 8, and 9, comprising Part III, focus on specific issues pertinent to Third World economic growth and development. Chapter 6 analyzes foreign aid; Chapter 7 examines the role of multinational corporations and foreign investment; Chapter 8 looks at migration; and Chapter 9 focuses on the impact of political corruption. Finally, Chapter 10 advances the proposition that economic development requires the creation of a wall of separation between government and the economy and presents a strategy by which this separation might be achieved and maintained.

I would like to thank David Boaz, Ted Carpenter, and Melanie Tammen of the Cato Institute for their unflagging interest in the manuscript. Their suggestions and comments made this a better book. I am grateful to the Cato Institute for its generosity. Without its support, this book would not have been possible. I must acknowledge my debt to my colleague, Robert Schenk. Whenever I encountered a problem, and I encountered them frequently, I would barge unannounced into his office. He would invariably stop what he was doing, listen, and then suggest. More often than not his suggestions have found their way into the manuscript. I am indebted to him for both his intelligence and his patience. The former I relied on shamelessly; the latter I stretched to the limit. I would also like to thank Donald Davison, whose relentless search for a particular piece of information yielded results long after I had given up in despair. Finally, I want to acknowledge my secretary, Annette Carter, for her valuable bibliographical assistance. Compiling and checking scores of references is a tedious task that she handled with a good deal of skill and never a hint of complaint.

Although I have been influenced by the work and ideas of many individuals too numerous to mention, four in particular stand out. The two noted Austrian economists, Ludwig von Mises and Friedrich A. Hayek, have influenced the way that I have come to interpret the world. Their impact is evident on every page of this manuscript. My view of the so-called Third World has been shaped in large part by the writings of Lord Peter Bauer. And my work in the area of resource availability, agriculture, and population growth has been heavily influenced by the writings of Julian Simon.

Needless to say, I bear sole responsibility for all the mistakes contained in this manuscript.

My most profound acknowledgment, however, is to my wife, Emmy. Far too many times I left her alone, always using the same refrain: I've got to get this thing done. For her understanding, forbearance, and encouragement, I am eternally grateful.

Rensselaer, Ind.   D. O.
June 1992

CONTENTS

I

THEORETICAL FRAMEWORK

1

The Three Worlds

The Evolution of Terminology

In currently fashionable terminology, *Third World* refers to those states, comprising about two-thirds of the world's population, that are poor. But this was not always so. The term was coined in the early days of the Cold War to designate those states that were aligned with neither the *First World* nor the *Second World.* The First World referred to those countries, largely in the West, whose political systems were democratic and whose economic systems were, by and large, market oriented. The Second World referred to those countries, largely in the East, whose political systems tended to be authoritarian and whose economies were highly interventionist. Thus the term *Third World* did not originally imply anything more than a proclamation of noninvolvement in the bipolarism of the Cold War (Harris, 1987, pp. 7,11–12; Henkin, 1979, pp. 119–121). While the terms *First* and *Second Worlds* helped to distinguish between two contrasting and competing ideologies or ways of life, the term *Third World* did not imply that its members shared anything in common other than the desire to remain independent of the struggles of the first two worlds. The term referred neither to a particular political or economic ideology that its members shared, nor, for that matter, to the economic status of its members.

As the tensions between the first two "worlds" were gradually relaxed, the East–West conflict was overshadowed by what became known as the "North–South" conflict. It was only at this point that the identifying feature of the Third World, or the South, became that of poverty, as distinguished from the wealth of the so-called North, which in fact was actually the First World, or the West (Bauer, 1987; Bauer and Yamey, 1980, pp. 116–119). The Second World, or the East (most of whose members were clearly in the North both geographically and, insofar as their standard of living was concerned, economically) tended to align itself with the South against the North. Thus the meaning of the term Third World has evolved over the past two decades from the political notion of nonalignment in Cold War rivalries to an economic notion based on its members' low standard of living.

This transformation from a political to an economic concept has produced some rather interesting anomalies. Most obvious are the geographical anomalies. Such countries as Australia and New Zealand are considered part of the "North" even though they are farther south than most of the members of the "South." In fact, many "Southern" countries, including Mongolia, Iran, Turkey, Tunisia,

3

Afghanistan, and even the so-called leader of the Third World, China, are well north of the equator and some are at least partially north of the United States, the clear leader of the so-called North. Japan, which is not only south of Mongolia but located in the Far East, is regarded as part of the West (i.e., the North), whereas such western countries as Haiti, the Dominican Republic, and Cuba are viewed as members of the South. South Africa is not considered a member of the South, although it probably will be if and when it has a black government. West Germany was regarded as part of the North while East Germany was not. The Soviet Union, most of which lies farther north than the United States, was not regarded as part of the North and regularly portrayed itself as the champion of the South. For example, the Brandt Commission Report (Brandt et al., 1980, p. 31) defines the North as "the market-economy industrialized countries," thereby specifically excluding the Soviet Union and the Eastern bloc countries, which, it observes, "do not want to be lumped together with the West, or to be contrasted with the South in a division which they see as the consequence of colonial history."

Economic anomalies likewise abound. While poverty is supposed to be the distinguishing characteristic of the Third World, some of its members are better off than the affluent First World countries. There is no denying the grinding poverty in Ethiopia, Bangladesh, Mali, and Zaire, to name but a few. But, according to its original definition, the Third World would also include the United Arab Emirates, Qatar, and Kuwait, oil-rich Mideast nations that, according to official statistics, have the highest per capita gross national products (GNPs) in the world (see World Bank, 1986, pp. 180–181, Table 1). Other relatively prosperous Third World countries include Hong Kong (technically, of course, a colony), Taiwan, Venezuela, and Trinidad and Tobago. As Bauer and Yamey have pointed out (1980, p. 58), "The idea of a world one-third rich (the North) and two-thirds hungry (the South) is pure fiction. There is a continuous range of incomes in the world, both between and within countries."

Politically, while many Third World nations are authoritarian dictatorships, some, such as India and Costa Rica, are democracies. The demographic contrasts are also striking. China has over a billion people and India has about 800 million, while the Maldives has a population of 150,000, the Seychelles only 67,000. In terms of religion, India is Hindu; Pakistan is Muslim; Korea is Buddhist; much of the Mideast is Muslim; Latin America is Catholic, as are the Philippines and the African nation of Rwanda. Ideologically, many have been socialist or communist while some, such as Hong Kong, Singapore, and Taiwan, lean toward capitalism—although these latter have developed so rapidly that many no longer regard them as part of the Third World but as newly industrializing countries, or NICs, a transitional group whose levels of development place them somewhere between the Third and First Worlds (see Harris, 1987, pp. 200–203).

A Proposal for Conceptual Clarity

It is clear that the Third World or the South, is, as Thompson has commented (1983, p. 5), neither politically, economically, nor analytically a coherent entity.[1]

In contrast, distinctions based squarely on income differences, such as those between the more and less developed countries, are analytically coherent, as are those between the First and Second Worlds, or West and East, since, traditionally at least, they represented two conceptually distinct economic systems: capitalism, or the market system, and a *planned,* or *non-market,* system. It is true, of course, that there is not a perfect correspondence between the terms and the operation of the actual economies. And historically there has been neither a pure market system nor a pure non-market system. Yet every actual economy has been some blend of the two. It could not be otherwise, for there are, in fact, no other possibilities. It is precisely for this reason that conceptual purity is indispensable: given the complexity of the real world, controlled experiments regarding the operation of entire systems, or even parts of those systems, are not possible. Thus, variables can be isolated and "tested" only by using the laboratory of the mind. While all historically extant economic systems have blended or "mixed" market and non-market elements, it is only by isolating the market from the non-market factors that one is able to attribute a particular outcome of a particular economy to a particular economic process at work in that economy. But in the sciences of human action, such factors can only be isolated and examined mentally. This does not mean that empirical data are irrelevant. While such data cannot, strictly speaking, either refute or confirm a theory, if the results expected from a theory do not occur, then the conditions that would make the theory applicable are either not present or have been overridden by the presence of other, more powerful conditions. If this latter is consistently true, then one can conclude that the theory, although valid, is trivial. Conversely, if expected results regularly occur, the necessary conditions are powerful enough to consistently override the multitude of other factors that are present. The data do not refute the theory; it is the theory that allows one to interpret and understand the data.[2]

Moreover, the argument that there are only two distinct economic modes does not mean that economies lying between the two extremes are automatically to be disregarded. On the contrary, mentally isolating the two basic economic processes may indicate that it is possible to have "too much of a good thing." Analysis may show, for example, that some markets may function best when left unregulated, while satisfactory performance in others may require regulation. The result would be that economic development might if not require at least proceed optimally through a judicious blending of market and non-market factors, that is, that the best economic order from the standpoint of economic development would be a mixed, or mercantilist, system. This conclusion could be arrived at only by isolation and analysis of the various factors in the two pure economic types.

Thus, while the Third World is not a coherent entity, the First and Second Worlds are. In fact, since there are only two possible economic systems, one symbolized by the term *First World* or the *West* and the other by *Second World* or the *East,* all Third World countries can, for the purpose of economic analysis, be classified as belonging to either the First or Second World. This, it is obvious, would provide a means for making sense out of what is now little more than an incoherent conglomeration of disparate units. Unfortunately, the term *Third World* has become so much a part of common discourse and, somewhat inaccurately, little more than a surrogate for poverty, that its use cannot be entirely avoided in any study whose focus is economic development. Whenever this term is used within this book, it will be as a synonym for the "less developed world," unless otherwise noted.

Market and "Non-market" Economies: The Data

It is reasonable to suppose that the type of economic system would have an impact on economic development. Since the Third World has been dissolved into the First and Second Worlds, this assumption can be examined by comparing data available from countries that can be classified as relatively market oriented with data from those that are highly interventionist or relatively less market oriented. One can, to a limited degree, control for other factors, such as culture and history, by selecting countries that, except for their economic systems, are otherwise quite similar. Table 1-1 provides at least prima facie evidence of the impact of economic systems on economic performance. Those countries that are more market oriented have clearly outperformed their less market-oriented sister states. The evidence on this point is overwhelming.[3] As the socialist economist Robert Heilbroner recently acknowledged (1989, p. 98)

> Less than seventy-five years after it officially began, the contest between capitalism and socialism is over: capitalism has won. The Soviet Union, China, and Eastern Europe have given us the clearest possible proof that capitalism organizes the material affairs of humankind more satisfactorily than socialism: that however inequitably or irresponsibly the marketplace may distribute goods, it does so better than the queues of a planned economy.

Another Evolution of Terminology

Another significant evolution of terminology has taken place, of even greater importance than that of the Third World. It is the evolution in the meaning of such

TABLE 1-1.   Per Capita Gross Domestic Product (GDP), 1988

Capitalist Countries		Socialist Countries	
United States	$20,000	Soviet Union	$ 6,490
West Germany	18,000	East Germany	12,500
South Korea	4,045	North Korea	910
Taiwan	4,325	China	320
Hong Kong	8,260		
Ivory Coast	960	Ghana	410t
Kenya	370	Tanzania	258
Thailand	915	Burma	200

Source: Compiled from Central Intelligence Agency, 1989.

key terms as *socialism, communism, non-market,* and *central planning.* These words are typically used more or less interchangeably both in the popular press and in professional literature. But terms such as socialism and communism no longer mean what they originally meant. When both proponents and critics of socialism and communism in the nineteenth century used these terms, they meant something very definite: a non-market economy. This is clearly evident in the writings of Marx and Engels. In a market system, "commodities" are products produced not for direct consumption or use but for exchange (Marx [1867], 1906, p. 94). Socialism and communism were distinguished from capitalism precisely by the absence of commodity production, and thus the market. Marx stated quite clearly in *Critique of the Gotha Programme* ([1875] 1972, p. 14) that "with the cooperative society based on common ownership of the means of production producers do not exchange their products." And Engels, in *Socialism: Utopian and Scientific* (1972, pp. 72–75), said that "with the seizing of the means of production, the production of commodities is done away with. . . . Socialized production upon a predetermined plan becomes henceforth possible." (Also see Roberts and Stephenson, 1973.)

This was the way socialism was understood by its critics as well. The critique by the Austrian economist Ludwig von Mises in the early twentieth century ([1920] 1975) was precisely that, for any economy beyond the most primitive level, markets were indispensable for economic rationality. Since by definition socialism would replace the market with central planning, it would eliminate the possibility for economically rational decisions, and therefore would collapse. This argument will be presented more fully in Chapter 2.

In their zeal to defend socialism from the Misesian critique, as well as to exonerate it from blame for the horrible debacle of "war communism" in the Soviet Union between 1918 and 1921 (see Farbman, 1923; Lawton, 1927, 1932; Richman, 1981; Roberts, 1971, pp. 20–47; Steele, 1981), such proponents of socialism as Oscar Lange and H. D. Dickinson argued that market socialism, that is, markets controlled by a central planning agency, would produce better results than the free markets of capitalism. What is significant here is not whether the Lange–Dickinson rebuttal succeeded in rescuing socialism from the Misesian critique but that, whether intentional or not, these proponents of socialism introduced a radical change in the meaning of the term. Since, for Marx as well as for most other nineteenth-century socialists, socialism quite literally was incompatible with the market, they would regard market socialism as a contradiction in terms.

Moreover, there was little doubt that the Soviet economy, whatever it was, differed fundamentally from the economies of the Western countries. Because the Soviet Union proclaimed itself a socialist society, it rather quickly became common practice to refer to its economy as socialist or communist. This practice had an interesting consequence. Since the Soviet Union still had markets and market prices, however distorted these were, and since whatever happened in the Soviet Union was by definition socialist, it became impossible to argue that such phenomena were not really socialist. Thus with the passage of time the meaning of the words *socialism* and *communism* came to refer less to a particular economic doctrine and became more a mere description of economic processes in the Soviet Union and other self-proclaimed communist countries.

Nowadays, the meaning commonly attached to such terms as *non-market* and *central planning* seldom bears any close congruence with what the words actually mean. Non-market rarely, if ever, means that there literally is no market; centrally planned rarely, if ever, is used to mean that the economy is really planned by a central planning board, even though one may officially exist (see Lavoie, 1985, p. 3). As Gary Anderson (1988, pp. 485–486) notes:

> The Soviet economy is clearly not centrally planned in the strict sense. Even among Western experts in comparative economic systems, the notion of "planning" applied to the Soviet economy is extremely murky. The consensus judgement seems to be that the Soviet economy is characterized by a very high level of government intervention, but that at best only a relatively small portion of the economy is centrally planned in any detail. . . . Also scholars of the Soviet economy widely recognize that "central planning" is, practically speaking, observed mostly in the breach. Nevertheless, it is commonly asserted that virtually the entire Soviet economy is centrally planned.

Similarly, Steele (1981, p. 108) has observed that since the Soviet "planners ask the enterprises what they intend to do, and then instruct them to do it," the planning process was the exact reverse of what would be required if central planning were actually to take place. "Whatever it is," Steele has commented, "Soviet 'central planning' is certainly not central planning."

Roberts noted (1971, pp. 78–85) that what goes on under the rather pretentious claim of central planning in the socialist countries was merely "the forecasting of a target for a forthcoming few months by adding to the results of the previous months a percentage increase." Yet even this plan was "changed so often that it is not congruous to say that it controls the development of events in the economy." The planning bureaucracy, he went on, simply functioned as "supply agents for enterprises in order to avoid free price formation and exchange on the free market." While this appearance of central planning "satisfies the ideology," the result has been "irrational signals for managerial interpretation, and the irrationality of production in the Soviet Union has been the consequence."

In short, today such terms as *socialism* and *communism* no longer mean non-market economies. Rather they are generally used to refer to nothing more than economies characterized by extensive government controls. Similarly, the terms *non-market* and *centrally planned* do not mean economies that are *literally* non-market or *literally* centrally planned—they refer only to economies characterized by extensive controls.

Unless otherwise noted, words such as *socialism, communism,* and *central planning* will, following current usage, refer to highly interventionist, or command, economies. The term *non-market* will be reserved for use when "no market" in its literal sense is intended. The terms *capitalism* or *market economy* will be used to refer to those economies characterized by relatively little intervention. And *mercantilism* will be used to refer to those economies with a moderate amount of government control. The term *interventionism* will be used to cover both mercantilist and socialist systems.

Figure 1-1 shows these four concepts as a continuum, beginning with a pure market system and ending with the complete absence of the market. The cutoffs between capitalism, mercantilism, and socialism are admittedly somewhat arbitrary, especially in practice. One can legitimately disagree about whether an actual system or country is properly characterized as capitalist or mercantilist, or is more accurately placed in the socialist camp. Suffice it to say that the fewer the controls and the greater the reliance on the free market, the more capitalist the economy. Conversely, the more extensive the controls and the smaller the reliance on the free market, the more socialist the system.

A Caveat Regarding Aggregate Data

It needs to be pointed out that, while certainly not meaningless, aggregate data are often notoriously inaccurate. Even for the United States, which employs the most sophisticated methods of data gathering and analysis, the margin of error is still significant. Kuznets (1967) has estimated that the average margin of error for national income statistics is about 10 percent. Others have placed it as high as plus or minus 20 percent (Morgenstern, 1979, pp. 15–17). Morgenstern has shown (pp. 30–31) that, within an error margin of plus or minus 10 percent, it is possible to plot a hypothetical business cycle exactly the reverse of that determined by the National Bureau of Economic Research (NBER). That is, for every business upturn or downturn as reported by the NBER, one can plot an opposite turn of equal intensity and duration and remain within the rather conservative error margin, or "uncertainty zone," of plus or minus 10 percent. But if this is characteristic for the United States, imagine, says Morgenstern, what the size of the margin of error must be in other, especially less developed, countries.

So far we have dealt solely with data for single countries. When one tries to com-

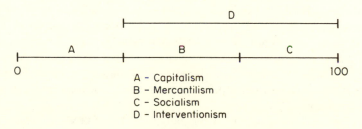

FIGURE 1-1. Taxonomy of economic systems.

pare data for different countries, and especially for countries with different economic systems, the difficulties become truly stupendous. This is so for two basic reasons: (1) the purely technical problem endemic in the attempt to fit the data from incompatible economic systems into a common, comparable, conceptual framework, and (2) the political difficulty resulting from the incentives present for countries to doctor the statistics to suit their needs. Each will be dealt with briefly.

Technical Problems with the Data

Purely technical difficulties tend to understate income data for the less developed countries, or LDCs, and may well overstate them for the more developed countries, or MDCs. There are several reasons why statistical reporting techniques understate income in the LDCs.

Perhaps the most obvious is that income statistics are generally based on those goods bought and sold on the market. But the subsistence sector, where goods are not marketed but are consumed by the producer or are bartered, comprises a large part of economic activity in the LDCs, especially relative to the MDCs. This means that an enormous volume of the economic activity in the LDCs is severely underestimated or completely ignored.[4]

Second, the average age of the population in the LDCs tends to be much lower than that in the MDCs. Children are not only less productive than adults but also, and especially so in the MDCs, much more costly to sustain. Income data that do not take into account the differences in the age compositions of the populations reflect nominal income levels but not the cost of living. Thus, they deflate real incomes in the LDCs while exaggerating them in the MDCs.

Third, where development has occurred in the LDCs it has resulted in the introduction of more and better medical facilities and a better and more varied diet. The result has been a substantial decline in infant mortality and a much longer life expectancy. As the survival rate has risen, population has sometimes increased faster than the GNP. This situation has appeared in official statistics as a decline in per capita income. Even where population growth has not outstripped growth in GNP, the impact of reduced mortality on per capita income statistics has still made it appear that the position of the poor was improving more slowly than it actually was. As Bauer noted (1972, pp. 60–64; 1984, p. 80), while "the position of those who failed to die has certainly improved, as has the situation of those whose children continued to live," not only did per capita income statistics not register this as an improvement, they actually recorded it as a deterioration. Conversely, a rise in infant mortality, or an increase in mortality generally, would be registered as an increase in per capita income and thus an improvement. As Lal has dryly observed (1989, p. 19), based on "the pure arithmetic of calculating per capita income . . . if an infant is born to a cow per capita income goes up, but if an infant is born to a human it goes down!"

Fourth, at least some of what is officially recorded in GNP statistics, and thus as per capita income, is not income at all but rather the cost of earning an income. This includes such things as boots, work shoes, uniforms, tools, business suits, and even (partially) automobiles, since one of their major uses is in transportation to and from work. These costs tend to be much heavier in the MDCs than the LDCs.

Finally, it is enough simply to note that the use of such figures as per capita income can be quite misleading when, as is more often the case in the LDCs than the MDCs, wealth is highly skewed, that is, concentrated in the hands of a few individuals.

In brief, while GNP statistics in the LDCs tend to understate the real per capita income of the LDCs—estimates are off by as much as several hundred percent (see, e.g., Bauer, 1984, p. 176, fn. 5)—they tend to overstate income in the MDCs. Other technical difficulties occur in attempting to compare data from different economic systems.

Probably the most perplexing problem in moving from a market to a socialist or command economy is that of determining the value of the medium of exchange. As Morgenstern (1979, p. 44) noted in regard to the Soviet economy:

> It is clear that the arbitrariness in valuation, partly due to the attempted use of the obsolete Marxist labor value theory, is greater than any country possessing a functioning price system. . . . There can be no statistic of national income without measuring or postulating money streams, since there must be a common denominator and no one has as yet found a substitute for the money measure. That is why the Soviet national income is also given in terms of rubles, though what a ruble means is obscure: There is no free market and no free exchange rate at which to make comparisons.

The process of assigning monetary expressions "on the basis of assumed, imputed values," he continued, creates difficulties that exceed even "those in underdeveloped countries" where, though the market sector is usually small, the market is nevertheless permitted more latitude in allocating resources.

A second problem is the volume of economic waste. As both Nutter (1983, p. 177) and Goldman (1983, pp. 30–35) have noted, in terms of sheer industrial output, command economies such as that of the Soviet Union have shown themselves the peer of market economies like that of the United States. In fact, the Soviet Union produced more steel, oil, coal, and cement than the United States. Growth, as Nutter points out (p. 178), "is measured in terms of things 'produced,' not in terms of things usefully consumed." Of course, mistakes are made in a market economy, but since the firm must be able to sell the goods it produces or face bankruptcy, waste is kept to a minimum. In contrast, in a command economy such as the Soviet Union, the plant manager did not face the problem of selling the goods produced. He or she was assigned production quotas or quantitative success indicators, based on the total weight or number of units produced in a given period, and received a wage bonus if that quote was achieved or exceeded. It made no difference to a manager whether the goods were needed. The job was to meet a quota. The result was what Michael Polanyi (1960) termed "conspicuous production"—production for the sake of production—which in turn led to a "phobic reaction to innovation" (Goldman, 1983, p. 43), since innovation would necessitate some revamping of the production routine, thereby endangering plan fulfillment. Consequently, plans focussed on producing more of what had been traditionally produced. But, as Goldman asks (p. 33), what good does it do to increase steel production by 10 percent if there is no need for additional steel? Nevertheless, the planners were satisfied because the additional output meant that the economy had recorded a "growth" and the managers were happy because they received bonuses. As one observer has noted (Goldman, 1983, p. 37), the Soviet economy "produces mainly for itself." As a result, "a disproportionate share of production never sees its way to the ultimate consumer but is diverted, instead, to a needless increase in the capital intensity of industry, or just waste." In brief, there is very strong reason to believe that the percentage of the aggregate data representing sheer economic waste is considerably greater in command economies than in market economies.

Quality is a related consideration. The quality of goods produced in socialist economies is notoriously poor. Aside from other considerations, one reason is the rhythm of the monthly production cycle. Very little is accomplished during the first third of the month. The work force is in a state of exhaustion from the feverish pace of production during the last few days of the previous month. Materials needed for production seldom arrive before the 10th or 12th of the month. Production begins to pick up during the middle of the month and reaches a frantic pace, commonly known as "storming," during the final third of the month, as workers desperately try to meet their monthly production quotas. As a Russian worker described the process (in H. Smith, 1984, pp. 287–288):

> In other countries production normally goes on throughout the month, but here, it can only begin on the 14th or 20th when all materials have been received. So factories must fulfill about 80 percent of the Plan [quotas] in the last 10–15 days. No one cares about quality any longer. Volume is the main thing. . . . The whole population knows all about this because everyone works. So normally, when someone buys a household appliance, he tries to buy one with a certificate saying that it was produced before the 15th of the month.

Of course, low quality goods are produced in market countries as well. But the market automatically compensates for quality differences by ensuring that inferior goods do not command as high a price as goods of higher quality. With the unit-pricing system used in the Soviet Union, all goods were treated as equal: a television is a television, an oven is an oven. The method of accounting thus tends to overstate the value of many of the goods produced, thereby inflating such an aggregate datum as the GNP.

Finally, there is the problem of the so-called second economy. The second economy has two components: (1) the legal, or tolerated but ideologically offensive, market, which is confined primarily to the agricultural sector, and (2) the illegal or black market. The second economy operates, in varying degrees, in all communist countries (see Goldman, 1983, pp. 55, 96–99); Grossman, 1972; Mosher, 1983a, pp. 76–103; Simis, 1982; H. Smith, 1984, pp. 106–134; Zafanolli, 1985). Some (Goldman, 1983, p. 55; Grossman, 1972, pp. 27–28) believe that the second economy may have accounted for as much as 25 percent of the Soviet Union's GNP and that participation in this economy was universal among the population.[5] This presents an interesting issue. Generally the GNP data reflect the legal component of the second economy but not the illegal component. But if one is interested in the actual standard of living of the average citizen living in a socialist society, then both components would have to be considered. However, if one is interested in evaluating the performance of a socialist economy, then neither component should be considered since it represents capitalist or market production. This means that, to ascertain the actual performance of a communist economy, that portion of the GNP representing market production should be deducted. There is abundant evidence that that figure would be quite large.

Political Problems with the Data

In addition to the technical difficulties of aggregate economic data, there are severe political problems.

First, political decisions involving the distribution of literally billions of dollars are routinely made by international organizations, such as the United Nations and the Organization for Economic Cooperation and Development, on the basis of aggregate data, especially per capita income. For example, the U.N.'s International Development Agency provides interest-free loans to the most poverty-stricken countries of the world. Countries with a reported per capita income level above $835 in 1986 dollars (Banks, 1988, p. 808) are no longer eligible for IDA money. There is no doubt that data from Third World countries are quite often doctored to ensure continued eligibility. This has, in fact, been admitted by Third World leaders. While impartial estimates placed Nigeria's population in 1963 at 37.1 million, Nigerian officials insisted that it was 55.6 million, which was eventually accepted by the United Nations. Oskar Morgenstern reported that a Nigerian civil servant, who for obvious reasons preferred to remain anonymous, commented to him, "We shall produce any statistics that we think will help us to get as much money out of the United States as we possibly can" (in Bauer, 1984, pp. 116, 178, fn. 19). A similar controversy erupted much more recently regarding the size of the population of Ethiopia (Bauer, 1986, p. 23).

Second, communist countries, and in particular the Soviet Union, are likewise notorious for manipulating their data, although the motives differ from those of Third World countries. Morgenstern (1979, pp. 42–43), for example, noted that while Soviet statistics "are exceedingly difficult to assess, . . . they are seldom what they purport to be. . . . There has been a great deal of deliberate doctoring of statistics at many levels." Traditionally, Soviet and East European statistics have been inflated because the Soviets viewed the communist East as being in a race with the capitalist West and wanted statistical "proof" of the superiority of their economic system. In addition, plant managers received bonuses and even promotions as rewards for fulfilling their quotas. Thus, both the economic planners and the plant managers have had, and since "the gross output indicator still reigns supreme" (Roberts and LaFollette, 1990, p. 9), continue to have, even under *perestroika,* very strong incentives to inflate the data in their reports. Multiple accounting provides a good example of how this is done. The final price of a good automatically incorporates the value added in each of the stages of production. To count each stage, therefore, greatly inflates the national product statistics.

While multiple accounting is not limited to socialist countries, their governments have raised it to an art form. Morgenstern (p. 43) believes that such methods have inflated the growth of industrial production in the Soviet Union by at least one-third. But Morgenstern's conclusions may be quite conservative. According to Nutter's detailed studies (1983, p. 179), while the official index of Soviet production shows industrial output as multiplying 77 times between 1913 and 1955, Nutter notes that if conventional Western methods of construction are utilized, industrial output multiplied only 5 to 6 times.

This means that such aggregate data as per capita GNP statistics understate the average income of the LDCs relative to the MDCs and overstate it for command or socialist countries relative to market or capitalist countries.

Conditions in the First and Third Worlds

These difficulties do not mean that one should not use such data. Their use is probably unavoidable. What they do mean is that the data must be used with care. Often such data obscure as much as they reveal. Whenever possible, therefore, other statistical indicators should be used to help clarify their meaning. For example, countries such as the United Arab Emirates, Qatar, and Kuwait have the highest per capita incomes in the world. Other data, however, such as literacy and mortality rates, life expectancies, and the number of physicians, hospital beds, TVs, telephones, and automobiles per person, show just how highly skewed wealth is in these countries (see Kurian, 1984; Osterfeld, 1989c, pp. 38–39).

Another indication of the magnitude of the differences in aggregate data can be obtained by contrasting the 20 wealthiest MDCs, excluding the oil-rich Arab countries, with the poorest of the LDCs, that is, those 23 countries with official 1980 per capita incomes below $300. Not surprisingly, the data show that the wealthiest MDCs are at or very near the top of every category and the poorest of the LDCs are consistently at or near the very bottom. But they also reveal some striking differences among the LDCs themselves. Let us take, for example, male literacy rates. Nearly every MDC has an "official" male literacy rate at or above 97 percent. In contrast, if one looks just at the 23 LDCs with 1980 per capita income levels below $300, Zaire is highest with a rate of 49 percent, followed closely by India with a rate of 47 percent. China has a rate of 25 percent; Ethiopia and Mali have rates of 8 and 4 percent, respectively.

The percentage of the relevant population in the LDCs enrolled in secondary school is extremely low. China is the highest with 43 percent, followed by India with 28 percent. Mali has 9 percent and Tanzania 4 percent. Practically all developed countries rank above 75 percent, and most are well above that figure. With regard to educational expenditures per capita, China ranks highest with $16; Ethiopia and Bangladesh rank at the bottom with $3 and $2, respectively. In contrast, most MDCs spend over $350 (Kurian, 1984).

In terms of such measures as cars per 1,000 people, the differences are, again, striking but not surprising: Zaire ranks highest with 3.1; the Western MDCs average more than 200. The United States ranks first with 530 cars per 1,000 people. One finds equally significant differences with such things as TVs, radios, and telephones (Kurian, 1984).

Turning to health measures, India had a male life expectancy in 1980 of 46.4 years, Zaire's was 41.9, Mali's 39.4, and Ethiopia's 37.0. Gabon's, at 25.0 years, was the lowest. For the developed countries male life expectancy was close to 70 years. Zambia had the highest infant mortality rate at 259 per 1,000 births. Gabon was second with 229. India's was 122, Zaire's 104. The MDCs averaged about 10 (Kurian, 1984).

These data show that, even allowing for an error margin of several hundred percent, there are significant differences between the so-called less developed and the more developed countries. The differences are severe enough to say that the two groups of countries inhabit very different worlds. But it must also be emphasized that the data compared here are the extremes. There is no clear dichotomy between the more and less developed countries but a very gradual transition in which the MDCs shade into the LDCs. There are also huge differences among even the poorest of the LDCs, especially in the area of life expectancies.

Conditions in the First and Second Worlds

Further, the data reveal important differences between the First World and the Second World, or what traditionally have been referred to as market and command economies. In cars per 1,000 population, the United States has 530, West Germany 384, France 368, and England 272. This contrasts with the Soviet Union's 29 cars per 1,000 inhabitants. In fact, even blacks in South Africa now own more cars per capita than do all the citizens in the Soviet Union (Adelman, 1990, pp. 5–6). Other Eastern European countries, while generally higher in this ranking than the Soviet Union, are still far behind the West. East Germany is highest with 151, Hungary 103, and Rumania 11 (Kurian, 1984; United Nations, 1981). Generally similar differences exist with such things as radios, TVs, and telephones (Kurian, 1984; Osterfeld, 1989b; United Nations, 1981). Interestingly, Second World countries tend to have higher rates of TV ownership than, say, telephone ownership. This is undoubtedly because TVs are perfect vehicles for the dissemination of state information and propaganda, while phones are for private communication, something Second World governments have actively discouraged.

Measures such as life expectancy and infant mortality are the most interesting. The Soviet Union has the most physicians in the world, and over twice as many as the United States (896,600 to 361,443). But other health indicators paint a very different picture. Life expectancy is higher among Western countries than Eastern countries. For example, in 1984 life expectancy in the United States was 76 years, the same as the average for what the *World Development Report* terms the "industrial market countries." In the Soviet Union it was only 67 years, and 62 for men, the latter three years below the figure reported for 1965. Average life expectancy for what the *World Development Report* terms the "Eastern European nonmarket economies" was 68 (World Bank, 1986, p. 181). What is most significant is that while life expectancy continues to increase in the United States and other Western nations, and to increase rapidly in Third World nations, *it has held steady or actually declined in the Soviet Union and the East European countries.* According to the *World Development Report,* life expectancy in the Soviet Union stood at 70 years in 1978 and reached 72 years in 1981; male life expectancy had reached 66 years in the 1970s (World Bank, 1980, p. 151; 1983, p. 193; 1986, pp. 181,233; Eberstadt, 1987, pp. 12–13; 1988, pp. 11–13). Thus, over the past decade Soviet life expectancy declined about five years; male life expectancy declined four years. But these are official figures, which are commonly viewed as having been doctored to make things appear better than they actually are. According to unofficial Soviet sources, male life expectancy may be as low as 55 years (see Roberts and LaFollette, 1990, p. 62). Such a decline is simply unprecedented, especially for a "modern" industrialized nation. Moreover, the situation in Eastern Europe is not much better. The official average male life expectancy for the Eastern European nations was only 66 in 1984; that for the Western nations was 73 (World Bank, 1986, p. 233).

Associated with this are the astonishingly high infant mortality rates in the Soviet Union and the Eastern European nations. In 1960 the Soviet rate was 41 per 1,000 births. By 1965 it had dropped to 30, after which it began to rise. In 1975, the last year the Soviet Union publicly reported its figures,[6] the rate was 31. Careful studies, based on admittedly fragmentary evidence, by such authorities on the subject as Murray Feshbach (Eberstadt, 1988, p. 12) have indicated that by 1981 the infant mortality rate in the Soviet Union may have been as high as 40 per 1,000 births.[7] Officially, the rates for East European nations range from a high in 1984 of 43 in Albania to a low of 11 in East Germany. Western European countries range between a high of 12 in Italy to a low of 6 in Finland. The average for the Eastern nations is 19; that for Western nations is 9 (World Bank, 1986, p. 233). As Eberstadt (1988, p. 13) has summarized,

> life expectancy in the U.S.S.R. is about the same as the average for Costa Rica, Jamaica, Malaysia, Mexico, and Sri Lanka. By the same token, the Soviet infant mortality rates could be replicated in a nation composed in equal parts of Chile, the Dominican Republic, Panama, Taiwan, and Trinidad. These countries, however, are moving up, while the Soviet Union is moving down. If current trends persist, most of Latin America and East Asia will surpass the Soviet Union in a matter of years.

The data show that, even allowing for problems of error and comparability, there have traditionally been, and continue to be—even after the Eastern bloc's collapse of 1989— significant differences between the Western market economies and the Eastern command economies. If anything, the data indicate that per capita income figures may actually have *understated* the magnitude of the differences. For example, some scholars who have examined the data closely (Nutter, 1983, p. 148) have placed Soviet income at no more than 20 percent of U.S. income. It is certainly interesting that East Germany, the wealthiest socialist country, ranked only twenty-ninth in per capita income. It is also noteworthy that East Germany has traditionally been the least communist of the Eastern bloc nations. The percentages of its industrial production and retail trade controlled by the socialist sector were well below those of any other Eastern bloc nation, including Yugoslavia (Gripp, 1973, p. 78).

Conclusions

Aggregate data, as unreliable as they may be, still show two things quite conclusively: (1) The nations of the Western or First World are far more productive and wealthier than those in either the Second or Third Worlds. This was not always so. Just a few hundred years ago all areas of the world were poor. In fact, the West was probably poorer and less advanced than most other areas at that time, especially China (Rosenberg and Birdzell, 1986, p. 37). (2) The West, over the past few hundred years, has traditionally been far more market oriented than the other areas of the world. The likely relationship between the West's economic institutions and its economic growth and development cannot be ignored. It is the principal concern of this analysis.

In the chapters that follow, the focus will be on examining the principles and problems of economic growth and development. Though related, the two terms are not identical. Economic growth is simply a measurement of things produced. It is quantitative. Economic development, on the other hand, is far more qualitative. Economic development, or wealth, can be defined

> as a wide range of choice of what to buy. The individual perceives growth in wealth as a widening of his or her range of choice. The extension cannot be purely quantitative, because, by ordinary notions of marginal utility, too much of a good thing speedily loses its value. The extension has to be qualitative as well. (Rosenberg and Birdzell, 1986, pp. 275–276)

That is, while economic growth may be seen as an increase in the quantity of available goods, economic development consists in the expansion of "the qualitative range of the consumer's choice" (Rosenberg and Birdzell, 1986; also see Bauer 1984, p. 22). For example, refrigeration vastly increases the variety and quality of foods available. Automobiles increase mobility. Radios, TVs, newspapers, and telephones broaden horizons and literally open up new worlds to entire populations. Better medical care likewise means qualitative change in people's lives. Infant mortality rates decline, life expectancy increases, and people tend to live longer, healthier, and happier lives. In short, the tremendous variety of goods and services available to inhabitants of developed, compared with less developed, countries is astonishing. It constitutes a fundamental difference in the quality of life, and this needs to be kept in mind. As Rosenberg and Birdzell aptly note (1986, p. 275):

> Observers who have compared the very limited variety of products available in East European economies to the much more extensive variety available in the West find the difference profoundly impressive—a difference between a gray world of monotony and a brighter world of wide-ranging choices and prospects. The differences . . . are not measured so much by cash paid as by what can be bought with that cash.

Notes

1. There is a great deal of truth to Bauer and Yamey's barbed comment (1980, p. 80) that the members of the Third World share only "one common characteristic": the desire to get as much "aid" from the First World as possible.

2. For an in-depth presentation of this methodological viewpoint, which Ludwig von Mises has termed "praxeology," see Mises, 1966, especially pp. 1–142; Mises, 1962, especially pp. 41–46; Mises, 1981, especially pp. 12–17. Also relevant are Hayek, 1979; and Rothbard, 1951, 1973.

3. In fact, partially as a result of *glasnost* (openness), very recent and more accurate data coming out of the Soviet Union strongly suggest that the official statistics, bleak as they are, actually depict a far more optimistic picture of conditions in the Soviet Union and the Eastern European countries than is the case. See, for example, Roberts and LaFollette (1990, pp. 32–74), Brzezinski (1989), T. Palmer (1990), and *U.S. News and World Report* (1990, pp. 34–39).

4. This belief is challenged by Hill, who maintains that rather than deflating actual incomes, "self-consumption" in fact significantly inflates official per capita income statistics. Her argument (Hill, 1986, p. 40) is that statisticians "presumably" compute the value of self-consumption by recourse to "ex-farm rates," which would include such things as transportation and handling costs in their prices, thereby statistically inflating the value of the economic activity of the subsistence sector. Interestingly, just a few pages prior to this (p. 32) she notes that intercropping, which is "very common" in many parts of the Third World, has increased yields per acre by as much as 62 percent. Yet, she points out, the Food and Agriculture Organization's instructions are to ignore these increased yields in their computations. Such an omission means that official statistics would significantly deflate peasant incomes. The latter seems far more likely, since a country with an average per capita yearly income that in fact was equal to, say, $300 in the United States, would mean that the great bulk of the population could not survive past the first two or three months of the year, regardless of their frugality. It should also be pointed out that Hill objects to both the term *peasant* (pp. 8–15) and to the term *subsistence economy* (pp. 17–19, 51–53). She does make a convincing case that the degree of subsistence farming has been considerably less extensive than development economists think (pp. 51–65).

5. The black market operates in market countries as well (see Gutmann, 1977; Sennholz, 1984). But there can be no doubt that it is dwarfed by the size of the second economy in the socialist counties. The impact of corruption will be dealt with in detail in Chapter 9.

6. The Soviet Union resumed official reporting in 1987, at which time the infant mortality rate was reported to be 29 (World Bank, 1987, p. 259). But some authorities (see, e.g., Eberstadt, 1988, p. 7) believe that due to the peculiarities in the Soviet method of calculating such data, the official figures paint an overly optimistic picture of the true state of Soviet health. Also see Maltsev, 1990; Roberts and LaFollette, 1990, pp. 32–37,62.

7. Kurian (1984, pp. 330–331) gives very different figures for this. But see Goldman, 1983, p. 101. Also see Eberstadt, 1988, pp. 34–42.

2

Economy, Government, and Culture

Economic growth and development are products of a multitude of factors. Among the most important are economic and political institutions and cultural values. An examination of these three factors will be the focus of this chapter. In practice, the three are obviously interrelated and mutually influencing. However, for purposes of analysis they will, as much as is possible, be treated separately.

Economic Institutions

All societies must have some method for coordinating the economic actions of their individual members. The larger and more complex the society, the more difficult and crucial this problem becomes. The impact of economic institutions on economic growth and development can be illustrated by contrasting the operation of a pure, free market, capitalist order with that of a pure, non-market, socialist order and the mixed order of mercantilism.

Pure (Free Market) Capitalism

There are three problems of coordination that must be solved, in fact continually solved, in *any* economic system: (1) the problem of *priorities*, that is, what goods and services should be produced, and in what quality and quantity; (2) the problem of *efficiency*, that is, what combination of factors used in the production of a commodity will (a) not impede the production of goods desired more intensely by consumers and (b) leave the largest bundle of factors left over for the production of other goods and services; and (3) the problem of *distribution*, that is, how should each participant in the productive process be compensated. The pure capitalist order will be *briefly* examined in an effort to highlight how it would approach and deal with these three problems.

It should be pointed out at the outset that since consumers buy only what they intend to use, one can, on the pure, free market, make a profit only by producing what is usable. Hence there can be no distinction between production for use and production for profit.

Priorities

Within a market system, priorities are set by consumers' buying and abstention from buying. Entrepreneurs, eager to maximize profits, will tend to produce those goods that when sold give them the greatest difference between total revenue and total cost. It is through the fluctuation of prices and costs that the unhampered market system is able to disseminate the relevant information to market participants. People need only to be concerned with the prices that are pertinent to them. If consumer demand for any good increases or its supply decreases, then, ceteris paribus, its price would rise, thereby encouraging its increased production. Conversely, if consumer demand decreased or the supply increased, again, other things being equal, the price would fall, thereby discouraging production of that particular good. Thus the market process works in such a way as to produce those goods and services that consumers wish to buy in the quantity and quality desired by them.

Efficiency

On the market the problem of the efficient allocation of resources is handled in the same way that the problem of priorities is handled: the price system. To produce their goods the entrepreneurs must bid for the needed factors. They therefore stand in the same relation to the sellers of factors as the consumers do to the sellers of final goods and services. Thus, prices for the various factors of production reflect the demand for them by entrepreneurs. Since what entrepreneurs can bid is limited by their expected yield from the final sale of their products, factors of production are channeled into the production of those goods most demanded by consumers. Those who best serve consumers earn the greatest profits and therefore are able to offer the highest bids for the factors they need. If returns are not high enough to cover the cost of a particular operation, consumers have found a more productive use for those factors of production elsewhere. The market therefore allocates factors to their most value-productive point, *relative to the priority system that the consumers have established.*

This can be demonstrated by the following: assume, for purposes of analysis, that the market is in equilibrium. Also assume that a technological breakthrough has enabled the production of a new commodity that is highly valued by consumers. The production of the commodity, however, requires the use of factor A. Those entrepreneurs who perceive this new profit opportunity will begin to bid for the factor. The increased competition for the available supply of A will cause its price to rise, forcing some of the current users of A to curtail their purchases of this factor. Who will these users be? Clearly it will be those who are employing A in its least productive way. Units of A thus are channeled, spontaneously as it were, from uses that consumers value less highly into uses that they value more highly. Further, the rise in the price and therefore the profit margins for factor A will encourage other entrepreneurs, also eager to earn profits, to expand their supply of A or to discover and provide suitable substitutes for it.

In brief, the price fluctuations of the market process spontaneously coordinate the actions of all participants in the system by transmitting the relevant information precisely to those who require that particular information to guide their actions.

Distribution

Since under the free market system those eager to earn profits can do so only by producing better than their competitors what consumers desire to buy, the more satisfactorily entrepreneurs serve consumers, the more profits they will earn.

Moreover, there is a natural tendency for entrepreneurs to invest in areas with a low wage level, thereby forcing those wages up to a level commensurate with that in other areas where the same work is done, while workers in low-pay jobs tend to migrate to areas where pay is higher. Similarly, entrepreneurs invest in areas manifesting high profits. But the increased output forces prices and profits to fall. Thus, contrary to popular notions, the market process, provided it is free, actually tends to reduce the extremes of wealth and poverty.

Finally, wealth on the free market is not dispersed on the basis of personal moral merit or "need" but purely according to one's ability to provide others with what they want. While this may be considered unjust from some higher point of view, the attempt to allocate wealth according to moral merit, need, or other non-market criteria is largely incompatible with economic growth, since the interventions required by such a policy not only distort the price structure and thus the signals conveyed by those prices but also penalize those who are the most efficient at serving the consumers. The result can only be to impede or even prevent economic development.

The Entrepreneur

The foregoing presentation of the market process was highly simplified, and the market was depicted as operating mechanistically. But as Mises has stressed (1966, p. 332), "there is nothing automatic or mechanical in the operation of the market." It was assumed for purposes of analysis that the market was in equilibrium. This is *never* the case. While the market is always heading toward equilibrium, it never reaches it, since that level is forever being upset by changes in the relevant data. A particular market price is the result of an array of factors existing in society at a given moment. Since the same confluence of factors could never reappear in exactly the same combination again, each market price is, in fact, a unique historical datum. While it may accurately reflect economic conditions today, the same price may not be an accurate reflection of economic conditions next month or even tomorrow.

The fact that scientific knowledge, availability of resources, consumer preferences, and hundreds of other factors are in a constant state of change means that, for the economy to operate with a reasonable degree of efficiency in satisfying the demands of consumers, it must be able to spot these changes and adjust promptly to them. This is precisely the role of the entrepreneur. As Kirzner has argued (1973, p. 81), the important feature of entrepreneurship is not so much the ability to break away from routine as the ability to perceive new opportunities which others have not yet noticed. Entrepreneurship . . . is not so much the introduction of new products or of new techniques of production as the ability to *see* where new products have become unsuspectedly valuable to consumers and where new methods of production have, unknown to others, become feasible.

"It is only through the entrepreneur that changes can arise," according to Kirzner. Entrepreneurship is essentially a *discovery* process and not simply a method of "mechanically" choosing the most efficient method of producing a given set of goods by the use of a given number of alternative methods (Kirzner, 1973, p. 70). There was no consumer demand for books before the invention of the printing press; there was no demand for air travel prior to the invention of the airplane; nor was there any demand for video tapes prior to the development of videocassette recorders. It was the entrepreneur who perceived that things had changed, who understood that there was a "consumer demand" for such things before the consumers themselves were even aware of their existence. It was the entrepreneur who, acting on his or her discovery, his or her creative insight, that the satisfaction of a demand for new products or for new methods of producing old products had become economically feasible, was able to move the economy toward this new equilibrium.

But in the very process of moving the economy toward the new equilibrium, the decisions of the entrepreneur change the economic conditions facing others, thereby necessitating further entrepreneurial decision-making. These decisions, in turn, change the economic conditions for still others, necessitating yet additional economic decisions. The result is an *ongoing process of discovery and adjustment to never-ending, often unexpected, and thus unpredictable changes in economic data.*

The entrepreneur is both the motor and the rudder of the capitalist economic process. It is he who ensures that the proper innovations will in fact be introduced. It is he whose recognition of and reaction to changes in economic conditions "brings *into mutual adjustment* those discordant elements which resulted from prior ignorance" (Kirzner, 1973, p. 74). It is, in short, the entrepreneur who notices that changes have occurred and whose activities move the economy toward a *new* equilibrium.

Conclusions

The purely free or unhampered market not only is a self-regulating system, it also works to maximize the production of goods and services. Equally, if not more important, since exchange on the open market is voluntary,[1] and since any voluntary exchange must be to the, at least ex ante, mutual benefit of all participating parties, and since the market spontaneously rewards with profits those who produce what consumers want and imposes losses on those supplying unwanted goods and services, it also works to *maximize the value of the goods produced*, that is, it maximizes what may be termed "social utility."[2]

Pure (Non-Market) Socialism

At the opposite end of the spectrum is the pure, non-market order. It was this that
Marx and the other socialists of the nineteenth century meant when they wrote of
socialism. It was also a purely non-market order that Mises had in mind when he
argued in his classic 1920 article, "Economic Calculation in the Socialist Commonwealth" (1975, pp. 87–130), that socialism was not a feasible economic order
because it lacked the indispensable mechanism for economic rationality: economic
calculation. As Mises put it (1975, p. 111), "where there is no free market, there is
no pricing mechanism; without a pricing mechanism, there is no economic calculation." And in the absence of calculation, he added, there is no rational economics.

Economic Calculation

For Mises the impossibility of economic calculation under socialism did not stem
so much from the problem of obtaining or even processing adequate information
or data on either the desires of the citizens or the existing factors of production,
available stocks of resources, and even the latest scientific knowledge. Although the
technical problem of data gathering and processing may well be insoluble, the
essential problem of socialism lay in the inability of the planning board to choose
the appropriate means to attain the desired ends (Mises, 1966, pp. 696–697).

Since consumption goods provide us with immediate benefits, we can value
them directly, without monetary calculation. However, the means of production
are valued only *indirectly*. As production grows more and more complex it becomes
impossible to ascertain, intuitively, the contribution of factors of production to
attaining the ends sought. Thus a method of calculation is required. Calculation
presupposes the ability to reduce the multitude of disparate physical stocks of
resources to a common denominator. This, however, depends on the existence of
free markets and a common medium of exchange, that is, money. Both of these, in
turn, presuppose the existence of private property throughout the society. Only
under these conditions can one determine the appropriate methods of production.
Without the ability to calculate and compare relative costs of production, Mises
argued, there would be no rational way to choose between the plethora of possible
alternatives. The current state of science and technology, Mises commented (1966,
p. 699), makes it possible to produce just about anything out of just about anything.
Consequently, "no single man can ever master all the possibilities of production,
innumerable as they are, as to be in a position to make straightaway evident judg-
ments of value without the aid of some system of computation" (Mises, 1975, p.
102). Thus, economic calculation is the sine qua non of all but the most primitive
of societies. Since a goal of socialism was to eliminate buying and selling, or in
Marxist terminology "commodity production," at least for the means of production, there would be no method of calculation. The consequences would be catastrophic. Modern civilization is based on the division of labor, specialization, and
economies of scale. Since these depend on economic calculation, and since economic calculation is not possible under socialism, socialism is incompatible with
modern civilization.

It is commonly thought that whatever problems might exist under socialism will be engineering problems that can be solved though the application of modern technology. But the technological or engineering problem is of a completely different order from the economic problem. The engineer is faced with the technical problem of selecting the appropriate means to attain a *given end*. The technological problem is characterized by its singleness of purpose. In society, however, there exists a multiplicity of constantly changing and competing ends, and the economic problem is that of allocating scarce factors such that (1) resources are not wasted and (2) the production of less intensely desired goods does not prevent the production of more intensely desired goods.

The differences can be easily illustrated. Good A can be produced through the use of one of three resources, X, Y, or Z, which are substitutable for one another. X is superior to either Y or Z in the technological sense, that is, its use will result in a higher quality product. However, X costs $25 per unit whereas Y costs $10 per unit and Z costs $5 per unit. If the gain in utility derived from the reduction in the final price of A permitted by the use of Y or Z exceeds, in the eyes of consumers, the loss of utility stemming from the reduction in the quality of A, then the economically best course is to use either factor Y or Z. This determination can be made *only* in a world where relative contributions to production can be ascertained and compared, which in turn presupposes the existence of factor prices. In the absence of private ownership of the means of production, however, factors cannot be bought and sold, in which case there can be neither factor markets nor factor prices. Thus, socialism would have no rational means to allocate resources.

It is a mistake to believe that a socialist society can calculate by summing labor costs. Aside from the fact that labor is not the only factor of production, costs are subjective, not objective. This does not mean that costs are arbitrary. It means that they are determined by their contribution to the production of a final good, the price of which is determined by the use-value that good has for individual consumers. And use-value is subjective. Put differently, the prices of factors are determined by their *opportunity costs*. For example, the reason that one factor (say X) costs so much more than, say, Y and Z is because users of factors are willing to pay a price up to the price that equals the value of the factor's contribution to the productive process. If the contribution of units of X is greater in alternative uses than is the contribution of units of Y or Z in their alternative uses, the price of X will be higher than the prices of Y and Z. The purchasers of X thus are the ones employing X in its most value-productive uses. Opportunity costs can only be ascertained in a system of private property and free markets.

In fact, the actual problem of socialism is much more complex than this. In the real world different people have different needs, and the real issue therefore is not whether to use X, Y, or Z but how many units of A to produce with X, how many with Y, and how many with Z. Even disregarding the problem of the choice of what is to be produced (Mises, 1966, pp. 698–699),

> there is the embarrassing multitude of producers' goods and the infinite variety of procedures that can be resorted to for manufacturing definite consumers' goods. The most advantageous location of each industry and the optimum size of each

plant and of each piece of equipment must be determined. One must determine what kind of mechanical power should be employed in each of them, and which of the various formulas for the production of this energy should be applied. All of these problems are raised daily in thousands of cases. Each case offers special conditions and requires an individual solution appropriate to these special data. The number of elements with which the director's decision has to deal is much greater than would be indicated by a merely technological description of the various producers' goods in terms of physics or chemistry. The location of each of them must be taken into consideration as well as the serviceableness of the capital investments made in the past for their utilization. The director does not simply have to deal with coal as such, but with thousands and thousands of pits already in operation in various places, and with the possibilities for digging new pits, with the various methods of mining each of them, with the different qualities of coal in the various deposits, with the various methods for utilizing the coal for the production of heat, power and a great number of derivatives.

Further, even if the proper proportions and methods could somehow be established in a socialist society, this would be just the beginning of the problem, since the real world is not one of static relationships but of ceaseless change in economic conditions. Even if a socialist society could miraculously establish the appropriate allocation of all resources today, the allocation would be inappropriate tomorrow and become ever more inappropriate with the passage of time. It is the entrepreneur who, under capitalism, spots these changes and causes the economy to adapt to them. Socialism has eliminated the role of the entrepreneur: he or she cannot operate in the absence of prices and private property.

Material outputs are interdependent. Thus, any change in one area has ramifications that affect the entire economy. A technological breakthrough in the production of factor X would, if the cost of X declined enough, make it economically feasible for producers of A to substitute factor X for, say, factor Z. Or the development of a new use for factor Z could, by increasing demand for it, cause its price to rise, thereby encouraging some of the current users of Z to begin to switch to Y or X. In either case, the substitution would itself cause price changes in these other factors, thereby affecting *their* employment in alternative uses. In fact, by changing their opportunity costs, the demand and thus the prices of those factors necessary to produce, or extract, X, Y, and Z would also be affected. For example, increased demand for X or Y would increase the demand for labor in those areas, causing wages for those producing X or Y to rise, while the decreased demand for Z would cause wages for those producing Z to decline.

Similarly, the sinking of an oil tanker or the destruction of a refinery by an earthquake will not merely affect the price of oil and the price of those goods using oil. It will also affect the price of those energy sources that can substitute for oil, as well as the price of those sources that, while not directly substitutable for oil, can be substituted for sources that *are* substituted for oil, and so on. It will also affect the price of the factors necessary to increase the production of oil. By changing the opportunity costs of these factors, it will therefore affect costs in those areas of production that compete for these factors.

Since economic conditions are in a constant state of change, and since such things as technological breakthroughs and accidents caused by humans or by nature cannot be anticipated and thus cannot be programmed into a socialist plan, the idea of a planned economy is a chimera. The irony is that, in order to plan, one must have cost and price data. But in the very process of planning, such data are systematically eliminated.

Precisely because socialism endeavors to eliminate exchange, money, and private ownership of the means of production, economic calculation is impossible. Hence a socialist society is unable to determine what is profitable and what is not. The resulting inefficiencies and distortions, Mises felt, lead to capital consumption or decumulation, in turn resulting in progressive impoverishment. The paradox of planning, Mises concluded (1966, p. 700), "is that it cannot plan, because of the absence of economic calculation. What is called a planned economy is no economy at all. It is just a system of groping about in the dark."

Mises' argument sparked what became known in Europe during the 1920s and 1930s as the "economic calculation" debate. Socialists such as Dickinson, Lange, Taylor, and Lerner responded to Mises' challenge by advancing proposals for what is commonly referred to as "market socialism." Mises' student F. A. Hayek joined the debate in the 1930s with several articles dealing with the weaknesses of the market socialist proposals.

Despite the differences in their individual proposals, the market socialists argued *not* that markets could be dispensed with but rather that, in one way or another, they could be made to operate more efficiently than they did on the unhampered market; that through the judicious manipulation of prices the "imperfections" of the free market could be replaced by a close approximation of the perfect competition model. It was to these proposals that Hayek directed his critique.

One proposal was to solve the allocation problem by use of simultaneous equations. The Central Planning Board, or CPB, would construct demand and production functions for goods that, when combined with given stocks of resources, would permit the determination of factor prices (Dickinson, 1933, pp. 237–250). A second proposal was to arrive at correct factor prices through a process of trial and error. While there would be a market for consumer goods, prices for factors would be set by the CPB. The CPB would then periodically adjust prices to ensure an equilibrium between demand and supply (Lange, 1972, pp. 92–110).

Hayek responded with comprehensive critiques of both proposals, only the barest outlines of which can be provided here. First, reiterating the essential point made earlier by Mises, he noted that since the efficiency of any given method of production or combination of factors is dependent on time and location,

> every machine, tool, or building is not just . . . one of a class of physically similar objects, but . . . an individual whose usefulness is determined by its particular state of wear and tear, its location, and so on. The same applies to every batch of commodities which is situated at a different spot or which differs in any other respect from other batches   (Hayek, 1975, p. 209)

Since endowing individual plant managers with the discretionary authority to adapt to local conditions by authorizing them to substitute one resource for another would upset the plan, "all this immense mass of different units would necessarily have to enter *separately* into the calculations of the planning authority." This would create not only the formidable problem of data gathering but also the even more formidable task of solving the literally millions of equations necessary to discover an even relatively efficient combination of methods of production for any complex society. Either of these probably lies well beyond the capacity of human beings, even with the use of high-speed computers, to achieve in a lifetime. Together they constitute a problem that is "humanly impracticable and impossible" to solve (Hayek, 1972, pp. 181–182; 1975, pp. 209–210).

In fact, Hayek argued, the problem is even more fundamental than it at first appears. The belief that the CPB can arrive at an efficient allocation of resources, either through the use of simultaneous equations or via a process of trial and error, assumes that all of the relevant data are given and that they can be objectively articulated in a plan. But this is not only not the case, it *cannot ever be the case*. The relevant knowledge, the knowledge that individuals use to guide their activities, is not only information that is unique to the particular circumstances of time and place, and therefore changes with every change in these conditions; it is also radically subjective—it lies within and is dispersed among the minds of millions of individuals. In fact, much, perhaps most, of the relevant information is tacit knowledge, which *by its nature* defies objective articulation. It is this that Hayek had in mind when he referred to the "technique of thought" (1975, p. 210) that enables an engineer or manager to use his or her expertise to adapt to the unique problems created for his particular firm at a particular time resulting from changes in economic conditions. While such knowledge, which is a product of experience and the mastery of largely "unarticulated" rules, would have to be completely specified (articulated) in order for the mathematical formulas to lead to acceptable solutions, such complete articulation is impossible even *in principle*. This means that the CPB would be forced to rely on general categories of goods. An automobile would have to be treated as an automobile; a toaster as a toaster. Distinctions between the numerous types, sizes, ages, conditions of repair, and so on of automobiles or toasters must be glossed over. *Consequently, prices under "market socialism" could not contain the same amount of information, either quantitatively or qualitatively, as prices in a free market economy.* The result must be major inefficiencies (Hayek, 1972, p. 193).

The market socialist proposals, Hayek argued, contained other serious flaws. On the market, economic changes are spotted or discovered and the proper adjustments are promptly introduced by the entrepreneur. True, entrepreneurs do make mistakes. But those who do so regularly, or who do not spot changes early enough, suffer losses and are automatically removed from their positions. In this way the market spontaneously transfers resources from those who are less adept to those who are more adept at spotting changes. But under the market socialist proposals a price could not be changed until (1) the disequilibrium was spotted by the purchaser or seller of a factor, (2) this information was conveyed to the CPB, (3) the information was verified by the CPB, (4) a new price was determined by the CPB, and (5) all the parties concerned had been notified of the date at which the new price would go into effect. The result is that given the delays (endemic in the proposal) between the emergence of disequilibrium and the response to it, official prices would be in disequilibrium much longer and more severely than free market prices, and this would

> prolong excess demands and supplies and also prolong resource misallocation. . . . Markets enable buyers and sellers to react more quickly to changing data because the path by which information must travel in order for corrective price changes to be effected is shorter than it would be under socialism.   (K. Vaughn, 1980, p. 546)

Moreover, market socialism could be even reasonably efficient *only* if the CPB introduced price changes as quickly, frequently, and systematically as occurs in a free market. But this would render the entire notion of "price fixing" meaningless (Hayek, 1975, pp. 213–214. Also see Roberts, 1971, pp. 89–103).

Further, Hayek argued that the proposals lacked precisely that mechanism by which methods of reducing costs are discovered: price competition. Hayek's argument (1972, pp. 196–197) is worth quoting at some length:

> What is forgotten is that the method which under given conditions is the cheapest is a thing which has to be discovered, and to be discovered anew, sometimes almost from day to day, by the entrepreneur, and that, in spite of the strong inducement, it is by no means the regularly established entrepreneur, the man in charge of the existing plant, who will discover what is the best method. The force which in a competitive society brings about the reduction in price to the lowest cost at which the quantity salable at the cost can be produced is the opportunity for anybody who knows a cheaper method to come in at his own risk and to attract consumers by underbidding the other producers. But if prices are fixed by the authority, this method is excluded. Any improvement, any adjustment, of the technique of production to changed conditions will be dependent upon somebody's capacity of convincing the [CPB] that the commodity in question can be produced cheaper and that therefore the price ought to be lowered. Since the man with the new idea will have no possibility of establishing himself by undercutting, the new idea cannot be proved by experiment until he has convinced the [CPB] that his way of producing the thing is cheaper. Or, in other words, every calculation by an outsider who believes that he can do better will have to be examined and approved by the authority, which in this connection will have to take over all the function of the entrepreneur.

The problem facing the CPB is how to evaluate the performance of the managers. There is simply no objective means to do this. Could another manager produce more with the same inputs in the same location? Should more be invested? What if another believes that he or she can do better? Is the current manager to be removed? How long is the new manager to be given to make good on his claim? How are new investments to be handled? Capital is scarce. If the CPB decides to produce a new product, how will it decide which plants are to have their resource allocations restricted? How much risk is acceptable? What if a new investment turns out to be mistaken? Is the manager at fault, or the CPB that made the decision to fund the product? After all, Hayek notes, "even the best entrepreneurs will occasionally make losses and sometimes even very heavy losses" (1975, p. 234). What if a manager's losses stem from a new invention? What if they stem from a change in price decreed by the CPB? What if they stem from a reduction in output resulting from the use of obsolete equipment, which in turn was caused by heavy demand resulting from the inability of the CPB to arrive soon enough at the decision to raise the price?

By the nature of a centrally directed economy, the entrepreneurial function devolves on the CPB. The CPB, however, cannot duplicate the actions of the entrepreneur in the free market. The CPB is a government agency assigned the task of coordinating the economic activities of the entire economy. It is, in every sense of the term, a monopoly—a single agency performs all entrepreneurial decisions. But it is the competition between entrepreneurs that brings the discordant plans into mutual adjustment. It is also through entrepreneurial competition that the most efficient methods of production are discovered and employed. And on the market the entrepreneur invests either his or her own funds or funds that have been voluntarily loaned and can therefore be withdrawn anytime capitalists become dissatisfied with the entrepreneur's performance. The CPB is not investing its own funds. It in fact determines how much society will invest. Losses from poor investments can be covered by increasing the amount invested. Since the CPB's decisions are backed by the coercive arm of the state, dissatisfied "investors" cannot withdraw their funds.

The real question here is how much responsibility the manager is to have for the operation of a plant when the ultimate decisions are to be made by the CPB. In brief, as Hayek rather tersely summarized the contradiction in the various market socialist proposals (1977, p. 241), the entire concept of market socialism is contradictory. Prices must be either arrived at by competition *or* dictated by the planning board. The two methods are mutually exclusive.

Finally, Hayek recalled (1975, p. 212) the critical insight of Mises that even if the solutions to all of these problems could somehow be found, this would still be merely the beginning. Economic data are constantly changing, and thus all of these problems would have to be solved not just once but continuously.

In his 1920 article, Ludwig von Mises demonstrated that a non-market society was a logical impossibility. In the ensuing debate, socialists such as H. D. Dickinson, Oscar Lange, and Abba Lerner allegedly refuted Mises. Hayek, goes the interpretation, "retreated to a second line of defense" in arguing that socialism was logically possible but merely objecting that there were technical or practical problems to its implementation (see K. Vaughn, 1980). In fact, this is a complete reversal of the truth. It is true that Hayek's arguments were quite different from Mises'. But this is hardly unexpected, since Hayek's purpose was quite different. Mises argued that a marketless economy was not possible; Hayek was dealing with the contention of market socialists that directed or controlled markets could outperform free markets. There was a retreat, and a retreat of massive proportions. But it was a retreat on the part of the socialists who refuted Mises not by demonstrating that a marketless economy was possible but by shifting the definition of socialism from that of a non-market economy to a centrally directed market economy. As Hayek asked, "Is this not rather a case of covering up their own retreat by creating confusion about the issue?" (1972, p. 183). In the process they implicitly conceded that Mises was correct.

Hayek's arguments were, until recently, largely ignored. Yet, just as the War Communism period in the Soviet Union provided empirical confirmation of Mises, Hayek's critique has received empirical verification in the universal and continued poor economic performance of the market socialist countries as well as in the recent worldwide retreat from socialism.

Incentives

Socialism is beset by a second serious problem, that of incentives. Socialism not only endeavors to generate greater material prosperity, it is also committed to a more "just" distribution of wealth, which is usually interpreted to mean greater equalization. This goal is summarized in the appealing phrase "from each according to his ability, to each according to his need."

Incentives cannot be eliminated. They are omnipresent. Every politico-economic system generates a set of incentives. The question is whether a particular set of incentives is right or wrong, that is, whether the set is appropriate to attain the goals sought or claimed for it by those implementing the political and economic policies. The problem is that the two goals conflict. The incentives created by the attempt to bring about what many believe to be a more moral, or equal, distribution of wealth are in conflict with the incentives needed to generate increased material prosperity.

Assume that individual A lives in a market society and owns his own farm. If A increases his annual production from 100 to 150 bushels of wheat, he will receive the full benefit of the additional output. If the selling price of wheat is $5 per bushel, A's income will increase from $500 to $750, an increase of 50 percent. Conversely, by reducing his output from 100 to only 50 bushels, A's income will fall from $500 to only $250. Thus, private property and the market automatically "internalize the externalities"—they channel both the costs and the benefits of each individual's actions to that particular individual. They thus create incentives that reward hard work and productivity.

Now assume that A is a member of a socialist society, that there are 1,000 members, and that the output is divided equally among the members. Further assume that the output of the commune totals 100,000 bushels of wheat a year. At the price of $5 per bushel, total receipts for the society are $500,000, or $500 per member. The question is: How will A behave? Will he work hard? Will he shirk?

Assume that A is both naturally industrious and socially conscientious, that he works very hard and increases his production from 100 to 150 bushels. This increases the output for the society from 100,000 to 100,050 bushels per year, raising the income of the society to $500,250, and the income of each member from $500 to $500.25 a year. Thus, while A's output rose 50 percent, his income increased by a mere $0.25, or by 0.05 percent. Moreover, the income of the other 999 members also increased by $0.25 even though they did not work any harder and their output did not increase.

Clearly, A's hard work benefited everyone in the society *except himself*. While the *benefits* of A's extra production *were diffused throughout the society*, the *costs were concentrated on A*. Given the distributional policies of the socialist society it is clear that A's decision to increase his work was irrational, and it is highly unlikely that he would continue his Stakhanovite exertions, thereby subjecting himself to continued "exploitation" by other members of the society.

Conversely, assume the same conditions except that instead of being socially conscientious A is a shirker, who reduces his output from 100 bushels to only 50. What are the effects? The total output of the society drops from 100,000 bushels to 99,950. Its total receipts therefore fall from $500,000 to $499,750, causing each member's income to decline by $0.25, from $500 to $499.75. The other workers have not reduced their work loads, while A has cut his work load in half. A has obtained a major increase in leisure at a cost to himself of only $0.25. Since the *cost* of A's shirking *is diffused among all the members* of the socialist society while the *benefits are channeled to A*, socialism creates a strong incentive to shirk. The incentive is is not limited only to A, it is equal for all members of the society. If all members shirk, little or nothing will be produced and the commune will quickly find itself in dire straits. In short, *the distributional policies of socialism penalize industrious behavior.*

The dilemma of socialism is that individuals who respond rationally to the incentives confronting them will produce results that are irrational for the community as a whole. And there is little doubt that individuals living under socialism have responded rationally. Mosher, for example (1983a, pp. 39–40), quotes a Chinese peasant as saying that "People aren't lazy all the time, just when they do collective labor. When they work on their private plots they work hard. There is a saying, 'Energetic as dragons on private plots, sluggish as worms on the public fields.'" Others (Goldman, 1983, pp. 63–87; Rydenfelt, 1983, pp. 27–45; H. Smith, 1984, pp. 264–84) have found that the same sort of behavior is common in the Soviet Union and other socialist countries.

Because of the dual problems of economic calculation and incentives, the dispute between the market order and socialism is not only *the* major issue in any theory of economic development. It is, in fact, "no less than a matter of survival. To follow socialist morality would destroy much of present humankind and impoverish much of the rest" (Hayek, 1988, p.7).

Mercantilism

The third economic system, mercantilism, is a mixed or "middle of the road" order. A problem in using this term is that it is commonly attached to a particular historical period, Europe between the fifteenth and eighteenth centuries. However, insofar as it is meant to describe the highly interventionist policies pursued by European nations during this period, what is significant is not so much the historical period itself as the particular set of economic policies. Countries that follow the same or very similar policies can legitimately be labeled mercantilist, regardless of the historical period in which they exist.

The Peruvian economist Hernando de Soto (1989, pp. 201–229) has pointed to the striking parallels between the economic and political policies pursued in Peru and numerous other Third World countries in the twentieth century and the practices of the European nations during the historical period of mercantilism. Others (e.g., G. Anderson, 1988) have noted important parallels between the policies of the European nations during the mercantilist period and those pursued by the socialist countries such as the Soviet Union and the Eastern bloc nations of the twentieth century.

A second problem is that if, as was contended earlier in this chapter, a pure socialist or non-market economy is not feasible, does it make sense to argue that mercantilism blends elements of a feasible economic order, the market system, with those of an unfeasible order, a non-market system? I don't believe that this poses a difficulty. Subsidies, price and wage controls, licensing restrictions, tariffs, and the like are antimarket or non-market policies. If applied to every aspect of the economy they would effectively eliminate the market. Intervention of this type on a large scale would lead to pure socialism and economic collapse. While socialism, or universal intervention, is not feasible, mercantilism, or partial intervention, is a *feasible* system. In fact, all historically extant economies have been blends of market and non-market elements, and thus can be called mercantilist. The degree of intervention has varied immensely, from the predominantly laissez-faire economy of nineteenth-century America, in which interventionism was relatively limited, to the Soviet economy of the twentieth century, in which it has been quite extensive.

A laissez-faire, or free-market, economy is a lot like a furnace operating with the vents open wide. The heat pours out. A mercantilist economy would be similar to the furnace operating with the vents partially closed; only some heat gets through. While inefficient, this mode of operation is far superior to closing the vents entirely and keeping any heat from escaping (the case with the socialist economy). In brief, mercantilism is a blend of two economic systems, only one of which is feasible. Logically it would seem that the further one moved from the pure free market pole, the less efficiently the economy would operate until, at the pole of the pure non-market economy, it would collapse entirely. In fact, however, proponents of mercantilism see the government as able or even needed to stimulate the economy. Thus, for mercantilists, government is the indispensable agent in economic development.

The problem is that government has no resources that it has not first taken from others. Consequently, as Mises repeatedly stressed (1966, pp. 743–744), government cannot stimulate one branch of production except by curtailing production elsewhere. If the government spends $100 million to stimulate the automobile industry, it must first acquire that money in taxes. What it stimulates in one sector is therefore offset by the reduced purchases of taxpayers in other areas. No overall economic stimulus has occurred. All that has happened is that wealth has been transferred from taxpayers to tax recipients.

But, some argue, this is not necessarily the case. Government pump priming, the printing of money, can stimulate the economy as a whole. In fact, such pump priming measures are only a more prosaic form of taxation whose consequences in this regard do not differ from direct taxation. Assume that there are only two individuals, A and B, and that each has $1,000. They would have equal purchasing power and would be able to buy goods of equal total value. Now assume that the government decides to stimulate the economy by printing an extra $1,000 and giving it to B. Will this stimulate the economy? It is clear that it will increase B's purchasing power. But it has not, in itself, changed the volume of goods for sale. As both A and B enter the marketplace, the increased demand will cause prices to rise. This will stimulate the economy in those areas where B spends her *additional* money. On the other hand, A will not be able to purchase as much as before and the economy will be depressed in those areas where he is forced to curtail his purchases. Factors will therefore be bid away from areas formerly patronized by A and into areas where B expands her purchases. Thus, while the additional money has changed what is being demanded and thus what is being produced, it has not changed the overall level of demand. And the effect is as if the government taxed A in order to benefit B.

In fact, since inflation renders calculation more difficult, the number and magnitude of entrepreneurial errors will increase, thereby consuming scarce capital goods and impeding economic growth. Thus, far from stimulating aggregate production, such policies are more likely to retard it.

Still, some maintain that pump priming will increase prices only when there is full employment but not, as is likely to be the case, when there is unemployment and "excess capacity." This too is incorrect. If workers are unemployed or factors are not being utilized, one must ask why. This can only be because wages are too high or the "wrong" goods, that is, goods not demanded by consumers, are being produced. If so, one must ask why entrepreneurs, whose job it is to spot such maladjustments, do not hire the unemployed workers to produce goods and services demanded by consumers? In fact, they could hire unemployed workers at wages that would permit them to produce and sell goods that consumers are currently purchasing at prices that are below those consumers are currently paying. The cheaper prices would leave consumers with additional money that they could spend in other areas, thereby stimulating employment in these areas. In this way, the maladjustments would be eliminated and full employment would return. If these adjustments do not occur, the reason must be that there exist non-market obstacles preventing the adjustments from being made. The inflationary policies of the government do nothing to remove these obstacles; they merely introduce an additional set of obstacles, thereby compounding the very problem they were intended to solve.[3]

Even if government cannot stimulate economic growth, what of its capacity to contribute to economic development, that is, the widening of the range of individual choice, by adopting policies that will increase the economic position of the poor while not harming, at least in any significant degree, the position of the wealthy?

What if the government attempts to benefit the poor by setting a limit on prices for goods of particular importance to the poor, such as housing and food? The consequences of price controls are well known. Without exception the results have been contrary to the (official) intention of their proponents. If the government establishes a maximum price for milk, then at the lower price more is demanded. But since profit margins are now lower in this area than elsewhere, capital will flow out of this area into areas where it will reap higher returns. The result will be a shortage of exactly the good that the government thought so important that it desired to provide it to people at lower prices. To ensure its continued supply the government would have to restore the previous profit margins by ensuring lower prices for all the factors used in the production of milk. But this would cause profit margins for those factors to fall, resulting in a scarcity of the factors needed to produce the milk. The government would then have to fix the prices of those factors required to produce the factors that are needed to produce milk, and so on in ever widening circles. Eventually the government would have to fix the prices of *all* consumer goods and *all* factors of production, because if some were permitted to be determined by the open market, the higher returns in these areas would cause capital and labor to flow into them and away from production of the goods the government believed so indispensable that it intervened in their production (Mises, 1969b, pp. 18–35).

The result of price controls is that the government must either abandon its interventionist policies or eventually fix the prices of all goods and services, including labor. In this case it would have evolved from mercantilism to pure socialism.

This process can be halted by the use of subsidies to maintain the profit margins for the products whose prices have been fixed. But this creates its own set of problems. First, the amount of revenue required to maintain the profit margins is directly related to the number of goods whose prices are fixed and the extent to which the prices are below the would-be market price. The greater the number of such goods and the more the official price departs from the would-be market price, the greater the revenue required, and therefore the higher the tax.

But if taxes are proportional, so that everyone pays the same percentage of income in taxes, then most of what the poor gain in terms of lower prices is offset by the additional taxes they must pay. If, however, the tax system is "progressive" so that the wealthier pay a greater percentage of their income in taxes than those who are less well off, the result is that those who, as determined by the decision of the marketplace, are most adept at serving consumers are penalized. Penalizing those who are productive and successful while rewarding those who are indolent and/or unsuccessful establishes a set of incentives that is inimical to increased production and economic growth.

The argument is sometimes made that the wealthy can or should be taxed to provide the poor with a guaranteed minimum income. The key point here is that those who continued to work would be working solely for the difference between their wage and the legal minimum. If the minimum is set high enough to eliminate poverty, it would also be high enough to have a disincentive effect on those whose incomes are only slightly above the minimum. If some of this group quit working, not only would this increase the number of those receiving government benefits, it would also impose increased taxes on those who continued to work, thereby encouraging still others to quit. The result would be an ever-increasing number of "beneficiaries" living off an ever-dwindling number of producers. The logical outcome of a lucrative guaranteed minimum-income policy would be the collapse of the whole pyramid. If the minimum were set low enough to preserve the incentive to work, it would be too low to eliminate poverty.

Empirical studies (B. Bartlett, 1986a; 1986b; Krauss, 1984; Marsden, 1986; Morrisson and Schneider, 1987; Phaup and Lewis, 1985; Rabushka, 1987b; Utt and Orzechowski, 1985; World Bank, 1983, pp. 60–61) confirm the relation between high tax rates and poor economic performance:

> In *all* cases the countries that imposed a lower effective average tax burden on their populations achieved substantially higher rates of growth in real gross domestic product (GDP) than did their more highly taxed counterparts. The average (unweighted) annual rate of growth of GDP was 7.3 percent in the low-tax group and 1.1 percent in the high-tax group. (Marsden, 1986, pp. 3–5)

Moreover, numerous studies (Eberstadt, 1987; Fields, 1962, pp. 159–160; Krauss, 1984, pp. 38–40; Marsden, 1986, p. 5; Osterfeld, 1988c, pp. 13–19; Rabushka, 1987a; *U.S. News*, 1986, pp. 26–32) also show that the chief beneficiaries of economic growth are the poor. As Bartlett (1986b, p. 46) has summarized the evidence, "rapid economic growth based on free markets and low taxes has narrowed the distribution of income between the highest and lowest income classes." This means that, regardless of their intent, policies that slow economic growth actually hurt the poor, at least in the long run. This is shown in Figure 2-1, which depicts the position of the poor under free market conditions and with altruistic intervention. Assume that at time *t* the government implements a policy of transferring wealth from the rich to the poor. It is clear that the poor would benefit from the transfer with their income rising from the free market level, P_m, to the interventionist level, P_i. However, due to the disincentive effect and the misallocation of resources, aggregate output in the interventionist economy (line *Y*, Y_i) increases

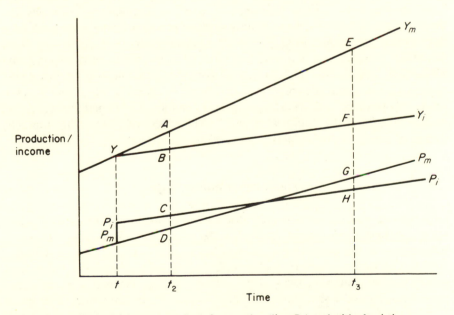

FIGURE 2-1. Income of the poor under a free market (line P_m) and with altruistic intervention (line P_i). (See text.)

more slowly than it would have under free market conditions (line Y, Y_m). By time t_2, economic output with intervention is at B, whereas output would have been at A in the absence of intervention. However, the position of the poor is better than it would have been without the intervention by the amount $C - D$. At time t_3, aggregate output with intervention is at F whereas output would have been at E without intervention. Significantly, the poor are now worse off than they would have been in the absence of intervention by the amount $G - H$, and this difference increases over time.

How long the long run will be is impossible to say. It depends on how severely the interventionist policies retard productivity. Given the above differences in growth rates between the less interventionist, low-tax economies and their higher tax, more interventionist counterparts, output would double about every 9.5 years for the former but only once every 64 years for the latter. If this is correct, then the long run would actually be quite short.

In fact, the plight of the poor is likely to be even worse than that depicted here, for there are good reasons to believe that government policies will not be designed to attain such altruistic goals. Rather than achieving a larger part of a smaller pie, the poor, in an interventionist system such as mercantilism, will in fact receive a smaller part of a smaller economic pie. The reasons for this will be dealt with in the next section.

Political Institutions

There are only two means through which human beings can satisfy their needs, and these two are mutually exclusive. One is work, or production; the other is robbery, or predation (Chodorov, 1980, pp. 84–92; Oppenheimer, 1975, pp. 1–41). Work can be defined as the use of one's labor, physical or mental, to produce goods and services for oneself or for voluntary exchange (or, on occasion, as gifts). By robbery or predation is meant the coercive or involuntary appropriation of that which is produced by others. Following Oppenheimer, the former is termed the "economic means," the latter the "political means." While these two *means* are mutually exclusive, their purpose is identical: the acquisition of wealth.

The Interventionist State

Government, that agency that possesses a legal monopoly on the use of force in society, is the ideal institution for the transfer of wealth from producers to predators. In fact, as the nineteenth-century political theorist and U.S. Vice President John C. Calhoun pointed out, such transfers are in the very nature of the governmental process (Calhoun, 1953). The fiscal action of government consists of two parts: taxation and disbursement. What is collected from each individual in the form of taxes cannot equal what is returned individually in the form of disbursements, since, said Calhoun, "that would make the process nugatory and absurd."

"It must necessarily follow," he continued, "that some one portion of the community must pay more than it receives back in disbursements, while another receives in disbursements more than it pays in taxes" (p. 16). Thus, taxation *by its nature* is a process by which wealth is coercively redistributed. An important question is: What is the direction of these transfers? Does government tend to transfer wealth from the rich to the poor, from the poor to the rich, or does the money remain within the same economic class?

The popular view is that through such measures as welfare payments and the progressive income tax, governments transfer wealth from the rich to the poor. Neither theory nor the empirical data support this conclusion. Calhoun saw this clearly. The "necessary result" of the inevitable inequality between taxes and disbursements

> is to divide the community into two great classes: one consisting of those who, in reality, pay the taxes and of course bear exclusively the burden of supporting the government; and the other, of those who are the recipients of their proceeds through disbursements, and who are, in fact, supported by the government. (Calhoun, 1953, pp. 17–18)

The interests of these two classes, those who are the net tax beneficiaries and those who are net taxpayers, are antagonistic. "The greater the taxes and disbursements," Calhoun wrote, "the greater the gain of the one and the loss of the other." Consequently, the larger and more active the government, the higher the stakes and thus the more bitter and more antagonistic the struggle between the classes.

One significant consequence of an interventionist state is that as the government acquires greater say over who gets what, enormous amounts of time, effort, and resources are diverted from economics to politics, from the process of production to that of redistribution, an activity referred to by economists as "rent seeking." The result, as Olson has observed (1982, p. 47), is not only to "generate resentment," thereby making society "more divisive," but, by diverting resources away from production and impeding the efficient allocation of resources, to also "reduce the efficiency and aggregate income."

Further, the net tax beneficiaries will favor expanding the scope of government's activities as well as increasing the size of its disbursements. And since the beneficiaries are also the ones in possession of government power, the result, "in an outcome so unequal," is not open to doubt (Calhoun, 1953, pp. 25–26). It is therefore *in the very nature of both man and government*, according to Calhoun, that (1) there will be a ruling group and (2) government will be run in the interests of that group.

If one asks who is likely to control the government, the wealthy or the poor, the answer is clear: the wealthy. There is a natural affinity between wealth and power. Those who have political power can use it to obtain wealth. On the other hand, the wealthy are usually able to use their wealth to obtain political power. Once in control of the state, they are in a position to use the political functions to perpetuate and even enhance their own positions, since they have at their disposal the entire panoply of government resources, from the use of tax revenues to purchase the allegiance of important, potentially rival groups to political indoctrination through public school systems and the news media, to the use of physical force to quash any challenge to their rule.

While the circle is seldom completely closed, and certainly not everyone who is wealthy is part of the ruling elite, its opening, especially in the interventionist state, is quite small. The "rise to the top" by those from the lower strata usually cannot be ruled out completely. However, such a rise, difficult under any circumstances, is rendered far more so by the *artificial obstacles* imposed by the elite. What is important is that the more interventionist the state, the more numerous the obstacles the elite is able to impose.

But what of economic power? Couldn't the wealthy just as easily exercise their economic power independent of the political means? The fact is that there is no such thing as economic power. The free market is nothing more than the sum of all voluntary transactions. In such a situation no one is in a position to *compel* anyone to do anything. All anyone can do on the unhampered market is offer to make a transaction or accept or reject a proffered transaction. Since no transaction will be consummated unless the parties to it benefit, ex ante, any and all free market transactions must be to the mutual benefit of all parties involved. Of course, one or even both parties will often sweeten their offers to influence the other to accept. But influence is one thing, coercion is something else. While all economic transactions are positive-sum, political transactions are either zero-sum or even negative-sum, since they take place *at the expense* of at least one of the parties involved. If it were otherwise the transaction would have been consummated voluntarily and coercion would not have been needed.

It is, in fact, precisely the absence of economic power that makes the acquisition of political power so important. For it is only through the latter that the rich can really solidify their wealth. The position of the entrepreneur on the market is always insecure. Capitalism is *not* a profit system; it is a *profit and loss system*. Just as the market provides opportunities for the acquisition of wealth, it also presents the possibility of loss. This means that the entrepreneur can never relax. No sooner would he triumph over one competitor than he would be met by others intent on cutting into "his" share of the market. No sooner would she uncover a lucrative area for returns on investment than other entrepreneurs would follow suit, the increasing production forcing profits down. And as soon as the entrepreneur failed to take advantage of the latest investment opportunities or adopt the latest methods of production, he would risk losing his position to those who did. The situation remains unchanged even in the case of a naturally formed, or free market, monopoly. For the moment the monopolist tried to extract profits by raising prices, she would attract new competitors intent on obtaining a share of the lucrative profits (Armentano, 1972; Osterfeld, 1987b).

Behind all of this there is the ever present possibility of entrepreneurial error. Since the first concern of capitalists is to realize a profit, and since the rigors of the market mean that this is a difficult and perpetual struggle, capitalists have no concern for the market as such. It is only natural that they should, whenever possible, turn to the state, which, with its monopoly on the use of force, can institutionalize profits by implementing statist measures such as tariffs, licensing restrictions, and so on to keep out competition, raise prices, and keep wage rates low. As Gary

Anderson puts it (1988, p. 487), "monopoly rents flow to those . . . in the fortunate position" of being able to manipulate government policy in such a way as to "transfer resources from consumers to themselves."

The distinction between political and economic means is important. It is characteristic of the market process that wealth is dispersed unevenly. But if the market is free, there are no external impediments that prevent an individual or a group from rising from a lower to a higher position. Historically, one finds a great deal of social and economic mobility in the relatively open societies of the West. For example, the vast majority of immigrants to the relatively open, free-market United States of the nineteenth century were penniless on arrival. This was a strictly *temporary* phase. Very quickly these individuals, and in fact entire ethnic groups, began to ascend the economic ladder, their places at the bottom being taken by succeeding generations of immigrants. Thus, while there was always a statistical bottom 20 percent, the individual occupants of that category were constantly changing (see Sowell, 1981a; 1981b, p. 344). In brief, *markets produce classes.*

In contrast to the openness and fluidity of classes, a caste is characterized by its rigidity: one born into a caste remains in it for life. If the wealthy are able to use government to institutionalize their positions, one can say that class is transformed into caste. It is important to emphasize that it is only through the state—the political means—that a socioeconomic position can be institutionalized. Hence, while *markets produce classes, states produce castes.* The concepts are pure types. The question is not which is present, classes or castes. Elements of both can be found in all existing societies. The key issue is the cause of the relative mix of class and caste. If the analysis is correct, one would expect to find an inverse relationship between government control and social and economic mobility: the more interventionist the state, the smaller the incidence of social and economic mobility.

There is considerable empirical support for the theoretical proposition that markets produce classes while states create castes. It has already been pointed out that the low-tax, market-oriented Third World countries have experienced significantly more rapid economic growth than the higher tax, more interventionist Third World economies. Moreover, evidence also indicates that while *all* economic groups benefited, in almost every case the chief beneficiaries were the poorer economic groups.

The evidence further indicates not merely that real economic growth has been sluggish to nonexistent among the high-tax, interventionist economies but that it is precisely in these economies that the poor have experienced little if any economic improvement and may even have been victims of economic deterioration. For example, per capita income for the 41 sub-Saharan African nations (excluding South Africa) declined 15 percent during the postcolonial period (World Bank, 1983, Table 1, p. 148). And both public and private agencies placed the decline in per capita income in the Philippines at 14 percent between 1983 and 1985 (Villegas, 1986, p. 135). Yet many of these countries are, or have been, ruled by some of the wealthiest people in the world. The estimated worth of such current or past rulers as Zaire's Mobutu, Indonesia's Sukarno, and the Philippines' Marcos, to name but a few, is counted in the billions of dollars (Ayittey, 1987c, p. 216. Also see Andreski, 1986, pp. 65–66).

The reason for this anomaly is not hard to find. While government controls, through high tax rates and an extensive network of economic regulations, stifle economic growth, they nevertheless enable the rulers to divert vast sums of wealth from the producers into their own and their cronies' pockets. Through the use of the political means, the rulers are in a position to benefit themselves *at the expense of the rest of society.* They are able to use their political power to entrench and perpetuate themselves at the very top of the politico-economic hierarchy. In the process, they consign the poor to a life of continued and grinding poverty.

The mercantilist state transforms a society characterized by movement between classes and general economic advance for all economic groups into a stratified caste society characterized by a permanent ruling elite and an equally permanent poverty-stricken underclass. Since the interventionist state is far more likely to transfer wealth not from the rich to the poor but from the poor to the rich, the result is not only that the size of the economic pie is smaller than it would be in the absence of intervention but that the portion going to the poor is also smaller. Thus, *the poor receive a smaller part of a smaller pie.* This is illustrated in Figure 2-2. Y, Y_m depicts aggregate output under free-market conditions, Y, Y_i under interventionism. Since the intervention transfers income from the poor to the rich, the income of the poor at the time of the initial intervention, t, falls from P_m to P_i. Since the interventionist economy is less efficient than a free-market, the difference between the position of the poor under intervention and what it would have been under free market conditions expands with time. Thus, by time t_2 the economic output is smaller than it would have been by the amount $A - B$. And the difference between the position of the poor and what it would have been without the intervention has increased to the size $C - D$.

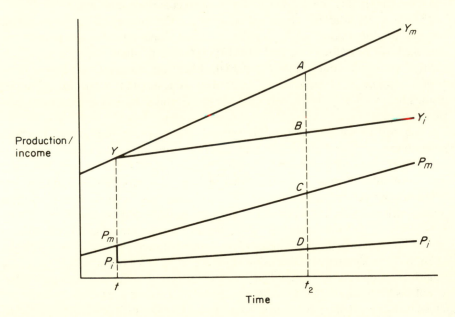

FIGURE 2-2. Income of the poor under a free market (line P_m) and with realistic intervention (line P_i). (See text.)

This raises an interesting and important question. Tax rates in most Third World countries are notoriously high. Table 2-1 shows marginal tax rates at the "poverty level." For an American family of four the poverty level is $12,000, in 1983 dollars, and the marginal rate is 12 percent. For a Tanzanian family with an equivalent income the tax rate is 85 percent; in Sierra Leone and Mali it is 70 percent; in Tunisia 63 percent, and in India and Sri Lanka 62 percent. Since high taxes and extensive government controls impede economic growth, why don't Third World rulers reduce taxes, abandon their interventionist measures, and allow the market to propel their countries to prosperity? After all, as the Laffer curve (Figure 2-3, bottom) shows, as taxes increase government revenues will also increase but at a slower rate until a point is reached at A when, because of the disincentive effect, further increases in the tax rate will actually reduce government revenues. Thus, government revenues will be no larger at tax rate K than at rate M. While the evidence indicates that tax rates in most MDCs are low enough that reduced taxes will

TABLE 2-1. Marginal Tax Rates for $12,000[a] and $6,000 Incomes

Country	$12,000 Rate	$6,000 Rate	Country	$12,000 Rate	$6,000 Rate
Low-Income Economies					
Ethiopia	49.0	29.0	Morocco	39.8	18.6
Bangladesh	60.0	55.0	Philippines	24.0	15.0
Mali	70.0	60.0	Nigeria	25.0	15.0
Zaire	60.0	60.0	Thailand	22.0	10.0
Burkino Faso	25.8	23.2	Peru	26.0	8.0
Burma	50.0	35.0	Guatemala	7.0	0.0
Malawi	45.0	30.0	Turkey	40.0	40.0
Niger	45.8	10.8	Tunisia	63.3	42.6
Tanzania	85.0	65.0	Jamaica	57.5	45.0
Somalia	56.1	56.1	Ecuador	24.0	17.0
India	61.9	65.0	Colombia	35.0	21.1
Benin	27.2	23.6	*Upper Middle-Income Economies*		
Ghana	60.0	60.0			
Madagascar	26.8	14.5	Jordan	15.0	5.0
Sierra Leone	70.0	57.5	Malaysia	25.0	9.0
Sri Lanka	61.6	61.6	Chile	8.0	0.0
Kenya	50.0	25.0	Brazil	25.0	10.0
Pakistan	60.0	50.0	South Korea	23.0	7.5
Sudan	60.0	50.0	Argentina	0.0	0.0
Chad	38.4	21.6	Portugal	41.5	21.5
Lower Middle-Income Economies			Mexico	36.5	16.8
			Greece	43.7	22.0
Senegal	24.1	19.4	Hong Kong	10.0	0.0
Liberia	34.0	27.5	Singapore	12.6	6.3
Yemen	15.0	15.0			
Indonesia	15.0	15.0	*Industrial Market Economies*		
Zambia	45.0	15.0			
Egypt	32.1	25.4	Ireland	35.0	35.0
Ivory Coast	19.0	12.4	Japan	25.0	4.0
Zimbabwe	34.0	22.0	USA	12.0	0.0

Source: B. Bartlett, 1986b, p. 47. Reprinted by permission of the Heritage Foundation.
[a]U.S. poverty level for family of four in 1983.

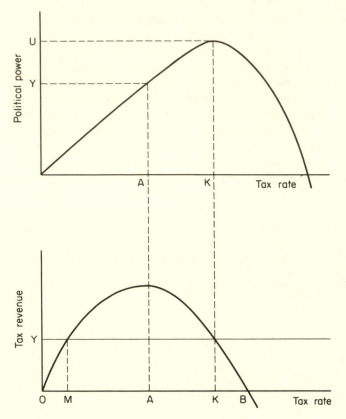

FIGURE 2-3. Curves showing where government revenues and political power are maximized. (See text.)

not increase government revenues, this is patently not the case in most LDCs. Why then do so many LDCs remain on what economists refer to as the wrong side of the Laffer curve?

Whether one is on the "right" or the "wrong" side depends on what it is that one wants to achieve. There are quite good reasons why political rulers would want to be on the wrong side. While economic growth rates vary inversely with tax rates, political power tends to vary positively. Thus, what is the wrong side of the Laffer curve economically may be the right side politically (Figure 2-3).

Political rulers value power either as an end in itself or as a means to other ends such as wealth. Since the greater their power the more secure their position, rulers will desire to maximize their power. Political power is a combination of two countervailing forces: (1) the size of the economy and (2) the extent of the ruler's control over it. The former creates an incentive to reduce taxes; the latter to raise them. Thus, a ruler's power would be determined by the *absolute* size of the wealth at his disposal. A ruler with a 70-percent control over a $10 billion economy would be far more powerful than a ruler with a 90-percent control over a $1 billion economy (control over $7 billion versus $900 million).

Consequently, if marginal tax rates of 25 and 75 percent yield the same revenue, the higher rate would be preferable. A larger percentage of the population is dependent on the ruler for its livelihood when the tax rate is high than when it is lower. The greater their dependence, the less likely they will be to place themselves in jeopardy by opposing the ruler. Similarly, the greater the ruler's control over the economy, the fewer the areas independent of such control, and thus the fewer the opportunities for potential adversaries to organize and finance an effective opposition.

Moreover, even if lower tax rates and fewer controls would increase the ruler's revenues in the long run, the fact is that the future is necessarily uncertain. It is therefore quite rational for political rulers to sacrifice a larger but very uncertain payoff in the future for a certain, if perhaps somewhat smaller, payoff in the present.

> Countries and societies may be immortal . . . but *governments* certainly are not. Concerned about its tenure, which is likely to be much shorter than the average individual's lifetime . . . the government's rate of time preference is likely to be much higher than that of private individuals.   (Lal, 1987, p. 59)

As a result, government policies tend much more often to be predatory than altruistic.

The tendency to sacrifice long- for short-run gains is reinforced by other factors. For instance, establishing tax rates so high that they reduce per capita GNP qualifies the country for larger sums of foreign aid, which not only will offset most or even all of the loss in domestic tax revenues, it can also be used to line the pockets of the rulers and their cronies.

Why Interventionism Is Less in the First World than in Other Worlds

Political rulers in all parts of the world face the same incentives. Why is it that tax rates tend to be high and intervention greater in the Second and Third Worlds than in the First World?

One key reason is that the West has historically been far more open, more politically and religiously decentralized, and less tradition bound than any other culture of which we know. Although the reasons for this decentralization are largely fortuitous, the crucial fact is that the existence of such independent entities posed an obvious upper limit on the ability of government rulers to solidify their hold on power by controlling the political and economic environment. Feudalism, which emerged in the wake of the decline of the Roman Empire, was itself a highly decentralized system.

Within the fief, power was centralized in the hands of the lord. It was also unified, with the lord controlling the political, legal, and even religious spheres. But the fourteenth century was a watershed in European history. Rosenberg and Birdzell (1986) described it as "a time of disaster in European society." An "apocalypse of wars, plagues and famine resulted in a major reduction in population and a contraction in the land area inhabited and under cultivation" (p. 37). One significant effect of the decline in population, a decline estimated at between one-fourth and one-third of the population of Europe (McEvedy and Jones, 1978, p. 25), was to create a labor shortage that shifted the terms of trade in favor of the peasant. The multiple centers of authority endemic in European feudalism presented the ever-present possibility of flight to another fief or even to an independent town, thereby limiting the ability of the lord to exploit the serf. Tullock (1987, p. 3), for example, points out that while the lord was nominally the peasant's superior, and while the peasant was legally bound to the land, he could "decamp quietly at night feeling fairly confident that about twenty miles down the road there would be another lord who would welcome him because he needed additional peasants to operate his land. There were, of course, also the Church and the free cities, both of which would offer him protection." And North and Thomas state (in Tullock, 1987, p. 14) that "would-be founders of new manors had to seek out peasants aggressively, even to the point of limiting their own powers by offering grants and privileges to entice potential emigrants." The idea that there were limits to the power of the lord gradually gained acceptance in theory as well as in practice, as did the notion that obligations were to be reached voluntarily, by negotiation and contract.

Towns grew in importance during the Middle Ages either as trading centers or for military, administrative, or even ecclesiastical purposes. Although towns were part of medieval society, they too contributed to the decentralization, diffusion, and limits of power. Despite trying, neither the feudal lords nor the emerging monarchies were powerful enough to exercise effective control over the city-states. As a result the towns became at a relatively early time independent, politically autonomous, self-governing entities. The power of the town rulers, however, did not extend beyond the boundaries of their own towns. Thus, while the guilds exercised monopolistic power within their town, trade beyond the city limits placed them in competition with merchants from other city-states. Moreover, as Europe recovered from the Black Death and the population of the cities began to grow, it became increasingly difficult for the rulers to suppress "unfair competition" with the merchant and craft guilds (Osterfeld, 1989b).

All of this "was without exact parallel in other cultures. . . . Nothing very similar can be found in the great civilizations of Asia or the Muslim world" (Rosenberg and Birdzell, 1986, p. 59). As late as the fifteenth century, Chinese technology was superior to the West's, yet the monopoly of power enjoyed by the Chinese leaders, in contrast to the political competition found in the West, resulted in a stifling political environment designed to preserve the status quo but which, in the process, worked to discourage the individual initiative that is necessary to translate the "troublesome innovations" into economic advancement.

The development of the scientific method, the work primarily of Bacon, Galileo, and Newton, reinforced the trend toward the diffusion and limitation of power. By using the experimental method, Galileo was able to refute the teaching of Aristotle regarding the speed of falling bodies. Since the Church, through Aquinas, had wedded itself to Aristotle, Galileo's successful refutation of Aristotle undercut the power of the Church (see, e.g., Greer, 1987, pp. 363–372).

The experimental method was vitally important in another respect. By providing a rigorous method of ascertaining truth it could combine the specialization of disciplines with the general accumulation and development of knowledge. The claims of one theory, propounded in one region or emanating from a particular discipline, could be scientifically tested in other geographical areas or even by practitioners in other disciplines. This, of course, went hand in hand with the political diffusion of power, for a multiplicity of independent funding sources is all but a prerequisite for scientific innovation. Since a great deal of uncertainty is attendant on any innovation, there must be some means of deciding which projects will be pursued and which will not. When science is hierarchically organized and the state is the sole source of scientific funding, and when pressure can be brought to bear on scientists espousing unpopular ideas, mistaken theories cannot be adequately tested and those proven wrong discarded. It was precisely the multiplicity of sources of money in the West that facilitated, indeed stimulated, scientific advances, for, as Rosenberg and Birdzell point out (p. 258),

> The rejection of a meritorious proposal by a half-dozen decision-making centers is presumably less probable that its rejection by only one. The system is thus biased toward the acceptance of proposals, but with the cautionary qualification that the costs are borne by the decision maker, and all the rewards go to the programs which succeed.

In short, the evolution of Western society after the fourteenth century was characterized by increasing decentralization and diffusion of power, by what Landes (1969, p. 15) referred to as the "context of multiple, competing centers of power," and by the gradual emergence of the notions of the limited state and inviolable individual rights. What gradually emerged was something that had not been consciously planned by anyone, was vigorously opposed by those in power, and received systematic philosophical justification only decades, even centuries later. It was the achievement of increasing security to person and property that more than anything else formed the foundation for the material development of the West. As Landes commented (p. 15),

> The role of private economic enterprise in the West is perhaps unique: more than any other, it made the modern world. It was primarily the rise of trade that dissolved the subsistence economy of the medieval manor and generated the cities and towns that became the political and cultural, as well as the economic, modes of the new society. And it was the new men of commerce, banking and industry who provided the increment of resources that financed the ambitions of the rulers and statesmen who invented the polity of the nation-state. Business, in other words, made kings. . . . To be sure kings could, and did, make or break the men of business; but the power of the sovereign was constrained by the requirements of state (money was the sinews of war) and international competition. Capitalists could take their wealth and enterprise elsewhere; and even if they could not leave, the capitalists of other realms would not be slow to profit from their discomfiture.

In short, social and economic independence is a necessary condition for effective opposition to the expansion of government control. Unfortunately, this condition is seldom present in the Third World. Very few Third World political leaders have permitted open opposition. One-man rule by decree rather than rule of law has been the norm, and criticism of government has usually been dealt with ruth-lessly. Bauer, for example, observed (1972, pp. 529–530) that the environment

> has for centuries been less authoritarian in the West than in Africa and Asia and thus more conducive to experimentation, a questioning turn of mind and an inter-est in material advance. The subjection of the individual in Africa and Asia to polit-ical authority and to tradition has discouraged these qualities.

The Ghananian economist George Ayittey has noted that most African soci-eties have become even less open during the postindependence period. Of the 51 African countries, only Botswana and Senegal permit freedom of the press and crit-icism of government policies. "Hundreds of African writers are currently languish-ing in jails," he writes (1987d, p. A7), and

> freedom of expression and speech—so vital in helping Africans develop their tal-ents and skills to . . . search for and debate solutions to their problems—is anath-ema to most black leaders. In much of Africa, the media are under government control. . . . The least deviation elicits sanctions, often fatal, against writers and journalists.

In his study of the sociopolitical environment in Latin America, Lawrence Har-rison, former director of the U.S. Agency for International Development missions to that region, arrived at similar conclusions. An "authoritarian view of human relationships," he writes (1986, p. 24), "is manifest at all levels" of Latin American society. The result is

> a reluctance to think independently, to take initiative, to run risks and to tolerate dissent. I am convinced that this is why Latin America—like the Third World in general—produces a disproportionately small number of entrepreneurs.

The Liberal Order

The evidence is clear. The interventionist state generates obstacles that prevent sus-tained economic growth and development. A drastic reduction in state activity, a wall of separation between economics and politics, is necessary to create what Rich-ardson and Ahmed (1987, p. 23) call an "enabling environment," an environment that would allow economic growth and development to occur. The enabling envi-ronment is, they point out, nothing more nor less than the traditional nineteenth-century "liberal economic environment."

The essential component of a liberal order is the limitation of government's functions to the protection of the person and property of each individual. The laws or rules imposed by the liberal state are negative, or purpose independent. They are restricted to telling individuals what they may *not* do. This means that in a liberal order each individual possesses a "protected domain" (Hayek, 1969, p. 167) within which he or she has complete autonomy. No one, not even the state, is permitted to intervene. Individuals have the right to do anything they wish as long as they do not violate or invade the protected domains of other individuals. It follows that all interactions between individuals are voluntary; they are the result of mutual consent and thus redound to the mutual advantage of all parties concerned.

A social order can be based on one of three schemes: (1) the cooperative pursuit by its members of a common goal, (2) manual or conscious coordination based on collective ownership, (3) or spontaneous coordination based on private ownership. It is obvious that the first scheme presupposes a large measure of agreement on both the ends to be pursued and the means to be employed. Short of resorting to the widespread use of coercion to achieve the necessary agreement, this method places severe limits on the size of the social order. Voluntary agreement seldom extends beyond the family or tribe and often does not exist even there. Studies of the extended family indicate that disagreements among members create "many pressures toward fission" that regularly result in the splitting of the family into several smaller units (Goode, 1964, pp. 47–50). Thus, if a society is to be based on voluntary personal cooperation in the pursuit of a common set of goals, it would necessarily be severely limited in size. As a result, division of labor and specialization would not be possible. The corresponding elimination of most opportunities for gains from trade and exploitation of economies of scale would reduce its members to a life of poverty.

A social order based on the manual or conscious centrally planned coordination of its parts likewise would not be possible for any society beyond the most primitive level since, as already discussed, it would lack the means of economic calculation. This scheme, too, would entail a life of severe hardship for its members.

The third scheme is based on private ownership of property. Individuals not only possess different goals, they also have different talents. The recognition of these different talents gives rise to the division of labor and the exchange of services for mutual benefit. The greater the number of exchanges, the greater the degree of specialization. The prices or exchange ratios that emerge from the network of exchanges reveal what goods and services are most urgently needed by the society. And the pull and push of profits and losses ensure that precisely those things are produced. Since specialization increases individual productivity, and since efficient resource allocation is a product of the prices stemming from the network of exchanges, the result is that what individuals produce through this method of social interaction far exceeds, in quantity, quality, and variety, the sum of what all these individuals could produce separately. It also far exceeds the sum of what can be produced in any other known scheme of economic organization.

One of the chief advantages of a society based on private property is that, unlike a society based on the pursuit of common goals, there is no upper limit to its size. The network of exchanges can, quite literally, cover the entire earth (and perhaps some day more than the earth). Private property facilitates voluntary cooperation among millions of individuals who may have no particular goals in common and do not even know one another. Gasoline, made from Mideast oil, is regularly pumped into American-owned cars, many of which have been designed in Japan and manufactured in Malaysia. Many people in the Third World may dislike Americans but they purchase such American-made products as pharmaceuticals and agricultural equipment. The United States and the Soviet Union may not have gotten along politically, but the Russians were eager customers for American grain and computers. Private property not only permits cooperation among people who are not even aware of each other's existence but encourages cooperation among people who possess vastly different cultural values and have virtually nothing in common. The result is a massive increase in productivity stemming from the deepening of the division of labor and the ability to take advantage of economies of scale.

An empirical study of 115 countries between 1960 and 1980 showed the impact of political and economic freedom on economic growth. Societies that were "politically open" had an annual real per capita growth rate of 2.53 percent; those that were "politically closed" had an average growth rate of 1.41 percent. Societies that respected individual rights and subscribed to a rule of law had an average real annual per capita growth rate of 2.75 percent; those where the right of the government to intervene transcended individual rights had an average per capita growth rate of 1.23 percent. And societies that relied heavily on the free market grew at an average real annual rate of 2.76, compared with a growth rate of 1.10 for command economies. The average rate of real per capita growth for those societies that possessed political, social, and economic liberty was 2.73 percent; those that were politically closed, in which the rights of the state transcended individual rights and the government intervened heavily in the economy, had a growth rate of 0.91 percent (Scully, 1988, pp. 7–8).

For private property to perform its function, property rights must be clearly specified. Otherwise, individuals may be able to shift the cost of their actions onto others. Failure to take into account the full costs of one's actions will impede the process of economic calculation, thereby bringing about a misallocation of resources. A good example is air pollution. If a firm is able to pollute, it is in a position to shift some of the costs of its operations to others in the form of impaired health and damaged property. The result is that the costs to the firm are lower than they would be if it had to take into account the full costs of its operations. Permitting property rights to be extended into air space would "internalize the externalities." It would mean that a firm that polluted would be violating the property rights, the protected domain, of others and would have to make full restitution. This outcome would not only force the firm to take into account all of its costs of production, it would also encourage the firm to search for methods to eliminate or contain the pollution, so as to avoid having to pay these costs in the future.

Individuals have a natural desire to live the most comfortable lives they can or, as Mises was fond of putting it, to reduce their "felt uneasiness." If such means as theft, either direct or indirect (i.e., through the use of government), are ruled out, and if the major externalities are internalized, as they would be in a private property system, then the only way in which individuals can achieve an actual reduction in their felt uneasiness is to produce. It is for this reason that classical liberalism results in prosperity: in contrast to all other politico-economic systems, it places a premium on creative, productive behavior. By eliminating wealth transfers, it promotes wealth production.

In a society based on private ownership, those who believe that they are being harmed by this method of social organization have the freedom to "drop out" and adopt the type of lifestyle or establish the type of society they desire. The fact that very few people adopt this course of action means that they realize, *consciously or implicitly*, that they are able to attain far more of their individual goals in society than out of it. It is not the effort to achieve some common end, the psychological need for companionship, or the conscious efforts of some grand planner that explains the existence of *modern* society, but the presence of an immense and complicated network of voluntary exchange for mutual benefit.

Culture

The free market and the liberal state do not necessarily result in economic growth and development. Rather, they constitute an institutional framework, an enabling environment, within which development may take place. They are necessary but not sufficient conditions for economic growth. What is required is for individuals to respond rationally or appropriately to the incentives generated by that institutional framework. If the opportunity for profit is present and individuals do not respond, or do not respond appropriately, growth will not occur. Nevertheless, one can be fairly certain that when the appropriate institutional framework is present, the responses necessary to ensure economic development will be forthcoming.

This is not to imply that cultural attitudes and values are irrelevant. On the contrary, they are critical. As Bauer has written (1981, p. 22), "some policies, popular beliefs and mores affect income differences between societies so greatly that they are central to any sensible discussion of such differences." Beliefs and attitudes inimical to economic development include such things as the relative importance of a passive or contemplative life compared with an active life; lack of such qualities as a sense of personal responsibility for one's actions, curiosity, and experimentation; high preference for leisure; emphasis on the performance of duties rather than the assertion of personal rights; the focus on group status rather than individual achievement; and the belief in a preordained and unchanging universe and in reincarnation, the former removing a sense of responsibility for one's position and the notion that one's actions can affect one's future position, the latter reducing the importance of one's present life (Bauer, 1972, pp. 78–79). This list could be greatly extended. Since such attitudes, Bauer notes, "are so deeply felt and strongly held that they have become an integral part of the spiritual and emotional life of many millions, probably hundreds of millions," of people living in the Third World, they will not be overcome in the short space of a few years.

Nevertheless, neither Bauer nor others, such as Sowell (1981a, b; 1983), Novak (1982), Harrison (1985, 1986), and Smiley (1982), who place great emphasis on cultural factors to explain the differences in economic performances between countries and, within countries, between different ethnic groups, really treat culture as an independent variable, but as the result primarily of historical factors. As such, despite the fact that there may be a large measure of cultural inertia present as these attitudes are handed down from generation to generation, the culture is not immune to change. Attitudes and beliefs accommodate themselves to changing situations.

Self-interested and Altruistic Behavior

This raises important questions regarding the nature of incentives. People desire to make their lives better. They act to maximize their utility. This means that while individuals respond rationally to the incentives confronting them, what is rational, in terms of both goals and the means to attain those goals, is in part a product of the particular beliefs dominant in a society. For example, the Hindu belief in the sacred status of cows creates a religious incentive to not slaughter cattle that is usually powerful enough to override the narrowly economic incentive for slaughter. A materialistic society may encourage the development of an acquisitive spirit by rewarding conduct that results in economic progress. Conversely, the belief that wealth is evil will result in an environment in which the (at least outward) display of acquisitiveness will be suppressed.

This is not to suggest that human nature is plastic. History suggests, I think, that, for practical purposes at least, human nature is immutable. Attitudes and beliefs may evolve, but the *principle* that motivates action remains unchanged. One's beliefs and attitudes will change as one's information and knowledge change, as the conditions within one's life change, as the environment—in particular the beliefs and attitudes held by others—changes. For example, immediately following the Ayatollah Khomeini's ascension to power in Iran, the number of individuals entering the religious life in that country rose dramatically. It is scarcely convincing to attribute this to an immediate and dramatic transformation in the nature of the citizens of Iran. The Iranian people did not suddenly become more religious. It is far more convincing to interpret this movement as a recognition by Iranians that the road to power, and thus to the good things in that society, which under the Shah lay through the cultivation of political or military connections, now lay through Islam. They would have to adapt to these changed conditions.

This does not mean that human beings are solely self-interested. In fact, Adam Smith, in the very first sentences of *The Theory of Moral Sentiments* (1969, p. 3), published in 1759, emphasized that people do exhibit a genuine concern for the well-being of others: "How selfish soever man may be supposed there are evidently some principles in his nature which interest him in the fortune of others, though he derives nothing from it, except the pleasure of seeing it." This natural interest in the fortune of others, Smith added, extends to some degree even to complete strangers. "When we see a stroke aimed, and just ready to fall upon the leg or arm of another person," he wrote (1969, pp. 4–5),

> we naturally draw back our own leg or our own arm; and when it does fall we feel it in some measure, and are hurt by it as well as the sufferer. The mob, when they are gazing at a dancer on the slack rope, naturally writhe and twist and balance their own bodies as they see him do, and as they feel that they themselves must do if in his situation. Persons of delicate fibres and a weak constitution of body complain, that in looking on the sores and ulcers which are exposed by beggars in the streets, they are apt to feel an itching or uneasy sensation in the corresponding part of their own bodies. The horror they conceive at the misery of those wretches affects that particular part in themselves more than any other; because that horror arises from

conceiving what they themselves would suffer, if they really were the wretches whom they are looking upon.

Humans are far from unidimensional, and Smith saw no necessary conflict between self-love and benevolence. Not only did he accept self-interest as a fact of nature rather than something to be combatted, he viewed it, along with benevolence and justice, as one of the three great virtues. Self-interest, or prudence as Smith usually referred to it, is concerned with the preservation of one's life and health (1969, p. 310). The methods of prudence are not only learned in childhood, they "may be considered as lessons delivered by the voice of Nature herself, directing him what he ought to choose, and what he ought to avoid, for this purpose. . . . Their principal object is to teach him how to keep out of harm's way" (1969, p. 310). Smith's observations led him to conclude not only that prudence was a *stronger* motive than benevolence, but also that it was *fortunate* that this was so. Beneficence, he said, "is an ornament which embellishes." Prudence, however, is the "foundation which supports the building." An excess of benevolence, the desire to right all wrongs will inevitably result in great mischief:

> The administration of the great system of the universe, . . . the care of the universal happiness of all rational and sensible beings, is the business of God, and not of man. To man is allotted a much humbler department, but one much more suitable to his weakness and powers, and to the narrowness of his comprehension—the care of his own happiness, of that of his family, his friends, his country: that he is occupied in contemplating the more sublime, can never be an excuse for his neglecting the more humble department.   (A. Smith, 1969, p. 348).

Human beings, Smith also observed, desire the approbation of others while simultaneously seeking to avoid their disapproval. "Society" is the great regulator of behavior. We learn how to conduct ourselves by observing the reactions of others and adjusting our behavior accordingly. The fear of social disapproval supplies the incentive for us to *moderate* our more antisocial dispositions. Behavior that is excessively self-interested, that is too self-centered, is met with social disapproval and is in this way moderated spontaneously. This is far from perfect, of course. But Smith felt that this natural system of morality was far superior to any known alternative.

Finally, Smith made the vitally important observation that those closest to us, our spouses and children, are normally so much a part of our lives as to be virtual extensions of ourselves. It is for this reason that we are willing to sacrifice for them, often even giving up our very lives. However, the further removed people are from us, the less intense is our fellow-feeling, or sympathy, for them. Thus, while we may sympathize with the plight of the starving in Africa, we feel their sorrow much less strongly than a minor cut or bruise suffered by our own child (1969, pp. 321–326). "Nature, it seems, when she loaded us with our own sorrows," Smith dryly commented (1969, p. 66), "thought that they were enough, and therefore did not command us to take any further share in those of others, than what was necessary to prompt us to relieve them."

Smith believed that human nature has natural, built-in moral limitations. While we have a natural propensity to sympathize with the misfortune and misery of others, the greater the distance, psychological and physical, between ourselves and those with whom we sympathize, the greater the asymmetry between their pain and ours; between what they feel pungently and our own "languid emotions." It is for this reason that like any other good or service, the incidence of other-interested, or altruistic, behavior will become more scarce as its cost rises. In fact, given the asymmetry between the two pains, the decline will be quite rapid. Thus, most people walking past an empty automobile and noticing that the lights are on will stop and turn them off. Few, however, will walk a half mile to do so. For the same reason, an individual will work hard if she can retain the fruits of her labor or to help her family, but will not work hard for the benefit of society. The benefits, material and psychological, that accrue to an individual from such altruistic behavior are so minute that they are invariably outweighed by the costs to him.

There can be little doubt that Smith's observations are correct. Human nature is not plastic, and individuals act overwhelmingly in their own self-interest. For example, one need merely recall the unspeakable horrors that have been inflicted on people in the name of universal benevolence, in the effort to improve human nature by cleansing it of the "evil" of self-interest. These horrors range from the mere tens of thousands executed during the French Revolution in the effort to create Robespierre's "moral citizen" (see, e.g., Palmer and Colton, 1978, pp. 367–370; Talmon, 1970) to the millions and even scores of millions murdered in the Soviet Union, China, Kampuchea, and other communist countries in the name of building the Marxist "new socialist man" (see Heller and Nekrich, 1986, pp. 222–276; Solzhenitsyn, 1973; U.S Senate, Subcommittee on Internal Security, 1977[4]). Yet despite the ruthless determination with which such schemes were carried out, and despite the unimaginable suffering they wrought, they accomplished nothing. Human nature remained unchanged. Self-interest was not expunged; no "new man" emerged.

Similarly, it was obvious to the eighteenth-century Scottish philosophers and economists, Adam Smith and David Hume to mention only the best known, that any tolerably workable social order had to be based on a system of incentives. "We may conclude," Hume wrote ([1777] 1976, pp. 194–195, italics in original),

> that in order to establish laws for the regulation of property, we must be acquainted with the nature and situation of man, must reject appearances which may be false though specious, and must search for those rules which are on the whole most *useful* and *beneficial*. . . . Who sees not, for instance, that whatever is produced or improved by a man's art or industry *ought*, for ever, to be secured to him, in order to give him encouragement to such *useful* habits and accomplishments? That the property ought also to descend to children and relations for the same *useful* purpose? That it may be alienated by consent in order to beget that commerce and intercourse which is so beneficial to human society? And that all contracts and promises ought carefully to be fulfilled in order to secure mutual trust and confidence by which the general *interest* of mankind is so much promoted?

Unfortunately, what was obvious to Smith and Hume seems to have completely eluded most of the social philosophers and practical politicians of the modern age.

For example, the "structuralist" school, dominant in the 1950s and 1960s, maintained that people in the LDCs were fundamentally different from individuals in the West. They argued that individuals in the LDCs do not think in terms of market incentives and therefore do not respond to changes in prices and costs. Gunnar Myrdal, one of the chief spokesmen of this school, argued that "peasants were hardly economic men," that the inhabitants of the LDCs "must acquire an ambition that today is missing," and dismissed the notion that higher prices would encourage peasants in the LDCs to increase output as "a carelessly over-optimistic view" (in Phaup and Lewis, 1985, p. 78).

The data indicate that this view is incorrect. The correlation mentioned earlier in this chapter between economic output and the rate of taxation is a clear case in point. Olson has observed (1987, p. 95) that

> individuals from different cultural backgrounds are broadly similar in response to unambiguous market incentives: behavior in the bazaars and market squares of the developing world is not vastly different from behavior in the markets of the economically advanced nations.

Numerous other studies (Bauer and Yamey, 1957, pp. 89–101; G. Clark, 1988; Hill 1963, 1986; Popkin, 1979;[5] Rabushka 1987a) confirm this conclusion.

These findings have significant ramifications. Neither state control nor social pressure that has the effect of suppressing outwardly self-interested behavior alters the nature of that behavior; suppression merely drives it underground, as it were. When individuals are not permitted to retain what they have produced, as is the case when agriculture is collectivized, they stop producing. When individualism is derided as a display of "decadent bourgeois behavior," innovative ideas are no longer heard and innovative behavior ceases. When the desire for wealth is condemned as "crass materialism," hard work is discouraged. In all these cases, society is poorer by the amount of goods and services not invented and not produced.

The tragedy is that in all such cases individuals find themselves in positions where their utility is maximized by *not* producing. Individuals continue to respond rationally to the incentives confronting them. The attempt to stamp out self-interested behavior succeeds only in changing what is in the self-interest of individuals to do. By punishing or condemning productive behavior, that is, by increasing the cost of producing, less is produced. The result is destitution and misery. The government may attempt to stimulate production by resorting to punishment, but this does not eliminate self-interested behavior. It merely turns society into a prison. People will work to avoid punishment. But conscripts are not known for either the quantity or the quality of their work.

Unfortunately, it is precisely the culture of so many Third World countries that inhibits economic development. Lawrence Harrison, the former director of the Agency for International Development missions in the Dominican Republic, Costa Rica, Guatemala, Haiti, and Nicaragua, writes (1986, pp. 23–24; also see Novak, 1982) that Latin American culture is characterized by such things as:

1. *An authoritarian view of human relationships.* This view, which permeates all social institutions, creates an unbridgeable gap between the autocratic leaders

and their obedient followers. One consequence is "a reluctance to think independently, to take initiatives, to run risks and to tolerate dissent." There is no room for the entrepreneur in such an environment.

2. *The view that work is bad.* This has deep historical roots that extend back to the Spanish conquest of the New World. The Spanish came to America to get rich quick and return to Spain, freed from the need to work again. This attitude was reinforced by the enslavement of blacks and Indians. Slaves worked; masters did not. Hard work came to be associated with slavery and inferiority and therefore something to be assiduously avoided. Economic development cannot occur in the absence of hard work and perseverance.

3. *A Hobbesian individualism characterized by excessive mistrust and fear of others.* The radius of trust seldom extends beyond the confines of the family, says Harrison. Those outside the family are viewed as enemies to be combatted, not as individuals with whom one can trade and cooperate for mutual advantage. Development is integrally connected to the degree of specialization, which in turn depends on the extent of the market. It is obvious that in a society permeated by mistrust, the scope of the market must be quite limited. Mistrust constitutes a serious impediment to development.

Cultural attitudes such as these, which collectively culminate in a kind of fatalism—the belief that one has no control over one's future— make economic progress all but impossible. But where did such attitudes come from? They have emanated from a historical situation in which the ruling elite, that group that is either the government or firmly in control of the government, was able to implement policies designed to institutionalize its position and literally to live off the labor of the rest of society. From the recognition that individuals are placed in a position where they must work for others, where they have no hope of ever improving their situation regardless of their efforts, it is only a short jump to the conclusion that the rational response is to work as little as possible. Similarly, from the recognition that if individuals are somehow able to advance themselves economically they will be beaten or killed and their wealth seized by the elite, it is, once again, but a short step to the conclusion that such things as hard work and risk taking are irrational. Looking at things from the opposite perspective, if individuals are born into privileged positions and aware that they will remain in those positions regardless of how much or little they work or how improvident their lifestyle, it is but a short step to the conclusion that work is only for the foolish. The result is that work quickly comes to be excoriated by both groups, and cultural traditions emerge that discourage hard work. As Hume, Burke, and more recently Hayek have clearly recognized, traditions and customs represent the accumulated wisdom and experience of the society. They reflect what is rational for individuals to do in the social context within which they live.

If the LDCs would suddenly repeal their mercantilist restrictions and adopt a liberal, noninterventionist policy, such cultural traditions would begin to change. This is so, it should be clear, because with the change in the politico-economic framework, what is rational likewise changes. Such things as hard work and risk taking which, under a mercantilist order, were irrational become, under a liberal noninterventionist order, quite rational. While the causal relationship is obviously not one way, while culture can and does influence what governments can and will do, in today's world at least, where government plays such an immense role in shaping the environment in which people live, it has become the prime determinant of cultural traditions.

How long would a cultural transformation of the kind just mentioned take? There is always a degree of cultural lag. It is impossible to say specifically how long the change would take, especially in a case where no one could be sure that the change in government policy was not simply a ploy to stimulate production, which production would then be seized by the government. However, it seems likely that, once begun, the length of the transition would be shorter in the Third than in the Second World. The underground economy, or informal sector, is extensive in both worlds (see Chapter 9). Given the direct relationship in the underground economy between hard work and risk taking on the one hand and personal income on the other, the informal sector encourages both hard work and entrepreneurial activity (de Soto, 1988, pp. 19–21). However, the single biggest difference between the Second and Third Worlds lies in the degree to which cultural mores inimical to development have been inculcated. The technological superiority of the Second World has enabled it to be far more successful than the Third in using its monopoly of the news media and the schools in propounding its anticapitalist, antiprivate property, anti-individualist, and prosocialist messages. Thus, the cultural mores inimical to economic progress are likely to be far more ingrained in the Second World. For example, in Soviet schools the more identical childen's sketches were to those of their classmates, the better. Children whose art work deviated from the work of others were reprimanded for their nonconformity. Architects, even those with innovative plans, did not attach their names to the plans since this would be self-advertisement, a serious infraction of socialist morality. In all aspects of life the collective was applauded and glorified; the individual was denigrated. A Russian proverb illustrates this mentality: "In a field of wheat, only the stalk whose head is empty of grain stands above the rest." To many Russians, says former *New York Times* Moscow correspondent David Shipler (1989, p. 73), "this was a beautiful statement, one that touched the essence of human affairs." "The collective" Shipler notes, is a word that has acquired the aura of the sacred.

> The ethic of collectivism is much more than a fragment of Marx and Engels polished by Lenin and stuck like an irritating splinter into Russian flesh. It has been absorbed into the structure of values and mores so that its violation stimulates genuine revulsion in many people.   (Shipler, 1989, pp. 72–73)

In contrast, the often crude collectivism of Third World governments is something that has been foisted on the indigenous populations. They may have been smothered by it, but they have not absorbed it (Ayittey, 1987b). It is common to hear that the chief impediment to "nation-building" in sub-Saharan Africa is its extreme ethnic and tribal pluralism. There are, for example, between 250 and 300 groupings in Nigeria alone, at least 120 in Tanzania, and more than 40 in Zaire (Liebenow, 1986, p. 56). "These tribal loyalties," comments Smiley (1982, p. 73), "have predominated and, to the chagrin of the Marxists, they have proved far more resilient than class loyalties." Yet, as James Vaughan points out (1977, p. 181, emphasis in original), because "there is so much diversity in the structures and complexities of African political systems . . . a fundamental underlying principle may be overlooked. That is virtually all of these diverse political organizations are based upon the validity of public means of resolving disputes and conflicts, that is, upon the *rule of law*." While kingship is common to nearly every African tribe, the tribal king is not a source of the law. On the contrary, he is beneath the law and is held responsible for the well-being of "his" kingdom. He can be removed if things go badly. Although now illegal, regicide is not uncommon for a king who violates the customary law of the tribe (Vaughan, 1977, p. 186). Thus, tribalism and ethnic groupings remain vibrant. And to the extent that they operate as a barrier to the grasping arms of the centralizing and oppressive state, they may actually serve as bastions for the defense of individual liberty, economic growth, and the rule of law.

Material and Moral Rewards

Even if human nature is immutable, isn't it possible to substitute moral or nonmaterial rewards, such as public recognition, for material ones? The empirical evidence indicates that this is not the case. Where this was attempted, such as in the Soviet Union, some Eastern European nations, and Cuba following the communist revolutions, the results were uniformly bad and the experiments were rather quickly abandoned with material "bonuses" being substituted for nonmaterial rewards. The idea of nonmaterial incentives is beset by an internal contradiction. Everyone can receive material benefits. However, nonmaterial rewards are, by their nature, selective. They single people out for excellent performance. They set the recipients apart from their peers; they give them celebrity status. Their purpose is to stimulate production by playing on the desire of people to become celebrities. But everyone cannot become celebrities. To make everyone a celebrity is, in fact, to reduce everyone to anonymity. Thus, the idea of nonmaterial incentives is contradictory. It is supposed to stimulate people to be productive workers. But if it succeeded in doing this, then everyone would expect to be a celebrity. Since this would be impossible, its very success would mean mass disappointment, thereby eliminating the incentive to work hard. Thus, while specific incentives are influenced by culture, both empirical data and logical analysis indicate that material incentives cannot be fully replaced by moral or nonmaterial ones. In short, the fatal flaw in the attempt to substitute moral for material incentives is that, in the process, it transforms a positive-sum process, in which everyone can gain, into a zero-sum process, in which only a few can gain and can do so only at the expense of everyone else.

Since the enabling environment means that the institutional barriers to economic development have been removed, it follows that if the "appropriate" responses are not forthcoming the only conclusion one can draw is either that the members of that society value other things more highly than material prosperity or that those values that are necessary for material advance to occur are not widely held. In either case the enabling environment allows all members to maximize their utility. If individuals desire material prosperity but do not respond either because they do not have the appropriate values or because they fear that government will reverse course and seize their wealth, then "staying the course" will eventually convince individuals that it is safe to pursue economic wealth. If they are successful, their values and activities are likely to be emulated by others. If economic development does not occur because most people do not value material prosperity, they can continue to pursue a lifestyle of "genteel poverty" regardless of what others may do.

Notes

1. On the meaning of such crucial terms as *voluntarism, coercion, freedom*, and *power* see, for example, Hayek, 1960, pp. 11–21; Mises, 1966, pp. 279–87; Osterfeld, 1988b, pp. 283–94; and Rothbard, 1956.

2. This is merely a very brief presentation of the market process. For more extensive and sophisticated treatments see Mises, 1966; Rothbard, 1970a, b; and Hazlitt, 1969. Also see Mises' brilliant essay, "Profits and Losses," in Mises, 1969b, pp. 108–149.

3. On the nature and causes of the business cycle see Hayek, 1932, 1933; Mises, 1966, pp. 524–586, 1971; Rothbard, 1963, 1970a, pp. 850–879.

4. The subcommittee report significantly underreported the actual human cost. For example, on the basis of newer information, scholars now place the cost of the Great Leap Forward in China not at between 1 and 2 million but at between 25 and 30 million lives. See, e.g., Mosher 1983a, p. 50; Rydenfeldt, 1983, p. 87; U.S. Agency for International Development, 1989, p. 15.

5. Popkin's work (1979) is extremely important. Popkin contrasts the views of the moral economists with those of the political economists. The former see peasants as "communal oriented," who put the welfare of the closed or corporate village above, or at least equivalent with, the welfare of the individual. The latter see the typical peasant as putting his or her own welfare first. Popkin derives a systematic set of hypotheses to test the two views. In every case, Popkin finds that the actual behavior of the peasant refutes the viewpoint of the moral economists and supports that of the political economists. For example, the moral economists argue that peasants oppose market "penetration" of the village because it undermines village solidarity and reduces the security of the individual peasant. In fact, he finds that such penetration is favored by the peasants because it liberates them from nearly total dependence on the village leaders. It is the village leaders who oppose market penetration precisely because, by providing outside options, the market undermines their control over the peasants. That is, it substitutes a multistranded relationship for the traditional dyadic one.

II

THE KEY VARIABLES

3

Food

There are some things about the world that everyone knows. One is that the world food situation is deteriorating, that population is increasing more rapidly than food production. Another is that there is only a limited amount of arable land in the world and that much of this, the most fertile part, is already under cultivation. Thus as population grows it will become increasingly difficult and eventually impossible to feed the world even at today's level. This chapter will begin by examining both of these beliefs. It will then focus on the causes of the food crisis in Africa and conclude by analyzing various proposals for dealing with the ongoing task of feeding the growing world population.

World Food Trends

Despite the famine in Africa, world food data show not only huge increases in aggregate production but, more importantly, sustained increases in per capita food production. For example, studies by both the U.N. Food and Agriculture Organization (UNFAO) and the U.S. Department of Agriculture (USDA) show that at least from 1948, the first year for which U.N. data are available, world food production has surpassed population increases by, on average, just under 1 percent per year (see Figure 3-1 and Table 3-1). As Figure 3-2 shows, this is not simply a short-run phenomenon. The real-world price of food has been declining for well over a century and probably much longer, indicating that food output has been increasing more rapidly than population growth.

Of course, such aggregates can obscure as much as they reveal. For example, UNFAO data (1977, pp. 3–7) show that while the increase in per capita food production in the developed countries averaged 1.4 percent per year for the 15-year period from 1961 to 1976, the increase in production in the less developed countries declined from a yearly average of 0.7 percent in the 1960s to 0.3 percent between 1970 and 1976. However, two things are worthy of note here. First, a decline in the rate of improvement must not be confused with a deterioration in absolute terms. The fact is that the average individual in a less developed country was still better fed in 1980 than he or she was in 1960 or 1970. And second, the decline in the rate of improvement during the mid-1970s was temporary, due largely to the nearly

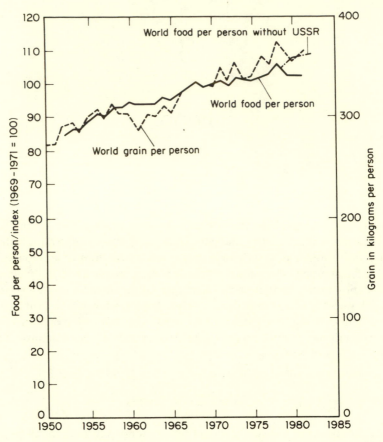

FIGURE 3-1. Per capita food production in the world. From Simon and Kahn, 1984, p. 17.
Reprinted by permission of Julian Simon.

TABLE 3-1.   World Food Production, 1980–1985 (1976 = 100)

	1980	1985	Annual % Change
Aggregate Food Production			
World	104	119	2.8
More developed countries	105	114	1.7
Less developed countries	107	126	3.6
Per Capital Food Production			
World	99	104	1.0
More developed countries	102	108	1.1
Less developed countries	100	103	0.6

Source: Adapted from U.S. Department of Commerce, 1988, p. 817, Table 1410.

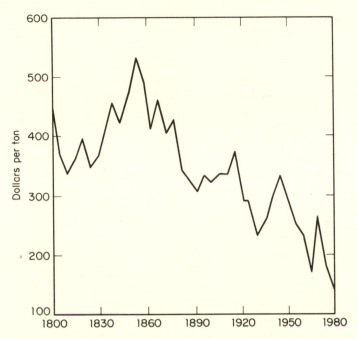

FIGURE 3-2. Real international price of wheat, 1800–1980, as deflated by the wholesale price index (1985 = 100). From U.S. Agency for International Development (USAID), 1989, p. 36. Reprinted by permission.

worldwide bad weather in 1971 and 1972, which caused widespread crop failures (UNFAO, 1977, p. 3). As Table 3-1 shows, during the 1980s, *even with the devastating famine in sub-Saharan Africa* where per capita food production declined by 1.2 percent per year during the first half of the 1980s, improvement in world per capita food production returned to its pre-1970 levels.

Most significantly, recent studies clearly show not only dramatic but even accelerating improvement over the past 20 years. In the 1964–1966 period, 59 countries (42%) of the world recorded an average daily caloric consumption of at least 100 percent of requirements. By 1974–1976 the number had risen to 72 countries (52%). And by 1982–1984 the figure stood at 92 (66%). This is a 56-percent increase in less than 20 years, an astonishing accomplishment especially when placed in its historical context. Of the 47 countries below the 100-percent level, 24 were making progress toward it. Of the 23 that have not made progress since 1964–1966, 14 (60%) are in sub-Saharan Africa. And fully 81 percent of the countries of the world, including China and India, now report average caloric consumption levels of at least 90 percent of daily requirements (see World Resources Institute, 1987, pp. 252–253, Table 16.3).

In short, as Ward Sinclair of the *Washington Post* has recently put it (1986, p. 23), far from deteriorating, "the world is producing more food than ever before believed possible." Since market-oriented reforms were introduced during the post-Mao period in China, food output has increased 40 percent, and China has now become a food exporter. Bangladesh, whose desperate plight inspired the first rock-music relief concert in 1971, is now self-sufficient in food grains. And India, until just recently regarded as a hopeless basket case, has doubled its wheat production in less than 20 years, increased its rice output by 30 percent and its per capita food grain production by 7 percent, and is now a net food exporter. Indonesia, traditionally one of the world's largest importers of rice, is now rice self-sufficient. It has also made impressive gains in the production of cassava, sugar, and other products. Between 1971 and 1982, agricultural output in the Philippines rose by 50 percent; rice and corn production more than doubled, the former through increased yields, the latter through expanded plantings. Between 1971 and 1982, agricultural output in Latin and South America rose nearly 38 percent, with per capita food output increasing by more than 10 percent. And in Africa, trends since the 1983 famine are encouraging. Serious problems remain, such as in Sudan. However, as one noted agricultural analyst (Avery, 1989, p. 8) has remarked, "more of Africa's countries are currently providing at least minimal caloric sufficiency to more of their populations now than at any time in recent decades." Given Africa's extensive agricultural resources, appropriate government policies would do much to expedite the rate of improvement.

As of 1985 the world surplus of grain stocks exceeded 190 million tons, or enough to feed all of the hungry people in sub-Saharan Africa for the next 50 years. The countries of Western Europe, the United States, Japan, and even Taiwan, Saudi Arabia, and the Philippines are all struggling with the problems of food surpluses. The world agricultural market is so glutted that world grain prices declined 50 percent in real terms during 1986–1987. As a result of depressed food prices, the United States diverted more than 70 million acres of cropland—over 10 percent of its total—during the 1980s. This is enough to supply more than 100 million tons of grain per year. The U.S. government pays farmers billions of dollars not to farm. It has also ordered the slaughter of 1.6 million cows in an effort to stabilize dairy prices. And one study recommended that the members of the European Community would be better off if they *destroyed* 20 million metric tons of beef, butter, and grain, since the surpluses reduce world prices, increase export subsidies, and entail storage costs of more than $4 billion per year (see, e.g., Armey, 1990; Avery, 1987, 1990; *The Economist*, 1985; Insell, 1985; Sinclair, 1986, pp. 23–25; U.S. Department of State, 1985).

In brief, as a recent report has stated (U.S. Department of State, 1985, p.i),

> World agricultural production rose about 25 percent between 1971 and 1982, despite droughts, energy shortages, and other problems. Agricultural output in the developing countries rose 33 percent in the period, raising per capita food output significantly in all major developing regions except Africa. World food prices are currently at historic lows, and commercial surpluses of virtually every important agricultural commodity are being held in storage around the globe.

The Availability of Arable Land

Can we sustain the progress? Isn't practically all of the world's arable land now under cultivation? And wouldn't the cost of clearing, draining, and fertilizing marginal land prove increasingly costly, thereby making it ever more difficult and eventually impossible to feed the world's population (L. Brown et al., 1989, pp. 12–16; Hewitt, 1985; Meadows et al., 1972, pp. 56–63; U.S. Council on Environmental Quality, 1982, pp. 16–17)?

The noted agricultural economist D. Gale Johnson has pointed out (1984, p. 89) that

> the view that there remains very little land to bring under cultivation in the world, and that this places a significant limitation on the expansion of food production, is both factually incorrect and, even if true, largely irrelevant.

The first point is whether the amount of land under cultivation is rapidly approaching its physical limitation. Revelle (1984, pp. 185–186) makes the telling point that "potentially arable land," that is, land that can produce an acceptable level of food crops, comprises only 24 percent of the total ice-free land mass of the world, or approximately 3.2 billion hectares (1 hectare = 2.47 acres). However, this is well over twice the amount cultivated in recent decades and more than triple the amount cultivated in any single year. Thus the widespread belief that there is very little land left to bring under cultivation is simply not true. Aside from the diversion of millions of acres of cropland in the United States and other developed countries already mentioned, in many other regions of the world land could be readily brought under cultivation if demand were sufficient. Brazil has approximately 200 million acres of unplanted arable land in the Cerrado Plateau south of Brasilia capable of producing an estimated 135 bushels of corn per acre. Other crops, including coffee and soybeans, could also be grown there. Argentina is currently pasturing nearly 80 million acres of some of the world's most fertile farmland. The Guatemalan government is opening up more than 2 million acres of new cropland, and Bolivia and Mexico both have millions of acres of unused farmland. Africa has hundreds of millions of acres of uncropped arable land. Sudan, for example, has tens of millions of acres of uncropped arable land.

Further, in every region of the developing world, large parts of the farmed areas are being underused. Brazil, for example, "probably has more food and agricultural production potential than any other country in the world." Yet its yields remain quite low by world standards (U.S. Department of State, 1985, pp. 10–11). Similarly, in Peru, Argentina, Jamaica, the Soviet Union, and the countries of Eastern Europe, yields are well below their potentials. And millions of farmers in sub-Saharan Africa still practice primitive methods of crop rotation, with fallow periods ranging from 6 to 20 years. With the adoption of more modern methods of farming, including the use of improved seeds and the application of chemical fertilizers, both of which are relatively inexpensive, outputs could be increased significantly. In many cases, such as in sub-Saharan Africa, the Philippines, the Soviet Union, and most of the countries of Eastern Europe, much could be accomplished simply by removing government price controls. Not only would this increase yields but, by reducing the need to cultivate marginal soils, it would also reduce both deforestation and soil erosion (see Avery, 1989, 1990; D. G. Johnson, 1984, pp. 67–112; Revelle, 1984, pp. 184–201; U.S. Department of State, 1985).

Moreover, the concept of arable land is not static. Indeed, the history of agriculture could be written largely in terms of transforming "unarable land" into "arable land." Much of the American Midwest was forest and swampland. No account of arable land in, say, 1800 would have included it. Now, after it has been cleared and drained, it is among the most fertile lands in the world. And the elimination of the tsetse fly would open up to cultivation about 200 million hectares of African land, an area larger than the total cropland in the United States (Gerster, 1986, pp. 814–833; Kahn, Brown, and Martel, 1976, pp. 123–124; Osterfeld, 1988a, p. 193). Today we literally have the technological ability to make nearly any land arable. For example, by the use of tariffs that enabled domestic soybean prices to rise to three times the world market level, Italy managed to increase its soybean output from practically zero in 1980 to more than 770,000 tons in 1986. Through the use of subsidies averaging $1,100 per ton, Saudi Arabia increased its production of wheat from 150,000 to 2.2 million metric tons in a decade (Avery, 1987, pp. 10–11). In fact, the technology now exists to enable practically every nation in the world to practice agricultural autarky, *provided cost is no object*. The question, of course, is whether agricultural autarky is worth the cost. Why, for example, should the Japanese consumer have to pay ten times the world price for rice just so Japan can be rice self-sufficient? Surely the resources expended in such efforts could be better utilized in other ways.

The point is that not only has the world not yet reached the limit of arable land, but what is arable is largely dependent on the state of technology and therefore expands as the level of technological development advances. This is rapidly occurring. In just the past decade, short-season corn hybrids have extended the corn belt 250 miles in each direction. Similarly, new varieties of soybeans have enabled China to grow them as far north as Manchuria. The discovery of a relatively simple method of redesigning bullock-drawn tools now makes it possible for primitive farmers in India, Ethiopia, and Sudan to cultivate the world's 750 million acres of "crackling clay" soils. In fact, the method makes it possible to cultivate the land with neither drainage nor erosion problems. A new hybrid, sorghum/sudangrass, releases carbon dioxide and acid in such quantities that it actually alters the chemistry of desert soil, making millions of acres of desert arable. And soil scientists have now determined that only about 4 percent of the Amazon Basin soil is laterite, which turns brick hard when exposed to sunlight. The reason cultivation in the area failed was that the soils lacked such minerals as boron and copper. When these mineral elements were added, good yields of rice, peanuts, soybeans, and corn were obtained for 15 consecutive years. Moreover, not only was there no deterioration, but with the mineral additives soil conditions actually improved during the period. This discovery will make arable millions of acres of land once thought to be unsuited for cultivation (Avery, 1987; U.S. Department of State, 1984, 1985).

The second point is that the amount of land under cultivation is less important than the yield per acre. As D. Gale Johnson has noted (1984, pp. 95–97), since irrigation increases yields twofold to fourfold, irrigating 1 hectare of land "is the same as 'finding' 1–3 hectares of cropland even when the irrigated area had been cultivated before." Revelle has estimated (1984, pp. 185–186) that simply by increasing the efficiency of water use in the less developed parts of Africa, Asia, and Latin

America, and assuming yields of less than one-half the present average in the corn belt of the United States, the cultivatable land on those parts of the continents outside the humid tropics could produce enough food to feed 18 billion people. When one includes the arable parts of the tropics as well, the figure for these three continents *alone* rises to about 35 to 40 billion people, or between seven and eight times the current population of the entire world.[1]

But this only scratches the surface. For centuries agriculture remained largely static. However, dating from about the time of the Industrial Revolution in the late eighteenth century, Western agriculture entered a period of rapid change. The invention of new types of plows and other farm implements dramatically increased farm output per worker per hour. As Evenson put it (1981, p. 62), the nineteenth century was "the age of invention for agricultural implements." The first patent issued by the U.S. Patent Office was for an improved plow. By the end of the nineteenth century close to 70,000 patents had been issued for "hundreds of types of plows, cultivators, specialized planting machines, and weed control devices, and for numerous types of harvesting and threshing machines" (Evenson, 1981, p. 62). In fact, Evenson noted, the largest industry in the United States during the nineteenth century was farm machinery. However, the real breakthrough occurred in the first part of the twentieth century with the replacement of ox and horse power by the gasoline-driven tractor. The mechanical revolution was quickly followed by the chemical revolution, occurring shortly after World War II. Through the development and use of fertilizers, herbicides, and pesticides, the chemical revolution, more commonly referred to as the "Green Revolution," also dramatically increased output.

One can gain some indication of the impact at least of the mechanical and chemical revolutions by looking at trends in food production in those countries where these revolutions have been allowed to operate. The mechanical revolution began and was given its freest expression in such Western or First World countries as the United States. In 1790 about 90 percent of the people in America were farmers. Today that figure is less than 3 percent. Similarly, a much greater proportion of the cleared land was devoted to agriculture in 1790 than today. Yet, there is little doubt that on average, Americans today, even with a much larger population, are much better fed than they were in 1776. Since, relative to population, there are only about 3 percent as many farmers today as in 1790, farm productivity must have increased by a factor of approximately 33. In fact, since the United States is now a major food exporter, this figure is probably an underestimate. Table 3-2 shows that between 1870 and 1985 farm output increased nearly ninefold. One must bear in mind that this increase was occurring with a drastically declining farm population and, at least in the 1980s, reduced amounts of land used for agriculture. Thus, while output was nearly 50 percent larger in 1985 than it was in 1960, the cropland used was identical, and the number of labor hours declined from 9.8 billion in 1960 to only 3.2 billion in 1985 (U.S. Department of Commerce, 1988, p. 623, Table 1089, p. 624, Table 1091).

A somewhat more direct measure of the increase in farm productivity is given in Table 3-3. Between 1800 and 1982-1986, man-hours per 100 bushels of wheat declined by 98 percent, per 100 bushels of corn by 99 percent, and per bale of cotton

TABLE 3-2.   Composite Index of Total
U.S. Farm Output (Crops and Livestock),
1870–1985 (1970 = 100)[2]

Year	Output
1985	142
1980	123
1970	100
1960	88
1950	72
1940	59
1930	51
1920	50
1910	43
1900	40
1890	31
1880	26
1870	16

Sources: Compiled from U.S. Bureau of the Census,
1975, pp. 498–499, Series K 414-429; U.S. Department of Commerce, 1988, p. 642, Table 1091.

by 99 percent. Table 3-4 shows the yield per acre for the same three crops. Between
1800 and 1985 yield per acre of wheat increased 150 percent, that for corn increased
nearly fivefold, and yield per acre of cotton more than quadrupled. In short, the
available data show remarkable increases in agricultural productivity. These trends
show no sign of slowing, much less reversing themselves. And since the result has

TABLE 3-3.   Man-Hours per Unit of Production in the
United States, 1800–1986

Year	Hours per 100 Bushel or per Bale		
	Wheat	Corn	Cotton
1982–86	7	3	5
1970–74	9	5	18
1970	9	7	26
1960	12	11	47
1950	27	34	107
1940	44	79	182
1930	70	123	252
1920	90	122	296
1910	106	135	274
1900	108	147	284
1880	152	180	303
1840	233	276	348
1800	373	344	601

Sources: U.S. Bureau of the Census, 1975, p. 500, Series K 445-59; U.S.
Department of Commerce, 1988, p. 624, Table 1090.

TABLE 3-4. Yields per Acre, United
States, 1800–1985

Year	Wheat (bu.)	Corn (bu.)	Cotton (lb.)
1985	37.5	118.0	630
1980	33.5	91.0	473[a]
1975	30.6	86.4	453
1970	31.0	71.6	438
1960	25.2	62.2	475
1950	17.3	39.4	296
1940	17.1	32.2	260
1930	13.5	23.0	184
1920	13.8	26.8	155
1910	14.4	26.0	201
1900	13.9	25.9	189
1880	13.2	25.6	188
1840	15.0	25.0	147
1800	15.0	25.0	147

Sources: U.S. Department of the Census, 1975, p.
500, Series K 445-89; U.S. Department of Agriculture, 1987.

[a]Figure is average of 1980/81.

been an actual reduction in the amount of acreage devoted to agriculture in the developed countries, there is little doubt that output could be increased significantly if there were sufficient demand.

To date, the mechanical revolution has had a relatively small impact on agriculture throughout most of the Third World. There are several reasons. A major one is that pricing and tax policies of LDC governments have typically contained an antifarmer bias, thereby making the cost of the machinery prohibitively expensive. Contrary to many observers, however, the reluctance of the Third World farmer to adopt the new machinery is a result neither of his alleged irrationality nor of his being too tradition bound to adopt new methods. In places like the United States, labor was always in short supply, and the high wage rates created a strong incentive to discover and introduce labor-saving technological improvements. It should hardly be surprising, then, that agriculture in the United States has been characterized by its mechanical orientation. But in most LDCs, human labor is the least-cost factor. Thus, far from the LDC farmer being irrational for not adopting the mechanical improvements employed in the West, it would be irrational for him to do so. Moreover, one finds, in fact, that when wage rates do rise, LDC farmers are quick not only to adopt labor-saving machines but to adapt them to their particular circumstances (Evenson, 1981, pp. 62–63; U.S. Department of State, 1984, p. 2).

The farmers had the same attitude toward the Green Revolution, which can be defined as the application of chemical fertilizers, pesticides, and irrigation to newly developed high-yield varieties (HYVs) of grain, especially wheat and rice. The new farm technology was developed in the MDCs and was designed specifically for conditions in those countries. Often it was not effective in the many parts of the LDCs that had different soil types, climatic conditions, and indigenous pests (U.S. Department of State, 1984, p. 2). Because of rainfall and climate patterns, the use of HYVs was largely confined to Asia and North America. But once farmers in those areas recognized the superiority of the HYVs over the traditional varieties, use of such grains became nearly universal within four years. As Pray (1981, p. 74) has observed, "these findings should have laid to rest the belief in the irrationality of Asian farmers once and for all." (Also see Wolf, 1986, pp. 16–17, Tables 1 and 2.)

The key question is: What impact did the Green Revolution have on the Third World? Estimates are difficult to make. But Wolf points out (p. 9) that the worldwide average yield per hectare of food grains rose from 1.1 tons in 1950 to 2.6 tons in 1985. Of course, not all of this can be attributed to the use of HYVs and chemical fertilizers. Much is a result of the increased use of irrigation and improved methods and tools. But Wolf also notes (p. 15) that while the cropland in the LDCs devoted to the production of rice and wheat increased by only 20 percent between 1965 and 1980, output rose by 75 percent. The result of such significant increases in grain production has been that world food prices are lower than *they would have been* in the absence of HYVs. This has been a tremendous benefit to the poorest segments of Asian society who spend 70 to 80 percent of their incomes on food (Pray, 1981, p. 76). As Michael Lipton wrote in 1985, "If farmers of the Third World today used the same cereal varieties as in 1963–64, and everything else were unchanged, then tens of millions of people would die this year of hunger" (in Wolf, 1986, p. 15).

Critics of the Green Revolution have argued that it has increased unemployment in the LDCs, caused greater income inequality, and generated environmental degradation. None of these appear to be true. First, the relative decline in the cost of food resulted in increased demand which, in turn, increased the demand for labor. In some places this has resulted in an absolute rise in employment and income. In other areas, the beneficial effect of HYVs on farm labor has been more than offset by other factors, including population growth. But this only means that in the absence of HYVs farm employment and wages would be even lower than they are currently (Pray, 1981, pp. 75–76; Johl, 1975). Second, to the extent that income inequality has increased in LDC villages, evidence indicates that this is not due to "economies of scale" inherent in the use of technologies but to inequalities in political power. The politically powerful use their positions to allocate inputs to themselves and their friends (Pray, 1981, pp. 76–77; also relevant on this point are Hill, 1986, pp. 16–29; and Popkin, 1979). Finally, although the evidence is scanty, it does seem to indicate that if anything, the Green Revolution has had a *positive* effect on the environment. According to Pinstrep-Anderson (in Pray, 1981, p. 77):

> Technological change resulting in higher yields reduces the pressures for expanding agricultural production into marginal lands and excessive exploitation of the land base. There is little doubt that the development and use of fertilizers, better production practices and other yield increasing factors have been of great importance in limiting land degradation in developing countries.

The world is now at the dawn of yet another revolution: biotechnology. Based on the discovery of the structure of DNA in 1953 and the development of recombinant DNA, or gene splicing, in 1973, scientists are in the process of breeding plants that are able to resist drought, insects, disease, and salinity. For example, a new, fast-maturing rice variety recently applied in Pakistan allows farmers to plant a crop of gram or peas after the rice is harvested. A new variety of sorghum is highly drought resistant and yields three to four times that of the traditional variety. A new corn variety has been tested in Nigeria and has provided yields more than nine times greater than that traditionally obtained in the region. A new variety of corn has been found to triple yields in northern Ghana. A new cassava is highly disease resistant and provides yields that more than triple those of current varieties. "Thanks to the chemical mutagenesis method," writes the Russian scientist Yuri Ovchinnikov (1985, pp. 110–111), "more than a hundred varieties of wheat, rice, oats, maize, sunflower and other crops have been developed" just in the Soviet Union. And this is only the harbinger of things to come. "The reality is that we are living in the age of the plant breeder," says Dennis Avery (1989, pp. 2–3):

> Plant breeders have produced a wide variety of new seed varieties that make better use of soil, sunlight and plant nutrients than any seeds in the previous history of mankind. Researchers have produced more cold-tolerant winter wheat and barley, shorter-season corn, short-stalked rice and wheat, hybrid sunflower seeds, low-acid rapeseed and pest-resistant cassava (in both West Africa and Asia). They have almost literally invented a high-protein grain called triticale for high yields under difficult crop conditions. They have cloned new oil palm tree varieties which double vegetable oil yields. They have produced high-protein food beans and field peas with higher yields and built in pest protection, to feed both humans and animals.

"All major crops," Avery concludes, "are now susceptible to biotechnology." (Also see Ovchinnikov, 1985, pp. 110–112; Ritter, 1984, Sect. 6, p. 1; Wolf, 1986, especially, pp. 29–31; U.S. Department of State, 1984.)

What makes biotechnology so significant is that its chief beneficiaries are likely to be the developing countries. In part because of cost, the major beneficiaries of the mechanical and chemical revolutions were the farmers in the more developed countries. However, the new varieties of seeds tend to be relatively inexpensive. Not only are relatively poor farmers in the LDCs able to employ these new miracle seeds, but their low cost often makes it possible for farmers to afford fertilizer and other inputs, as well (Avery, 1987, p. 2; Wolf, 1986, pp. 30–31).

To summarize, not only is the world not approaching the limits of arable land, but the increasing use of irrigation, development and use of miracle seeds, and improvement of technologies and methods are actually working to expand the amount of potentially arable land at the same time that they are reducing the importance of land for the production of food. Moreover, if Revelle is correct and the LDCs alone could produce enough food to feed seven to eight times the current population of the world through the adoption of such conventional methods as irrigation, then, especially when one considers the possibilities of biotechnology, aquaculture (Wise, 1984, pp. 113–127), currently "exotic" methods of agriculture (Kahn et al., 1976, pp. 127–132), and the general state of technological and scientific progress, it seems unlikely that the world population will ever approach, much less exceed, its *physical* ability to feed itself. "The progress of agricultural productivity," Avery has written (1987, p. 5),

> is no isolated series of events. It is a process. The process is erratic and unpredictable in both space and direction. . . . The individual parts of the research are also fragile. Insects adapt to new varieties and develop resistance to pesticides. . . . That warrants the greatest care on the part of researchers, and continuing research investments by the public to protect those gains. . . . But the process of agricultural research—indeed the advance of human knowledge in farming and all other fields of human endeavor—is anything but fragile. Over time and around the world, it has proven a permanent and nearly irresistible force.

Of course far from everyone in the world is adequately fed. Progress in this area is quite uneven, and conditions in a handful of countries have actually deteriorated. Since these countries tend to be concentrated in Africa, this will be the focus of the following section.

Africa's Economic Decline

A recent article dealing with the food problem in Africa lamented that "in 1984 140 million of its 531 million people were fed entirely with grain from abroad" and that "in 1985 the ranks of those fed with imported grain may have reached 170 million" (Brown and Wolf, 1986, pp. 177–178). The article is hardly unique. In fact, studies dealing with Africa's deteriorating economic plight almost invariably focus their attention on either the continent's declining per capita agricultural output or its increasing reliance on food imports. But, by themselves, the figures prove little or nothing. Since development has historically been associated with specialization, and since specialization in the production of nonfood products or in the production of one or a few food products would entail increasing levels of food imports, the above figures would be quite consistent with rapid economic development.

There is no doubt, however, that the economic situation in much of the African continent is perilous. The number of deaths from the 1983–1984 famine has been estimated, probably conservatively, at 1 million (World Resources Institute 1986, p. 55). The irony, in fact the tragedy, is that Africa has tremendous agricultural potential. In an article for the *New York Times*, Thomas Johnson noted (1975) that "agronomists say Ethiopia could easily become the breadbasket for much of Europe if her agriculture were better organized." And agronomist Doreen Warriner (in Ellis, 1980, p. 526), writing in 1973, commented that "Ethiopia is one of those rare countries so richly endowed by nature that the agrarian structure, feudal in every sense of the term, does appear to be the only constraint on development." In March 1975, the new Marxist government nationalized all land. Ethiopian feudalism ended; Ethiopian socialism began. But instead of development, agricultural performance, poor to begin with, deteriorated rapidly. In fact, not only did Ethiopia suffer two famines within the space of a single decade, it was the nation that suffered most from the brunt of the famine of the early 1980s. Ghana and Tanzania are just two other African countries that have managed to combine great agricultural potential with declining agricultural output (Rydenfelt, 1983, pp. 110–124; U.S. Department of State, 1985, pp. 27–30).

Africa's economic potential is not limited to agriculture. David Lamb (1983, p. 20), has pointed out that Africa

> has 40 percent of the world's potential hydroelectric power supply; the bulk of the world's gold; 90 percent of its cobalt; 50 percent of its phosphates; 40 percent of its platinum; 7.5 percent of its coal; 8 percent of its known petroleum reserves; 12 percent of its natural gas; 3 percent of its iron ores; and millions upon millions of acres of untilled farmland. There is not another continent blessed with such abundance.

Yet the countries of sub-Saharan Africa (excluding South Africa) have an average per capita income of only $210. And while Africa is the only continent in which incomes have declined, averaging a 0.1 percent decline per year for the last two decades, what is most alarming is that the rate of decline has been accelerating (World Bank, 1986, p. 180, Table 1). What has gone wrong?

It is clear that the real problem in Africa is not a "food problem" at all. It is a poverty problem. The reason so many in Africa are starving or suffering from malnutrition is not because there is a shortage of food in the world but because their productivity is so low that they lack the means to purchase it. This means that any analysis of the problems of "feeding Africa" cannot be restricted to agriculture alone, but must examine the broader causes of Africa's poverty. The real question is: How can a nation so richly endowed by nature be haunted by starvation and grinding poverty? How can one explain the tremendous discrepancy between potential and performance?

Comparative Advantage

While the reasons advanced to explain Africa's economic atrophy vary from the belief that the Western nations control international markets and have deliberately subjected the nations of Africa to unfavorable terms of trade (Chichilnisky, 1982), to the argument that Africa's work force is unskilled and capital is relatively scarce (Higgott, 1986), a common argument is that Africa is poor because it simply cannot compete on the world market. The conclusion that is then drawn is that since the nations of Africa are harmed by foreign trade, they would be better off severing their economic ties with the rest of the world (Mazrui, 1967, pp. 7497). This argument is fundamentally mistaken.

The economic argument for free trade is premised on the Ricardian "law of comparative advantage." This law demonstrates that for society to secure the greatest possible advantages of trade, everyone, including every nation, should devote itself to what it can do most cheaply. This means that even if it were found that *everything* that the African nations can produce can be produced better and more cheaply elsewhere, such a discovery would be irrelevant to the question of whether free trade would benefit Africa. What is relevant is not *absolute* but *relative* advantage. The two are quite different. For example, assume that Mary is both a better chef and a better dishwasher than Fred. Thus Mary possesses an absolute advantage over Fred in both jobs. But if Mary's advantage over Fred as a chef is greater than her advantage as a dishwasher, it would be in Mary's interest to specialize in cooking, leaving the dishwashing to Fred. Similarly, if Fred were, relative to Mary, a better dishwasher than a chef, even though inferior in both to Mary in absolute terms, it would be in Fred's interest to specialize in dishwashing, leaving the cooking to Mary. Thus, even though Mary were better at both cooking and dishwashing than Fred, Fred would still have a *comparative advantage* over Mary in dishwashing. And both would benefit by specializing in that area where their comparative or relative costs were cheaper.

What is true for individuals is just as true for nations and regions. As Harrod put it, the gain from free trade "depends on the relation between the ratio of the cost of production of A to that of B at home and the ratio of the cost of production of A to that of B abroad. *Gain is possible if the ratios are different*" (Harrod, 1963, p. 16; italics in original).

Government Intervention

We can now deal with the question of Africa's continuing poverty. Three sectors of the economy will be examined: (1) the farm sector, (2) the nonfarm sector, and (3) the investment sector.

The Farm Sector

There is general agreement that Africa has tremendous agricultural potential. For example, Kahn, Brown and Martel believed (1976, p. 124) that Africa contains as many as 700 million hectares of *potentially* cultivatable land, or about three and a half times the amount currently cultivated in the United States and more than double that in the industrialized countries of North America and Europe combined. The World Resources Institute (1986, p. 42, Table 4.2) puts the figure even higher, at 760 million hectares. But only about 160 million are being cultivated.

The controversy is not about Africa's agricultural potential but the cost of bringing those additional areas under cultivation. Some researchers, such as Nick Eberstadt (1985a), David Hopper (1976), D. Gale Johnson (1984), and Herman Kahn, William Brown, and Leon Martel (1976), believe that the elimination of the tsetse fly, which could be accomplished at an estimated cost of only $20 billion, would open up, as already noted, about 200 million hectares of land to cultivation. Proper irrigation would add an additional 300 million hectares. While cost estimates vary from a low of $218 per hectare to a high of just over $1,000 per hectare, Kahn, Brown, and Martel argued that, given the productivity of the new land, "such costs should be no great deterrent in a world of growing affluence, even if they should run as high as $2000 per hectare." In fact, since so much of the continent is located in tropical and semitropical regions where the growing season is quite long, much of Africa is ideally suited for multicropping (1976, p. 124; see also Revelle, 1984, pp. 189–191).

Others, such as Brown and Wolf (1986, pp. 177–198) and the World Resources Institute (1986, pp. 55–58) are not as sanguine. According to the World Resources Institute, "Africa is not particularly well suited to agriculture. Over 80 percent of its soils have fertility limitations and the climate in 47 percent of the continent is too dry for rainfed agriculture." Consequently, conversion to cropland would require massive irrigation or the introduction of new drought-resistant crops, both of which, the Institute believes, are far too expensive for African farmers. Moreover, multicropping would result in high levels of soil erosion and rapidly deplete the soil of its nutrients, both of which would have a "significant deleterious effect" on fertility. While this could be offset by the increased use of fertilizers and such methods as no-till and minimum-till agriculture coupled with the use of herbicides, the cost for most of these measures, they argue, is generally more than the African farmer can afford.

Who is right? At first blush it would appear that Brown and Wolf and the pessimists are correct. After all, if Africa does have a comparative advantage in agriculture, why isn't more land being cultivated? And why is Africa the only continent in which per capita food production has declined in recent years? But appearances can be deceiving. The simple fact is that following independence numerous African governments adopted highly interventionist if not outright socialist policies. The *official* purpose of these policies was to stimulate the industrial sector, although it is clear that in many cases the actual motives were political: to provide food at low prices in order to keep the urban populations, including the army, content. Regardless of the reason, the effect of such policies was to penalize the agricultural sector. These policies included high taxes, often in excess of 50 percent, on agricultural products; price controls on food; monopolistic marketing boards; the abolition of the private sale of food products and farm implements, often ruthlessly and brutally enforced; coercively established and maintained state farms; land reforms that placed farmers' land, especially that of the more prosperous farmers, in perpetual uncertainty; acreage limits placed on the size of "private farms" that were often so low as to preclude the use of mechanized equipment; and overvalued exchange rates that made imported food cheaper than locally produced crops at the same time that it made the cost of fertilizer and other farm inputs more expensive (Avery, 1989, p. 9; Ayittey, 1986a, p. 12; Clark, 1988, pp. 68–70; D. G. Johnson, 1984, p. 99; Morrisson and Schneider, 1987, pp. 4–6; Osterfeld, 1985, pp. 609–611; Richardson and Ahmed, 1987, pp. 16–25; U.S. Department of State, 1985, p. 21; Zinsmeister, 1988).

There is little doubt that these policies, which amounted to nothing short of an assault on agriculture, resulted in a drastic reduction in agricultural output. Africa was a net food exporter in the 1930s and was food self-sufficient in the early 1950s. But by the 1980s it was a major food importer (T. Jackson and Park, 1986, p. 127). Between 1960 and 1985 Africa's per capita food production declined by 25 percent (Figure 3-3). There is little doubt that much if not all of this decline was self-imposed.

Africa lost its comparative advantage in agriculture, but the reason for the loss was ill-advised government policies that penalized farmers and discouraged investment in the agricultural sector. This is easily seen. Not only was Africa a net

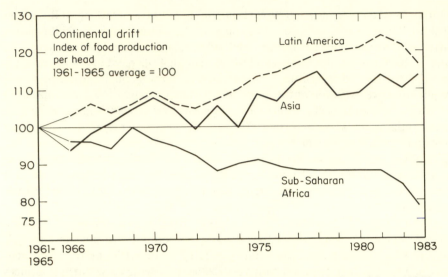

FIGURE 3-3. World food trends. From *The Economist,* 1985, p. 48. Copyright © 1985 by the Economist Newspaper Ltd. Reprinted by permission.

exporter of food prior to massive government involvement in agriculture but, in the wake of the 1983–1984 famine that racked the continent, several African nations, such as Zaire, Zambia, Ghana, Togo, Nigeria, Cameroon, Madagascar, and Guinea, introduced agricultural reforms. Marketing boards were abolished in some; price controls were lifted in others, and the private sale of farm produce was reintroduced in still others. In Nigeria and Ghana, for example, prices paid to cocoa farmers tripled. In Zaire, prices for cassava tripled; those for maize doubled. Agricultural output increased almost immediately. In Ghana, for example, maize production tripled; cotton production in Togo doubled; agricultural output in Zambia rose by 20 percent in two years (Richardson and Ahmed, 1987, pp. 19–21; U.S. Department of State, 1985, pp. 28–31; Osterfeld, 1987a). Similarly impressive results were obtained from the breakup of collective farms and the move to private property. When Mauritania began to permit private ownership of open land along the banks of the Senegal River in the mid-1980s, the new owners responded by digging their own irrigation canals and purchasing and installing their own water pumps. The result was that rice production in the area increased from just 3,000 to 80,000 metric tons in five years (Avery, 1989, p. 9).

Moreover, as already noted, one of the major benefits of the biotechnological revolution is precisely that it is able to make better drought- and pest-resistant seeds available inexpensively. And as the cost of seeds drops at the same time that yields not only increase but become more reliable, it becomes economical for African farmers to utilize fertilizers and other inputs. The data show that, while still low, the use of such seeds as well as the use of fertilizers, herbicides, and pesticides are becoming increasingly common in Africa as well as in other regions of the Third World, especially where government policies no longer discourage their use (U.S

Department of State, 1985, pp. 1–3). Avery estimates that "now, high-tech seeds and methods are available for 80–90 percent of the world's arable land" (1990, p. 6). As Ayittey (1986a, p. 13) has put it, "if all Black African leaders were to follow the examples of Malawi, Somalia, Zambia and Ghana and to lift price controls to permit their peasants to sell their produce in open, free markets, there would be no food crisis in the continent."

The evidence appears to indicate that Africa does have a natural comparative advantage in agriculture. Poor agricultural production has stemmed primarily from government policies that undermine the incentive to produce. As long as government policies continue to be biased against the agricultural sector, the African farmer will remain poor, the investments required to increase productivity will not occur, and farm output will remain low. In brief, government policies have turned African agriculture into an economic dead end.

The Nonfarm Sector

There are two possibilities for the nonfarm sector. First, if Africa has a natural comparative advantage in agriculture that has been blocked by ill-advised government policies, one would expect to find capital and labor being employed in those areas in the nonfarm sector that are the most productive alternatives to agriculture. One would expect incomes to rise as productivity in these areas increased.

If, however, Africa's comparative advantage lies not in agriculture but in one or more areas in the nonfarm sector, one would expect to find factors of production spontaneously entering those areas. As above, incomes would rise as productivity in these areas increased and output expanded.

Unfortunately, the governments of Africa have also intervened heavily in the nonfarm sector. In their attempts to stimulate industry they have enacted high tariffs and imposed an extensive network of licensing restrictions, subsidies, minimum wage rates, and the like (Berry, 1977, 168–177; Osterfeld, 1985, pp. 268–269). The results should have been predictable: since tariffs and licensing restrictions would not be required if the industries or firms had a comparative advantage, such protectionist measures mean that resources are transferred from areas in which they are more productive into areas where they are less productive. The result is the artificial substitution of relatively high-cost, inefficient local production for lower cost, more efficient foreign production, and everyone, except perhaps the domestic producers, is made less well off.

Similarly, since minimum wage laws increase the cost of labor, they artificially reduce the number of jobs available, that is, the number of individuals firms can afford to hire. The tragedy is that the ones most hurt by such laws are the poor. Since they are the least productive members of society they are the ones such laws price out of the job market. In short, in the name of stimulating industrialization, governments in Africa have enacted policies that benefit a privileged few while severely restricting income-earning opportunities for the members of society in general. Thus, regardless of their intent, such policies have retarded if not completely blocked economic development.

The Investment Sector

Given the relatively low cost of labor in Africa, one would expect to find capitalists investing heavily in the continent. In fact, about 80 percent of all foreign investments go to developed countries. Of the 20 percent invested in the LDCs, almost two-thirds is concentrated in 13 countries. None are African. The balance is scattered among the more than 100 remaining countries (Spero, 1985, p. 270; World Bank, 1986, pp. 206–207). This is not surprising in view of the extensive restrictions imposed on foreign capital, the ideological commitment of African governments to socialist policies, the ever present possibility of nationalization, and the loss of Africa's comparative advantage in cheap labor due to minimum wages and other interventionist measures.

In short, in the name of stimulating industrialization, African governments have pursued policies that have not only penalized economic activity in the farm sector but eliminated opportunities in the nonfarm sectors as well. By adopting policies that retard or even prevent economic development, African governments have needlessly condemned very large segments of their populations to permanent and grinding poverty.

Africa's Economic Future

There are three possible courses that African governments can pursue in the future: the continuation of the status quo; economic autarky; and laissez-faire. The recent famine and Africa's declining standard of living for 20 years has clearly shown the bankruptcy of the status quo and many countries are contemplating or have already adopted reforms of some type.

A second possibility would be to adopt policies of economic autarky, or self-sufficiency, that is, policies of import substitution designed to create a "fully diversified home economy" that, as fully as possible, is isolated from the world economy (Harris, 1987, p. 14). In fact some countries are actively pursuing policies with just that end in mind. The New International Economic Order, or NIEO, passed by the U.N. General Assembly in May 1974, encouraged the LDCs to adopt policies leading toward economic autarky. The declaration, which refers to the nationalization of foreign-owned property as an "inalienable right" that is nothing more than "an expression of the . . . sovereignty of every State," is replete with such phrases as the "full permanent sovereignty of every State over its natural resources and all economic activities" and "the right of every nation to adopt the economic and social system it deems most appropriate and not to be subjected to discrimination of any kind as a result" (in Henkin et al., 1980, p. 697). Such sentiments are obviously incompatible with the economic interdependence of nations. The NIEO clearly encourages the LDCs to adopt highly interventionist policies that, logically pursued, would result in economic autarky.

The Lagos Plan for Action, adopted in March 1982 by the Organization of African Unity, likewise calls for "the development of agriculture" with the goal of achieving economic, and in particular, food "self-sufficiency" for the African continent (Ravenhill, 1986, pp. 85–107). And some countries are pursuing national self-sufficiency. Nigeria, for example, has banned the importation of wheat, rice, corn, vegetable oil, and most other food items. The goal, according to the Minister of Information, is "to encourage local substitutes." Nigeria hopes to achieve food self-sufficiency. As a result of the ban, prices for some farm products such as cocoa have quadrupled (Brooke, 1987).

There is no doubt that a policy of agricultural self-sufficiency would stimulate food production. But this means only that resources formerly employed in the non-farm sector would be transferred to the agricultural sector. To the extent that this transfer is the result not of a natural comparative advantage in agriculture but of its artificial stimulation created by the ban on the importation of food products, domestic resources will have been transferred from more to less productive uses. The result in the long run will be that everyone involved, including farmers, will be less well off. That is, resources must be transferred from industries that produce goods at a comparative advantage, that is, from industries that are able to produce goods at relatively low cost, into the production of goods for which the country is at a comparative disadvantage; that is, into the production of goods for which the local cost of production exceeds the price that must be paid to import those same goods. Clearly, it would be better to produce and export those goods for which it has a comparative advantage and use the income obtained to purchase goods that either could not be produced domestically or produced only more expensively than it would cost to import them.

The larger the area of free trade, the greater the opportunities for specialization. And the greater the specialization, the more productive the economy. It follows that the smaller the area of free trade, the greater the harm. Thus the collective or continental autarky proposed by the Lagos Plan for Action would be less harmful than the policy of national self-sufficiency pursued by Nigeria. In brief, since a policy of economic autarky must, of necessity, forgo numerous possible gains from trade, it must render practically everyone, but especially the people of the nations pursuing such a policy, worse off.

Recent World Bank studies on the impact of protectionist measures support this conclusion. Both the industrialized market countries and the LDCs would reap significant benefits from "liberalization," that is, the elimination or reduction of tariffs and other protectionist measures. But "the main beneficiaries of unilateral liberalization," according to the World Bank (1986, p. 131), "are the liberalizers themselves." Since a national market must be smaller than the world market, the conclusion is just what one would expect from the above analysis. It follows, of course, that a move toward complete autarky by either a nation or a region can only increase the cost to the residents of the unit isolating itself—it can only make them poorer, not wealthier.

A final possibility is a move in the direction of laissez-faire, that is, the reduction or even elimination of all obstacles, domestic and foreign, to the free movement of people, goods, and capital. Such a policy would increase the efficiency of the world market by allowing all factors to be employed in their most value-productive use. The resulting increase in the size of the goods and services produced in the world, would benefit everyone, but once again the residents of the LDCs in particular, since they tend to be more interventionist than the more developed industrialized countries.

Again, studies by the World Bank support this conclusion. The Bank classified countries according to their degree of "price distortion," or market intervention. It found that the greater the degree of intervention, the slower the rate of growth. Those nations with a "low distortion index" had a rate of economic growth that was more than double that of those with a "high distortion index" (6.8% vs. 3.1%); the savings-to-income ratio in those countries with a low distortion index was almost twice as high as in those with a high distortion index (21% vs. 13%); the annual industrial growth rate in the low distortion countries was triple that in the high distortion countries (9% vs. 3%); the growth in agricultural production was considerably higher for the former countries than the latter (4.4% vs. 2.4%); and the annual export volume increased almost ten times faster in the low distortion countries than in the high distortion ones (6.7% vs. 0.7%) (1983, pp. 60–61. Also see Phaup and Lewis, 1985, pp. 80–81).

The conclusion seems inescapable. The solution to Africa's "food problem" lies in solving its "development problem." And the solution to its development problem lies in moving toward a policy of laissez-faire. Only through laissez faire is it possible to determine precisely where Africa's natural comparative advantage lies. Allowing individuals the freedom to pursue what is in their comparative advantage is the best and quickest road to economic development. Whether it lies in the production of food for domestic consumption, the production of food for export, or even in nonfood production is irrelevant.

If Africans can earn higher incomes by exporting food or other products than they can by growing food solely for domestic consumption, so much the better. For the higher incomes mean that they are in a better position to satisfy their own and their families' needs than they would be if they were to grow food strictly for domestic consumption. Even though it may seem paradoxical, growing food may not always be the best way for hungry people to feed themselves (Osterfeld, 1988a).

For the past two decades most African nations have pursued highly interventionist policies. The bankruptcy of interventionism has been graphically and gruesomely revealed by its needless but perennial famines. As a result, many nations have been forced to reassess their economic policies. Two alternative paths are possible. They can move further down the interventionist road to complete autarky, or they can reverse their course, begin to dismantle their interventionist programs, and move in the direction of laissez-faire. Both economic analysis and empirical data show that only a policy of laissez faire offers any real hope for improvement.

Conclusions: Agriculture, Socialism, and Capitalism

The unprecedented growth in agricultural output occurring during the twentieth century was the principal focus of the first two sections of this chapter. Many of these gains resulted from increased yields per acre, effected by technological advances. More tractors or combines are, however, *in themselves* not the cure for world hunger. Capital-intensive, highly sophisticated equipment has been tried in Africa and many other parts of the Third World and the results have often ranged from disappointing to disastrous. For example, peasant farmers in Ghana, using primitive tools, produced 0.49 ton of rice per acre. However, Ghana's state farms, using capital-intensive equipment, produced only 0.13 ton per acre (Ayittey, 1986a, p. 8). Food production is, at base, not a question of technology but of economics. More tractors and fertilizer do not automatically translate into more food.

Most food must be produced in relatively close proximity to where it will be consumed. This is especially true in LDCs, where transportation tends to be difficult and storage facilities inadequate. Large-scale, capital-intensive modern farms produce tremendous surpluses of one or a few types of food. The efficiency of modern large-scale farming is dependent on the existence of such high-cost, complementary factors as adequate transportation and storage facilities. Where these are absent, as they tend to be in African countries and other LDCs, one would expect to find numerous, highly dispersed small farms. This is precisely what one finds. And, since tractors tend to be uneconomic when the farm size is less than about one worker per 100 acres, and since the average farm size in Africa is nowhere near even half of this (Ayittey, 1986a, p. 9), capital-intensive, highly mechanized agriculture is simply uneconomical in much of Africa and the Third World at this time.

Again, *the point is not that Africa and other areas of the Third World should not use modern technology. It is that its use should be dictated by economic considerations.* The goal is to be able to feed people at reasonable costs. The only test of the efficiency of any particular agricultural method or technique is the market. Attempts artificially to stimulate the use of capital-intensive equipment, such as on the state farms in Ghana or, conversely, artificially to retard its use, as was done in Ethiopia with the 1975 land-reform measures that proclaimed maximum farm sizes so small as to make the use of mechanized equipment uneconomic (Osterfeld, 1985, pp. 270–271), can only harm agricultural productivity by misallocating scarce resources.

But even more fundamental is the need to restore market incentives. If one looks at those countries in which the food situation has actually deteriorated over the past two decades, such as in particular the countries in sub-Saharan Africa, or at those countries that have traditionally had serious food problems, such as the Soviet Union, China, India, and the countries of Eastern Europe, one fact stands out: the lack of market incentives.

The belief was widespread at one time that the typical LDC peasant simply did not, or would not, respond to economic incentives. Price levels, it was held, made little or no difference. The typical farmer would continue to produce as he had traditionally done. High prices would not stimulate production; low prices would not discourage it (see Phaup and Lewis, 1985, pp. 78–79). This view has been disproven many times over. Individuals, regardless of occupation, place, or economic position, respond to incentives in the same way (see Bauer and Yamey, 1957; Popkin, 1979; Rydenfeldt, 1983, to cite just a handful). Penalizing production reduces output; rewarding production increases it. This is the painful lesson of the African experience since independence. It may be understandable that, following independence, the African countries repudiated everything associated with colonialism, including "capitalism." However, aside from the fact that colonialism is not capitalistic but, as Adam Smith pointed out over two centuries ago, mercantilistic, repudiation does not repeal economic law.

The tragedy is that the results of the African adoption of socialism and statism were clearly predictable. Not only were they what one would expect from elementary economic theory; they were also what one could observe after a half century of experience with socialism in the Second World. The (former) Soviet Union contains some of the most fertile agricultural land in the world. Prior to the communist revolution in 1917 Russia was the world's largest exporter of grain. Collectivization of agriculture during the 1920s and 1930s was quickly followed by dramatic declines in output. Between 5 and 10 million Russians died of starvation during these years, with 12 to 13 million more saved by food donated by the Western capitalist countries. By the 1980s the Soviet Union employed 25 percent of its labor force and invested in excess of 25 percent of its capital in agriculture, both figures far higher than in any other industrialized country. Despite its tremendous agricultural potential, the Soviet Union became the world's largest food importer. It imported nearly one-third of its food, and this is despite having grudgingly permitted the establishment of private minifarms one-half to one acre in size. These private plots made up only 3 percent of the total cropland yet produced 27 percent of the nation's food. It was unlikely that the Soviet Union could exist without these plots (Goldman, 1983, pp. 63–87; Rydenfelt, 1983, pp. 27–45; H. Smith, 1984, pp. 264–284).

The pattern is repeated with monotonous regularity throughout socialist countries. Most of the Eastern European countries are blessed with fertile agricultural land and, prior to socialism, were food exporters. The adoption of socialist policies in most of these was quickly followed by declining production, food shortages, and bread lines (Rydenfelt, 1983, pp. 46–79). Zinsmeister (1987, p. 22) notes that "between 1960 and 1980 agricultural productivity declined by one-third in the Soviet Bloc."

Agricultural output in China was virtually stagnant during the 25-year reign of Mao Tse-tung. The Chinese government now acknowledges that during just one three-year period, the so-called Three Difficult Years from 1959–1962, between 25 and 30 million Chinese died from starvation. By the time of Mao's death in the mid-1970s, the average Chinese was less well fed than he was during the 1920s or even during the Japanese occupation of the 1930s (Mosher, 1983a, pp. 28–50; USAID, 1989, p. 15, Table 1.1; Zinsmeister, 1988, p. 28). Beginning in 1977, Mao's successors abandoned his "socialist experiment." As a result, says *The Economist* (1985, pp. 86–87; also see Prychitko, 1987), "food grain output has increased by 12% a year since then, despite bad weather in 1980."

After its highly interventionist if not socialist policy had resulted in famine in the early 1970s, India abandoned price controls on agriculture. By 1977 not only was this basket case self-sufficient, it was even exporting large quantities of grain. In addition it had built up a grain reserve of 22 million tons, which enabled it to manage the severe drought of 1979 without the need for food imports (Ohri, 1987; Simon, 1981b, pp. 64–65; World Bank, 1981, p. 80).

The lesson is clear. If African and other Third World leaders seriously desire to put an end to their food crises they would do well to compare the striking differences in the agricultural performances of the First and Second Worlds, abandon their commitment to interventionism, and allow the free market to operate within their countries' potentially rich lands.

Notes

1. The 35- to 40-billion figure was calculated from the figures given by Revelle (1984, p. 186) on the gross cultivated area in Asia, South America, and Africa for land inside as well as outside the tropics. Revelle estimates that there are on these continents the equivalent of 1.85 billion hectares of arable land outside the tropics. This is enough to feed, he estimates, 18 billion people. He also estimates the gross cultivated hectares inside the tropics on these three continents at 3.75 billion, or double that outside the tropics. If that is the case, the total feeding potential of these three continents alone should be at least 35 to 40 billion people (even assuming yields of less than 50 percent of the average yields in the United States). In an earlier article (1976, p. 175) Revelle in fact used the 40-billion figure, arguing that, even assuming a 10-percent harvest loss due to pests and nonfood uses, the world had the capacity to feed indefinitely a population of 40 billion people at 2,500 calories per day.

2. The data sets using 1967 and 1977 were converted into a composite index using 1970 as a base year by dividing 1967 data by 1.02 and 1977 data by 0.84 (their respective values for 1970). The data set using 1947 as a base year was converted into its 1970 equivalent by deflating each figure by 0.71.

4

Resources

A frequent theme in development literature is that the Third World is poor because the First World has "victimized" (ul Haq, 1983, p. 188), "mercilessly plundered" (Vorontsov, 1986, p. 73), or "exploited" (Manley, 1984, p. 249; Palmberg, 1986, p. 18) the Third World of its resources. Because of its "voracious appetite," the North, "unable of its very nature to draw sufficient sustenance from local resources, rapidly swallowed up the whole world" (Magdoff, 1968, p. 32). It has "controlled" (O'Connor, 1974, p. 172) or "completely dominated" (Chichilnisky, 1982, p. 2) all major resource markets, holding prices down to the benefit of itself but to the detriment of the Third World.

The North, Chichilnisky writes (pp. 6–9), "uses more than 80% of the annual flow of world resources, even though it has, at most, 25% of the world's population." And, "the North's disproportionate use of resources is increasing because of the relative changes in technology, consumption, and population growth in the North and South." The "development patterns of the North," she continues, "tend to deplete global resources," thereby impeding the South's economic development. Although "the North's right of unrestricted resource use" has generally gone "unquestioned," it is "inconsistent with ecological limits" as well as with international "equality and hence with the basic political stability of the planet."

A drastic reduction in resource use, at least by the North, and/or the transition from the use of "nonrenewable" to "renewable" resources are seen as the only solutions to the problem of resource depletion (Deudney and Flavin, 1985). While stating that "the problem of scarce resources is more a matter of successful management and market behavior, rather than of physical scarcity" (p. 8), Chichilnisky goes on to argue that economic development in the Third World requires a significant reduction in inequality. To achieve this she proposes, among other things, "that the rich countries contribute to relieving the long-run pressure on available resources by curtailing their own consumption," a low "rate of economic growth," at least for the wealthy nations, "a reduction in non-essential consumption," and the "implementation of an active policy to better distribute goods and services" (p. 28).

Similar proposals have been advanced by, among others, Daly (1974, 1979), who proposes the "steady-state economy," and Perlman (1976, pp. 46–47, 179–

181), who calls for "ecotopia" or "global equilibrium." Some of the components include "zero growth in the stock of human population," the reduction of "resource consumption per unit of industrial output . . . to a fraction of its current value," a "vastly more equitable distribution of wealth and power among all people of the world," and a redefinition of wealth so as to be "represented less by *things* and more by *knowledge* and *experience*, by the aggregation of wisdom and love." "Ecotopia" says Perlman, would be similar to that "suggested in [B. F. Skinner's] *Walden Two* and somewhat realized already in the People's Republic of China." It is clear, Perlman concludes, "that the longer we delay and the more lax we are in establishing the conditions for global equilibrium the less chance we have for escaping the coming global collapse." The same conclusion was reached by Chichilnisky (pp. 26–27).

The two most basic issues raised by these charges and proposals are: (1) Is Third World development impeded or even prevented by Northern resource consumption? Related to this, (2) Is the world facing the prospect of global collapse resulting from imminent resource depletion? These two questions will be the focus of this chapter.

Catastrophism: Predictions and Realities

Catastrophism in one form or another is nothing new. It can be traced back at least to the writings of Thomas Malthus and David Ricardo nearly two centuries ago. The catastrophists base their predictions of imminent catastrophe on the seemingly unobjectionable assumption that the supply of resources is finite. From this it follows that the more oil, copper, bauxite, or tungsten we use, the less there is left, and the more quickly we consume them the sooner we will run out. In 1865 William Stanley Jevons predicted "the impossibility of a long continuance of progress" due to the impending exhaustion of coal supplies. Since then hardly a year has gone by when an "expert" or an "official body" has not solemnly predicted the end of affluence or the dawn of the age of scarcity due to the exhaustion of nonrenewable energy supplies or the depletion of key raw materials. The most revealing thing about these predictions is that they have never come true.

Table 4-1 shows the vast and continued underestimation of oil resources between 1866 and 1950. As of 1990 about 145 billion barrels of oil have been produced in the United States since 1914, or almost 25 times the 5.7 billion barrels projected at that time by the Bureau of Mines as the "maximum" future production.[1] Although peaking at just over 3.5 billion barrels in 1970, U.S. production, representing between 18 and 20 percent of the world total during the 1980s (U.S. Department of Commerce, 1989, p. 678, Table 1182), has fluctuated between 3 and 3.5 billion barrels per year (U.S. Department of Commerce, 1989, p. 680, Table 1187).

Catastrophist predictions have proven no better for other resources. For example, the U.S. President's Materials Policy Commission, better known as the Paley Report, stated in 1952 that by the mid-1970s copper production could not exceed 800,000 tons. It was 1.6 million in 1973 (U.S. Bureau of Mines, 1985, p. 209). The Commission placed U.S. lead production at a maximum of 300,000 tons per year.

TABLE 4-1.   Oil Prophesies from Official Sources and the Corresponding Realities

Date	U.S. Oil Production Rate (billion bbls./yr)	Prophecy	Reality
1866	0.005	Synthetics available if oil production should end (U.S. Revenue Commission)	In next 82 years, 37 billion bbls. produced by U.S. with no need for synthetics
1885	0.02	Little or no chance for oil in California (U.S. Geological Survey)	8 billion bbls. produced in California since that date; important new findings in 1948
1891	0.05	Little or no chance for oil in Kansas or Texas (U.S. Geological Survey)	14 billion bbls. produced in these two states since 1891
1908	0.18	Maximum future supply of 22.5 billion bbls. (officials of U.S. Geological Survey)	35 billion bbls. produced since 1908, with 26.8 bbl. reserve proven and available on January 1 1949
1914	0.27	Total future production only 5.7 billion bbls. (official of U.S. Bureau of Mines)	34 billion bbls. produced since 1914, or six times this prediction
1920	0.45	U.S. needs foreign oil and synthetics; peak domestic production almost reached (Director of U.S. Geological Survey)	1948 U.S. production in excess of U.S. consumption and more than four times 1920 output
1931	0.85	Must import as much foreign oil as possible to save domestic supply (Secretary of the Interior)	During next 8 years imports discouraged and 14 billion bbls. found in U.S.
1939	1.3	U.S. oil supplies will last only 13 years (radio broadcasts by Interior Department)	New oil found since 1939 exceeds the 13 years' supply known at that time
1947	1.9	Sufficient oil cannot be found in U.S. (Chief of Petroleum Division, State Department)	4.3 billion bbls. found in 1948, the largest volume in history and twice our consumption
1949	2.0	End of U.S. oil supply almost in sight (Secretary of the Interior)	Petroleum industry demonstrated ability to increase U.S. production by more than a million bbls. daily in the next 5 years

Source: Kahn, Brown, and Martel, 1976, pp. 94–95. Reprinted by permission of the Hudson Institute.

It was 558,000 tons in 1973 and 614,000 tons in 1974 (U.S. Bureau of Mines, 1985, p. 442).

In fact, for at least the past 100 years and probably much longer, the prices of practically *all* minerals including coal, copper, iron, zinc, aluminum, and even petroleum have, despite short-term fluctuations, declined. In most cases the decline has been dramatic. This is true whether one compares mineral prices with wages for labor, as is done in Table 4-2 and Figure 4-1, panel a; with the consumer price index (Figure 4-1, panel b); or with any other relevant standard.[2] Declining prices imply that, in contrast to the much publicized predictions of imminent resource depletion, resources are actually becoming *less* scarce over time. Table 4-3, showing that the known reserves of nearly all important minerals have actually increased during the two decades between 1950 and 1970, confirms that inference.

Catastrophism and the Post-1970 Data

The late 1960s and early 1970s witnessed a revival of catastrophist studies, with most conceding that while reserves had increased in the past and prices had fallen, we had now reached a historical turning point. With increased consumption, resources would become more scarce and prices would rise, they argued. In 1968 Charles Park argued (pp. 15–16, 22) that maintaining past growth trends in mineral use "would be a difficult and probably impossible task." Because of rapid resource depletion "the assumption of a continually expanding economy cannot be made; any prognostication based on that assumption is invalid." Rather, the future will entail ever "greater shortages of all kinds" and "there will be more and greater poverty in the world than at present." In his dramatic article, "Eco-Catastrophe" (1969), biologist Paul Ehrlich predicted, among other things, rapid deterioration of the "raw material situation" during the decade of the 1970s. And the much-publicized 1972 *Limits to Growth* predicted complete depletion of known global reserves for practically all major resources within 30 years (Meadows et al., pp. 64–68). As a result of "nonrenewable resource depletion," the study concluded, "the industrial base collapses, taking with it the service and agricultural systems. . . . Population . . . decreases when the death rate is driven upward by lack of food and health services" (Meadows et al., 1972, p. 125).[3]

TABLE 4-2. Prices of Important Minerals Relative to Labor Costs

| | Labor Costs | | | | | |
Mineral	*1900*	*1920*	*1940*	*1950*	*1960*	*1970*
Coal	459	451	189	208	111	100
Copper	785	226	121	99	82	100
Iron	620	287	144	112	120	100
Phosphorus	—	—	—	130	120	100
Molybdenum	—	—	—	142	108	100
Lead	788	388	204	228	114	100
Zinc	794	400	272	256	126	100
Sulphur	—	—	—	215	145	100
Aluminum	3,150	859	287	166	134	100
Gold	—	—	595	258	143	100
Crude petroleum	1,034	726	198	213	135	100

Source: Nordhaus, 1974, p. 24. Reprinted by permission of the American Economic Association.

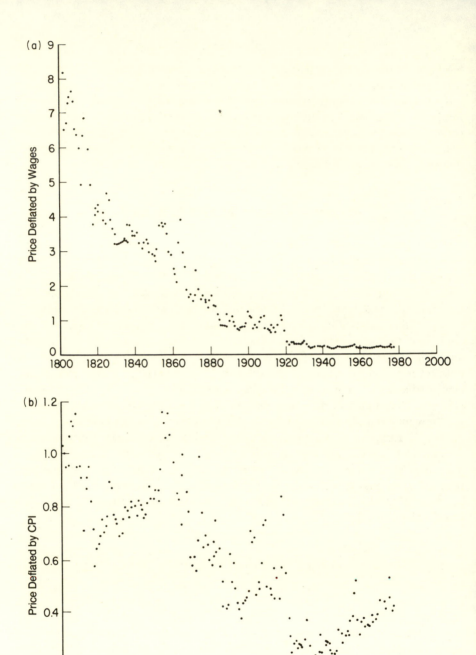

FIGURE 4-1. The scarcity of copper (a) as measured by its price relative to wages and (b) as measured by its price relative to the consumer index. The diagrams are typical of the pattern for each of the metals. From Simon and Kahn, 1984, p. 15. Reprinted by permission of Julian Simon.

TABLE 4-3.   Changes in "Known Reserves," 1950–1970

Ore	Known Reserves (1,000 Metric Tons) 1950	1970	Percentage Increase
Iron	19,000,000	251,000,000	1,221
Manganese	500,000	635,000	27
Chromite	100,000	700,000	675
Tungsten	1,903	1,328	−30
Copper	100,000	279,000	179
Lead	40,000	86,000	115
Zinc	70,000	113,000	61
Tin	6,000	6,600	10
Bauxite	1,400,000	5,300,000	279
Potash	5,000,000	118,000,000	2,360
Phosphates	26,000,000	1,178,000,000	4,430
Oil	75,000,000	455,000,000	507

Source: Kahn, Brown, and Martel, 1976, p. 92. Reprinted by permission of the Hudson Institute.

Are we now entering, or perhaps reentering, the "age of limits"? This view seems to stem, at least in part, from recent reports from the U.S. Bureau of Mines (1975, 1980, 1985) indicating that the dramatic increases in known reserves that occurred during the 1950s and 1960s have tapered off or in some cases have actually declined a bit. Were the catastrophists not wrong, merely premature?

The answer is a categorical no. If we are now facing serious resource depletion, one would expect this to be reflected by (1) rising resource prices and (2) increasing investment in the resource exploration and extraction industry. Table 4-4 shows recent real price trends for 13 of the more important resources. Eight show that prices have continued to decline and in some cases, coal and tungsten for instance, decline drastically. Three more show 1988 prices below their 1980 price levels. Only two minerals, nickel and aluminum, show real prices above those of 1975 or 1980. The rise in the price of aluminum of $0.07 per pound during the 1980s was quite modest. Moreover, since, as Table 4-2 shows, aluminum prices have fallen so drastically during this century, and since production of aluminum has exceeded consumption by about fivefold each year since 1973 (World Resources Institute, 1990, p. 322, Table 21.4), there is no reason to view the 1988 price as anything more than a temporary lull in a long-term, albeit somewhat erratic, downward trend. The high 1988 price for nickel also appears to be temporary. The Western world's largest producer of nickel, Inco, experienced labor difficulties, Falconbridge in the Dominican Republic found itself in a dispute with the government, and P. T. International of Indonesia experienced production difficulties. The uncertainty of the confluence of these three factors encouraged nickel consumers to increase their inventories, resulting in a suddenly tight market (U.S. Department of the Interior, 1990, pp. 694–695). By 1990 these problems were resolved and nickel prices had not only declined but were actually below their 1980 level (Tierney, 1990, p. 81).

In fact, far from increasing, mineral prices as a whole declined in real terms (1979–1981 = 100) from 97 in 1976 to 65 by 1986 (Ray, 1987, p. 40, Table 1). As

TABLE 4-4.   Real Prices of Selected Mineral Products, 1975–1988[a]

Mineral	Price			
	1975	1980	1985	1988
Aluminum (¢/lb)	67.5	83.2	75.0	90.7
Coal ($/ton)	32.60	28.51	22.82	18.14
Cobalt ($/lb)	6.68	29.17	10.31	5.85
Copper (¢/lb)	1.08	1.18	.60	.84
Gold ($/oz)	272.	715.	287.	361.
Lead (¢/lb)	36.4	49.6	17.2	30.5
Nat. Gas ($/1,000 ft^3)	.76	1.84	2.26	1.41
Nickel ($/lb)	3.71	3.45	2.03	5.15
Petroleum (crude) ($/bbl)	12.93	25.19	23.32	10.36
Platinum ($/oz)	277	512	428	494
Silver ($/oz)	7.45	24.08	5.54	5.39
Tungsten ($/lb)	8.94	9.78	3.81	2.37[b]
Zinc (¢/lb)	65.6	43.6	43.8	49.6

Sources: Compiled from U.S. Department of Commerce, 1990, p. 480, Table 775, and p. 483, Table 780)

[a]1982 = 100.

[b]Figure is from 1987; 1988 data is not available.

Ray put it (p. 40), "the middle years of this decade [1980s] will go down in economic history as a period when primary products hit rock bottom, whatever method is used to illustrate their real value or purchasing power. There have been hardly any exceptions to this general decline." The reason for the decline, according to Ray (p. 41) was "the excess of supply over demand." The phrase "hit rock bottom" is both unfortunate and misleading, since it implies that in the future resource prices will rise. Yet Ray provided no reason to believe that this would be the case. On the contrary, the trends he observed during the 1980s are consistent with the long-run historical trends shown in Table 4-2: short-run fluctuations coupled with long-run decline in real prices. In fact, the long-run decline in raw material prices is hardly a recent phenomenon, even when put in historical context. The price of copper, as expressed in labor time, was about 120 times greater in the year 1 AD than it is now, and the price of iron was 240 times greater. Going back even further, the price of copper was about 360 times higher in 800 BC and 1,620 times higher in 1800 BC (Simon, 1990, pp. 425–426). The decline in resource prices has been going on for centuries. There is no reason to believe that resource prices "hit rock bottom" during the decade of the 1980s, or that we have suddenly reached a historical turning point and prices will now begin to rise. The past is not, of course, a necessary harbinger of the future. However, the burden of proof lies on those who make such claims to explain why, after centuries of declining real prices, future resource prices will now reverse themselves and begin to rise.

As to investment in the resource exploration and extraction industries, the percent of the U.S. GNP devoted to mining activities did increase from about 2 percent in 1970 to 2.5 to 3 percent during the mid-1970s; it reached as much as 4.7 percent in the early 1980s. Since 85 percent of the total U.S. investment in the mining sector during this period was in the energy field, all of the increase is attributable to the "energy crises" of the mid- and late-1970s. But by the early 1980s, as energy prices stabilized and began to decline, so did investment in the mining sector. By 1987 mining investment as a percentage of GNP had fallen to just 1.9 percent (Department of Commerce, 1989, p. 688, Table 1205). Thus the increase was temporary and due to a single resource, oil. The U.S. experience is consistent with worldwide trends. The Mineral Production Index, a measure of the mining sector's contribution to gross product, declined from 116 in the late 1970s to 109 in the early 1980s (Kurian, 1984, pp. 200–201). Thus, not only did real prices continue to decline during the 1980s, but so too did the percentage of the world's investment devoted to mining activities.

The decline in both prices and investment during this period refutes the belief that resources are becoming more scarce. What is one to make of the reports indicating that the huge increases in reserves during the 1950s and 1960s have tapered off in recent years? First, it should be noted that this was actually predicted by Kahn two decades ago. Given the cost of exploration and the worldwide surplus of resources in the early 1970s, there was, he and his colleagues noted in 1976, little reason to expect reserves to continue to increase over the next few decades. "Since anything found today could not be sold for 30 years or so," any additional minerals "found in the next few years," he observed, "are more likely to be a fortuitous discovery than the result of a concerted exploration." It is only when reserves are "down to 10 years or less" that one should begin to worry. But if that were to happen, "then the marketplace would reflect that condition with increased prices until new mines are opened and reserves are expanded to higher levels" (pp. 92–93). The argument is not only consistent with the recent Bureau of Mines reports, it in fact *anticipates them.* It is also worth pointing out that tungsten, the only mineral that registered a reduction in reserves between 1950 and 1970, registered an increase in reserves of 90 percent between 1973 and 1983, the largest increase of any of the 12 minerals in Table 4-2. Oil is another example. Higher oil prices in 1973 stimulated increased exploration at the same time that it encouraged more efficient use of energy. Energy efficiency increased by about 30 percent between 1973 and 1987 (*Economic Report of the President,* 1991, pp. 84–85), holding demand down. The result is that while production rose by less than 10 percent between 1973 and 1990, proven reserves increased by 50 percent. Put differently, in 1973 the world had a 30-year supply of proven oil reserves; in 1990 it has a 45-year supply (*Economic Report of the President,* 1991, pp. 103–104).

Second, and complementary to the first point, periodic scarcity is, paradoxical as it may seem at first, an integral part of the process by which human progress in general and resource abundance in particular occur. As resources become more scarce, their prices begin to rise. This stimulates the search for solutions to the problem, the discovery of which almost invariably leaves us better off than before the problem occurred (see Simon, 1990, p. 422). Thus, short-run problems yield solutions that improve our situation in the long run. Short-run resource shortages result in long-run resource abundance. Energy is a good example. Wood was a common source of energy in seventeenth-century Europe. As it grew scarce and its price rose, it was replaced by peat and coal in the eighteenth century. The coal-fired steam engine was an important element in stimulating the industrial revolution. As peat supplies became depleted, again causing energy prices to rise, the search for alternative sources of energy led to the widespread use of whale oil. As the whales were killed off faster than they could spawn, prices once again rose, resulting in the development of the fossil fuel industry in the mid-nineteenth century. Similarly, the energy crisis a little over a century later stimulated the development of alternative energy sources, including nuclear power. What is noteworthy is that, even at the height of the energy crisis of the 1970s, energy was still considerably cheaper than it was a century before. The price of whale oil was about $10 per gallon in the 1870s. Allowing for inflation, that would be equivalent to about $200 a gallon today or approximately $4,000 to fill the tank of a medium-sized automobile (Louw, 1985, pp. 6–7).

Third, "reserves" are defined as that part of the resource base that, given current prices and technology, "could be economically extracted or produced at the time of determination" (Bureau of Mines, 1985, p. 3). They are just one part of the "reserve base," the others being "marginal" and "subeconomic" resources, that is, minerals that, while known to exist with a high degree of certainty, are not economically extractable at current prices and/or with current technology. The reserve base, as Figure 4-2 shows, is only a small part of the total resource base.

This definition makes the size of a mineral's reserves a function of the price of the mineral. By reducing costs of extraction, thereby making lower grade deposits economic, technological advance increases the reserves of a mineral. In addition to

RESOURCES OF (commodity name)

AREA: (mine, district, field, State, etc.)   UNITS: (tons, barrels, ounces, etc.)

Cumulative production	IDENTIFIED RESOURCES			UNDISCOVERED RESOURCES	
	Demonstrated		Inferred	Probability range (or)	
	Measured	Indicated		Hypothetical	Speculative
ECONOMIC	Reserves		Inferred reserves		
MARGINALLY ECONOMIC	Marginal reserves		Inferred marginal reserves		
SUB- ECONOMIC	Demonstrated subeconomic resources		Inferred subeconomic resources		

Other occurrences	Includes nonconventional and low-grade materials

FIGURE 4-2. Major elements of mineral reserve classification. From U.S. Bureau of Mines, 1985, p. 5.

stimulating exploration and development, price increases likewise increase reserves by making economic those deposits that were marginal or subeconomic at lower prices. Conversely, a fall in price means a *statistical* reduction in the size of a mineral's reserves. And since a rapid fall in price would be expected to more than offset any advance in technology, the result would be registered as a net *statistical* decline in reserves. The resources have not been consumed. They still exist, and they are extractable with current technology. It is simply that at the lower price some of the deposits have ceased to be economically viable. A price increase, *even without any additional exploration or technological advance*, would render them economic, thereby automatically increasing reserves. For example, the increases between 1973 and the late 1970s in prices for such minerals as iron, copper, bauxite, phosphate, and oil were accompanied by increasing reserves; the subsequent decline in their prices was accompanied by declines in reserves.

Thus, recent price-reserve data provide no support for the catastrophist belief that world resources are being rapidly depleted. On the contrary, the data support the hypothesis that the reserve reductions registered for several minerals is, in part, a statistical artifact resulting from price declines. But prices decline only when supply exceeds demand. Far from depletion, the data indicate that resources are actually becoming more abundant. This raises two questions: (1) How could the catastrophists have gone so far wrong?, and (2) How can resources actually increase?

Mistakes in the Catastrophist Methodology

Catastrophists arrive at their doomsday calculations by dividing known reserves by current consumption in order to calculate the date at which the supplies of a given resource will be depleted. Thus we are told, for example, that at current consumption rates the known reserves of copper will be exhausted in 2010, of petroleum in 1999, and of tin in 2003. A somewhat more sophisticated approach assumes that known reserves are a part, say 20 percent, of the total amount of a given resource. The resource supply is then increased by a factor of 5. Invariably coupled with this is the assumption that the consumption of the resource will increase "exponentially" (see Meadows et al., 1972; Park, 1968). Since whatever years of supply are added by the former assumption are reduced by the latter, the net effect is to keep the "exhaustion date" about where it was using the less sophisticated approach. Such a procedure is seriously flawed and guarantees the imminent exhaustion of whatever resource one wishes to examine.

Known reserves are only a very small part of the available resource base. According to Ridker and Cecelski (1982, p. 595), they are similar to inventories, "and since exploration and development are costly, little effort is made to find proof of new resources if what is already known is considered adequate to meet demands for the next ten to twenty years." The World Bank made the same point (Beckerman, 1975, p. 175): "The reason we do not know the absolute limits of the resources we have is quite simple . . . we do not know because no one has yet found it necessary to know and therefore went around taking an accurate inventory." In short, we find resources as we need them. Hence, calculations based on current or known reserves produce exhaustion dates that are unrealistically close at hand.

A flaw in the notion of exhaustion dates is that it ignores the "feedback mechanism." As current reserves are consumed and the exhaustion date for a given resource draws near, its price will begin to rise. This will reduce consumption and encourage recycling, exploration for new sources of supply, and the development of technological improvements that will make the mining of lower-grade ores economically feasible. So despite the predictions of imminent depletion of numerous resources over the years, their exhaustion dates never get any closer. In fact, as was shown in Table 4-3, improved methods of mineral detection have increased the reserves of practically all raw materials, causing their exhaustion dates to recede.

Put differently, there are always shortages of raw materials, just as there are always shortages of shoes, toilet paper, and automobiles. These shortages are *independent of any particular economic system*. Economic institutions, observed Sowell (1980, p. 45), "exist to introduce elements of rationality, or efficiency, into the use of inputs and outputs." A rational policy is one that ensures that adjustments to changing economic data are made incrementally, that is, "at the margin." As the supply of a resource increases relative to its demand, the exhaustion date will recede. It is rational for factors of production to be diverted from areas where the exhaustion date is relatively remote, and thus the demand for additional units of the resource is relatively less urgent, into areas where the exhaustion date is closer at hand, and thus the demand for additional units of those resources (or finished goods or services) is relatively more urgent. Consider, said Sowell (1980, p. 46), the consequences of alternative decision-making processes:

> The alternative would be to completely satisfy all of some category of needs—the most urgent, the moderately important, and the trivially marginal—thereby leaving still more unsatisfied (and more urgent) needs unmet elsewhere in the economy. . . . The mundane fact of insufficiency must be insisted upon and reiterated because so many discussions of "unmet needs" proceed as if "better" policies, practices, or attitudes would "solve" the problem at hand without creating deficiencies elsewhere.

The catastrophists tend to ignore the marginalist principle and take an all-or-nothing view of the world. It is this oversight that has led them to derive such erroneously alarmist conclusions from such mundane concepts as known reserves and exhaustion dates.[4]

Growing Abundance of Resources

The prospect of running out of resources such as iron, tin, or bauxite is not a matter of decades, as the doomsayers would have us believe, but lies hundreds, perhaps thousands, of years ahead for all vital resources. The World Bank has estimated the stock of metals in the top mile of the earth's crust to be a million times as great as the present known reserves. Beckerman (1975, p. 102) has calculated that "this means that we have enough to last about one hundred million years." Kahn, Brown, and Martel (1976, p. 102) determined that "over 95 percent of the world demand [for metals] is for five metals (iron, aluminum, silicon, magnesium, and titanium) which are not considered exhaustible." Another 4.85 percent of world demand is for seven metals—copper, zinc, manganese, chromium, lead, nickel, and tin—that are "probably inexhaustible." Thus 99.9 percent of world demand is for metals whose supply is either clearly or probably inexhaustible.

Goeller and Weinberg (1976, pp. 683–689) have shown that of the 13 most widely used resources, only fossil fuels and phosphorus are "not essentially inexhaustible." Phosphorus, they write, has a "present resource-to-demand ratio [of] 500 years for world reserves and an additional 800 years for potential resources." They further argued that the development of alternatives to fossil fuels, such as the fission breeder, fusion, solar energy and the like, would provide the world with inexhaustible sources of energy.

Nordhaus (1974, pp. 22–26) arrived at similar conclusions. Using U.S. Geological Survey data, he presented resource availability according to three measures: "known reserves," "ultimate recoverable resources," (0.01% of the materials estimated to be in the top kilometer of the earth's crust), and "crustal abundance" (the total amount estimated to be in the earth's crust). Dividing each measure by the current (i.e., early 1970s) consumption rates, Nordhaus provided an estimate for resource availability in years (Table 4-5). He dismissed the known reserve measure as unduly pessimistic, for reasons already discussed. The crustal abundance measure was rejected as "unduly optimistic because it assumes that everything [in the earth's crust] can be recovered." "Ultimate recoverable resources" was therefore left as the most reasonable measure. According to Nordhaus, the catastrophist concern about imminent resource exhaustion is without foundation, especially since these findings are based on existing technology and "do not take into account the

TABLE 4-5.   Measures of Mineral Consumption (in years)

Mineral	Known Reserves ÷ Annual Consumption	U.S. Geological Survey's Estimate of "Ultimate Recoverable Resources" (= 0.01% of Materials in Top Kilometer of Earth's Crust) ÷ Annual Consumption	Amount Estimated in Earth's Crust ÷ Annual Consumption
Copper	45	340	242,000,000
Iron	117	2,657	1,815,000,000
Phosphorus	481	1,601	870,000,000
Molybdenum	65	630	422,000,000
Lead	10	162	85,000,000
Zinc	21	618	409,000,000
Sulphur	30	6,897	NA
Uranium	50	8,455	1,855,000,000
Aluminum	23	68,066	38,500,000,000
Gold	9	102	57,000,000

Source: Nordhaus, 1974, p. 23. Reprinted by permission of the American Economic Association.

economic feasibility of mining lower grade ores as prices rise or techniques improve." The clear evidence, Nordhaus concludes, "is that the future will not be limited by the sheer availability of important materials." Nordhaus reached similar conclusions for energy. Ignoring, for the moment, the question of price, there would be sufficient supplies of fossil fuel—from conventional as well as such unconventional sources as oil shale, which is technologically, but at current prices not economically, feasible—to last for over 500 years (Table 4-6, line 1). And, even with only current technology, "there are resources for more than 8,000 years at the current rate of consumption" (Table 4-6, line 2). With breeder reactors, and more dramatically with fusion technology, Nordhaus concluded, "there is virtually unlimited energy available."

But what of cost? Nordhaus and others (W. Brown, 1984, pp. 360,367; Kahn, Brown, and Martel, 1976, pp. 58–65; Kaysen, 1972, pp. 664–665; Opel, 1987; Simon, 1981b, pp. 95–110) believe that, with a relatively free market in energy and assuming that the advance of technology continues at its historical pace, with productivity increasing by 2.0 to 2.5 percent annually, that is, that productivity doubles in about 35 years, then any tendency toward higher energy prices will be more than offset by increased productivity. Consequently, "energy prices would continue to fall relative to labor's price and average incomes" (Nordhaus, 1974, p. 25).

Some mention should also be made of geothermal energy, that is, energy obtained by tapping into the heat generated by radioactive decay in the earth's interior. Geothermal energy represents a virtually unlimited alternative source, and advances in drilling technology may well make this a reality by the mid-twenty-first century (Beckmann, 1984, p. 425).

Finally, even the pessimistic *Global 2000 Report* (U.S. Council on Environmental Quality, 1982, p. 2) acknowledges that the depletion of important resources is not an immediate concern: "The world's finite fuel resources—coal, oil, gas, oil shale, tar sands, and uranium—are theoretically sufficient for centuries. . . . Nonfuel mineral resources generally appear sufficient to meet projected demands through 2000."

One of the pillars of catastrophist thought is the Second Law of Thermodynamics, the law of entropy (Commoner, 1976; Daly, 1974, 1979; Georgescu-Roegen 1971, 1977). This law points out that although the quantity of energy in the universe is constant, the "usable stuff" is low-entropy energy. As energy is used it is transformed from useful (low-entropy) to useless (high-entropy) energy. This process is irreversible. The law of entropy, claim the catastrophists, proves that the

TABLE 4-6.   Energy Resource Supply-Consumption Ratio, 1979

Energy/Technology	Years
Fossil fuels only	520
Fossil fuels plus current nuclear technology	8,400
Fossil fuels, current nuclear, and breeder technology	1.1×10^6
Fossil fuels, current nuclear, breeder, and fusion technology	5.3×10^{10}

Source: Nordhaus, 1974, p. 24. Reprinted by permission of the American Economic Association.

world is inexorably headed toward the disaster of energy depletion. But if the studies of Nordhaus, Kahn, Simon, and Goeller and Weinberg are correct, we have, even with *current* technology, enough energy to last for over a million years. And then there is, of course, the sun. While the catastrophists admit that the sun will be a steady source of energy for 5 to 6 billion years, they emphasize that solar energy "is strictly limited in the rate at which it reaches the earth" (Daly, 1979, p. 74). But the amount of direct solar energy absorbed by the earth is about 4,500 times the world's current energy consumption rate (Beckmann, 1984, p. 415).

The point is not that the law of entropy is wrong but that the conditions that would make the law a concern in the area of energy accessibility are so remote as to render the law irrelevant for the foreseeable future. The real issue concerning direct solar energy lies not with its volume but with its "diluteness," or density. Beckmann (1984, p. 418) notes that the history of human energy use "is a history of increasing energy concentrations." Direct solar energy is so dilute that one must question whether it can ever become an economically viable energy source. The difficulty lies with the diluteness of solar energy and not, as the catastrophists would have it, with "the rate at which it reaches the earth."

In fact, one can go even further and question whether the Second Law of Thermodynamics would ever become relevant. The history of human energy production and use is one of increasing efficiency, and there is no reason to assume that this trend will not continue indefinitely. Given the time-span of several *billion* years, who is to say that we could not reach a point at which we would become so energy efficient that we could supply the world's energy needs by using virtually no energy at all? As William James commented, "Though the *ultimate* state of the universe may be its vital and physical extinction, there is nothing in physics to interfere with the hypothesis that the penultimate state might be the millennium" (in Simon, 1990, p. 459). Of course one cannot guarantee such a result. But one cannot rule it out either.

Science, Technology, and Resources

If the depletion of the earth's stock of a vital raw material such as oil ever did appear imminent, we can be confident that it would not have serious consequences, provided the market is unhampered. As the exhaustion date drew near and exploration failed to yield new reserves, the price of oil would rise. Not only would this stretch the supply by encouraging conservation, but the rising price would also encourage the search for both resource substitutes, such as nuclear, solar, and geothermal energy, and factor substitutes, such as capital and labor. It would also stimulate the search for technological developments that might permit us not just to produce oil synthetically but to produce it at economically feasible prices. In such a case, the physical exhaustion of even a key natural resource would be, as Solow (1974, p. 11) has phrased it, "just an event, not a catastrophe."[5]

Kahn, Brown, and Martel (1976, p. 59) observed that the steep increase in the price of oil during the early 1970s generated just such responses. The oil crisis "represented an energy watershed, but it was not a watershed from abundance to scarcity, or even from cheap to expensive, but rather from cheap to inexpensive." These authors argued that the effect of the sudden price hike "was to increase the rate at which the new energy came on the market and to decrease the rate at which energy was used—that is, the cartel's moves actually decreased the possibility of future energy shortages." This conclusion, as already pointed out, has received considerable empirical support. And the 1986 oil price crash, when the price of oil was more than halved, falling, in 1980 dollars, from more than $30 per barrel in 1985 to only $14 the following year, was a result of both the world oil glut and the rapid development of alternative energy sources (Louw, 1985; Osterfeld, 1984, 1987b.).

The earth is a physically finite place, but its resources are neither fixed nor finite. The concept of resources is a dynamic one. While it is common knowledge that technology consumes resources, a more important fact is often overlooked: technological advances permit us to use existing resources more efficiently. For example, in 1900 the lowest grade of copper ore economically mineable was about 3 percent. Today the cut-off point has fallen to 0.35 percent. Similarly, although much of the coal closest to the surface has been extracted, advances in mining technology have actually reduced the cost of obtaining coal despite having to go much deeper to extract it. And Opel (1987, p. 51) has pointed out that, because of technological advances, the United States now has "a larger quantity of usable iron ore deposits within its borders than it did fifty years ago."

More importantly, technological advances actually create resources by finding uses for previously useless materials. Uranium is one example; hydroelectric power is another. But oil is, perhaps, the most dramatic. Prior to the mid-nineteenth century oil was a liability, and land known to possess this slimy ooze was worth very little. Only with the dawn of the machine age did oil become a resource. Aluminum is another example. Throughout the nineteenth century aluminum was a precious metal on a par with gold and silver; with advances in technology aluminum can now be extracted from bauxite quite cheaply. Bauxite, and other materials containing aluminum such as clay and shale, are so plentiful that we now have a nearly inexhaustible supply of aluminum at relatively low prices (Beckerman, 1975, pp. 185–186).

By enabling us to find and use resources more efficiently and by discovering uses for heretofore useless materials, technology creates resources. As Earl Cook (1976, pp. 677–678) succinctly put it,

> During the past 150 years large increases in the earth-resource base of industrialized society have been attained. By increasing the efficiencies of discovery, recovery, processing and application of such resources, we have been able to find and exploit leaner, deeper, and more remote deposits. By discovering and developing new methods of utilizing previously worthless materials we have created resources where none existed.

Although the notion that resources are becoming more abundant may appear counter to common sense, it has solid empirical foundation. How else can one explain that, by whatever index one chooses, the costs of all important raw materials have declined for at least the last 100 years (see Figure 4-1 and Table 4-2)? But while technology creates resources, it must be remembered that technology itself is created by the human mind, which Julian Simon (1981b) aptly dubs "the ultimate resource." The supply of resources, therefore, is limited only by human ingenuity. Although this, too, runs counter to conventional wisdom, there is strong empirical evidence for it. That the possession of physical stocks of resources is not necessary for economic development is illustrated by Hong Kong, Singapore, Switzerland, and Japan, all of which have few physical resources yet are highly developed economies. That the possession of physical resources does not guarantee economic development is demonstrated by the Soviet Union as well as numerous African countries that possess an abundance of physical resources yet are economically backward.

The flaw in the catastrophist outlook is the seemingly plausible but erroneous assumption that the stock of resources is fixed, that the size of the resource pie is determined by nature. What is important, however, is not the actual physical substance itself, but the services we are able to derive from it. What is relevant to us, Simon writes (1981b, pp. 46–47),

> is not whether we can find any lead in existing lead mines but whether we can have the services of lead batteries at a reasonable price; it does not matter to us whether this is accomplished by recycling lead, making batteries that last forever, or by replacing lead batteries with another contraption.

Viewing resources as "services" rather than stocks leads to the important conclusion that the resource pie is not fixed but changeable, and thus there is no inherent reason for the stocks of resources to diminish over time. On the contrary, since resources are a function of knowledge, and since our stock of knowledge has increased over time, it should come as no surprise that the stock of physical resources has also been expanding.

Resources, the Market, and the Entrepreneur

Scientists and technicians, of course, are not merely sitting around waiting for shortages to appear. How is it that they are directed to the areas where their services are most needed? Here we come to a very different but perhaps even more indispensable type of information, that provided through the market, and to the vital but often neglected role of the entrepreneur acting on that information.

In contrast to scientific and technological knowledge, which may be viewed as an expanding body of knowledge, market information is fleeting and ever changing. This is so by its very nature. Consumer wants change. It would be of little interest or help to a businessperson concerned with consumer wants in the 1990s to be told that crew cuts, string ties, and cars with tail fins were popular in the 1950s. In contrast to a particular scientific field, such as physics or even economics, where one can be fairly sure that the general body of principles will not change to any significant degree, economic data must be forever learned anew. But these changes, however haphazard and chaotic they may appear to be, are connected, or coordinated, spontaneously through the market.

Profits and losses are indicators of maladjustments; the structure of production is not completely synchronized with consumers' preferences. Losses occur because what is being produced is not what consumers desire at the time of their decisions. This means that, in the eyes of consumers, those factors can be more usefully employed elsewhere. The adjustment will be made because production cannot be continued at a loss. Conversely, profits are an indication that, in the eyes of consumers, too little of a good is being produced. Profits also serve to attract resources into the field. Thus it is the changes in relative prices, caused by consumer buying and abstention from buying, that determine the entire process, from the search for raw materials to the completion of the finished product. Changes in consumer preferences causes changes in profit margins and thus in the allocation of resources. In a free market, therefore, profits are automatically correlated with serving consumers, while losses indicate a failure to serve.

But why does this adjustment process occur? If the consumer is the "sovereign," the entrepreneur is the motor. As noted in Chapter 2, it is the misallocation of resources resulting from changes in economic data that creates profit opportunities. It is the entrepreneur who, by spotting and exploiting these opportunities, moves the economy toward a more efficient allocation.

The market and the entrepreneur are the opposite sides of the same coin. Neither can function without the other. Their critical role in the area of resources is evident. Scientists and technicians are drawn into those areas where they are most needed because entrepreneurs, perceiving the signals conveyed by price changes in the market, bid those scientists and technicians away from areas where their contributions are less urgently needed and into areas where they are more intensely needed.

It is instructive to consider the only alternative to the market: the centrally planned, nonmarket economy. Without the market there would be neither signals conveyed by market prices nor profit-seeking entrepreneurs to act on those signals. The closest example was the USSR, where decisions, at least in theory, were made by a single central planning board, Gosplan. The Soviet economy was notoriously inefficient and would have been even more so if it were not for extensive black markets. The standard of living was the lowest of any developed country and Soviet products were noteworthy for their shoddiness.

Since consumer goods are directly valued, the demand for them can be at least roughly determined by planners. But resources are valued only indirectly, that is, for their contribution to the production of a final good. This renders the problem of the efficient allocation of resources particularly acute. The number of alternative technologies and different ways of utilizing scarce resources for an economy the size of the Soviet Union's was in the billions. Without accurate price data, the choices made by Gosplan were little more than guesses. There is little doubt that this is the case. Producers in the Soviet Union had no direct link to consumers. They were assigned quantity production targets of so much steel, so many nails, and so on, and were then evaluated according to whether or not they had met their targets. Because these targets rarely coincide with "improvement in the country's economic well-being," the planning process, notes Goldman (1983, pp. 46–47) resulted in a great deal of waste of both human labor and natural resources. A few examples will make this clear.

When production targets were given in weights, factory managers in the nail industry produced large construction nails and no small finishing nails. Shoe manufacturers produced adult shoes but no children's shoes. When production targets were switched from weights to quantities, the result was a glut of finishing nails and children's shoes. The same sort of distortions occurred regularly in the area of energy resources. The Soviet oil industry, for example, was evaluated not according to the amount of oil discovered but the number of meters drilled each month, making the discovery of oil only incidental to the primary goal of drilling the number of meters assigned as the quota. Since the deeper the well the slower the drilling process, geologists responded by digging numerous wells too shallow to hit oil (Roberts and LaFollette, 1990, pp. 10–14). As *Pravda* (Goldman, 1983, p. 38–39) noted, "there are geological expeditions that have not discovered a valuable deposit for many years but are counted among the successful expeditions because they have fulfilled their assignment in terms of meters." The result has been the waste of resources and labor.

Another incentive method used by the Soviet planners was the *valovaia producktsia*, or "val," which was intended to be a measure of gross ruble output. Since plant managers were rewarded for increasing the gross value of their factories' outputs, they responded by intentionally increasing production costs. Hence the val unwittingly provided an incentive to squander scarce resources by rewarding managers for using large quantities of the most expensive resources they could find.

These problems impede the search for substitutes. Soviet managers, Goldman has noted (p. 42), had an "almost phobic reaction to innovation." This is so because to produce a new product the plant manager would have to shut down the plant to revamp the production process. But shutting down the plant meant that the factory would not be able to meet its production quota, in which case the manager and his or her workers would not qualify for their bonuses. In fact, falling short of their quotas resulted in punishment. Thus, says Goldman (p. 42) "there is little in the way of extra inducement for innovation, but considerable disincentive."

In brief, central planning as it worked in the Soviet Union was notoriously inefficient. This inefficiency was not the result of incompetence. For even if the factor allocation established in the plans had been optimal, changes in data during the plan period would have meant that the allocation would no longer have been optimal at the end of the period. Inefficiency was particularly acute in the area of resources, when the incentives created by the plan encouraged their squandering (such as oil) while simultaneously impeding innovations and the search for substitutes and additional sources of supply.

Conclusions

If what has been said is at all correct, then the common view that Third World economic development is being impeded or even prevented because it is being systematically drained of its resources by the First World is exactly the reverse of the truth. The deserts of the Mideast became valuable only in the nineteenth century when oil became a resource. And oil became a resource only after (1) important uses for it were discovered and (2) reasonably efficient extraction technologies were developed. Both were primarily products of the West.

The characteristic, in fact unique, feature of the West has been its openness. This, as noted in Chapter 2, has had a tremendous impact in both science and economics. The free exchange of ideas has stimulated scientific advance and technological innovation. By allowing a close interaction between scientists and innovators on the one hand and economic entrepreneurs on the other, it has enabled science and technology to be used in the satisfaction of consumer desires. Thus it is the Western institutions of limited government and its free market corollary that have permitted the resource base to increase more rapidly than resource consumption, thereby actually expanding the resource pie.

Conversely, rigid state controls stifle the exchange of ideas. The absence of such an exchange has ominous consequences, for it means that there can be little or no scientific advance and few if any technological innovations. Since the *creation* of resources is slowed or even prevented altogether, "closed" societies are therefore condemned to live off their *existing* stock of physical resources. Further, because of the inefficiencies resulting from impediments placed in the way of entrepreneurial activity by governments and/or customs, closed societies consume those resources more rapidly than open ones. This means that the resource pie can be expanded *or* reduced. It also means that its size is determined not by nature but by social and economic institutions. Perhaps the kernel of truth in the catastrophist position is that a completely closed or controlled society would, in fact, face the ominous prospect of resource depletion. Unfortunately, precisely such authoritarian state controls and the brutal suppression of ideas are distinguishing features of so many Third World countries.

The answers to the two questions raised at the beginning of this chapter are evident. The activities of both experimental scientists and entrepreneurs, acting largely in the West, have actually created resources where none had existed. Thus, far from draining the Third World of its resources, the West has, in fact, provided the Third World with a greater supply of resources than it had prior to its contact with the West. In that sense, the Second and Third Worlds are beneficiaries of the First World. The answer to the second question follows directly from the first. Far from the prospect of imminent collapse resulting from worldwide resource depletion, the world, thanks to the Western "development patterns" so deplored by Chichilnisky and others, is actually moving farther away from that prospect.

Notes

1. The figure was calculated from data obtained from the following sources: the U.S. Bureau of the Census, 1975, p. 593; U.S. Department of Commerce, 1987, p. 683; and the U.S. Department of Energy, 1983, p. 7.

2. Also see H. Barnett, 1982, pp. 167–173, Tables 8.1–8.7; H. Barnett et al., 1984, pp. 319–321.

3. Critics such as Kaysen (1972) demonstrated that the book's assumptions and methodology were so flawed that its conclusions were worthless. The study was so discredited that even its own sponsor, the Club of Rome, disavowed the book.

4. Two decades have now passed since the publication of *The Limits to Growth* in 1972. There is, perhaps, no more telling commentary on this highly influential book than to see how its prognostications have fared. Its authors gave several variations regarding methods of projecting resource availability. It is clear, however, that they believed the most reasonable was to assume that most of the resources in the earth have already been discovered and that, as population increases, resource consumption will continue to expand. Thus, they determined exhaustion dates by dividing known reserves by the exponential index of consumption. On the basis of these projections (pp. 64–67), the world should already have run out of gold, mercury, petroleum, silver, and zinc. It is scheduled to run out of copper and lead in 1993 and natural gas in 1994. It is interesting to note that Meadows et al.'s "exhaustion date" for lead was 21 years. Today, despite a significant increase in consumption during the past two decades, it now stands at 22 years (World Resources Institute, 1990, p. 322, Table 21.4). The exhaustion dates for most other resources listed by Meadows et al. have likewise receded. For example, they listed the exhaustion date for aluminum at 31 years, or 2003. Today it stands at 224 years if one uses proven reserves and at 2,388 years if one relies on the reserve base (World Resources Institute, 1990, p. 322, Table 21.4). Increased resource production has been accompanied by increased reserves and falling prices, something Meadows et al. would find inexplicable.

5. A staple of catastrophism is that we are consuming resources too fast. The reasoning is that since life is short, individuals discount future for present consumption. But society does not die. Therefore, in social decision-making "there is no excuse for treating generations unequally" (Solow, 1974, p. 9). Hence, "we ought to act as if the social rate of time preference were zero." Solow (p. 9) says that "I find the reasoning persuasive." This is a curious conclusion, for he also states that "if the future is anything like the past," resources will become more abundant over time, they will be used with increasing efficiency and, with technological improvements, substitutions will become progressively easier so that the exhaustion of a natural resource will be "just an event," and an unlikely one at that. If so, why should we be concerned about saving resources for future generations? Indeed, if "intergenerational equity" is a concern at all, it would be the reverse of what is commonly thought. To the extent that government policies are successful in artificially reducing current resource consumption, it follows that the present generation is being exploited by future generations, that is, that we are consuming resources "too slowly."

6. In discussing the plight of the Soviet Union, Brzezinski (1989, p. 39) has commented that "It literally took a political decision on the level of the ruling Politburo to produce a single quality consumer item. . . . In the seventy years of Soviet rule not a single such item capable of competing on the world market has yet been produced." Brzezinski also quoted the Soviet historian Leonid Batkin (p. 34): "[W]hile the Stalin system was exterminating people in the millions, people like Bohr, Wiener, Watson, and Crick were at work. While the Brezhnev system was reducing our country to mediocrity, the world [i.e., the West, including Japan] was developing lasers and personal computers and witnessing the explosion of the postindustrial revolution."

5

Population

There is a great deal of concern, both among professionals and in the popular press, over the "population crisis." According to biologist Paul Ehrlich in a 1970 interview (1973, pp. 13–28), "the death of the world is imminent" because

> the human population of the planet is about five times too large, and we're managing to support all these people—at today's level of misery—only by spending our capital, burning our fossil fuels, dispersing our mineral resources and turning our fresh water into salt water. We have not only overpopulated but overstretched our environment.

The basic problem, said Ehrlich, is "too many people. And nothing else can be solved unless we solve that problem." The "population of the United States should eventually be reduced to well under 50,000,000 and that of the world to an absolute maximum of 500,000,000." (Also see Watson and Smith, 1973.) In his 1968 book *The Population Bomb* (p. 17), Ehrlich stated that "each year food production in undeveloped countries falls a bit further behind burgeoning population growth." The "inevitable" result is "mass starvation. . . . A minimum of three and one-half million will starve this year [1968], mostly children. But this is merely a handful compared to the numbers that will be starving in a decade or so. And it is now too late to take action to save many of those people."[1]

In a similar vein the famous *Limits to Growth* (Meadows et al., 1972) characterized population growth as "'super' exponential" (p. 41) and concluded, much like Ehrlich, that the inevitable consequence is resource depletion, massive pollution, soil erosion, and a reduction in the amount of arable land. "The basic behavioral mode of the world system is exponential growth of population and capital, followed by collapse" sometime before the year 2100 (pp. 148–149).

In his 1973 book, *One Hundred Countries, Two Billion People*, Robert McNamara wrote (cited in Zinsmeister, 1987, p. 18):

> The greatest single obstacle to the economic and social advancement of the majority of the peoples in the underdeveloped world is rampant population growth . . .
> the threat of unmanageable population pressures is very much like the threat of

nuclear war. . . . Both threats can and will have catastrophic consequences unless they are dealt with rapidly. (Also see McNamara, 1984.)

And the 1980 *Global 2000 Report to the President* (U.S. Council on Environmental Quality, 1982, pp. 1–4) concluded that "rapid population growth will hardly have altered by 2000." Since some areas of the world—sub-Saharan Africa and the Himalayan hills of Asia—have already "exceeded the carrying capacity of the immediate area," the projected population growth will result in the

> erosion of the land's capacity to support life. Unless this circle of interlinked problems is broken soon, population growth in such areas will unfortunately be slowed for reasons other than declining birth rates. Hunger and disease will claim more babies and young children, and more of those surviving will be mentally and physically handicapped by childhood malnutrition.

The popular press is literally glutted with articles dealing with the population crisis. "Earth Headed for the Breaking Point" (McLaughlin, 1982), "UN Tries to Defuse Population Bomb" (Atlas, 1984), and "Population Bomb Ticks More Loudly than Ever" (Bukro, 1987) are just three, all from the same newspaper.[2]

But concern over the "population crisis" is nothing new. It was a matter of concern in the 1930s and 1940s. At that time, however, "population crisis" did not refer to an "explosion" but to a "birth dearth." There were numerous articles in both the professional and popular literature with such titles as "World Suicide by Birth Control," "Are We to Disappear?," "Where Are the Children?," "Population Going Down?," and "Parents Go on Strike" (Pohlman, 1973, pp. 8–10). A. M. Carr-Saunders' 1936 book, *World Population* (1973, pp. 2–3), is fairly typical:

> The most essential thing at the present time is to implant in the members of a modern community a firm grasp of the fact that they are responsible for its future in the sense that if they do not replace themselves, the community will be extinguished. . . . Therefore, if things remain as they are, the reproduction rate will fall, and the prospect will be a reduction of the population to less than a quarter of its present size a century from now. . . . The prospect of so catastrophic a fall makes it urgent that steps should be taken at once, and the difficulties, which will be encountered in undertaking the social reconstruction that is necessary are so formidable that the urgency is much enhanced.

The 1938 *Report of the Committee on Population Problems* (U.S. National Resources Committee, 1973, p. 7) lamented the fact that "the birth *rate* has been declining for decades," observed that the United States was in the midst of a "transition from an era of rapid growth to a period of stationary or decreasing numbers," and predicted that "even with the highest rates that can reasonably be assumed, there would be a natural increase of less than 50,000,000 from 1935 to 1980." In fact, by 1980 the population of the United States was close to 100 million *more* than it was in 1935, or nearly double the Committee's *highest* projection.

Conclusions such as these, as Simon has noted (1990, p. 165), "give us reason to be humble about turning forecasts into policy." We cannot simply project past population trends into the future. We need to learn from our mistakes. After examining the historical trends, we should try to derive from them principles or determinants of population growth that are consistent with the empirical data. We then need to examine the consequences of these principles. That is the goal of this chapter.

The Dynamics of Population Growth

Numbers and Trends

Figure 5-1 and Tables 5-1 and 5-2 leave no doubt that the world is in the midst of a population explosion. They also show that world population history can be divided into two distinct periods: a very long period of slow population growth and a short period of rapid population growth.

Anthropologists estimate that, prior to the development of agriculture and the domestication of animals about 10,000 to 12,000 years ago, the world could not have supported a population based on hunting and gathering of more than 10 million. Most estimates place the actual population at 5 to 8 million (Coale, 1964, pp. 42–43; Merrick, 1986, p. 8). Interestingly, the introduction of agriculture did not have much of an *immediate* impact on the rate of population growth. Between 10,000 BC and 1 AD, population increased only by about 250 million, or by an annual rate of 0.04 percent. Between 1 AD and 1650, world population increased by less than 300 million, or by the identical rate of 0.04 percent per annum. Between 1650 and 1750, population increased by about 180 million, or by a rate of 0.29 percent. In the 200-year period from 1750 to 1950, world population increased by about 1.7 billion. But in just the 30-year period from 1950 to 1980, world population increased by more than 75 percent, going from 2.5 billion to 4.4 billion.

TABLE 5-1.   Estimated Population Growth Through History

Year	Estimated Population	Percent Annual Increase in the Intervening Period
Circa 10,000 B.C.	5,000,000	
1 AD	250,000,000	0.04
1650	545,000,000	0.04
1750	728,000,000	0.29
1800	906,000,000	0.45
1850	1,171,000,000	0.53
1900	1,608,000,000	0.65
1950	2,486,000,000	0.91
1970	3,632,000,000	2.09
1980	4,390,000,000	1.73
1990	5,390,200,000	1.70

Sources: Adapted from Thompson and Lewis, 1965, p. 384; Todaro, 1981, p. 159; and World Resources Institute, 1990, p. 254.

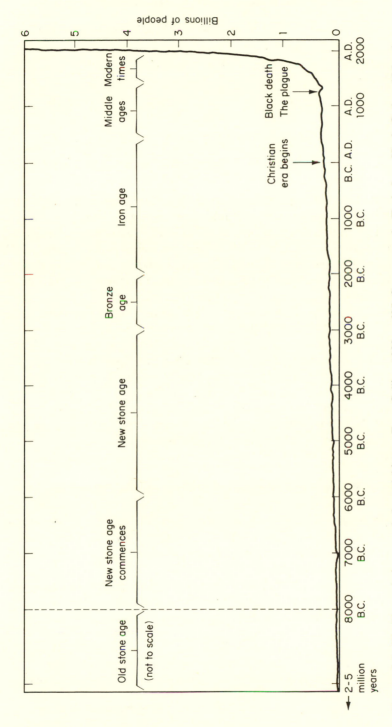

FIGURE 5-1. World population growth through history. From Collins, 1982, p. 697. *Source:* van der Taak, Jean, Haub, Carl, and Murphy, Elaine (1979). "Our Population Predicament: A New Look." *Population Bulletin* (December), p. 2. Reprinted by permission of Population Reference Bureau.

TABLE 5-2   World Population Growth Through History

Period	Average Annual Rate (%)	Doubling Time (years)
Appearance of man to early historical times	0.002	35,000
1650–1750	0.3	243
1850–1900	0.6	116
1930–1940	1.0	73
1965–1970	2.06	35
1975–1980	1.74	41.9
1985–1990	1.73	42.2

Sources: Adapted from Todaro, 1981, p. 161, and World Resources Institute, 1990, p. 254.

What is striking is not so much the absolute magnitude of the increases but their rate and the trend. For 99.9 percent of human history, population grew at a rate of 0.002 percent per year, a doubling time of about 35,000 years. Between 1650 and 1750 the rate of growth increased to 0.3 percent per year, a doubling time of 240 years. Between 1850 and 1900 the rate of growth increased to 0.6 percent, for a doubling time of 115 years. And by 1970 the rate of growth reached 2.1 percent per year and the doubling time fell to just 35 years. Put somewhat differently, even if one began with a hypothetical Adam and Eve, as Ansley Coale pointed out in the 1960s (Coale, 1964, p. 43), world population has doubled only 31 times or, on average, about once every 30,000 years. But by 1970 doubling time was just 35 years. The trend is clear: a dramatic increase in the rate of increase. Since this rate was itself based on an ever-expanding population base, it produced a population trend like that shown in Figure 5-1. Simple projections of this trend into the not too distant future conjured up horror stories of an earth literally swamped with people, of a world with "about 100 persons for each square yard of the Earth's surface, land and sea" (Ehrlich, 1968, p. 18). In short, it spelled disaster.

The Demographic Transition: The Data and the Projections

While the world is now experiencing a population explosion, there are very strong reasons to believe that the explosion is temporary, that population extrapolations based on its continuation are therefore seriously flawed, and that the earth is not in danger of becoming overpopulated.

Thomas Merrick, president of the Population Reference Bureau and former director of the Center for Population Research at Georgetown University, has recently written (1986, pp. 3,7,30) that

Human demographic history has reached an important turning point. World population in the spring of 1986 stands at about 4.9 billion and is growing at about 1.7 percent a year. . . . After accelerating for more than two centuries, the annual *rate* of world population growth is slowing: today's rate of 1.7 percent is down from a peak of about 2.04 percent in the late 1960s and is expected to continue to decline, to between 1.4 and 1.5 percent in 2000 and zero toward the end of the 21st century, according to the United Nations. . . . Because they generally occur at a glacially slow pace, demographic changes rarely make the headlines. Yet the decline of a third or more in the fertility rates of many LDCs between the early 1960s and the early 1980s is headline news. . . . World population is on the path toward stabilization.

Ben Wattenberg and Karl Zinsmeister (1986, pp. 1–2) have noted that

> As recently as 1970, women in the less-developed world were bearing a lifetime average of 6.1 children. Today it is 4.1 children. When you consider that eventually 2.1 children will produce stable populations in the Less Developed Countries, it can be seen that *in 15 years, the less developed world moved more than halfway toward a rate that yields "zero-population growth."* [emphasis in original]

And Herman Kahn and colleagues argued vigorously (1976, p. 30) that on the basis of available data and demographic theory, "fears of a population explosion should disappear within the next half-century." If one takes a long-term perspective, they believe, the current population growth rates will "appear as a momentary spike, or blip, in an otherwise smooth line."

The basis for these rather confident assessments is illustrated in Table 5-3, which shows that from 1950–1955 to 1980–1985 the world moved nearly halfway (48%) toward a fertility rate—the average number of children born per woman—that would result in zero population growth. During this period the more developed

TABLE 5-3.   Total Fertility Rate (TFR)[a] for World and Regions

	1950–55 (lifetime children per woman)	1980–85 (lifetime children per woman)	Goal for Population Stability[b] (lifetime children per woman)	Decline in TFR since 1950–55 as % of Total Needed to Reach Population Stability
World	5.0	3.6	2.1	48
More developed countries	2.8	2.0	2.1	114
Less developed countries	6.2	4.1	2.1	51
Africa	6.5	6.4	2.1	2
Caribbean	5.2	3.4	2.1	58
Central America	6.8	4.8	2.1	43
Temperate So. America	3.5	3.2	2.1	21
Tropical So. America	6.4	4.1	2.1	53
Asia	6.0	3.6	2.1	61
East Asia	5.5	2.3	2.1	94
South Asia	6.4	4.7	2.1	40

Source: Wattenberg and Zinsmeister, 1986, p. 49. Reprinted with the permission of the American Enterprise Institute for Public Policy Research, Washington, D.C.

[a]The TRF is the average number of children that would be born per woman per lifetime at current birth rates. TFR is among the more refined demographic measures. Unlike growth rates and crude birth rates, it measures fertility trends without the distortions created by prior population developments. It measures what is actually happening among families. It may be seen that the more developed nations have already gone below population stabilty and that the less developed nations have gone roughly half the way toward achieving population stability.

[b]Assumes mortality levels will continue to decline, and absence of net immigration.

countries went 114 percent of the way toward zero population fertility rates and the less developed countries have gone more than halfway (51%) toward a fertility rate that would produce population stability. These are truly astonishing figures for a period as historically short as just 30 years. Figure 5-2 shows that population growth rates are now declining not only in the developed countries but in the less developed countries as well, where they peaked at about 2.35 percent per year in the late 1960s and are now down to just over 2.0 percent.

But population will continue to grow for some time. This is because the age structure of the world population, especially that in the LDCs, is so young—often with nearly 50 percent at or below 15 years—that it will still take a full generation for population to stabilize, even *after* fertility rates have been reduced to replacement levels. This phenomenon, known as demographic momentum, can be easily demonstrated. To use Todaro's illustration (1981, p. 169), assume that a country has a population of 600, consisting of 100 married couples each with four children, two boys and two girls. Assume that all 400 children eventually marry, producing 200 married couples. If each couple has only two children, the population of the country, assuming the deaths of the first generation, will now be 800—200 couples with two children each. If all 400 children of these two-child families marry and also have two children of their own, there will again be 200 families of four people each, or 800 people. The population will now be stabilized. Of course fertility rates will not fall to replacement levels that quickly. The data indicate a more or less gradual although increasingly rapid reduction over several generations.

The question is: Why, beginning about 200 years ago, have fertility rates begun to decline so suddenly, drastically, and quickly all over the world after being so high for practically all of human history? The answer is that it is one part of a process known as the demographic transition.

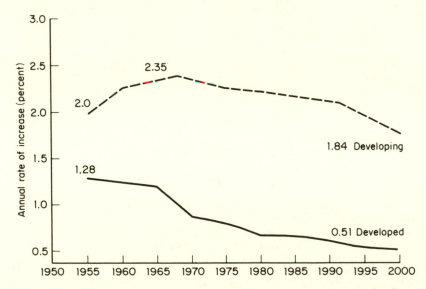

FIGURE 5-2. Population growth rates in developed and less developed countries. From Todaro, 1981, p. 164. Reprinted by permission of Longman Publishing Group.

Demographic transition theory "typically supposes either that fertility decline is a lagged response to a mortality decline, the latter presumably induced by economic growth or associated public health measures, or that mortality and fertility respond (not necessarily together) to changes brought about by social and economic development" (McNicoll, 1982, p. 519). There is some controversy about the exact relationship between the key variables in the process, in particular about how fertility decisions made by spouses, or even by the extended family or clan, are made to conform to the broader interests of society. This will be discussed in some depth later in the chapter. However, "that fertility and mortality fall in the course of socioeconomic development is," McNicoll notes (p. 519), "a well-established fact." This is illustrated in Figure 5-3, which shows the birth and death rates for a typical developed country, like Sweden, and a fairly typical less developed country, like Mexico. Despite their differences, the transition from high birth and death rates to low birth and death rates is evident for each. It is also shown in Figure 5-4, which indicates a clear, inverse relationship between economic development and fertility rates.

The conclusion drawn from these empirical observations is that the population explosion is a purely temporary phenomenon, of probably no more than 300 years' duration, resulting from the lagged response between the decline in death rates and the decline in birth rates. The data seem to indicate that the latter is adjusting to the former. And once that adjustment is completed, population will be stabilized (Figure 5-5). Given the observed decline in fertility rates offset by the impact of the demographic momentum, most authorities expect population to stabilize at between 8.2 and 10.5 billion by the year 2100 (Brandt et al., 1980, p. 106; Collins, 1982, p. 680; McEvedy and Jones, 1978, p. 349; Merrick, 1986, p. 15; World Resources Institute, 1987, pp. 7–10). These estimates are well below the estimated maximum population that the earth can comfortably support, an estimate that is usually placed, probably conservatively, at 20 billion (McEvedy and Jones, 1978, p. 351). Thus, even if these estimates are upset by decisions by couples, for whatever reason, to have larger families, or by a series of medical breakthroughs that double or even triple life expectancies, the impact would still fall well short of what the earth could support even assuming no advance in technology. In fact, more people mean both more ideas and more workers. And these, in turn, mean more resources and more food, thereby increasing the ability of the earth to support a larger population (Simon, 1990, pp. 166–198).

But the data, themselves, shed no light on the nature of the relationship between such variables as mortality, fertility, and income. They do not, for example, say anything about *why* fertility rates accommodate themselves to mortality rates. Nor do they indicate whether a decline in fertility rates causes a rise in average per capita income, whether the rise in per capita income causes a decline in fertility rates, or whether both are a consequence of some third factor. It is to these questions that we now turn.

The Demographic Transition: The Theory

The overwhelming bulk of human history has been characterized by short life expectancies and high mortality rates. Many believe that among hunting and gath-

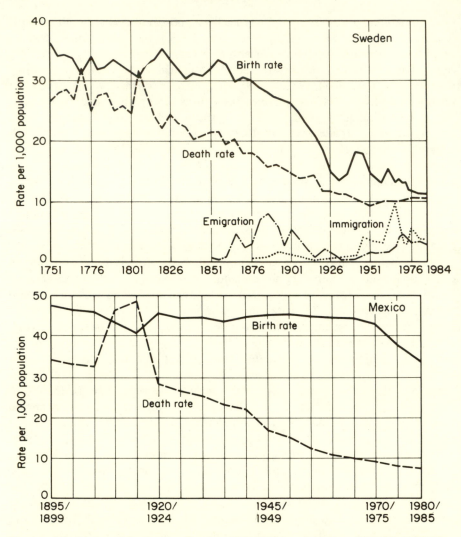

FIGURE 5-3. Birth and death rates: Sweden, 1751–1984, and Mexico, 1895/99–1980/85. *Source:* From Thomas Merrick, 1986, p. 9. Reprinted by permission of the Population Reference Bureau.

ering societies prior to about 8000 BC life expectancy was less than 20 years (Coale, 1964, p. 47; Collins, 1982, p. 679). As late as the eighteenth century life expectancy even in the more advanced countries was still no more than 35 years and was considerably less in many countries. Today it is well above 70 years for all developed countries and close to 60 years for the LDCs. During the same period fertility rates declined from about 7.5 to less than 2.5 in what are now the developed countries. As Coale has put it (p. 48), "virtually all the more developed nations have, during the past two centuries, doubled the average life expectancy and halved the total fertility rate."

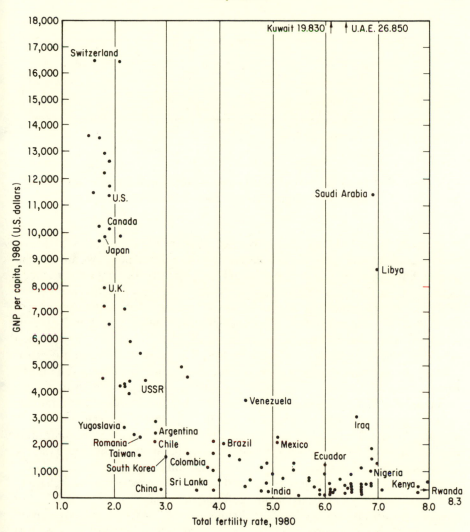

FIGURE 5-4. Fertility rates in developed and developing countries. From Nafziger, 1984, p. 207. Reprinted by permission of Prentice-Hall and Oxford University Press.

The reasons seem fairly clear cut. High fertility rates were necessary to offset the high mortality rates. In both preindustrial societies of historical times and nonindustrial societies of today, nearly all the incentives are to have large families. First, the cost of rearing children is minimal and by the time they are 5 or 6 years old they are working in the fields or doing other odd jobs and more than "paying their way." "The man with many children controls much wealth. In terms of economic production more children mean an increased supply of food and perhaps the production of surpluses for trade" (Benedict, 1970, p. 177). In such societies children also provide the only support for parents in their old age (C. Clark, 1970, p. 227; Freed-

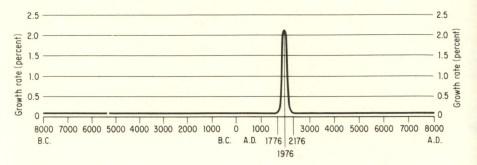

FIGURE 5-5. Population growth rate in the long-term historical perspective. From Kahn, Brown, and Martel, 1976, p. 29. Copyright © by Hudson Institute. Reprinted by Permission.

man and Berelson, 1974, pp. 36–37; Merrick, 1986, p. 30; Mosher, 1983b). Moreover, not only may children provide the family with political power within the clan or tribe but they also often provide the only real security: the larger the number, especially men, the better able the family, clan, or tribe to protect itself from bands of thieves and marauders or attacks by other clans or tribes. As Caldwell put it (1976, pp. 338–339), in primitive societies "the size of the group is often the means of safety." All of these considerations, regardless of whether the decisions regarding family size are made by the husband and wife or, as is common in primitive societies, by the extended family or clan, provide strong incentives for large families. Many children, especially where mortality rates are high, provide an important hedge against the uncertainties of the future; it is a rational way both to minimize risks and to maximize the possibility for wealth. "The very poor even in industrial societies," wrote Benedict (1970, p. 178), "can often see no advantage in limiting their children. At the lowest levels 10 children are no more of a handicap than 9. The child as yet unborn may be the very one who will help his parents."

It is hardly surprising that, given the risks of primitive society, social, religious, and moral "props" emerged to encourage fertility (see Caldwell, 1976, p. 323). For example, not only is there the familiar religious inducement to "be fruitful and multiply," but there are important cultural practices as well. In various places, such as in sub-Saharan Africa, the wife does not bring a dowry into a marriage but is exchanged for a brideprice, which is remitted to the wife's parents or lineage. The brideprice entitles the husband to all children borne by the wife, regardless of whether they are the husband's. The brideprice is often paid in installments, following the birth of each child. Childlessness is grounds for dissolution of the marriage and full repayment of any portion of the brideprice paid by the husband (Benedict, 1970, p. 176; Frank and McNicoll, 1987, pp. 213–216). Moreover, in many cultures it is the duty of the wife to supply food for the family. The wife is permitted to "recruit" her children for farming and household tasks. The fertility incentive is obvious. As Frank and McNicoll have summarized (p. 217):

By continuing to bear children a woman confirms her status in the marriage (in competition with existing or potential co-wives), makes more secure her continued access to land, and serves the family and lineage interests of her husband (as well as ensuring that her own family can keep the brideprice that was given for her). That she also accumulates a very large family is a byproduct of this economically and culturally defined and socially enforced obligation.

Thus in primitive societies practically all the incentives, both individually and collectively, were for high fertility. This should not be surprising. Given the fact that high mortality was the norm, it is clear that high fertility *had* to be present as well. Those societies maintaining low fertility while mortality remained high perished.

This is not to say that attempts were never made to control fertility. Nor is it meant to imply that each subsequent period in history was invariably less hazardous and had a lower mortality rate than its predecessor. Through abortion, infanticide, and the use of contraceptive measures of varying degrees of effectiveness, some primitive societies did try to regulate fertility at some times. But these attempts were generally made by peoples living in very harsh environments, such as the Eskimos; peoples living in very restricted environments, such as the Polynesians; and those living in extreme poverty, such as the Chinese. Female infanticide was practiced among the Eskimos because food was often scarce and Eskimo women did not hunt and thus were consumers rather than providers of food. Since outward expansion was not possible in Polynesia, infanticide seems to have been used to control population densities, although it also appears that girls were more often the victims than boys. As one Polynesian remarked, "men go out and catch fish and do other work" (in Benedict, 1970, p. 174). In China the smallness of individual property holdings encouraged attempts to regulate fertility, while patrilineal and patrilocal marriage meant that girls were an economic burden on their biological parents. When food was scarce, it was usually the girls who starved (Benedict, 1970, pp. 174–175). Infanticide was also used for noneconomic reasons, such as illegitimacy. But as Benedict has put it (p. 175), "the fact is that in most primitive societies people do not wish to restrict fertility. On the contrary they desire to produce the maximum number of children possible."

While history clearly shows that life has become increasingly less hazardous and that life expectancies have increased, this trend has certainly not been unilinear or without disruption. For example, many authorities believe that the early agriculturists had a longer life expectancy than hunters and gatherers; many others dispute this. Polgar, for example (1972, pp. 201–06), believed that rather than living in "utter misery," hunters and gatherers were "well nourished and healthy" and had a low mortality rate and a relatively long life expectancy. Yet they were able to maintain a balance between natality and mortality that prevented population growth. There were a number of incentives to keep fertility low in such a society, the most important being the difficulty of taking care of several infants in a hunting and gathering mode of life. Infanticide was apparently widely used for this end, with perhaps as many as 50 percent of all children killed. Coale believed that agriculture, by bringing relatively large numbers of people into rather close proximity with each other, not only created the possibility for the easy transmission of diseases but also increased the potential for water, food, and soil contamination. The result is that the mortality rate among early cultivators may have been above the rates for hunters and gatherers. But if this is the case, then the fertility rate must have risen as well, and by a margin more than the mortality rate, since evidence indicates that population did increase if only slowly (Coale, 1964, pp. 47–48; McEvedy and Jones, 1978, p. 343; Merrick, 1986, p. 8). And Coale suggested that "the cultivation of crops could have increased fertility by increasing body weight and possibly by promoting earlier weaning of infants so that mothers could work in the fields." If this is in fact what happened, then the passage from a hunting and gathering stage to an agricultural stage was characterized by a demographic transition of its own: a transition from a period of relatively low birth rates and long life spans among hunters and gatherers to a period of higher birth rates and shorter life spans among the early cultivators.

Despite many reversals and setbacks, however, the overall direction is clear: longer life expectancies and lower mortality and fertility rates.

The mortality revolution began to occur in the West about two centuries ago. Mortality rates began a dramatic decline in the West during the seventeenth century and have reached the point that now about 98 percent of all those born are likely to reach adulthood (Brass, 1970, p. 139). There are three broad causes for the decline in mortality and the increase in life expectancy: (1) improved economic conditions including, in particular, significant advances in both the production and supply of food; (2) improvements in general health resulting from advances in sanitation facilities, water purification, the development of immunizations, and so on, and (3) medical advances, including the establishment of hospitals and the development of new drugs (Brass, 1970, p. 140; Merrick, 1986, p. 10). Historically, the first two have been the most important.

The implications of the decline in mortality rates are significant. The immediate effect was a spurt in population growth. Between 1750 and 1845 the population of Europe increased from 140 million to 250 million, an increase of 80 percent (McEvedy and Jones, 1978, p. 29). But as life grew more secure, people realized that high fertility rates were neither necessary nor desirable and adjusted their behavior accordingly. Today the population of Europe is practically stable, increasing at a yearly rate of just 0.27 percent. In fact, several nations, including Sweden, the United Kingdom, Austria, Germany, and Luxembourg, have either stable or declining populations (World Resources Institute, 1987, p. 249, Table 16.1). Figure 5-3 (top panel) shows the pattern of birth and death rates for Sweden, a pattern typical of most European countries after 1750.

The impact of the Industrial Revolution cannot be ignored, for it is a significant cause of the decline in both mortality and fertility rates. Indeed, to focus on the population explosion while ignoring the even more important productivity explosion of the Industrial Revolution is to completely misunderstand the nature of the demographic changes that have occurred over the past two and a half centuries. It was largely the increased productivity brought about by the Industrial Revolution that improved health, thereby making possible a sustained decline in mortality rates (Ashton, 1965, pp. 153–155; Hayek, 1988, pp. 130–131; Rosenberg and Birdzell, 1986, pp. 172–178). It also resulted in a quantum leap in the number of people the earth could adequately sustain. Between 1776 and 1975 world population increased sixfold. But real gross world product *rose no less than 80-fold* (Macrae, 1975, p. 19).

The skills demanded in a modern industrialized society often require years of formal training. Thus, as society modernizes and children are sent to schools rather than the fields, the flow of wealth reverses itself. In a preindustrial society children support their parents; in an industrial society parents support their children. It is this reversal of the flow of wealth, the transformation of children from the economic assets they were in preindustrial society into economic liabilities in industrial societies, that constitutes a strong incentive to reduce fertility. Indeed, if economics were the sole consideration, fertility in industrial societies would be zero. As Caldwell has noted (1976, p. 346):

> This does not happen, and fertility falls slowly and even irregularly . . . for social and psychological reasons—the extent to which alternative roles are available to women, the degree to which child-centeredness renders children relatively expensive, the climate of opinion, and so on. Fertility does not reach zero for reasons that are entirely psychological and social.

Both Caldwell and Bauer have argued with a good deal of justification that the economic divide is determined by neither industrialization nor urbanization, as such, but by "Westernization." "Adoption of Western attitudes will induce people to restrict the number of their children," says Bauer (1981, p. 58), "but neither higher incomes nor increased urbanization by themselves will bring this about." And Caldwell has pointed out (1976, p. 348) that urbanization is not necessarily incompatible with a flow of wealth from children to parents. For example, studies of such places as Ibadan, Nigeria, show that while the cost of rearing children is higher in urban than rural areas, the return on the parents' "investment"—the child's wages—is also much larger. Since the flow of wealth continues to be from the children to the parents, fertility rates remain high, even in urban areas. It is the emphasis in Western culture on the primacy of the individual that, according to Caldwell, is the primary cause of the reversal in the flow of wealth and the corresponding trend to family nucleation and reduced fertility. The importance accorded in Western culture to the individual relative to other social entities such as the tribe, city, or nation "put much store on self-sufficiency of all types." It allowed a man

> to tell his relatives that they should be more careful in their expenditures, more frugal in their wants, and more farsighted in planning for times of need. More importantly, it allowed him to do this and cautiously refuse to give any (or much) assistance while retaining his pride and even preaching his practice. (Caldwell, 1976, p. 347)

In brief, the primacy of the individual in Western culture generated a view of the family as a tiny, emotional unit. This was incompatible with the extended-family economic system. It thus simultaneously generated forces resulting in a corresponding economic nucleation. Spouses became the final decision-makers in all matters, economic as well as fertility. In a culture that places tremendous emphasis on individual autonomy and the satisfaction of individual desires, children become significant economic and personal burdens:

> The typical working class mother of the 1890s, married in her teens or early twenties and experiencing ten pregnancies, spent about fifteen years in a state of pregnancy and in nursing a child for the first years of its life. She was tied, for this period of time, to the wheel of childbearing. Today, for the typical mother, the time so spent would be about four years. A reduction of this magnitude in only two generations in the time devoted to childbearing represents nothing less than a revolutionary enlargement of freedom for women.   (Titmuss, in Easterlin and Crimmins, 1985, p. 5)

Significantly, Caldwell found that in the Third World "demographic innovators," that is, women with low fertility rates in a society characterized by high fertility rates, are far more likely to have been to school, and especially to secondary school, than their more traditional counterparts. They are also more likely to have husbands who work in nonmanual occupations, and to work in such occupations themselves. The primary determinant, Caldwell found, was education. What is significant is that educational systems in most of the Third World reflect and even inculcate the values and lifestyles of the modern West. They rarely present the values of the rural, communal village as something to be emulated. This message is constantly reinforced, since education is likely to lead to higher incomes and thus the purchase of radios and televisions.

> All cinema films, most television films that portray family life, much of the magazine content, and a considerable proportion of the newspaper feature content are imported, and the models on which they are based are wholly imported from the West. The same message of nuclear family structure is relayed as is imparted by the schools.   (Caldwell, 1976, p. 354)

While there is no doubt a great deal of truth to this, Bauer and Caldwell appear to exaggerate the role of Westernization in reducing fertility. Urbanization and industrialization are not neutral in their effects on fertility, as these two authors imply. They have their own dynamic and that dynamic encourages reduced fertility.

As Caldwell has noted, it is *possible* for the flow of wealth to continue in the child-to-parent direction even in an urban setting. But this is unusual. The cost of rearing a child is much greater in an urban than in a rural environment. Thus even if the expected return on the "investment" is positive, only the very wealthy could afford the outlay. This is especially the case if, as is common in an urban environment, the expected payback does not begin for as long as two decades following the initial investment. Relatedly, an urban setting, with its competition for jobs and thus its need for adequate job skills, will tend to encourage parents to emphasize the "quality" of children over their quantity. Finally, while the cost of raising children is higher in urban than in rural settings, the cost of goods is lower, thereby making goods, other things being equal, relatively more attractive than children.

This attraction is reinforced by the fact that children are an "old" good while life in the city exposes one to a wide variety of exciting "new" goods. Further, since children hinder their parents from enjoying these "new" goods and lifestyles, the goods are substitutes for, rather than complementary with, children. All of these factors tend to encourage an "antinatal life style" (Easterlin and Crimmins, 1985, pp. 20–24).[3]

Urbanization also reduces both the market and subjective cost of fertility regulation. Like other new goods, contraceptive devices tend to cost less in urban than in rural areas, and urban areas are less tradition bound and more open to innovative lifestyles, both of which encourage lower fertility (Easterlin and Crimmins, 1985, p. 24).

Thus, while Westernization and urbanization are largely separable in terms of influence on fertility rates, they are not completely so. Urbanization has its own dynamic that militates against high fertility, thereby reinforcing the impact of Westernization.

The demographic transition is a complex phenomenon. That historically mortality and fertility rates have adjusted themselves to one another is an empirical fact. There is, however, little consensus on the reasons for this adjustment. Some place primary emphasis on culture, others on economic factors. It seems likely that both have played a role. For example, fertility decline in Europe began first in eighteenth century France, which means it preceded urbanization and industrialization; decline in England did not occur until a century later, after the onset of both. This *seems* to indicate that while fertility decline in England may have been largely a result of the transition from a rural-agrarian economy to an urban-based economy, fertility decline in France was primarily a product of cultural changes, that is, of changes in attitudes about such things as childbearing, the morality of birth control, and the status of women (Merrick, 1986, p. 10). Some have noted that the standard of living in preindustrial France was rising and have argued that parents restricted fertility out of fear that large families would "undermine the good life" (Freedman, 1968, p. 376; McEvedy and Jones, 1978, p. 56). It is not clear what exactly these authors mean by "undermining the good life." It could mean that the flow of wealth had reversed itself and that children had become economic liabilities. But this is highly unlikely for a preurban society. It could also mean that the time required to rear children had begun to interfere with parents' ability to enjoy their higher standard of living.

Whatever its causes, the demographic transition has largely run its course in the West. The transition from high to low birth rates and death rates took about two centuries but is now essentially complete. The population of the Western world has been stabilized; birth and death rates have once again been equalized.

The Demographic Transition and the Less Developed World

By the end of World War II demographers were confident that world population growth was rapidly coming to an end. The demographic transition had run its course in the West and in fact some were expressing alarm that fertility rates had fallen below replacement levels. Most authorities were confident that the transition would quickly spread throughout the rest of the world. But then the "explosion" began.

The population explosion is attributable to two separate events occurring more or less simultaneously. First was the unexpected rise in fertility rates in the West, commonly known as the postwar "baby boom." Fertility rates in the United States rose from a low in 1935–1939 of 2.0, or slightly below the replacement level, to 3.7 in 1955–1959, the equivalent of a population increase of 2.1 percent per year (Table 5-4). The second and far more important factor was the dramatic decline in infant mortality rates and the increase in life expectancies throughout the less developed countries (Tables 5-5 and 5-6). During the 30-year period from 1950–1955 to 1980–1985, infant mortality fell almost 42 percent for the world as a whole. For the LDCs it fell from 159 to 92 deaths per 1,000 births, a decline of over 42 percent. Life expectancies during the same period rose by 29 percent for the world and by 30 percent in the LDCs, rising from an average of 41 years in 1950–1955 to 56.6 years in 1980–1985.

The first event proved to be a temporary phenomenon. By 1975–1979, in fact, fertility rates in the United States had declined to just 1.8, equivalent to a population decrease of 0.7 percent per year. The reasons for the baby boom are not completely understood. However, long-run swings in fertility patterns seem to be characteristic of developed countries. Easterlin hypothesizes that the substantial improvement in economic conditions following the depression of the 1930s, and especially the increase in disposable income, made larger families more affordable in the 1940s and 1950s. The result was an increase in fertility rates. The population bulge created by the baby boom generation created a number of economic pressures as that generation matured and entered the work force. For example, the rising demand for such things as housing and education increased their costs. This, coupled with the relatively expensive consumer tastes this generation acquired during

TABLE 5-4.   U.S. Fertility Rates, 1930–1979

Year	Total Fertility Rate[a] (children/woman)	Intrinsic Rate of Natural Increase per Year[b] (%)
1930–34	2.1	0
1935–39	2.0	−0.2
1940–44	2.5	+0.5
1945–49	3.0	+1.2
1950–54	3.3	+1.7
1955–59	3.7	+2.1
1960–64	3.4	+1.9
1965–69	2.6	+0.8
1970–74	2.1	0.0
1975–79	1.8	−0.7

Source: Wattenberg, 1984, p. 63. Reprinted by permission of Simon and Schuster, Inc.

[a]Expressed as lifetime births.

[b]The annual rate at which a population will grow or shrink if given fertility and mortality rates remain in effect over a long period of time.

TABLE 5-5.   Infant Mortality Rates (infant deaths per 1,000 live births)

	1950–1955	*1980–1985*	*Percent Change*
World	139	81	−41.7
More developed	56	17	−69.6
Less developed	159	92	−42.1
Africa	185	115	−38
Caribbean	124	58	−53
Central America	122	57	−53
Temperate So. America	83	37	−55
Tropical So. America	136	70	−49
Asia	155	87	−44
East Asia	124	36	−71
South Asia	182	109	−40

Source: Wattenberg and Zinsmeister, 1986, p. 49. Reprinted by permission of American Enterprise Institute.

the economic boom times of their youth, reduced their disposable incomes, thereby making children relatively more expensive. The result was that couples began to delay having children and to have fewer of them (Easterlin, 1986, pp. 77–138; Schultz, 1976, p. 94, fn. 1).

The second event, occurring in the LDCs, is of much greater long-term importance. Between 1750 and approximately 1940, population growth rates for the West were about 50 to 100 percent higher than for the rest of the world. But after World War II that trend was reversed, with population growth rates for the LDCs about doubling those of the West. The change was caused not so much by the decline in growth rates in the West, although that did occur, but rather by the tripling of growth rates for the rest of the world (Kuznets, 1967, pp. 170–171, fn. 1, 2; Merrick, 1986, pp. 10–11). As stated, this can be accounted for by the precipitous decline in mortality rates and the dramatic increase in life expectancies in the LDCs. The technology required to increase life expectancies was invented in the West with a great

TABLE 5-6.   Life Expectancy at Birth (years)

	1950–1955	*1980–1985*	*Gain (Years)*	*Gain (%)*
World	45.8	58.9	+13.1	29
More developed	65.1	73.0	+ 7.9	12
Less developed	41.0	56.6	+15.6	38
Africa	37.5	49.7	+12.2	33
Caribbean	51.9	64.0	+12.1	23
Central America	49.3	65.0	+15.7	32
Temperate So. America	60.3	69.0	+ 8.7	14
Tropical So. America	49.9	62.9	+13.0	26
Asia	41.2	57.9	+16.7	41
East Asia	42.5	68.0	+25.5	60
South Asia	40.1	53.6	+13.5	34

Source: Wattenberg and Zinsmeister, 1986, p. 49. Reprinted by permission of American Enterprise Institute.

deal of time and effort. When the technology reached the LDCs, they had only to apply it. As an example, in the 1950s the World Health Organization sprayed the insecticide DDT over large areas of Sri Lanka to destroy malaria-carrying mosquitos. The experiment was highly successful and between 1945 and 1959 Sri Lanka's death rate fell from 21.7 to only 9.1 per 1,000 people (Nafziger, 1984, p. 204).

At the same time that death rates were declining, fertility rates in quite a few of the LDCs, including Pakistan, Lebanon, Benin, Cameroon, Kenya, Chad, Ethiopia, Tanzania, Togo, and Argentina, actually began to rise (World Resources Institute, 1986, pp. 238–239, Table 2.2). The consequence of the combination of rapidly declining death rates with stable or rising fertility rates was a population explosion that dwarfed anything that had ever occurred before. According to demographic transition theory, such a thing was not supposed to occur. Birth rates were supposed to accommodate themselves to death rates, as they had in the West. What happened?

Birth rates are in large part a result of culture—of religious, social, and legal "props" that emerged centuries ago and have been in existence ever since. It takes time for cultural attitudes to change, for the props to be eroded. In the LDCs the decline in mortality rates was too rapid for birth rates to adjust immediately. A second, related factor is that marriage patterns in Europe were "unique or almost unique in the world" (Hajnal, 1965, p. 101). In 1900, for example, about 40 percent of all women remained single at the age of 25; about 15 percent never married at all. In contrast, fewer than 10 percent of Asian and African women were single at age 25, and only about 2 percent never married (Hajnal, 1965, pp. 102, 104). Given that mortality rates declined slowly in the West with new technological discoveries, and birth rates were lower than elsewhere in the world, the demographic changes had a smaller impact on population growth in the West than they did when they occurred later in the rest of the world.

But why did fertility rates actually rise in many LDCs after World War II? Rising fertility is not unique to the LDCs. It is a common first effect of modernization. The key analytical concept is what Easterlin and Crimmins (1985, p. 15) term "the potential supply of children" (Cn), that is, "the number of surviving children a household would have if fertility were not deliberately limited." This in turn depends on the relationship between natural fertility (N) and the probability of child survival (S). Natural fertility is a product of the interaction of biological and cultural factors, and tends to be below the physiological maximum because of biological constraints, such as sterility or malnutrition and disease, and cultural constraints regarding such things as the frequency of intercourse, the length of postpartum abstinence, prohibitions on remarriage by widows, and fetal mortality (Benedict, 1970; Easterlin and Crimmins, 1985, p. 16). One would expect that improvements in nutrition and public health measures and easier access to medical care would increase both natural fertility (N), by increasing the number of births per woman, and the survival ratio (S) of the children born. This is what happened. For example, between 1951 and 1975 N increased 4.9 percent in rural Karnataka, India, and S increased 16.3 percent. As a result, the potential supply of children (Cn) rose 22.1 percent. In Bangalore, India, during the same period N rose 15.3 percent; S was up 17.1 percent. Cn thus increased by 35.1 percent (Easterlin and Crimmins, 1985, p. 127). Clearly, if cultural factors remain unchanged, any increase in *N* and/or *S* will increase *Cn*. The rapid onset of modernization in the LDCs had precisely that *initial* effect.

The demand for fertility regulation is not simply a response to high fertility. The supply of children must exceed the demand for them. If fertility is high but the demand for children is even higher, there will be no push to regulate fertility. Moreover, even if demand exceeds the supply, attempts to regulate fertility will not be made if the cost of fertility regulation exceeds the cost of rearing another child. Thus, demand for regulation is not simply a product of the number of children deemed necessary but is also affected by the cost of regulation vis-à-vis the cost of child rearing (Figure 5-6). To the left of point *m* in Figure 5-6 the demand for children (*Cd*) exceeds the natural supply (*Cn*), which is also the actual supply (*C*). As society modernizes, the demand for children begins to fall while the supply increases. But fertility regulation is not adopted until point *h*, when the cost of child rearing exceeds the cost of fertility regulation. As modernization reduces the cost of regulation and increases that of child rearing, both the number of children demanded (*Cd*) and the number actually born (*C*) decline. They stabilize at point *p*, when *Cd* corresponds to *C*, although further declines are likely because modernization also tends to reduce the preference for children relative to goods.

This theory has a great deal of plausibility. It explains, for example, why birth control tends to be most frequently used where the fertility rate is highest and least used where the fertility rate is lower. It also means that, contrary to the conclusions drawn by many authorities on the subject, fertility control was not ineffective in the LDCs:

> The most important point argue is that a rise in observed fertility should not be taken to mean that the fertility transition is not underway or that fertility control

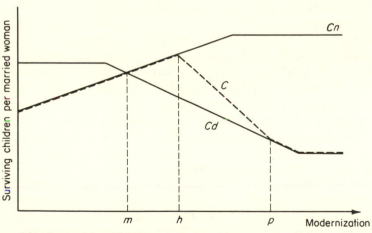

Cd = Demand for children
Cn = Natural (unregulated) supply of children
C = Actual supply of children

FIGURE 5-6. The fertility transition. (See text.) From Easterlin and Crimmins, 1985, p. 27. Copyright © by The University of Chicago Press 1985. Reprinted by permission.

is ineffective. . . . The increase in [fertility control] use resulted in more births averted . . . but the tendency of this to reduce fertility was defeated by an even greater rise in natural fertility. (Easterlin and Crimmins, 1985, p. 132)

Easterlin and Crimmins estimate that fertility control reduced natural fertility by 0.5 births in 1951 and by 1.5 births in 1975 (p. 132).

In brief, the dramatic decline in mortality rates coupled with stable or even rising fertility rates in the LDCs produced a tremendous spurt in population growth. This trend, especially the increase in fertility rates, led many authorities to conclude that the demographic transition was not occurring in the LDCs. In fact, rising fertility was not restricted to the LDCs; it is a common initial feature of modernization, resulting from improved health. Once the supply of children exceeded their demand and access to methods of fertility regulation became widespread and their costs declined, fertility rates in the LDCs began a rapid decline, moving in the last 15 years as much as 60 percent of the way toward levels that would result in population stability (Zinsmeister, 1987, p. 19; also see Table 5-3, above). The speed at which first mortality rates and later fertility rates declined in the LDCs was largely a result of the fact that the technology for both had already been invented in the West and needed only to be applied in the LDCs. At any rate, the initial despair at the magnitude of the population increases in the LDCs was followed by astonishment at the speed at which fertility rates declined.

The "Dependency Burden"

A word should be said about the highly touted "dependency ratio," which is regarded by some as a significant factor holding back economic growth in the LDCs. The dependency ratio is the ratio of the population age 0 to 14 and 65 and over to the persons of working ages, or economically active adults (Nafziger, 1984, p. 212–214; Todaro, 1981, p. 165). For example, while about two-thirds of the population of the United States is between 15 and 64 years of age, in many of the LDCs the number is under 50 percent. As a result of the age structure in the LDCs, many argue, "very little is left over for saving and capital formation" (Nafziger, 1984, p. 214). Thus, economic development is retarded.

Far too much has been made of the age structure. Age categories have relevance in the MDCs with children in school until at least age 16 and retirement occurring at age 65, both often because of legal compulsion. These events are irrelevant for the LDCs, where children, as noted, are important economic assets, not liabilities, and where adults do not cease to be economic contributors on reaching the age of 65. Thus, using age to construct a dependency ratio entails considerations that are ethnocentric and results in conclusions that are highly misleading. To be sure, there is a great deal of dependency. But it has little to do with age—it is a result of occupation. The real dependency burden, and one that does retard economic development, is that of political bureaucrats and others protected by political privileges. This group neither produces goods nor provides services. Its members are not economically productive persons. Rather, they use their positions of political power to systematically exploit those who are producers, including the very young and the old.

Children and Externalities

References to an "optimum population" are common in the literature (Singer, 1973; Watson and Smith, 1973). But this concept only has meaning when each couple is able to have the number of children it desires, given the costs of raising children. The determination of actual demand requires, therefore, accurate cost data. Such data are precisely what is missing in practically all societies, developed as well as developing.

What is relevant for family decision-making of any sort is not the cost to society but the cost to the family. There can be no doubt that the provision of such goods as free public education by all MDCs and by many LDCs encourages higher fertility rates. For example, if the cost of education is $1,000 per child and there are 100 tax-paying families, the cost of public schooling per child per taxpayer is $10. (Assume for simplicity that these are the only taxes and that they are adjusted according to the total cost of the school budget.) If the 100 familes each have one child, then everyone pays $1,000 in taxes, $10 for the family's child and $10 for each of the other 99 children. In this case, each family actually pays the full cost of its own child's schooling. The decision by one family to have an additional child will increase that family's budget by only $10, while it will increase the cost to society by $990. It is clear that "internalizing" the cost of education—making each family pay the entire cost of educating its children—would encourage fewer births.

What is of special importance for the LDCs is the nature of their tax structure. Most LDCs impose heavy taxes on rural areas to provide subsidies for urbanites. The subsidies reduce the cost of raising children, thereby encouraging higher fertility rates. The relationship is not symmetrical. The higher tax rates on rural residents do not reduce fertility; they actually increase it, because in rural areas children are economic assets. If the tax reduces a rural family's income by, say, $100, the family can recoup the loss by having another child. Interestingly, imposing higher taxes on urban areas to subsidize rural areas would tend to discourage fertility—it would increase the cost of living in urban areas, thereby making children less affordable, and increase the income of rural residents, thereby reducing the economic incentive to have children.

The important point is that population growth is neither good nor bad in itself. A family with six or eight children is a burden on society only when others are required to help support these children. Thus, not only can an optimum population be achieved through internalizing the external costs, but in this case control over fertility decisions can then be left safely in the hands of the family. A couple desiring a large family would be able to "purchase" the children at the cost of a lower standard of living, while another couple having few or no children could purchase a higher standard of living. The "optimum population" would be *whatever* the population happened to be when each family was permitted to decide for itself how many children it wished to have, provided these decisions were made in an environment in which the major externalized costs had been internalized.

Population Growth, Technological Improvements, and Economic Development

Part I showed that world population grew very slowly until the eighteenth century when, largely because of the productivity unleashed by the Industrial Revolution, general health, especially in the Western world, improved. Mortality rates then began a period of rapid decline, causing a temporary population spurt. As birth rates declined to accommodate themselves to mortality rates, the population explosion came to an end in the West. By this time, however, the demographic transition had begun to spread to other parts of the world, and mortality rates elsewhere were plummeting. Once again the world was subject to a tremendous but temporary spurt in population growth rates. This is now beginning to slow down. Once the demographic momentum caused by the age structure in Third World countries has run its course, the population explosion in the Third World will, like that in the West, come to a halt.

Population Growth and Economic Development: The Data

The question is: Is the world in danger of becoming overpopulated? Conventional economic theory, dating at least from the first edition of Thomas Malthus's *Essay on Population* in 1798, maintains that it is.[4] Malthus was one of the first discoverers of the law of diminishing returns. The proposition can be stated succinctly: ceteris paribus, the more people, the lower both per capita income and marginal productivity. Income, and with it consumption, must decline as population increases *if* economic output either remains unchanged or increases more slowly than population. Similarly, marginal output per worker must decrease *if* factor availability either remains the same or increases more slowly than population. This, according to Malthus, was precisely what had happened and would continue to happen, especially since the best lands and most readily available resources were naturally utilized first. The conclusion was inescapable: as population increased, marginal productivity and the standard of living had to decrease, and eventually population would exceed the ability of the world to support it. As Malthus put it, population grew geometrically while agricultural output increased only arithmetically. Thus, more people, according to the logic of the Malthusian argument, are a bad thing. Overpopulation is the natural state of mankind (Hayek, 1988, pp. 120–122; Simon, 1986a, pp. 13–15).

But even a cursory review of the historical evidence shows that the Malthusian conclusions do not fit the data:

> Modern economic growth, as revealed by the experience of the developed countries
> since the late eighteenth or early nineteenth century, reflects a continuing capacity

to supply a growing population with an increased volume of commodities and services per capita. The increase in both population and per capita product is not the unique feature of recent growth: even in pre-modern times the population and per capita product of several countries grew and enjoyed a rising per capita product. The distinctive features of modern economic growth are the extremely high rates of increase—at least five times as high for population and at least ten times as high for per capita product as in the observable past. (Kuznets, 1967, p. 170)

Similarly,

There are many more people alive today than in earlier epochs, and yet most people are better off in most material ways than in the past. The last 300 years, during which the Western world has had the most rapid population growth in history, has also been the period of the most rapid economic growth in history. And in the quarter century from 1950 to 1975 during which the population in the less-developed countries (LDCs) has grown very rapidly, *per capita* income has grown rapidly—at least as rapidly as in the MDC world. (Simon, 1986a, p. 3)

There are, of course, many anomalies. China and India are relatively densely populated countries that are poor; Canada is sparsely populated but wealthy. Such examples mean that a multitude of factors are involved in economic development and population density is only one, and perhaps not the most important one (D. Johnson, 1987). The data do make it clear, however, that there is no necessary relationship between population density or population growth and poverty.

Thus the historical data are actually the reverse of what one would expect if Malthus's position were correct. The element omitted by Malthus is the impact of population growth on the advance of technological and scientific knowledge. Studies by Kuznets, Simon, Boserup, and others show a positive relationship between population density and the rate of population growth, on the one hand, and the rate of technological advance on the other. For example, Simon has shown that for both ancient Greece and Rome, the number of scientific discoveries and technological inventions varied positively with changes in both total population and the rate of population change. As population increased, so did the number of scientific discoveries and technological inventions; as the former decreased, so did the latter. Studies of medieval Europe also indicate that the rate of scientific advance coincided with population growth rates. The number of scientific discoveries rose as population increased and declined as population declined (Simon, 1986a, pp. 67–69).

According to Boserup (1981, p. 129),

before the industrial revolution one densely populated area after another became the technological leader. During the whole of this part of human history, the main advantage of a dense population, i.e., the better possibilities to create infrastructure, seems to have outbalanced the disadvantage of a less favorable ratio between population and natural resources. Europe succeeded Asia as the technological leader, but only after it arrived at relatively high population densities. . . . [T]he inhabitants of large sparsely populated continents were doomed to be illiterate subsistence producers.

The historical data indicate that as population increased it induced changes in economic, political, and cultural institutions, thereby making Malthus's ceteris paribus assumption increasingly untenable. As Kuznets put it (1967, pp. 171–172),

> More population means more creators and producers, both of goods along estab-
> lished production patterns and of new knowledge and inventions. . . . [T]he dis-
> parity between the reality of rapid growth of population and per capita product and
> the vision of the Malthusian threat has become progressively wider.

The real question is: Is there any reason to suppose that science and technology *must* advance more rapidly than population? That is, is there any reason to suppose that the historical trend is anything more than a fortuitous but short-lived phenomenon? Is there any reason to believe that the historical trend will continue?

The answer is yes. The correlation between population size and scientific and technological advance is not coincidental.

The Relationship between Population Density and Productivity

Other things being equal, population density is positively correlated with improved communications and transportation and thus the exchange of ideas. And the exchange of ideas is, of course, indispensable for scientific advancement and additions to our stock of knowledge, which in turn bring about increases in productivity. Moreover, not only does improved communication stimulate the advance of knowledge directly by facilitating the exchange of ideas, it also stimulates knowledge indirectly by reducing the duplication of effort. It is not accidental, for example, that agriculture was independently invented by many primitive societies. "This invention repeatedly had to be made independently because of the lack of communication among groups, and because of the lack of means to 'store' the idea in writing" (Simon, 1986a, p. 111). It is precisely for this reason that many authorities (Bauer, 1981, p. 45; C. Clark, 1970, p. 233–236; Samir Amin [in Todaro, 1981, pp. 173–174]) believe that Africa is actually *underpopulated*. Africa is the world's most sparsely populated continent (although it now has the most rapid population growth rate) and many parts of it are so sparsely populated that it is unable to support anything more than very rudimentary communications and transportation networks. The result is that the distribution and diffusion of goods, services, and ideas are severely retarded. As a Red Cross officer observed during a famine in Africa, "Sure the food is pouring in, but how the hell are we going to get it to the people who need it? There isn't a tarred road within a thousand miles of Juba" (in Simon, 1981b, pp. 62–63).

Moreover, as Adam Smith recognized (1937, p. 17), the extent of the division of labor is limited by the size of the market. Thus the larger the market, the deeper the division of labor and, accordingly, the greater the specialization in society. And specialization, the focusing of one's efforts on one or a few tasks, increases productivity.

It is, then, not simply more men, but more different men, which brings about an increase in productivity. Men become powerful because they have become so different: new possibilities of specialization—depending not so much on any increase in individual intelligence but on growing differentiation of individuals—provide the basis for a more successful use of the earth's resources. (Hayek, 1988, pp. 122–123)

Related to specialization is the phenomenon of "learning-by-doing." Numerous studies have shown that how efficiently a good is produced corresponds with how many units of the good are produced. The more units produced, the more the people involved spot better and easier ways to produce the good. Since every doubling of the output of a particular good results in an approximate 20-percent reduction in the amount of labor involved, it is known as the "20 percent curve." Thus, average per capita productivity will be higher in a larger than a smaller market (Simon, 1986a, pp. 73–74).

Further, larger populations make possible the realization of economies of scale, thereby facilitating the more efficient utilization of the earth's resources. "A denser population can . . . employ techniques and technology that would have been useless in more thinly occupied regions" (Hayek, 1988, p. 122).

Finally, there is what may be called the direct relationship between population density and the growth of scientific and technological knowledge. This has been noted by numerous authorities including Hayek, Kuznets, Machlup, and Simon. The basic idea is simple: even if the proportion of geniuses remains the same, a larger population will have a larger number of geniuses, in absolute terms, than a smaller one. And the larger the number of geniuses and talented and clever individuals in society, the more rapidly our overall stock of knowledge will increase (Simon, 1986a, pp. 16–17, 53–56).

What is significant is that each individual has a mind and is therefore a potential supplier of new knowledge. But minds don't operate in a vacuum. They are stimulated by their environment. Consequently, as Machlup says (in Simon, 1986a, pp. 55–56), "every new invention furnishes a new idea for potential combination with vast numbers of existing ideas . . . [and] the number of possible combinations increases geometrically with the elements at hand." This means, as Table 5-7 illustrates, that a society with only, say, a sum total of five ideas would contain 120 permutations or possibilities for combinations of those existing ideas, which would result in the discovery of a new idea. But if a new idea is uncovered, the number of

TABLE 5-7.   Table of Permutations

Number of Ideas	Number of Permutations
5	120
6	720
7	5,040
8	40,320
9	362,880
10	3,628,800

existing ideas would increase to six, which would increase the number of permutations to 720. The discovery of a seventh idea would increase the number of permutations to 5,040, and so on. The number of permutations with ten ideas would be 3,628,800. The geometric increase in the number of possible combinations of ideas as the stock of ideas increases not only reduces the likelihood of duplication of effort but simultaneously increases the likelihood that advances in productive technology will occur more rapidly.

The historical record seems to confirm this:

> There have been many more discoveries and a faster rate of growth of productivity in the past century, say, than in previous centuries, when there were fewer people alive. True, 10,000 years ago there was not much knowledge upon which to build new ideas. Seen differently, it should have been all the easier 10,000 years ago than now to find important improvements because so much still lay undiscovered. Progress surely was agonizingly slow in prehistory, however. Whereas we develop new materials (metals and plastic) almost every day, it was centuries or thousands of years between the discovery and use of, say, copper and iron. It makes sense that, if there had been a larger population then, the pace of increase in technological practice would have been faster.   (Simon, 1982, pp. 327–328)

Similarly, the advances in such things as medical technology in the twentieth century probably exceed the sum total of medical advances in human history prior to this century. The increase in average life expectancy during the twentieth century equals or exceeds the gains made in all the preceding centuries combined. And the first airplane did not get off the ground until 1903. The flight lasted 12 seconds and traveled 120 feet. Human beings were walking on the moon just 66 years later. Additional examples could be provided ad infinitum.

Given the fact that each new idea increases the number of possible combinations of ideas geometrically, and that this increases the likelihood of the development of yet additional new ideas, there is no reason to expect either an eventual reduction in the rate of technological and scientific advance or diminishing returns. If anything, the data suggest that returns are increasing. Studies indicate not only that the doubling time for the growth of scientific knowledge has been decreasing over the centuries and now stands at 30 years, but that productivity has been increasing at an ever faster rate. The data therefore suggest that economic productivity per unit of scientific knowledge is increasing over time (Simon, 1986a, p. 40).

For all of these reasons, larger populations are more productive than smaller ones, *other things being equal.*

The Relationship Between Technological Advancement and Economic Systems

Of course, other things are *not* equal. The principal theme of this book is that the impact of political and economic institutions is far from neutral. "Neither socialism nor any other known substitute for the market order," Hayek stresses (1988, p. 121), "could sustain the current population of the world."[5] Large populations make possible the increases in per capita productivity discussed above. But since these increases are brought about through increased specialization and thus reduced capacity for self-sufficiency, such population densities themselves entail greater interdependence and increased reliance on the exchange of goods and services. And it is only the signaling mechanism of market prices, that is, of economic calculation, that enables factors, including labor, to be spontaneously and voluntarily shifted to precisely those areas where their use will increase productivity. It is only the market order that allows society to adapt immediately and efficiently to changes in economic and social conditions. Thus the market order both produces and is produced by large populations.

Economies characterized by stringent economic controls will not be able to adapt to changing conditions. This makes them inherently inefficient, and drastically reduces the number of people they can support. As was noted in Chapter 2, in a market order a shortage of good A causes its price to rise, which in turn induces factors to flow into the production of A. Since all factors are fixed in the short run, who will surrender his or her use of these factors to A? The answer is, those consumers of factors with the smallest gap between total price and total cost. This is precisely what is needed, since the small price-cost gap means that the factors either are being used inefficiently or are being used in the production of goods least valued by consumers. Thus their transfer will increase both the efficiency and the value of their use. Moreover, the transfer will occur spontaneously, as it were, for as the heightened demand for these factors causes their prices to rise, the producers of A will be in a position to bid them away from other, less efficient, producers.

With a highly restricted market, this process may not occur, since the movement of factors could be obstructed by price controls or other measures. (In a pure socialist, i.e., non-market, economy it *could not occur,* because by definition there would be no prices at all.) Even if the authorities decided to expand the production of A, they still would have to decide who would have their allocation of factors reduced. An examination of profit margins would be of no help in this matter, since these would not be an accurate reflection of efficiency or consumer satisfaction but a result of price controls, licensing restrictions, and other interventionist measures. Moreover, the shifting of factors from B to A would, in turn, necessitate further changes in ever widening circles. If A were, say, an automobile producer, then an increase in the output of A would likewise entail an increase in such things as tires, roads, traffic signs, and so on. Thus the authorities would also have to adjust their allocation of factors necessary to produce these goods and services. It is obvious that, as society becomes larger and more complex, the ability to handle such decisions becomes correspondingly more difficult. This problem becomes especially acute when one recalls that consumer tastes are radically subjective and resource availability and factor demand depend on many things, including the state of knowledge. The economic decisions that must be made *each day* in any complex society quite literally number in millions. Since these decisions themselves change economic conditions, they make necessary additional decisions in a never-ending process. It is not hyperbole to say that the *very existence* of a modern complex order depends on a socioeconomic system that is able to coordinate the activities of millions of individuals and to automatically adjust, quickly and efficiently, to the day-to-day alterations in economic data that, while individually may be quite small, cumulatively are of major importance. Nor is it hyperbole to suggest that neither socialism, where prices are entirely absent, nor mercantilism, where prices do not accurately reflect economic conditions, can achieve the efficiency required to sustain a complex order.

Moreover, while factors are fixed in the short run, they are expandable in the long run. And, as shown in Chapter 4, not only does the market ensure the efficient utilization of resources, it also automatically attracts knowledge, or more accurately knowledge producers, that is, scientists and technicians, into precisely those areas where their services are most needed. The process by which this demand-induced increase in knowledge works is identical to the process by which other factors are allocated: the fluctuation of relative prices. The high price of a scarce good encourages scientists and technicians to search for ways to increase the supply or to find substitutes for the existing good. It was precisely the high cost of whale oil that led to the search for alternative energy sources in the nineteenth century. The result was the development of fossil oil as an energy source. Similarly, the energy crunch of the 1970s stimulated research in the development of such alternative energy sources as solar and wind power, alcohol, and nuclear fission (Osterfeld, 1987b). There is no guarantee of success, of course. But the concentration of effort by many scientists on the same problem certainly increases the likelihood of finding solutions.

However, a society characterized by oppressive social regulations on speech and press, a society in which the propagation of unconventional ideas is punished, must *artificially* retard the dissemination of information and the development of new scientific ideas, with potentially disastrous results.

As Hayek has tersely put it (1988, pp. 120,133),

> Like it or not, the current world population already exists. Destroying its material foundation in order to attain the "ethical" or instinctually gratifying improvements advocated by socialists would be tantamount to condoning the death of billions and the impoverishment of the rest. . . . Whatever men live *for*, today most men live only *because* of the market order.

It is the major differences in socioeconomic systems that account for the anomalies mentioned above. China and India are poor primarily because they have for centuries been subjected to stultifying and rigid controls; Canada is wealthy not only because its socioeconomic system is open, but also because of its access to the huge markets in more densely populated countries like the United States.

Conclusions

According to Malthus, increasing population size reduces marginal productivity and per capita income, *other things being equal*. It is this ceteris paribus assumption that is crucial.

It is common to find references to historical periods when population is said to be approaching or even exceeding its "Malthusian limits" (McEvedy and Jones, 1978, pp. 20, 24, 25, 41–42, 55, etc.). But one must make a clear distinction between *natural* carrying capacity, which is the number of people a given society can support utilizing the technology available at that particular time, and what may be termed *actual* carrying capacity, which is the number of people the society can support given the existing social, political, and economic institutions and policies. Since government economic intervention almost invariably reduces productivity to below what it would have been on the free market, the actual carrying capacity of most existing societies is usually well below its natural, or Malthusian, limits. The problem is not so much that there is a natural tendency for population to increase more rapidly than production. It is that too often productivity is *artificially* reduced to below what is required to support an existing population.

As was noted in Chapter 3, practically every famine in the last century or so was not a result of population exceeding the natural limits of productivity. It was the result of government policies that reduced production. Quite often, in fact, this was the *intended result*. Similarly, one cannot understand the severe population problems of the Middle Ages without realizing that one of the principal reasons the ancient Roman civilization collapsed was that currency debasement (inflation) coupled with price controls created a situation in which "big-scale farming . . . lost its rationality completely [because] the opportunity to sell at remunerative prices disappeared" (Mises, 1966, p. 768). Farmers began to revert from cash cropping to subsistence farming. As food shipments to the cities ceased, urbanites were forced to flee to the countryside where they eventually were employed by the landlords to work on their manors. Thus, as a direct result of government policies, the ancient farmer

> discontinued big-scale farming and became a landlord receiving rents from tenants or sharecroppers . . . . A tendency toward the establishment of autarky of each landlord's estate emerged. The economic function of the cities, of commerce, trade and urban handicrafts, shrank. Italy and the provinces of the empire returned to a less advanced state of social division of labor. The highly developed economic structure of ancient civilization retrograded to what is now known as the manorial organization of the Middle Ages.   (Mises, 1966, pp. 768–769)

The lowered nutrition and health levels of the Middle Ages were not a result of population approaching or passing its Malthusian limits but of government policies that restricted productivity, thereby artificially reducing the carrying capacity of the society.

Nor is such a historically monumental event as the transition from hunting and gathering to agriculture explained by Malthusian principles. While population pressure probably stimulated the adoption of agriculture, it was not the type of population pressure that Malthus had in mind. Agriculture was invented about 8000 BC when the estimated world population was 5 to 8 million, or well below the carrying capacity of about 10 million for that mode of existence. But agriculture did not come into common use in, say, England until 5000 BC. The reason seems to be that by that time the population of England had reached about 15,000, the maximum that a hunting and gathering society could support. It was only then that tribes began to make the transition to agriculture. Agriculture was no doubt resisted as long as possible and adopted only reluctantly, since it requires a great deal more work than a hunting and gathering mode of existence. There was no point in trading off leisure for additional food until such a trade-off became necessary. Colin Clark (1970, p. 232) also pointed out that many of the improvements in agriculture commonly attributed to the agricultural revolution of seventeenth- and eighteenth-century Europe were known in the ancient world but not implemented until much later when population pressures and economic conditions made their use necessary.

The conclusion is that rather than population increasing until it reaches Malthusian limits, at which time further expansion halts until unexpected technological discoveries increase productivity,

> in most cases, . . . population increase generally comes first, and then, usually with great reluctance, people adopt technically more efficient methods because they have to provide for the increased population. The strongest reason for believing that things work this way round is that almost every technical improvement in agriculture involves, in its initial stage, harder and more disagreeable work than the methods previously used. Technical knowledge, in most countries, is available well ahead of the actual adoption of technical improvements.   (C. Clark, 1970, p. 231)

There can be little doubt that this has continued to the present day. The slowing down of the growth in population, coupled with the continued rapid expansion of scientific and technological knowledge, has drastically increased the gap between the existing population and its Malthusian limits.

Many are alarmed by the prospect of overpopulation. But overpopulation must be overpopulation relative to something. Chapter 3 demonstrated that we now have the capacity to feed many times the current world population. Chapter 4 presented evidence, both empirical and theoretical, that resources are becoming more rather than less plentiful. Nor is the availability of space a problem. If the entire population of the world were placed in the state of Texas, Thomas Sowell has remarked (1983, p. 209), each person could have 1,700 square feet. Thus a family of four would have 6,800 square feet, "about the size of a typical middle class American home with front and back yards."

In short, while world population is increasing in absolute terms, far from becoming overpopulated relative to such key variables as food and resources, *the world is actually becoming relatively less populated.*

Notes

1. Thomas Sowell (1983, p. 215) pointed out that Ehrlich juxtaposed two phenomena, the number of children being born and the number of people (allegedly) dying from famine, thereby insinuating that there is some relationship between the two. However, famines are a

result of spot shortages in backward areas. Often food surpluses are nearby but, because communication and transportation facilities are poor, it is difficult or even impossible to transport and distribute the food in time. Famines are not the result, as Ehrlich stated, of population increasing more rapidly than food production.

2. Everyone is an authority in this area. In a recent column, "Dear Abby" wrote that "since the world's resources are limited we can't continue to provide for a population that daily produces 185,000 new mouths to feed. Either we must decrease our birth rate or increase our death rate. The choice is up to us" (Van Buren, 1989). "Dear Abby" felt the message was so important that, by her own acknowledgment, she reprinted a column that she originally published in 1975.

3. As agriculture becomes more sophisticated one would expect the flow of wealth to reverse itself in the rural area as well.

4. Malthus was not the first to advance fears regarding overpopulation. As Schumpeter pointed out (1954, pp. 254–255), "the 'Malthusian' Principle of Population sprang fully developed from the brain of Botero in 1589. . . . There was nothing left for Malthus to say that had not been said before." It is also noteworthy that Malthus modified his conclusions in each subsequent edition. And these modifications were not minor. Schumpeter said (p. 579) that the second edition of the *Essay on Population* was, in fact, "a completely new work which . . . contains an entirely different theory."

5. Empirical data might appear to refute this argument, since some of the more densely populated countries are socialist. In fact, their socialism was a result, usually, of revolutions or coups that, in a historical context, were extremely recent. When one considers the millions who have died just from malnutrition and famine, as well as the high and often rising infant mortality rates and declining life expectancies, it is clear that the data support rather than refute the argument.

III

ECONOMIC DEVELOPMENT: ENGINES AND OBSTACLES

6

Foreign Aid

The case for foreign aid is seldom made; foreign aid is taken as axiomatic. In its 1980 report, *North–South: A Program for Survival,* the Brandt Commission stated that "The poorer and weaker countries have not been able to raise much money on commercial terms. For them, Official Development Assistance or aid is the principal source of funds" (Brandt et al., 1980, p. 224). Such questions as why some countries remain poor and weak while others progress, or why these countries are unable to raise money on commercial terms, are never raised. Aid is simply assumed to be essential. The Commission lamented the "disappointing record" of such developed countries as the United States that have not met the 0.7-percent target for official development assistance (ODA) established by the United Nations in the early 1970s. "An increase in total aid must remain a high priority . . . the overall flow of wealth must increase" (pp. 226–227). In its 1983 follow-up report, *Common Crisis North–South,* the Brandt Commission reiterated its call for increased aid. The Commission asserted that despite "a few glaring examples of misused or unsuccessful aid loans," most aid was effectively used (Brandt et al., 1983, p. 78); observed that there remained substantial unmet needs, especially in the poorest of the LDCs (p. 75); deplored the "strong current mood in the donor community to require greater efforts by aid recipients to improve their own economic performance"; pointed out that the Articles of the World Bank "enjoin it to respect its members' different economic systems" (p. 73); and urged "donors to double by 1985, in real terms, the aid flows which the poorest countries received in the five years up to 1981." The Commission also called on the donor countries to waive all official debt for the least developed countries (pp. 76–77). And, just in case there was any doubt, the Commission emphasized that even if the LDCs did implement the policy reforms called for by the World Bank and many donor countries, such "reform is not a substitute for more assistance; it *requires* more assistance to be successful" (p. 74, emphasis in original). Nowhere in either of the Brandt Commission reports is the question of whether aid is the appropriate vehicle for stimulating economic development even considered.

Similarly, in its recent report, *Development and the National Interest: U.S. Economic Assistance into the 21st Century* (1989), the U.S. Agency for International Development (USAID) acknowledges (pp. 111–113) that aid has all too often resulted in dependency rather than development, that "though there is no steady stream of new nations coming on line, demands for development assistance seem only to increase; certainly they show no signs of abating," and that where economic growth and development have occurred, "U.S. development assistance, overall, has played a secondary role and has not always succeeded in fostering growth-oriented policies among recipient states." Yet despite these candid admissions of failure, the report called not for the reduction, much less the termination, of the approximately $15 billion in assistance that the United States extends each year to other governments in the form of grants and loans of various types. It called rather for "radically reshaping future official assistance programs to face new realities" (p. 121). And despite the privatization rhetoric that permeates the report, a radical reshaping of USAID in no way rules out increased budgets. In fact, the report states that reduced resources in recent years coupled with closer congressional oversight of its activities "have often limited USAID's ability to use its field presence to best advantage" (p. 16). In other words, while acknowledging that USAID programs have often retarded development in the past, what USAID is calling for is a larger budget, an increase in personnel, and even greater discretionary authority for the future.

Indeed, that any but the misanthropic could oppose programs whose stated goal is to provide aid to the less fortunate is generally met with incredulity. For example, in December 1983, at a conference entitled "Liberation Theology and Third World Development" at the University of Regina in Saskatchewan, Canada, Peter Bauer presented a critique of foreign aid. Murdith McLean, who followed Bauer on the panel, opened by commenting that "I was going to begin by saying that everyone thinks foreign aid is at least a good thing to those less well off than ourselves. It may appear that we have at least one disagreement on that contention in the panel" (McLean, 1985, p. 39).

But, like so many other government terms, ranging from Aid to Families with Dependent Children (AFDC) to Peacekeeper missiles, the term *foreign aid* used to describe the political process of transferring wealth from First World taxpayers to Third World governments both prejudges the results and disarms critics. There is, as Thomas Sowell has noted (1983, p. 239), no more a priori justification for calling it "foreign aid" than "foreign hindrance." Whether wealth transfer is an aid or a hindrance is, Sowell points out, an empirical question, not a foregone conclusion.

This point is well taken. What are the results of foreign aid?

The Record

In *The Economics of Developing Countries,* Wayne Nafziger asks, "How effective has aid been?" After listing several criticisms, he concludes (1984, pp. 396–397), "Nevertheless, the evidence suggests that aid has been essential to many low-income countries in reducing savings and foreign exchange gaps." However, he presents no evidence to support this assessment. A few pages later Nafziger acknowledges several criticisms of food aid but again concludes (p. 401) that "Nevertheless, food aid has frequently been highly effective" and "plays a vital role in saving human lives during famine or crisis." Again, no supporting evidence is provided.

Similarly, in its 1989 report (p. 113), USAID claims that "there have been development success stories as well as failures," but is able to cite only three such success stories. "The impressive development of first Japan and later Taiwan and South Korea in East Asia is proof positive that the right donor program and guidance, when matched by the right recipient policies, can result in a smoothly phased transition from dependency to self-sufficiency." Yet even this handful of successes is ,dubious at best. Japan is a case not so much of development as of reconstruction. The task in the late 1940s was the relatively simple one of rebuilding an already developed economy that had been destroyed by war, not the far more complex problem of stimulating development itself. And the impressive economic performances of both Taiwan and South Korea began only *after* large-scale economic aid from the United States was discontinued (Krauss, 1984, p. 190).

Whether bilateral or multilateral, the official original purpose of foreign aid, defined here as the transfer of resources from one government to another, was to stimulate economic development. However, with passage of the U.S. Foreign Assistance Act of 1973, commonly known as the Reforms of '73 or the New Directions Initiative, and the adoption of the New International Economic Order (NIEO) by the General Assembly of the United Nations the following year, the additional goal of directly increasing the living standards of the poorest strata in the recipient countries, that is, of meeting basic human needs, was added to, if it did not in fact replace, the original goal (Eberstadt, 1985b, pp. 25–26; Erickson and Sumner, 1984, pp. 1–21; Lappe, Collins, and Kinley, 1981, p. 169). Clearly, aid, at least according to its original intent, was to be temporary. Once the capacity for self-sustaining economic growth had been achieved, aid would no longer be required. Yet, as Paul Craig Roberts commented (1985, p. 20), "Far from developing, most Third World countries seem to be more dependent than ever on aid." In fact, it was precisely because of the growing dissatisfaction with the results of foreign aid that the NIEO and the Reforms of '73 altered the focus of the program. Aid had come increasingly to be viewed, by recipient as well as donor countries, not as something freely granted but as something owed. That is, the MDCs have a moral if not in fact a legal obligation to ensure that the people of the LDCs have their basic needs provided for. This was to be done, according to the Presidential Commission on World Hunger in its report to President Carter, by "redirecting income from the rich to the poor" (in Eberstadt, 1985b, p. 28). Thus, what began as a temporary economic development program has been transformed into a permanent, ongoing, international welfare system.

Yet by either goal—that of generating self-sustaining economic growth or of improving the lot of the poorest segments of the recipient countries—the evidence lends precious little support for the contention that aid actually aids.

Approximately $60 billion is spent on foreign aid, or Official Development Assistance (ODA), each year. Of course the amount of assistance money actually provided is considerably larger, since ODA by definition excludes contributions from private voluntary organizations such as Oxfam, Save the Children Fund, and World Vision. Further, to be classified as ODA the resource transfer must have "the promotion of economic development and welfare of the developing countries as its main objective." It must also contain "a grant element of at least 25 percent." Thus loans to Third World countries are classified as ODA only if they are soft, or concessional; military assistance, even if it is in the form of grants or concessional loans, is excluded (Hancock, 1989, pp. 42–43). What has this massive transfer of resources accomplished?

In practically every case, the influx of aid has been immediately followed by the emergence of a massive, unproductive, parasitic government bureaucracy whose very existence undercuts the recipient's ability for sustained economic growth. For example, Tanzania and the U.S. trust territory of Micronesia receive more aid per capita than any other nations in the world. While the Tanzanian economy collapsed during the decade of the 1970s, its bureaucracy grew by 14 percent per year, more than doubling during the decade (Sowell, 1983, p. 240). The Micronesian island of Palau has "more elected officials per capita than any other nation on earth." With only 8,000 voters it has 16 state governments. Palau is not an anomaly. Sixty-seven percent of the taxable wages of Micronesia come from government employment (Fitzgerald, 1980, pp. 283, 285–286; Manhard, 1981, p. 209). The U.N. Development Program (UNDP) concluded that "this large cadre of highly paid government workers . . . is far beyond the ability of the economy to support" (in Fitzgerald, p. 281). In other words, the size of the government bureaucracy in Micronesia is a direct result of foreign aid. Further, aid has been directly responsible for the pauperization of large segments of the population, and again Micronesia is a prime example (Bauer, 1981, p. 113; Fitzgerald, 1980, pp. 275–284; Manhard, 1981, pp. 207–214).

Aid has in many places actually destroyed the possibility for sustained economic growth by driving local producers, especially farmers, out of business. Such was the case in Micronesia, Bangladesh, India, Egypt, Haiti, Peru, Guatemala, Kenya, Jamaica, and many other places (Bandow, 1985, p. xiv; Bovard, 1984, p. 18; 1989, pp. 128–131; Eberstadt, 1985b, p. 22; Fitzgerald, 1980, pp. 278, 288; Lappe et al., 1981, pp. 93–102).

Former U.S. Assistant Secretary of Agriculture George Dunlop acknowledged in 1984 that the dumping of massive quantities of U.S. wheat on India in the 1950s and 1960s so disrupted the Indian agriculture market that the food aid may have been responsible for the starvation of millions of Indians (in Bovard, 1989, p. 129). Other studies have shown that malnutrition in Bangladesh actually rose as food aid to that country increased (Krauss, 1984, p. 160). It is unlikely that these are isolated occurrences. Countries such as Peru, Haiti, and Guatemala have either refused to accept U.S. food aid or pleaded with the U.S. government to restrict such aid (Bovard, 1984, p. 18; Lappe et al., 1981, pp. 116–118).

In the 1950s and 1960s the World Bank and other aid agencies funded the construction of the Akosombo dam on the Volta River in Ghana. The dam has been the source of very inexpensive hydroelectric power for the U.S.-owned VALCO aluminum plant as well as for the most prosperous inhabitants of Accra, the capital of Ghana. Not only does the dam not provide power for the poor inhabitants of the rural villages, it is they who have borne the cost of the dam. Thousands of Ghanaian villagers were displaced, without compensation, when the dam flooded their lands. Moreover, the dam has been responsible for the spread of river blindness and other diseases. Over 100,000 people living in the vicinity of the dam have been inflicted with river blindness since the completion of the dam. Of these, 70,000 have been rendered totally sightless. In addition, "at least 80,000 more people have been permanently disabled as a result of schistosomasis, a parasitic water-borne disease carried by two species of snail that are now the commonest molluscus in the Volta reservoir" (Hancock, 1989, pp. 140–41). The World Bank and other agencies have funded thousands of giant dams over the past decade. The Ghanaian experience is the rule rather than the exception (Bovard, 1988, p. 187; Lappe et al., 1981, pp. 35–39).

During the 1983–1984 famine, the World Bank and other aid agencies provided the Ethiopian government with millions of dollars in loans and outright grants. According to a World Bank report, the assistance was to provide for "relief and rehabilitation services to alleviate the impact of drought and famine on human welfare" (in Bandow, 1989, pp. 78–79). The government used much of this money to purchase trucks. The trucks were the principal means used by the government to implement its "resettlement" program, that is, the seizure and forcible transportation of hundreds of thousands of Ethiopians from the rebel-dominated northern region to government-controlled villages in the south. According to the French medical group Doctors Without Borders, more Ethiopians died from the resettlement program than from the famine. One World Bank employee described the Bank's Ethiopian policy as "genocide with a human face" (Bandow, 1989, pp. 76–77; Bovard, 1988, p. 185; Keyes, 1986, p. 2). The Ethiopian government continued this program until it fell in 1991, with the goal of resettling 33 million Ethiopians, 75 percent of the population. Yet it continued to receive massive aid from the World Bank (Bovard, 1988, p. 185).

This is not the only such program that the World Bank has sponsored. Between 1982 and 1985 the Bank funded a massive resettlement program in Brazil. The program encouraged hundreds of thousands of Brazilians to relocate themselves in the Amazon Basin where, as farmers, they were forced to adopt slash-and-burn agriculture. The result was both massive loss of life and the wholesale destruction of large areas of the ecologically sensitive Amazon jungle (Hancock, 1989, pp. 131–133). Brazil possesses an estimated 125 million acres of unused but very fertile land (Avery, 1989, p. 4), and there was no economic reason to go into the Amazon basin. The World Bank now admits the program was "an ecological, human and economic disaster of tremendous dimensions" (Hancock, p. 131). Yet the Bank, in conjunction with numerous other aid agencies, including USAID, is currently financing a similar but much more massive resettlement program in East Timor, Indonesia. More than 6 million have already been relocated, most in what are largely rain forest areas. Millions more are scheduled for resettlement by 1994. Resistance is met with brutal repression—approximately 150,000 of the 700,000 inhabitants of East Timor have either been killed in the fighting or have died of starvation. And 2.3 million hectares of Indonesia's tropical rain forest have been destroyed and millions more are scheduled for destruction to make way for resettlement sites (Bovard, 1988, p. 185; Hancock, 1989, p. 133–138).

Africa, traditionally a food exporter, "lost its historic ability to feed itself," notes Sowell (1983, p. 239), precisely when donor agencies began to "smother Africa with project aid." Many observers believe that the relationship is not accidental and that Africa's economic deterioration, and in particular its tragic agricultural situation, was caused in part by aid (Ayittey, 1988a; Bandow, 1989, pp. 75, 80; Bauer, 1984, pp. 46, 51–52; Fitzgerald, 1980, pp. 287–289). Between 1973 and 1980 the World Bank invested $2.4 billion in Africa for the stated purpose of boosting agricultural output. Yet between 1960 and 1985 per capita food production fell nearly 20 percent. A 1986 World Bank study concluded that the Bank-funded enterprises "represent a depressing picture of inefficiency, losses, budgetary burdens, poor products and services and minimal accomplishment of the noncommercial objectives so frequently used to excuse their poor economic performance" (in Bovard, 1988, p. 185). A 1987 World Bank study admitted that fully 75 percent of its African agricultural projects had failed (Hancock, 1989, p. 145).

Another 1987 World Bank study classified nearly 60 percent of its projects around the world as either having "serious shortcomings" or being "complete failures." It also concluded that another 60 percent, including many otherwise judged to be successes, were not sustainable after completion (Bandow, 1989, pp. 77–79; Hancock, 1989, p. 145).

The World Bank has noted (1983, p. 18) that ODA totaled just 5 percent of the gross domestic investment of the low-income countries of South Asia but over 40 percent in the low-income countries of Africa. It also pointed out (1980, Table 2.8, p. 11) that for the decade of the 1970s, per capita income in South Asia's low-income countries grew over five times faster than it did in the low-income countries of Africa. Conversely, the most economically developed areas in the world—Western Europe, the United States, and Japan—developed without aid. Similarly, Hong Kong and Singapore, two of the most economically vibrant areas over the past two decades, received only negligible aid. And, as already noted, although Taiwan and South Korea are often touted as foreign aid success stories, their impressive economic performances began only *after* large-scale economic aid from the United States was discontinued.

In short, despite the truly massive aid effort, there is little to suggest that aid has succeeded in either stimulating self-sustaining economic growth or improving the plight of the poorest strata of people in the recipient countries.

Reforming Foreign Aid

Many who acknowledge that foreign aid has done little or nothing to help the people of the LDCs believe that the solution lies in reforming the program. The proposals are numerous and not often consistent with one another. They include, to cite just a few, providing a clearer description of the aid objectives (Ottaway, 1985, p. A5; USAID, 1989, p. 25); placing greater emphasis on "decentralized decision-making," thereby both reducing the "necessity for joint action" and enabling aid to be tailored to the specific needs of the villages within the recipient countries (Hart, 1986, p. 50; Tendler, 1977, p. 107); placing greater emphasis on the selection of "good leaders" who can inspire others by their "strong, personal commitments to program goals" (Gow and Morse, 1988, pp. 1415–1416); "somehow" achieving greater "independence" for donor agencies from the pressures imposed by both donor and recipient governments (Tendler, 1977, pp. 108–110); and, rather ambiguously and grandiloquently, "radically reshaping future official assistance programs to face new realities" (USAID, 1989, p. 121).

It is no doubt true that some reforms, if implemented and followed, could eliminate some of the more unsavory aspects of the aid program, such as the blatant waste, mismanagement, and corruption that has been a part of foreign aid since its inception. But the real problem is far more fundamental. Proposals to reform foreign aid do not call into question the program itself. They assume that, if only the programs could be successfully administered or properly restructured, beneficial results would follow. In fact, even if the proposed reforms were implemented, few of the expected beneficial results would appear. As will be shown below, the basic problem lies not in the way the programs are either administered or structured; it lies in the nature of the programs themselves. Foreign aid, *by its very nature,* retards economic growth and development.

The Economic Problems of Foreign Aid

The economic problems facing foreign aid can be subdivided into two categories: (1) the problem of incentives and (2) the problem of calculation.

Incentives

Individuals act to maximize their utility. One of the ways they do this is by making trade-offs between additional units of wealth, and thus work, and additional units of leisure. Each individual must decide whether an additional unit of wealth is more valuable than the unit of leisure that he or she would have to forgo to obtain that wealth. If it is more valuable, the individual will prefer to increase his or her wealth at the expense of leisure; if not, the individual will prefer to increase his or her leisure by reducing work units.

The implications are significant. If individuals find themselves in positions where the benefit from a unit of leisure exceeds the benefit from an additional unit of work, it will be rational for them to choose leisure over work. For example, it is safe to assume that a 100-percent tax on all production would eliminate all productive behavior—it would sever any connection between individuals' economic behavior and their economic position. While each increment of leisure would be less valuable than each preceding increment, leisure would retain at least some value, whereas work would have none. Similarly, assuring individuals of a certain level of wealth or supplying them with certain economic goods, regardless of circumstances, artificially reduces the value of work relative to leisure. One would expect to find that the more lucrative such benefits become, the greater the amount of leisure individuals would choose.

The evidence bears this out. The Great Society and War on Poverty programs of the 1960s not only failed to eliminate poverty in the United States but actually led to an increase not only in the number but in the percentage of poor people. The poor, noted sociologist Charles Murray (1984, p. 9),

> continued to respond, as they always had, to the world as they found it, but we . . .
> changed the rules of their world. . . . The first effect of the new rules was to make
> it profitable for the poor to behave in the short term in ways which were destructive
> in the long run. Their second effect was to mask these long-term losses—to subsi-
> dize irretrievable mistakes. We tried to provide more for the poor and produced
> more poor instead.

In short, as a result of efforts to aid the poor, a large segment of American society
has been pauperized.

There is no reason to believe that the disincentive effects of aid are limited to
domestic programs. The pauperization of Micronesia was a direct result of foreign
aid. The United States acquired Micronesia as a trust territory in 1945 following its
liberation from the Japanese. Outside private investment was discouraged because
it would, according to U.S. Navy officials, "reduce the people to cheap labor" (in
Fitzgerald, 1980, p. 276–277). Instead, the people of Micronesia were given free
food, clothes, and other supplies. The result was bankruptcy of many local stores
and undermining of the incentive to work. Not surprisingly, Micronesians pre-
ferred "to accept free and usually gratuitous welfare, thus avoiding the work and
sacrifice required for real economic progress" (Manhard, 1981, pp. 213–214). As
productivity plummeted, Micronesia became entangled in a vicious circle: the
more the economy deteriorated, the more aid it received, and the more aid it
received, the more the economy deteriorated. Between 1947 and 1985 this territory
of less than 150,000 people received $2.4 billion, and its inhabitants were eligible
for close to 500 government programs (Fitzgerald, 1980, p. 279; Manhard, 1981, p.
213). The statistics are indeed revealing. Nearly two-thirds of all Micronesians are
now employed by island governments financed by American taxpayers. In terms of
acreage cultivated, every category of agriculture declined. Between 1963 and 1973
acreage devoted to coconuts fell by 50 percent, to vegetables by 70 percent, and to
citrus fruit by nearly 60 percent. During the same period, imports of food that had
traditionally been produced locally rose fivefold while exports declined by half
(Fitzgerald, p. 279). And a 1984 U.S. State Department report lamented the fact
that despite massive infusion of funds the local fisheries sector was no more productive than it was in 1945 before Micronesia became a trust territory (Fitzgerald,
p. 282).

Minister of Administration Hauro Willter has publicly complained that "We
have no technicians, no plumbers, no electricians. We have no economic base to
be self-sufficient because the U.S. Government just handed us everything and
didn't ask us to do anything for ourselves" (in Fitzgerald, p. 275). Yet in the mid-
1980s, the U.S. government responded to the alarming deterioration by more than
doubling the amount of aid to Micronesia (Fitzgerald, p. 282).

The point, of course, is not that Micronesians are inherently lazy. It is that they
behaved rationally given the context within which they found themselves. There
was no need for them to trade off leisure for wealth since they could have as much
or more wealth, at least in the short run, without sacrificing leisure than they could
obtain by working.

What makes Micronesia so pertinent is precisely that it is composed of more
than 2,100 islands with numerous cultures and nine distinct languages. One might

expect to find that the more lucrative such benefits become, the greater the amount of leisure individuals would choose.

> What should confound sociologists but vindicate free-market enthusiasts is that nothing of the sort occurred. The uniform application of government in Micronesia, placing it at the center of economic life, produced in every culture and among every island group a uniform result—stagnation, dependence, disaster and despair.

There is little doubt about the disincentive effect of foreign aid. The Food for Peace program, or PL-480, which was created mainly to deal with the growing problem of U.S. surplus food (Bandow, 1988, p. 36), began in 1954. The program distributes surplus U.S. food overseas. In country after country, including Bangladesh, India, Haiti, and Guatemala, the result, Bovard has noted (1984, p. 18), is that the program "has fed the same people for more than a decade, thereby permanently decreasing the demand for locally produced food and creating an entrenched welfare class."

Perhaps even more tragic is that since "consumers naturally will not pay for what they can get free" (Bandow, 1985, p. xiv), the program has driven local producers out of business. Thus, not only has food aid pauperized large segments of the Third World, it has also penalized local producers, thereby resulting in a "deskilling" of the local population as well as retarding the development of those attitudes—thrift, industry, and self-reliance—that are essential for economic development.

But what of emergency relief such as that extended to famine-stricken countries like Ethiopia? Even there the record speaks for itself. During the 1973–1974 famine, Ethiopia received large amounts of food from Europe and America. Although the provinces of Eritrea and Tigre were most affected, food was diverted away from them to starve the rebels there into submission. The government of Haile Selassie sold much of the donated food on the world market, the money going to line the pockets of regime members. The government even offered to sell the United States 4,000 tons of grain, which the United States would then donate back to Ethiopia, thereby helping the former to fulfill its pledge of 22,500 tons of donated food. The offer was declined (Legum, 1975; Shepard, 1975).

The actions of the Mengistu government during the 1984–1985 famine were remarkably similar. Though thousands starved, the government not only spent over $200 million to celebrate the tenth anniversary of the Marxist revolution, it also earned $15 million in revenues by charging ships loaded with donated food a port-entry fee of $50.50 a ton. Ships unable to pay the fee were turned away, cargo unloaded (Fenwick, 1987). The Eritrea-Tigre area was sealed off, and those smuggling food into the area were attacked by the army. Food shipments were seized and some of the food used to feed the army. Some was sold on the world market and the money earned used to buy munitions for the war against the rebels (Osterfeld, 1985).

"Most of the food destined for Eritrea—as much as 100,000 tons each month—has arrived at the Ethiopian-controlled port cities of Aseb and Mitsiwa." But, said Anthony Suau (1985, pp. 391,400), since "Ethiopia tries to prevent outside aid from reaching the people in Eritrea . . . food aid and medicine must enter the way

I did: from Sudan, crossing the border without official permission and moving only at night to avoid Ethiopian planes." The steady trickle of Eritrean refugees into Sudan, about 400,000 between 1967 and 1984, turned into a flood, with many of these either starving or wounded from strafing and the bombing of civilian centers by the Ethiopian military (Kaplan, 1985).

Even with the best intentions by donors, the benefits of emergency aid for victims of famine or other natural disasters may be only an illusion. First of all, as agricultural analyst Dennis Avery has stated in Congressional testimony (1989, p. 10), emergency food aid requirements are ordinarily much smaller than officially estimated, since such estimates tend to ignore the fact that farmers or local governments hold stocks as a matter of course. While individually these stocks may be small, cumulatively their impact is significant. "During the 1987–88 Asian monsoon failure," Avery noted, "India, Pakistan, Indonesia and Thailand all had their own rice reserves. India had wheat reserves as well. Only modest imports were needed to keep consumption at near-normal levels in the region, and the imports were available." Moreover, farmers adjust quite rationally to crop shortfalls by planting such fast-growing crops as peas and potatoes as soon as the rains arrive. One of the major problems of food aid is precisely that organization and shipment are not only costly, they are also time consuming. A study of the U.N. World Food Program's response to 84 emergencies disclosed that it took an average of 196 days to respond. It takes the European Economic Community (EEC) an average of 400 days to respond to emergency requests (Fauriol, 1984, p. 83; Hancock, 1989, pp. 21–22). The result, typically, is that the food arrives "too late to relieve hunger but in time to depress prices for local farmers who have tried their best to respond" (Avery, 1989, p. 12).

Moreover, if the food aid is distributed free of charge, it will, as already noted, drive local shops and markets out of business, thus retarding recovery or even preventing it altogether. If the food is sold at local predisaster price levels, it will tend to freeze domestic production at the disaster level. That is, if enough food is provided by outside aid programs to prevent food prices from rising, there will be little incentive for local farmers to return to their predisaster level of production, since they could sell their increased output only at low prices. Finally, as noted in Chapter 2, there is no shortage of food in the world; if necessary, food production could be expanded. Consequently the reduction in local output due to drought or other natural disasters would, if local prices were permitted to rise, stimulate the importation of food. Significantly, this would not disrupt the recovery process. On the contrary, the higher prices would actually stimulate it since they would encourage local producers to return to their predisaster levels of production. As these levels were reached, local prices would begin to fall, crowding out not the local producers but the foreign importers.

That is what would happen in the event of an actual natural disaster. But, Eberstadt has commented (1985a, p. 25), there is very little that is natural about today's natural disasters. "Acts of God," he writes, "cannot be prevented, but the quotient of human risk and suffering can be vastly and systematically reduced." During the first decade of the twentieth century more than 8,000 Americans died in hurricanes. During the last ten years there have been only 100 hurricane-related deaths. How does one explain this 99-percent decline despite a doubling of the population?

Improvements in communications, transportation, weather tracking, emergency management, rescue operations, and relief capabilities have made it possible to reduce dramatically the human price exacted by even the worst hurricanes in the most populated areas. Purposeful private and governmental actions can now substantially cut the toll from other natural disasters as well, even in the poorest nations. (Eberstadt, 1985a, p. 26)

Given the surplus of world food coupled with the use of early warning systems, ranging from aerial and meteorological surveillances to using price fluctuations in local markets as a barometer of the size of regional harvests, there is no reason in today's world for local crop failures due to such natural conditions as drought to result in famine. Where famine has occurred, it is traceable to government policies that have, intentionally or unintentionally, short-circuited both the early warning systems and the automatic transfer of food to the affected areas. In many cases, such as the starvation of millions of Russians in 1929–1930, of at least 1 million Ibos in Nigeria in the late 1960s, of 100,000 Timorese after its annexation by Indonesia in the mid-1970s, of an estimated 2 million Cambodians after the Khmer Rouge seized power in the late 1970s, the mass starvation in Afghanistan following the deliberate destruction of Afghanistan's food system after the 1979 invasion by the Soviet Union, and massive famines in Eritrea in the 1970s and 1980s, *starvation was the deliberate intention of the government* (Eberstadt, 1985a, pp. 25–27; Zinsmeister, 1988, pp. 22–30).

In other cases, such as the starvation of 25 to 30 million Chinese during the "Three Lean Years" from 1959 to 1962 and the massive famine in most of the sub-Saharan countries in the 1980s, starvation, while not the intention of the government, was nevertheless the direct consequence of ill-advised government policies such as price controls, collectivization, marketing boards, and other interventionist measures that not only reduced the production of food locally but discouraged or even prohibited the importation of food from abroad.

In the first case above, aid was not desired, since starvation was the direct intention of the government. In the second case, aid may have done more harm than good: by subsidizing the effects of ill-advised government policies it enabled, even encouraged, the governments to continue pursuing the very policies that were responsible for the catastrophies in the first place, thereby compounding the harm.

Calculation

Another problem inherent in the nature of foreign aid is that of economic calculation. It is economically rational to pursue a project only when the (expected) benefits exceed costs. Although this principle may occasionally be overridden by noneconomic considerations, any country interested in economic growth and development must adhere to it. This poses a serious problem for the recipients of aid. Since the transferred resources would be scarce, their transfer at *zero cost to the recipients* would seriously distort cost data. Thus, even assuming that public officials honestly desire to benefit their people, the artificial lowering of costs entailed by the transfers would make many economically unsound projects *appear* profitable. That is to say, trying to determine whether costs exceed benefits in the absence of accurate cost data is like trying to cut a piece of paper with a single scissors blade. Inevitably, numerous mistakes will be made and the waste of resources will be enormously high.

Moreover, private investors risking their own capital are under the economic constraint of serving consumers. Public officials to whom resources are transferred are largely relieved of this constraint. In fact, since they receive resources at *zero cost to themselves*, they are able to treat these as free goods. Even when public officials are not corrupt, they are human. Relief from the economic constraint of serving consumers enables public officials to substitute their own priorities, however well intentioned, for those of consumers. Since economic development is often confused with industrialization, the result has been the diversion of resources from the satisfaction of consumer desires to use in capital-intensive projects even when there is little or no demand for the subsequent products or such products can be bought more cheaply elsewhere. Examples are the construction of steel mills, hydroelectric dams, modern airports, double-deck suspension bridges for nonexistent railroads, giant oil refineries in countries that neither produce nor refine oil, giant crop-storage depots that have never been used because their locations are not accessible to local farmers, and numerous other white elephants (Ayittey, 1987c, pp. 210–211; Ayittey, 1988a; Bauer, 1987, p. 5; Chapman, 1986; Fitzgerald, 1980, pp. 284–285). Although these projects are undertaken in the name of industrialization, they do not contribute to economic growth. They are the modern counterpart of the Egyptian pyramids: colossal, impressive, and a wasteful drain on the resources of the country. As a result, foreign aid has historically led to a "notable increase in the amount of capital devoted to economically wasteful projects" (Fleming, 1966, pp. 78–79. See also Bauer and Yamey, 1980, p. 61; M. Friedman, 1958, pp. 205-206).

The Political Problems of Foreign Aid

There are also serious political problems endemic in foreign aid programs. These include the following.

Centralization

In spite of the free-market rhetoric that is so often utilized by both USAID and the World Bank to justify their loans, foreign aid—the transfer of resources from government to government—inevitably means the centralization of government power over the economic affairs of the country. Aside from the potential for serious restrictions on individual freedom that this centralization involves, there are other untoward ramifications.

One of these is the diversion of activity from economics to politics, from production to distribution. The percentage of their GNPs devoted to aid by the MDCs is almost invariably less than 0.5 percent per year. It would be a mistake to conclude from this, however, that aid is of negligible impact. For many recipient countries, ODA constitutes a large part of the government's budget. For example, ODA equals nearly 50 percent of government expenditure in Burundi, over 38 percent in Tanzania, more than 40 percent in Honduras, 49 percent in Zaire, 31 percent in Rwanda, 60 percent in Mali and in Malaysia, and 67 percent in both Niger and Somalia (USAID, 1989, Table IX, pp. 148–149). Consequently:

> The question of who runs the government has become paramount in many Third World countries and is especially so in multiracial societies, like those of much of Asia and Africa. In such a situation the energies and resources of people, particularly the most ambitious and energetic, are diverted from economic activity to political life, partly from choice and partly from necessity. Foreign aid has contributed substantially to the politicization of life in the Third World. It augments the resources of governments as compared to the private sector, and the criteria of allocation tend to favor governments trying to establish state controls.   (Bauer, 1978, p. 162)

This diversion of energies into political activity is especially pernicious, since what is not produced cannot be consumed. Thus, in contrast to market relations in which the economic output expands to the benefit of everyone, the politicization of economic life, by reducing the amount of energy devoted to production, reduces overall economic output (relative to what it would be in the absence of politicization). Moreover, the conflicts generated by the political process of distribution must likewise retard production. The result is that foreign aid transforms the economic process of production on the market with its corollary, *voluntary exchange for mutual benefit*, into the political process of transferring wealth from politically weak to politically powerful groups, with its corollary of coerced "exchange" where one group benefits itself *at the expense of another*. It transforms a process that is inherently positive-sum, where the sum of the gains exceeds the sum of the losses, into a process that is inherently negative-sum, where the sum of the losses exceeds the sum of the gains.

Environment

Further, it is a mistake to regard aid as a net addition to the capital stock of a country. The influx of aid not only centralizes economic control in the hands of the government, it simultaneously enables the recipient government to camouflage the ill effects of its statist policies, thereby reducing pressure on the government to maintain an environment favorable to private enterprise. Since this discourages private investment, both domestic and foreign, the result is often a net reduction in the amount of capital available (Bandow, 1989, pp. 383–385; Bauer, 1989, pp. 221–224; Bauer and Yamey, 1985, pp. 38–40; M. Friedman, 1958, p. 207).

This has been especially true following the change in the focus of foreign assistance that became symbolized in the early 1970s on the multilateral level by the NIEO and on the bilateral level by the Reforms of '73, which shifted the principal orientation of both the World Bank and USAID from economic development to the satisfaction of basic needs. The change of focus has discouraged private investment by encouraging LDCs to adopt policies that militate against protection of private property. The NIEO, for example, characterizes nationalization as an "inalienable right" and boldly states that "every country has the right to adopt the economic and social system that it deems to be the most appropriate for its own development and not to be subjected to discrimination of any kind." And "the soft-loan affiliate" of the World Bank, the International Development Association (IDA), has encouraged large-scale borrowing by making soft or concessional loans readily available to LDC governments. Private banks were encouraged to make loans to the LDCs by the availability of export credit insurance provided by government organizations such as the U.S. Export Import Bank (Ayittey, 1984, p. 32; Fitzgerald, 1980, p. 284), by less formal government pressures and assurances about the soundness of the loans (Meigs, 1984, p. 114), and by the inflationary macroeconomic policies of the U.S. government during the 1970s, designed to deal with the oil price shock and the resulting recession. The result, however, was to reduce real interest rates and thereby encourage lending, and especially foreign lending, by U.S. banks (Mussa, 1984, p. 82). As will be dealt with in greater detail in Chapter 7, the consequence of these policies was that many LDCs began systematically substituting foreign *borrowing* for foreign *investment*. Over the last three decades private investment in the LDCs as a share of total capital transfers from the First to the Third World has steadily fallen. It was almost 40 percent in the 1950s, about 25 percent in the 1960s, 16 percent in the 1970s and just 10 percent in the 1980s. (Eberstadt, 1985a, p. 28; Weigel, 1988, pp. 5–6).

This means that far from additional aid being necessary to relieve the foreign debt burden of the Third World, foreign aid in fact bears a large responsibility for the foreign debt crisis. While motives are difficult to document with any degree of certainty, it can hardly be an accident that the emergence of the Third World debt crisis coincided with the changing attitudes toward ODA that occurred in the early 1970s. For example, between 1975 and 1980 Argentina's debt rose by over 300 percent, Brazil's by 250 percent, and Mexico's by 280 percent (S. Bartlett, 1989, p. 207). The "capital flight" that has bedeviled so many Third World nations is due in part to the hostile environment for private investment and in part to the rampant corruption resulting from the politicization of economic life. Both are at least in part a consequence of foreign aid. As Ghanaian economist George Ayittey has observed (1988a, p. B-12), "More than $10 billion in capital leaves Africa every year. That is more than comes in as foreign aid. Much of this capital is booty, illegally shipped abroad by the ruling elites." The amount Zaire's President Mobutu places in his personal Swiss bank account exceeds the $45 million a year in U.S. aid to Zaire (Ayittey, 1986c, p. 9). And economist James Henry observed that "More than half the money borrowed by Mexico, Venezuela and Argentina during the last decade has effectively flowed right back out the door, often the same year or even month it flowed in" (in Ayittey, 1986b, p. 30).

In short, there would be neither a Third World debt crisis nor capital flight problem were the domestic environments in the LDCs more receptive to private investment. But since foreign aid not only removes the pressure on governments to institute such an environment but also, in fact, entails the politicization of the economy, it makes it neither necessary nor, in some cases, even possible to establish such an environment.

Bureaucratic Self-Interest

During the mid-1980s the Reagan Administration, as part of its attempt to reduce spending, significantly cut back its contributions to the United Nations. Since the United States is the largest single contributor, supplying approximately 25 percent of the U.N. budget, the cutback placed the United Nations in a financial crisis. As part of an economy move, Secretary General Javier Perez de Cuellar proposed a number of budget cuts, one of which was that the supply of carafes of iced water in 13 meeting rooms at U.N. headquarters in New York be halted. The proposal provoked a heated debate. A motion calling for the retention of iced water was promptly introduced followed by hours of debate by the Committee on Administrative and Budgetary Questions. The controller, Richard Foran, explained that since there were 159 delegates in each of the 13 rooms, and since the glasses had to be changed and the carafes refilled between meetings, the cost of the iced water was about $100,000 per year. Given the major cuts in the aid programs that were in the process of being made, it was argued that the restoration of the iced water at that time would appear unseemly. However, some of the delegates argued they were not going to surrender their water as long as those on the podium retained access to iced water. And since those on the podium were not about to give up their water, the debate lasted for hours. As the debate dragged on late into the night, one of the speakers warned that the total cost of the meeting, which would include overtime expenses such as those for guards and translators, could end up equaling or even exceeding the amount that would have been saved from the elimination of the iced water. The Committee, it should be noted, was unable to reach a decision (Hancock, 1989, pp. 89–90).

The great iced water debate is not important in itself. It is significant, however, in that it highlights just how tenaciously bureaucrats in the aid agencies, the "aristocrats of mercy" as Hancock calls them, cling to their perks and privileges. For example, even in the wake of the Secretary General's economy program, the United Nations continued to pay $60,000 a year for the services of a chauffeur-driven limousine for a single employee. It has also paid more than $200,000 to construct leisure facilities for the U.N. staff in New York (Hancock, 1989, p. 90).

An increasingly large part of the budget of practically all aid agencies, bilateral or multilateral, is for travel, most of which is not travel to poverty-stricken areas in the LDCs but to poverty seminars normally held at plush hotels in very attractive locations. A former ambassador to the United Nations acknowledged that the Economic and Social Council (ECOSOC) holds its summer meetings in Geneva rather than New York "just because the weather is more pleasant in Geneva during the summer than it is in New York" (in Hancock, 1989, p. 91). In just one year the Executive Board of the Educational, Scientific, and Cultural Organization received $1,759,548 for travel and lodging costs. During the same period it spent a grand total of $49,000 on education of handicapped children in Africa, $7,200 for curriculum development in Pakistan, and $1,000 to train teachers in Honduras (Heritage Foundation, 1984, pp. 6–7). The U.N. Food and Agriculture Organization (UNFAO) budgets $14 million annually for travel, while in 1989 the World Bank, whose members fly first class, spent $85 million on travel (Irwin, 1990b, p. A10). Indeed, travel has become so much a part of the life of the international development bureaucracy that in at least one U.N. agency "a number of officials are *permanently* registered as being on duty travel and are paid accordingly," and the U.N. Secretariat in New York employs no fewer than 20 people, full time, at a cost of more than $1 million a year, to make travel plans for U.N. staffers (Hancock, 1989, p. 91). Free trips to some of the most glamorous spots in the world are often merely the beginning of the perks that accrue to members of the international development bureaucracy. The simple fact is that travel is not merely free, it is quite lucrative. Food and lodging are covered by per diems that exceed $100 per day. As one thrifty world traveling development bureaucrat acknowledged, by economizing on such things as hotels, he could save as much as $50 per day or, he estimated, $3,000 per year in tax-free money.

In addition, flights of nine hours duration or more entitle senior U.N. officials to fly first class rather than, as the official regulations put it, "by the class immediately below first class" (Irwin, 1990a, p. 7). Finally, travel also entitles the U.N. staffer to a certain number of "rest days," the exact number determined by the length of the travel. As Hancock (p. 92) comments:

> It is surprising how many destinations are more than nine hours' flight from U.N. headquarters in New York. A list of 178 frequently visited cities contains no fewer than 130 which permit the nine-hour rule to be applied. . . . Long-haul travel also brings another privilege: a generous entitlement to "rest days" on full pay before starting work. Thus a UN staffer gets two days paid leave on top of his existing six-week vacation allowance every time he flies from New York to, say, Singapore, Nairobi or Bangkok, and two more days when he flies back. The compensation for the pain of visiting Tahiti, however, is just one day each way while those unfortunate enough to be sent on a mission to Nassau in the nearby Bahamas get no extra paid leave at all.

Perhaps some of this could be excused if it were compensation for the monetary sacrifices endured by the idealistic international poverty worker. This is hardly the case, however. Salaries for international civil servants are determined by the Noblemaire Principle, which stipulates that pay rates and conditions are to be sufficiently generous to attract as employees members of the best-paid national civil service. This means that salaries and working conditions for U.N. employees are to be better than those for the federal civil service in the United States. This is clearly the case. It would take, for example, more than 14 years for a U.S. government employee to accumulate as much sick pay as the U.N. staff member obtains on his or her very first day on the job. The average U.N. staffer is promoted at a rate twice as fast as a U.S. civil servant. The U.N. employee works an average of nearly 22 days less per year than the U.S. civil servant. U.N. pensions exceed those for the U.S. civil servant by 43 percent. And, discounting the considerable tax-free "fringe benefits" received by the U.N. staffer, base pay is higher *at every level* for the U.N. employee than it is for the U.S. civil servant. The difference averages 24 percent (Hancock, 1989, pp. 95–96; Irwin 1990a; Lichenstein et al., 1986, p. 12).

In fact, many aid workers frankly admit that they are in it for the money. "I hate this country," a worker stationed in one of the poorest Third World countries told Graham Hancock (p. 81),

> but that is why I am here. The main reason that people accept a job in a place like this is so they can stash away money—and I'm stashing away a small fortune. Because it's classified as a hardship post, I'm automatically on 25 percent above the basic salary for my grade. In addition it's a Muslim country, which means we work on Sundays—and that gets me another 25 percent. My housing's paid for, food is cheap, and there's really nothing much else to spend money on, so I'm building up a nest-egg.

This attitude is also common among natives of LDCs who find they can earn as much as a hundred times what they would receive by working for their own governments (Hancock, 1989, p. 81).

Even when the original reason for joining the poverty industry is idealistic, idealism almost invariably wanes over time. Individuals who enter the aid business in their teens often do so for altruistic reasons. Moreover, they usually work in private voluntary organizations such as Oxfam and Save the Children, where the pay is considerably less than that of official aid organizations. As they reach their late 20s or early 30s, they begin to think of their futures, of what they want in life. They want to get married, have children, own a home, have a secure future. This, they realize, requires money. And the official development agencies, especially the U.N. agencies, are where the money is. Thus, self-interest and concern for their own careers gradually become the primary motivation for even the most dedicated workers. They then begin to position themselves for a move to the United Nations or another official agency. As one writer put it,

> it is the United Nations . . . that offers the best prospect of a lasting compromise between altruism and self-interest. Whether you get a job in the Food and Agriculture Organization, in UNDP, in UNICEF or in any of the other agencies of the system, you will be entering a career that pays you a colossal salary to go on doing "humanitarian" and "socially valuable" work and that, furthermore, does so against a backdrop of liberal and progressive ideas with which you can feel comfortable. (in Hancock, 1989, pp. 81–82)

In short, a job with the United Nations allows you to have your cake and eat it too.

The result is what Peter Bauer once ironically referred to as Adam Smith's invisible hand in reverse: "those who sought the public good achieve what was no part of their intention, namely personal wealth" (Bauer, 1981, p. 144).

The Official Development Assistance–Multinational Corporation Complex

As noted already, about $60 billion per year is currently being spent on Third World aid and development. It would be a serious mistake, however, to suppose that $60 billion is actually transferred to LDCs. In fact, only a relatively small part of this ever reaches them.

Over the years the various development agencies have come to rely increasingly on "foreign experts." These experts have so permeated the aid agencies that Hancock (1989, p. 114) estimates their number at 80,000 in Africa alone (more foreigners than there ever were in Africa during the colonial period). Estimates place the number of experts, advisers, and consultants in the LDCs at any given time at a minimum of 150,000. The minimum cost per expert consultant for the United Nations is $100,000 per year, which puts the *minimum* cost for such activity at $15 billion. One consultant to the World Bank, Michael Macoby, was paid $3,000 per day (Irwin, 1990b, p. A10). Another U.N. official, an undersecretary general, retired with a lump-sum payment of nearly $500,000 and an annual pension of $50,000. He was then hired by the United Nations as a consultant, receiving $125,000 per year (Lichenstein et al., 1986, p. 12). The average cost is probably closer to $150,000 per consultant per year, which is what at least one U.N. agency budgets for. Thus, between a third and a half of all ODA is spent each year on expert consultants (Hancock, 1989, p. 115).[1]

But this is only the beginning. "Bureaucratic success" is measured by the size of an agency's budget or, in the case of transfer organizations, by the volume of loans dispensed. As one World Bank official admitted, "We're like a Soviet factory. The push is to maximize lending. The . . . pressures to lend are enormous and a lot of people spend sleepless nights wondering how they can unload projects. Our ability to influence in a way that makes sense is completely undermined" (in Bandow, 1989, p. 74; also see Tendler, 1977, p. 91). The result is that agencies have far more incentive to increase the amount of wealth transferred than to be concerned about how it is used (Irwin, 1990b, p. A10; Manhard, 1981, pp. 212–213; Sowell, 1983, p. 238). In fact, anything that slows down the allocation and spending of money, such as concern for *how* it is spent or even consulting with the people who are (ostensibly) the intended beneficiaries of a project, is quite logically regarded as an impediment.

> Finding outlets for prodigious sums of foreign exchange isn't exactly conducive to Bank officers reflecting on the social consequences of projects they are planning. "Anyone who stops to raise such questions," we were told by one Bank consultant who has worked with almost every department of the Bank, "is considered an obstructionist—not a good team man. . . . Similarly, AID's program in the African Sahel entails more dollars per capita than any other AID program in the world. One disillusioned AID officer said of the program, "we have more money available than we are able to use. . . . No one has a chance really to stop and look at what is happening because of the constant pressure to get more funds on the bottom line for the next fiscal year." (Lappe et al., 1981, pp. 85–86)

The World Bank's authorized capital increased from an initial $12 billion in 1944 to $86.4 billion in 1981 to $171 billion in April 1988 (Banks, 1988, p. 806). The IDA's authorized capital was initially established at $916 million in 1960. The seventh replenishment (1984–1987) established a target of $16 billion, which was not met because the United States decided to cut its annual contribution by 20 percent (Banks, pp. 809–810). A 1987 audit by the Operations Evaluations Department concluded that "the drive to reach lending targets . . . is a major cause of poor project performance" (in Bandow, 1989, p. 76).

The incentive to spend has other untoward consequences. One is that the easiest and fastest way to spend is on big projects. It is far easier and quicker to get rid of a million dollars by spending $200,000 on five projects than $10,000 each on 100 projects. Further, funding giant high-tech projects generally means lucrative contracts for Western-based multinational corporations (MNCs). This, it should be pointed out, in no way implies that there is a conspiracy between development agencies and the multinationals. On the contrary, it is merely the logical outcome of the incentives embedded in the foreign aid process.

To cite just a handful of examples of the results of this process, a $15 million high-tech irrigation project on the banks of the Niger River at Namasigoungou in Northwest Africa, paid for by an IDA grant and built by Western contractors, has been abandoned by the Niger government because it cannot afford the extraordinary operating costs of such a project. Yet just a few miles away aid money is being spent to finance the construction of another *identical* project. The only beneficiaries of either of these multimillion dollar projects are the Western consultants and Western contractors (Hancock, 1989, p. 155; Hodgkinson, 1988, p. 741).

Other aid-sponsored projects include rural road construction in Pakistan and Bangladesh at the cost of $62,500 per mile in the former and $133,000 per mile in the latter (in 1979 and 1980 dollars, respectively). These costs are approximately ten times the cost of road construction in other comparable countries (Lappe et al., 1981, p. 39). USAID spent $108 million to construct a huge, ultramodern grain silo complex in Egypt. On completion of the project it was discovered that the energy required to operate the plant dwarfed that available locally. USAID appropriated another $6.5 million to construct an appropriate power generating station (Hancock, 1989, p. 147). And the World Bank allocated $450 million for the construction of a huge hydroelectric project in Brazil that World Bank President A. W. Clausen, conceded was "an ill-conceived project which has had substantial negative effects on the environment and on the AmerIndian population" (in Bovard, 1988, p. 187).

Overall, the World Bank admits that about 70 percent of the money it loans out is actually spent on goods and services supplied by the wealthy industrialized countries (Hancock, 1989, p. 159; Lappe et al., 1981, p. 90). Not surprisingly, the figures are even higher when one looks at bilateral aid. For example, between 1960 and 1970, that is, during the "first development decade" as the United Nations and members of the Kennedy Administration optimistically referred to it, 99 percent of USAID money was actually spent in the United States and most was spent on products that were priced an average of 35 percent above their market value. Since then nearly 75 percent of USAID money has been spent in the United States to finance purchases from more than 3,500 U.S. corporations (Lappe et al., 1981, p. 90). And close to 80 percent of the money allocated by England for aid is spent in England. The figures are quite similar for Germany, Italy, and Japan (Hancock, 1989, pp. 156–159). It is hardly an accident that "multinational corporations are in the forefront of lobbying efforts for aid programs" (Lappe et al., 1981, p. 92).

The incentive to loan money for big projects also explains at least in part why, despite the free-market rhetoric of both the World Bank and USAID, they continue to lend large sums of money to parastatals, or government-owned, and usually very large, businesses. For example, much of the World Bank's agricultural investment in Africa has gone to finance such projects as monopolistic agricultural marketing boards and large state-run collectivization programs such as the *ujamaa* villages in Tanzania (Bandow, 1989, p. 75; Bovard, 1988, p. 185–187). During the decade of the seventies the World Bank, under Robert MacNamara, committed nearly 80 percent of its funds to government-owned businesses. Despite the nearly universally dismal performances of the parastatals and the pledge by McNamara's successors to promote private sector growth, there was no perceptible change in the Bank's priorities during the 1980s (Bandow, 1989, p. 75).[2]

Finally, the incentive for donor agencies to spend is in part responsible for the enormous corruption common to Third World recipient countries, where unscrupulous rulers all too often divert the money into their own and their cronies' pockets. It is not an accident that some of the world's wealthiest individuals are or were rulers of some of the world's poorest countries. The Marcos, Duvalier, and Mobutu fortunes, which total into the billions of dollars, are only the tip of the iceberg.

It is important to understand that foreign aid "goes not to the pitiable figures we see on aid posters or in aid advertisements" (Bauer and Yamey, 1983, p. 125), but rather to their rulers. Dispensing aid on the basis of need, which has become increasingly the case with both multilateral programs, after the adoption of the NIEO, and bilateral aid, following the passage of the Foreign Assistance Act of 1973, creates a perverse situation: it provides Third World rulers with an incentive to perpetuate the poverty of their subjects (Bauer and Yamey, 1985, pp. 38–90; Osterfeld, 1988c).

There is little doubt that this is the case. Throughout the Third World one finds entire occupations being outlawed and hard-working and industrious groups being subjected to brutal treatment ranging from discrimination to exclusion from choice occupations and to outright slaughter. An example of the former is Mobutu's expulsion of traders or middlemen, which promptly reduced Zaire's per capita income and thereby qualified Zaire, that is, President Mobutu, for increased aid (Bauer and Yamey, 1983, p. 125). Examples of the latter include the brutal mistreatment of economically wealthy but politically weak groups in Algeria, Burma, Burundi, Egypt, Ethiopia, Ghana, Indonesia, Iraq, Kenya, Malaysia, Nigeria, Sri Lanka, Tanzania, Uganda, Zaire, and Zambia. "Because the victims' incomes were above the national average," says Krauss (1984, p. 158), "their maltreatment promptly reduced average incomes and thereby widened income differences between these countries and the West." The result? Qualification for additional aid.

Moreover, even when the aid money filters down to the local level, it rarely if ever reaches those who are actually poor. For example, one aid project was designed to provide 3,000 mechanical tubewells, with each well intended to supply 25 to 50 small farmers. However, according to one Bank project worker on the scene,

> One hundred percent of these wells are going to the "fat boys." First priority goes to those with the most power and influence: judges, the magistrates, the members

of parliament, the union chairmen. If any tubewells are left over, the local authorities auction them off. The big landlords compete and whoever offers the biggest
bribe gets the tubewell. (Lappe et al., 1981, pp. 57–58)

The wealthy and powerful local "commission agents" are estimated to have
pocketed at least $136 million over an eight-year period (Hancock, 1989, p. 174).
This incident is the norm, not the exception (Lappe et al., p. 57–60).

ODA and Its Defenders

Some observers have defended World Bank and IDA activities. The Brandt Commission reported (1980, p. 226) that "the overwhelming proportion of aid money
has been usefully spent" and has "done much to diminish hardships in low-income
countries." Robert Ayres (1983, pp. 15,37,63) argues that while there have been
difficulties, World Bank and IDA loans have benefited the world's poor and that
any curtailment would cause "societies in transition" to suffer. Yet one finds little
in the way of concrete evidence to support these conclusions. On the contrary,
Ayres makes numerous references to such things as "benefit deflections" (pp.
103, 124, 193) and "shortfalls" (p. 126). He states that the World Bank always
"seeks assurances from the recipient country" about the way the loan will be used,
but then observes that "the Bank can obtain all of the assurances it wants, but it is
up to the recipient country to make good on them, and the Bank does not always
possess the leverage or supervisory capability for seeing to this" (pp. 43–44).

Elsewhere Ayres says that "the political elite in most recipient countries does
not care about the poor majority. Where there is the absence of political will and
commitment it is difficult for the Bank to be effective" (p. 57). He acknowledges
that "in several of the countries many of the housing units in the Bank-financed
projects had in fact been occupied by families with incomes higher than originally
intended by the Bank. In some instances . . . it reflected a deliberate decision by
the government" (p. 193). He further acknowledges that "World Bank resources
could free recipient-country resources for the pursuit of other projects" (p. 216).
When the Bank financed $23 million for a rural development project and $23.5
million for educational development,

> the Brazilian government has $46.5 million to spend on other, including non-
> developmental concerns. Seen in this light, Bank resources financed not only the
> projects that had been appraised and approved but also projects, perhaps even per-
> verse ones, that had not. Even the approved projects may have entailed side benefits
> going not to the poor but to those allied with the political regime. (Ayres, 1983,
> p. 217)

Finally, Ayres acknowledges that some Bank officials "admitted that they
cooked up the evidence" (p. 108).

Conclusion

Far from stimulating growth and development, as was its original intention, foreign aid actually retards development and perpetuates, even exacerbates, poverty. While reforms might reduce some of the damage caused by the program, the real causes for the failure of foreign aid lie in the nature of the program.

Foreign aid retards the development of those attitudes—thrift, industry, and self-reliance—that are essential for economic growth and development; it blurs lines of investment and distorts cost data, resulting in a massive waste of scarce resources; it politicizes life in the recipient country, thereby diverting energy from economic to political activities; it reduces pressure on the recipient governments to maintain an environment favorable to private enterprise, thereby discouraging private investment; and it gives the ruling elites in the recipient countries a vested interest in policies that impede or prevent economic development by providing money to governments on the basis of the poverty of its subjects.

Moreover, since there are large, politically powerful foreign aid bureaucracies in both donor and recipient countries, with vested interests in maintaining and even expanding the size of the aid programs, it is highly unlikely that effective reforms, even were such possible, could be implemented. For example, the occasional proposals made to reform the U.S. aid programs to Micronesia and elsewhere have never been seriously considered (Fitzgerald, 1980, pp. 289–290). Certainly one reason for the plethora of nearly 500 different welfare programs available in Micronesia is that it is a beautiful island chain that is a perfect vacation spot. Once a bureaucrat's agency has a program there, he or she naturally finds it necessary to visit the island chain to see that the agency's program is being operated properly (see, e.g., Manhard, 1981, pp. 212–213).

Finally, many maintain that the more fortunate have a moral obligation to help those who are less fortunate. As we have just seen, however, much of the wealth that is transferred remains in the wealthy countries. Moreover, transferring wealth from rich to poor *nations* is not the same as transferring wealth from rich to poor *individuals*. Many of the taxpayers in the rich nations are themselves either poor or middle-income wage earners; many of the recipients in the poor nations are the economic elite. As Hancock explains the process:

> Public money levied in the form of taxes from the poor in the rich countries is transferred in the form of "foreign aid" to the rich in the poor countries, who then hand it back for safe-keeping to the rich in the rich countries. The real trick, throughout the cycle of expropriation, is to maintain the pretense that it is the poor in the poor countries who are being helped all along.   (Hancock, 1989, p. 181)

In short, foreign aid generates incentives that, by their nature, militate against economic growth and development. This should hardly be surprising. Aid has been in existence for more than four decades. If it were in fact effective, by now the demand for it should be declining. In fact the demand for aid is only increasing (USAID, 1989, p. 111–112). Surely it is time to question the entire program.

Foreign aid is not aid at all, it is foreign harm. The sooner this is recognized the better. The capitalist countries of the West developed without aid, as did Japan and

Australia. The most rapidly developing Third World countries—Taiwan, Hong Kong, Singapore, and South Korea—received little aid or began developing only after massive amounts of aid were discontinued. What is needed, as Melvyn Krauss has perceptively pointed out (1984, p. 109), is not the transfer of wealth but the transfer of prosperity, that is, the "transfer of the ability to produce adequate amounts of real income." Since the public sector can only transfer wealth, while the private sector produces wealth, "the transfer of prosperity," Krauss points out, "depends greatly on private sector participation." Further,

> If all conditions for development other than capital are present, capital will soon be generated locally or will be available . . . from abroad. . . . If, however, the conditions for development are not present, then aid . . . will be necessarily unproductive and therefore ineffective. Thus, if the mainsprings of development are present, material progress will occur even without foreign aid. If they are absent, it will not occur even with aid. (Bauer, 1972, pp. 97–98)

Notes

1. One may, parenthetically, wonder about the need for outside consultants, since the justification for the high salaries of U.N. staffers is to attract the most competent experts in the field.

2. Structural adjustment loans (SALs) became quite popular during the 1980s. The purpose of SALs is to bribe LDC governments into instituting free-market reforms. The evidence indicates that they have not induced much in the way of reform. (See, for example, Bandow, 1989, pp. 82–87; Bovard, 1987, pp. 14–22.)

7

Multinationals

The multinational corporation is one of the most thoroughly misunderstood and criticized institutions in the contemporary world. MNCs are criticized for, among other things, exporting jobs to the LDCs in order to exploit LDC workers by paying them low wages (Barnet and Muller, 1974, p. 298; Cox, 1979, p. 416; Lall, 1983, pp. 621–622). They are also blamed for upsetting wage rates in the LDCs by paying higher than prevailing rates (Akinsanya, 1989, p. 58; Nafziger, 1984, p. 242). They are criticized for using the LDCs as dumping grounds for outdated technologies (Barnet and Muller, 1974, pp. 164–165; Hancock, 1989, pp. 162–168), as well as for introducing modern, capital-intensive, and often inappropriate technologies, which are then blamed for causing unemployment, hunger, and poverty (Akinsanya, 1989, p. 56–58; Barnet and Muller, 1974, pp. 166–172, 180–184; Muller, 1979, pp. 249–250; United Nations, 1979, p. 312). They are accused of charging both above-market prices, thereby reaping monopoly profits (Barnet and Muller, 1974, pp. 158–159; I. Frank, 1981, p. 73; Spero, 1984, p. 471), and below-market prices, thereby driving local competitors out of business (Akinsanya, 1989, p. 55; I. Frank, 1981, pp. 29–30). In fact, the MNC is perhaps the principal mechanism for the transfer of prosperity to the Third World.

The multinational corporation, as its name implies, is nothing more than a species of the corporation. What distinguishes the corporation from the MNC is not economic but political criteria. This can be easily shown. Assume that in 1964 the "Malaya Company" had two plants, one in Kuala Lampur and the other in Singapore. Since both were located within Malaysia, the Malaya Company would be a purely domestic operation. However, after Singapore's separation from the rest of Malaysia the following year, the Malaya Company would be regarded as a multinational corporation. The transformation of a domestic firm into a multinational corporation thus is a result not of any *economic* change on the part of the corporation but solely of a change in *political boundaries*. The MNC crosses at least one *political* boundary. This distinction is important.

Criticisms of the MNC can be divided into two categories: political and economic. The solution for those who criticize MNCs on political grounds is straightforward: the separation of economics entirely from politics, thereby permitting the MNC to allocate resources and produce goods and services unimpeded by political interference. However, the criticism of the second group, by far the more numerous

162

of the two, is of an entirely different character. The criticism of the MNC for its economic activities, that is, the argument that MNCs are concentrations of corporate power that, by their nature and the nature of the market process, are able to dictate prices and wages, exploit masses of people, undermine the sovereignty of the LDCs, create dependency of the LDCs on MDCs, and perpetuate poverty and economic backwardness in the host countries for their own gain, is in fact not just a criticism of the MNC but an attack on the existence of the firm itself.

The Multinational and Its Functions

Why the Firm?

Since there is no inherent economic difference between a firm and a MNC, one can best understand the functions performed by the MNC by looking first at the nature of the firm.

A theoretical but highly interesting and important consideration is, "Why the firm?" The market economy is commonly regarded as self-regulating. Movements of factors are determined by changes in relative prices. A shortage of factor A in operation O forces O to offer more for A. This will induce some of the owners of A to move to O until the price difference between O and alternative employments of A disappears.

The distinguishing mark of the firm, Ronald Coase has argued (1952, pp. 332–334), "is the suppression of the price mechanism." If in a firm "a workman moves from department Y to department X, he does not go because of a change in relative prices, but because he is ordered to do so." But, as Coase has asked, if the market is indeed so efficient, how does one explain the existence of the firm? Why is there any organization at all? Why isn't all economic activity handled through individual transactions? The reason, he argues, is that there is a cost to using the market. One of the major costs is that of negotiating contracts. As Coase put it (1952, p. 336),

> It is true that contracts are not eliminated when there is a firm but they are greatly reduced. A factor of production (or owner thereof) does not have to make a series of contracts with the factors with whom he is co-operating within the firm, as would be necessary, of course, if this co-operation were as a direct result of the working of the price mechanism. For this series of contracts is substituted one.

But this raises a consideration of a very different sort. If the firm is able to reduce costs by avoiding market transactions, why are there any market transactions at all? To this, Coase (1952, p. 340) and others (e.g., Downs, 1967, pp. 132–157; Williamson, 1981, pp. 1541–1542) point out that internal organization entails its own costs, such as the difficulty of preventing "subgoal pursuit," that is, of individuals pursuing their own goals at the expense of those of the firm. As the firm grows larger, "the cost of organizing additional transactions within the firm may rise. Naturally, a point must be reached where the costs of organizing an extra transaction within the firm are equal to the costs involved in carrying on the transaction in the open market." At this point, growth in the size of the firm ceases. However, an absolute limit to the size of the firm cannot be specified. The optimal size will vary over time as well as from industry to industry. Some "bundles of activities" may well be harder and more costly to organize than others. Similarly, improvements in transportation and communications facilities will increase the size of the firm *if* they reduce the cost of internal organization more than they reduce the cost of using the market; they will reduce the size of the firm if the reverse occurs (Coase, 1952, pp. 342–344).

None of this, of course, in any way implies that the market is being replaced by the firm. Regardless of the procedure used for determining the allocation of factors inside the firm, the market remains the indispensable touchstone. The reduction in the cost of production resulting from organizing certain activities within the firm means that the firm can now offer its goods or services on the market at a price below that of its competitors. This, in turn, places pressure on other firms or individuals to reduce costs, thereby reducing the market price for the good or service. But if the cost of the internal organization of activities exceeds the cost of individual transactions on the open market, the firm will suffer losses. Thus the market is indispensable for the efficient organization of economic activity. It determines how much economic activity should be handled directly through the market and how much should be handed indirectly through the firm. It thereby determines the optimal size of the firm for the given conditions. Thus, in the absence of the market it would be impossible to determine whether the internal organization was or was not efficient. As Coase acknowledged (1952, p. 334), the internal organization is "related to an outside network of relative prices and costs."

The Emergence of the Modern Corporation

According to Oliver Williamson (1981, p. 1551), "the 1840s mark the beginning of a great wave of organizational change that has evolved into the modern corporation." Firms in the late-nineteenth century tended to be organized along centralized, functionally departmentalized lines. This was an improvement over the more primitive older structures. However, as firms increased in size, control over the parts by the center began to break down. As Alfred Chandler expresses it (in Anderson, McCormick, and Tollison, 1983, pp. 222–223):

> The inherent weakness in the centralized, functionally departmentalized operating company . . . became critical only when the administrative load on the senior executives increased to such an extent that they were unable to handle their entrepreneurial responsibilities efficiently. This situation arose when the operations of the enterprise became too complex and too intricate for a small number of top officers to handle both long-run entrepreneurial, and short-run operational, activities.

Many of these problems were ameliorated, if not entirely overcome, by the development of the multidivisional (or M-form) structure, pioneered in the 1920s by Pierre S. du Pont at Du Pont and Alfred S. Sloan at General Motors (Williamson, 1981, p. 1555).

The M-form divided decision-making between day-to-day operating decisions and long-run strategic decisions. The former were made at the divisional level, thereby relieving the communications overload at the center. This proved doubly efficient. By allowing operating decisions to be made by lower level managers who possessed the requisite information about particulars, it permitted a more efficient adaptation of the enterprise's operations to local conditions. And by freeing senior executives from responsibility for day-to-day details of the operation, it enabled the general office to focus on "strategic decisions, involving planning, appraisal, and control, including the allocation of resources among the (competing) operating divisions" (G. Anderson et al., 1983, p. 223). Of course, for decentralized decision-making to work effectively a way had to be found to hold in check subgoal pursuit by divisional managers. This was handled through such devices as internal auditing and the tying of the fate of the local manager to the successful performance of his "quasi-firm." As G. Anderson et al. put it (1983, p. 224), "if the manager at the divisional level in the firm has economic interests which rise or fall with the corresponding rise or fall of the value of the firm, an incentive for the provision of services leading to the former end has been provided." (Also see Mises 1969a; Niskanen, 1973, pp. 37–59.) The M-form structure began to be adopted by American firms in the 1940s, and by firms in Europe and elsewhere in the late 1960s (Williamson, 1981, p. 1556).

By facilitating decentralized decision-making but with centralized control over the parts, the multidivisional structure has permitted an enormous expansion in the size of the firm. By allocating resources between the various competing quasi-firms that comprise the corporation, the multidivisional firm "takes on many of the properties (and is usefully regarded as) a miniature capital market" (Williamson, 1981, p. 1556). These are especially important considerations for economic development.

The Functions of the Multinational

"The key institution in the world economy facilitating the transfer of prosperity from the industrialized countries to the developing ones is the multinational corporation" (Krauss, 1984, p. 126). To understand how this process of prosperity transfer takes place, and the role of the multinational in it, it is necessary to assume, for analytical purposes, a world characterized by private property and its corollaries, freedom of trade and migration—thus a world in which states either do not exist or exist as simply administrative units. In such a hypothetical situation the world becomes a single customs area, and "the distinction between foreign investment and domestic investment disappears" (Aliber, 1970, p. 21). This assumption is necessary to examine the purely economic functions of the multinational. Only after this examination can the impact of government interference with multinationals and the international economy be understood.

In such an order, capitalists and entrepreneurs, anxious to maximize profits, would transfer capital from areas where it was more plentiful relative to other factors and thus returns to capital were low, to areas where capital, and related resources such as technology and management and marketing skills, were scarce relative to labor and returns to them were correspondingly higher. Similarly, workers anxious to maximize their earnings would migrate from those areas where wages were low to those where they were higher. This process would come to an end only when both wage rates and returns to capital were equalized between areas.

The process of capital and labor migration is just what served to transform the Western world in the nineteenth century. Since Great Britain began to save and invest earlier than other nations, it had a higher standard of living than all other European countries. But "something happened which caused the headstart of Great Britain to disappear." That something was the internationalization of capital. In 1817, wrote Ludwig von Mises (1979, pp. 78–80),

> the great British economist Ricardo still took it for granted that . . . capitalists would not try to invest abroad. But a few decades later, capital investment abroad began to play a most important role in world affairs. . . . Foreign investment meant that British capitalists invested in those European countries which, from the point of view of Great Britain, were short of capital and backward in their development. It is a well known fact that the railroads of most European countries . . . were built with the aid of British capital. The gas companies in all the cities of Europe were also British. . . . In the same way British capital developed railroads and many branches of industry in the United States.

Occurring at the same time was the "great migration" of individuals from Europe, which was relatively overpopulated and in which wages were therefore low, to America, which was underpopulated and where wages were higher. This dual process of capital and labor migration would be expected to continue until equilibrium was reached, that is, until the marginal utilities of both capital and labor were equalized. This is essentially what occurred in the Western world, although to the extent that tariff and migration barriers were present, complete equalization was prevented (see, e.g., Mises, 1983, pp. 65–72; 1985, pp. 136–142). But this dual migration played a vitally important role in transforming, within the space of just a couple of centuries, a stagnant and economically backward continent into the most vibrant and economically productive area in history. There is no reason to suppose that the peoples of America and the West are *inherently* different from the peoples in other parts of the world. Therefore, *other things being equal*, this is also what one would expect to occur throughout the world. And it has, in fact, begun if not already occurred in such places as Japan, Hong Kong, Taiwan, and South Korea, to name but a few (Krauss, 1984; Rabushka, 1987a).

In brief, the process of capital and labor migration is, in fact, the process through which prosperity is created and diffused. For expansion of the scope of the market order results in a deepening of the division of labor and increased specialization, and therefore in a more efficient allocation of factors, labor as well as capital. Increasing productivity and thus expanding world output is the result. This is of tremendous benefit to the LDCs, since it is they who can least afford the squandering of scarce resources.

What function does the firm have in this process? Assume that firm A generates a new product, or a new method of production for an established product. Given such uncertainties as the dimensions of the demand for the product, the reactions of competitors whose market the new product is jeopardizing, and the possible need to adjust input mixes or to modify the product itself, it is usually vital at the early stage of what Raymond Vernon calls the "product cycle" for the firm to be located close to its intended market. "In the choice of location, flexibility and swift response were given more weight than capital and labor cost" (Vernon, 1979, p. 109). As demand for the product grows, the firm's initial response is to satisfy this demand through exports. Eventually the more distant markets may reach a size at which it becomes more economical to service them through the establishment of new production facilities in those markets than through exports from the central site. This may especially be the case when the new product starts being imitated by the firm's competitors, which makes price considerations a more urgent concern than product differentiation. The firm may, in fact, have no alternative to establishing production facilities in distant markets since, if it does not, its competitors surely will. As Vernon summarized it (1979, p. 103),

> the enterprise, having lost its oligopoly advantage, finds that it can no longer claim any cost or other advantage over its imitators, local and foreign; even its overseas subsidiaries, operating in an economic environment no different from their competitors, begin to feel the pressure. At this stage, diseconomies associated with large size and an elaborate apparatus threatened to outweigh the economies.

Thus at this point the enterprise ceases growing and may begin to retrench. It is clear that many if not most of the additional operating facilities would be located in administrative units—states—different from that of the parent firm, thereby transforming the domestic corporation into a multinational.

What makes the multinational so important in the transfer of prosperity is precisely its role in connecting the LDCs with the MDCs through international trade. As already noted, the vast extension of the market that this linkage entails facilitates the efficient utilization of resources, thereby increasing world output. But other advantages follow. The MNC can, because of its function as a miniature capital market in which transaction costs are reduced or eliminated, facilitate the transfer of capital and technology to the LDCs less expensively than they could otherwise be obtained.[1] Moreover, the tremendous advantage the transfer of capital through MNCs or capital markets has over its acquisition through foreign aid is that it is far more likely to be productively used. Just as foreign aid is, *by its nature*, inefficient, foreign direct investment (FDI) is, *by its nature*, efficient. As Bauer and Yamey have pointed out (1957, p. 143), while mistakes will be made, "those providing the capital have a continuing interest in minimizing the chances of error and in taking remedial action when necessary. Their direct interest in the success of the investment and their power to control the use of their capital persist after the initial transfer of capital has been made."

This leads to another vitally important function of the MNC, that of serving as a buffer, or risk-reducing, vehicle for LDCs. The oil price shock of 1973–1974 resulted in a massive surplus of savings in the oil-exporting countries, which were recycled to banks in developed nations. Since the recession caused by the oil price shock reduced the demand in the developed nations for investment capital, interest rates declined (Figure 7-1). And since the 1974 U.N. Resolution on the Establishment of a New International Economic Order deliberately discouraged foreign direct investment and applauded nationalizations of MNCs as the means to liberate LDCs from dependence on MDCs, the result was a massive increase in commercial lending to LDCs. Significantly, "loans to central governments and state owned enterprises were especially favored by commercial banks. Because of their sovereign status these entities were considered to be low risk. Developing countries were happy to take advantage of this unaccustomed access to cheap loans with few strings attached" (World Bank, 1988, pp. 28–29). The result of the confluence of these two factors was to reinforce the decline of FDI's share of total foreign capital flows to the LDCs, as was pointed out in Chapter 6. The problem was that the borrowing and investment decisions were "often imprudent and resulted in excessive indebtedness in a number of countries. And in a number of countries borrowings fueled a flight of capital that drained the pool of resources for investment even as the burdens of foreign debt mounted" (Whitehead, 1987; Also see World Bank, 1988, p. 29) (see Figure 7-2). The burden of debt repayment is now being shouldered by the citizens of the LDCs in the form of both higher taxes and cutbacks in services. The

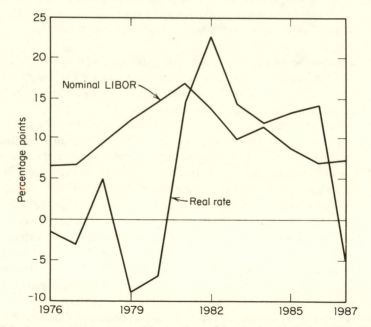

FIGURE 7-1. Interest rates on external borrowings of developing countries, 1976–1987. LIBOR = London interbank offered rate. The nominal rate is the average six-month dollar LIBOR during each year; the real rate is the nominal LIBOR deflated by the change in the export price index for developing countries. From World Bank, *World Development Report 1988,* Fig. 1.9, p. 29. Copyright © 1988 by the International Bank for Reconstruction and Development/The World Bank. Reprinted by permission of Oxford University Press, Inc.

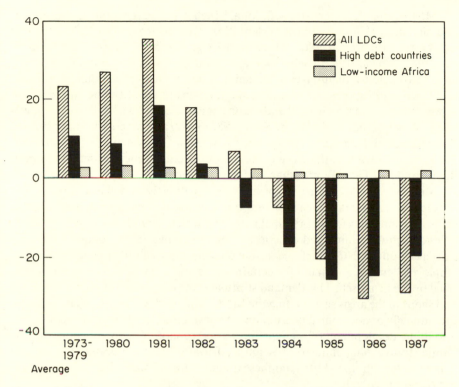

FIGURE 7-2. Net resource transfers to developing countries, 1973–1987. Net resource transfers are defined as disbursements of medium and long-term loans minus interest and amortization payments on medium and long-term external debt. From World Bank, *World Development Report 1988.* Copyright © 1988 by The International Bank for Reconstruction and Development/The World Bank. Reprinted by permission of Oxford University Press, Inc. Fig. 1.10, p. 30.

irony is that, far from liberating the LDCs, the switch from FDI to bank loans, from equity to debt, has placed the LDCs in a position of even greater dependency on the developed world.

The problem is not so much an external accounts deficit. After all, every developed country except Great Britain became developed only by borrowing from abroad. In fact, as *The Economist* (1984, pp. 15–16) pointed out, the United States in the nineteenth century was, relative to its gross domestic product, even more in debt, in terms of capital flows, than countries such as Brazil and Mexico are today. The difference, however, is twofold: (1) the flow of capital was primarily in the form of equity rather than bank loans, and (2) the flow was primarily to private investors rather than to governments. The advantage to the LDCs of allowing MNC investment in their countries is that if the MNC fails, it is the stockholders in the home country, and not, as is the case with bank loans, the citizens of the LDC, who must shoulder the loss. Thus MNCs shift the risk of investment away from the LDCs. Far from cultivating LDC dependency, MNCs are in fact liberating agents.

MNCs bring with them still additional benefits. Entrepreneurial, management, and marketing skills are, almost by definition, quite scarce in the LDCs. This may well be due primarily to cultural factors (see, e.g., Casson, 1987, pp. 56–57; Harrison, 1985; Novak, 1982; Richardson and Ahmed, 1987). But cultural traditions and customs adjust themselves to changing situations. Once the political environment ceases to suppress such skills, once it begins to reward rather than punish innovation and entrepreneurial and management talents, these skills will be developed. In fact, recent studies by de Soto (1988, 1989) and others who have studied the underground economy or the informal sector (Grossman, 1972; Zafanolli, 1985) have shown that there is a great deal more entrepreneurial activity in both the Second and Third Worlds than traditionally thought.

Moreover, the MNCs are the prime vehicles, directly as well as indirectly, not only for the transfer but, even more importantly, for the local development of these skills. The foreign firm is a principal means by which the indigenous population is able to acquire training and experience before striking out on its own. The very existence of the MNC, which means the concentration of rather large numbers of employees, creates a demand for certain goods and services that are seldom supplied by the firm itself. This demand stimulates the emergence of numerous stores and shops in the areas surrounding the MNC. The result is that the MNC, whether intentionally or not, contributes not only to developing local entrepreneurship but also to the development of such qualities as perception of economic opportunity, administrative skill, industry, discipline, frugality, and endurance (Bauer and Yamey, 1957, pp. 108–110). And these qualities are indispensable for self-sustaining economic growth.

In brief, MNCs not only transfer capital and technology but are usually able to utilize these far more efficiently than can be done by recourse to such alternative capital sources as foreign aid. Moreover, the firm, domestic or multinational, plays an important role in the process of resource allocation and indigenous skills development. And in contrast to the acquisition of capital via borrowing, MNC and foreign direct investment functions as a buffer or risk-reducing device for the LDCs.

Finally, it should be pointed out that, as is the case with any corporation, the MNC is not *inherently* beneficial. It is good only insofar as it is able to provide goods and services to people less expensively than these can be acquired elsewhere. Whether this is the case can be determined only through a market unimpeded by government restrictions.

Economic Criticisms of the Multinational

The MNC has been subjected to numerous criticisms. These criticisms relate in one way or another to the belief that MNCs, in and of themselves, retard or even prevent economic growth and development in the LDCs. An examination of the major criticisms of MNCs on purely economic grounds will help to shed further light on their operation in and impact on the LDCs. These criticisms include the following: (1) that MNCs transfer technology that is too capital intensive and thus inappropriate for the economic situation of the LDCs; (2) that the MNCs are major components of an international economic system that holds down prices and thus wages in the LDCs, thereby causing the terms of trade for the LDCs to deteriorate; (3) that MNCs pay higher salaries than can domestic competitors, thereby widening the income gap between the haves and have-nots; (4) that MNCs retard the development of local entrepreneurship by driving local firms out of business; (5) that MNCs do not transfer much capital to the LDCs but instead acquire most of their capital through local borrowing, thereby raising interest rates, squeezing local enterprises out of business, and retarding development by transferring more profits out of the LDC than they put in through investments; and (6) that MNCs jeopardize the sovereignty and independence of the LDCs and impede development by creating dependence on the MNCs, which impedes or prevents the development of local enterprises.

Each of these criticisms will be discussed in turn.

Inappropriate Technology

A common complaint against MNCs is that their investments in the LDCs are "inappropriate." While the LDCs have rapidly increasing labor forces, MNC investment, it is claimed, is capital rather than labor intensive, and thus does little or nothing to relieve the severe unemployment problems that plague these countries (Akinsanya, 1989, p. 58; Barnet and Muller, 1974, pp. 166–170; I. Frank, 1981, p. 73; Spero, 1984, p. 471). The reason usually cited is that the MNCs put profits before people.

First, the charge is not borne out by the data. A study of more than 200 manufacturing firms indicated that MNCs had a lower capital/labor ratio than their domestic counterparts (Schmidt, 1983, p. 274). Another study revealed that either there were no differences between foreign and domestic firms on this point or, "where differences are present it is the MNCs that typically show more adaptation of technology" (Pack, 1981, p. 34).

But even if the charge is true, one must ask why a company concerned solely with profits would employ expensive and sophisticated capital-intensive technologies and thus deliberately pass up the gains to be made from introducing labor-intensive technologies to take advantage of cheap labor? The answer is not hard to find. Many LDC governments have imposed minimum wage laws, prohibited the layoff of domestic workers during slack periods, or adopted other policies that increase the price of labor relative to that of capital. On the other hand, government restrictions on the importation of used machinery, coupled with host-country pressures on the MNCs to employ the most modern and sophisticated technologies, are common in the LDCs, as are overvalued exchange rates, ceilings on interest rates, and subsidies and tax breaks for the importation of capital equipment. The result is a systematic and substantial reduction in the cost of using capital. The net effect of such policies is to distort the price structure in such a way as to encourage firms operating in the LDCs, foreign as well as domestic, to employ unnecessarily complex, capital-intensive technologies (see I. Frank, 1981, pp. 76–77; Krauss, 1984, pp. 134–138; Nafziger, 1984, pp. 242–243; Pack, 1981, pp. 34–37; Ranis, 1981, p. 51).

For example, policies introduced in Peru by the government of Valesco Alvarado in the late 1960s, and which remain in effect to this day, have significantly distorted factor prices to the detriment of labor. Policies such as minimum wage rates and taxes on wages raised the real cost of labor, while other policies, including interest rate subsidies, tax exemptions on import duties, and overvalued exchange rates, reduced the cost of capital importation. As a result, the price of labor rose by 102 percent relative to the price of capital. The effect was to encourage the substitution of capital for labor, thereby reducing employment in the formal sector by nearly 40 percent. This figure, according to the World Bank (1987, p. 126), is probably an underestimate, since the effect of these distortions did not "take into account lost opportunities for exports of labor-intensive products. High labor costs reduced Peru's natural comparative advantage in these commodities." A recent World Bank study (1990, pp. 62–63) has noted that tax breaks for the importation of capital equipment, subsidized credit policies, and overvalued exchange rates artificially reduce the price of capital. This, coupled with minimum wage laws, job security laws, social security, and other "pro-labor" policies, has increased the price of labor relative to capital by 11 percent in Korea, as much as 50 percent in Argentina, Brazil, and Ivory Coast, 90 percent in Tunisia, and as much as 300 percent in Pakistan. The result has been an increase in the capital intensity of production and a reduction in the relative demand for labor. For example, studies of job securities regulations indicated that the demand for labor during the decade of the 1980s decreased by 18 percent in India and by 25 percent in Zimbabwe. To quote the World Bank (1990, p. 63), "by trying to improve the welfare of workers there, governments reduced formal sector employment, increased the supply of labor to the rural and urban informal sectors, and thus depressed labor incomes where most of the poor is found."

But government-spawned "inappropriate technology" is not solely a matter of foreign investment. Government-created factor distortions will likewise affect the investment of domestic capital. Through its policy of permitting fixed investments to be fully depreciated in the first year and then to be depreciated as much as six times over, Brazil has encouraged excessive capital investment in land. Brazil's tax policy, according to the World Bank (1990, p. 59), "encourages excessive mechanization, . . . reducing the demand for unskilled labor. . . . Opportunities for unskilled workers to acquire skills by becoming long-term workers have been substantially reduced by subsidized mechanization."

Inappropriate technology is therefore not an example of so-called market failure. It is a result of government failure. Misdiagnosing the problem as one of market failure has had significant ramifications. It has resulted in, or at least been used to justify, increased regulation of MNCs by many LDC governments. Both the U.N.'s Code of Conduct on the Transfer of Technology adopted in the early 1980s (see, e.g., McCulloch, 1981, pp. 121–122) and the Brandt Commission Report (1980, pp. 195–198) not only applaud these policies but call for increased international regulation of the MNCs in order to reduce "market imperfection." The tragedy is that since the basic cause of such market imperfections as inappropriate technology and the resulting high unemployment rates experienced by many LDCs is too much government interference in the market, additional regulation can only aggravate the very problems it was designed to solve. The only way to discover which technology is appropriate for any given LDC is for LDC governments to cease distorting the price structures in their countries by abandoning their interventionist measures and permitting the price mechanism of the market to perform its function of indicating relative scarcities.

Deteriorating Terms of Trade

Another common complaint is that the LDCs face deteriorating terms of trade, that is, that the prices of primary products fall relative to manufactured goods and, since LDCs are exporters of the former and importers of the latter, they must constantly produce more and more simply to remain where they are. Barnet and Muller have written (1974, p. 136) that the industrialized nations

> have used their technological and marketing superiority to obtain terms of trade which, not surprisingly, favor them at the expense of their weaker trading partners in the underdeveloped world. Thus, over the past twenty-five years, until the 1970s, because of the falling relative price of certain essential raw materials the countries of the underdeveloped world have had to exchange an ever increasing amount of such raw materials to get the finished goods and technological expertise they need. This steady worsening of the terms of trade between the rich countries and the poor is an important reason why the "gap" between them has continued to grow.

MNCs are important components in this process since they "control many of the most important export commodities of developing countries" (Akinsanya, 1989, p. 56).

The argument dates from the works of economists Raul Prebisch and Hans Singer in 1950. Their studies show that the ratio of the prices of primary commodities relative to manufactured goods declined from 100 for the period 1876–1880 to 64.1 for the period 1936–1938 (Cole, 1986, p. 32, Table 1).

There are numerous problems, statistical as well as theoretical, with the argument that there is an inherent tendency for the terms of trade for the LDCs to deteriorate. First, Prebisch's findings were generalized from data restricted to Great Britain, and their validity therefore depends on whether the British data are representative of all industrialized countries. Estimates by Charles Kindleberger, which show a modest 19 percent improvement in the terms of trade for the industrial European countries between 1900 and 1938 in contrast to Prebisch's 34 percent improvement for England during the same period, suggest that they are not (Cole, p. 32). Second, the available data, although scanty, show that the British terms of trade steadily declined throughout the first half of the nineteenth century and reached their nadir in the 1860–1880 period, precisely the period Prebisch chose as the base years for his study. Thus the choice of the base years biased Prebisch's results against the primary commodity exporting countries. Third, "the basic British export price index is on a F.O.B. (free on board) basis, while import prices are measured C.I.F. (cost, insurance and freight), that is, including transportation charges." Since freight rates declined by 50 percent between 1870 and 1913, this alone accounts for much and perhaps *all* of the decline in British import prices during the period. In fact, concludes Cole (1986, p. 33), "since the prices of British manufactured exports declined by 15 percent, the terms of trade of primary producing countries," far from declining, "may well have *improved* over that period."

There are further difficulties. The quality of primary goods like copper, iron ore, and cotton remains about the same. But that of such manufactured goods as tractors, automobiles, and computers has undergone tremendous improvement over the years. Failure to account for new products and quality improvements in existing manufactured goods introduces a serious upward statistical bias in the reporting of the prices of manufactured goods (Bauer, 1972, p. 242).

Further, it should be noted that while an improvement in the commodity terms of trade can be interpreted as an improvement in national welfare, the reverse is not necessarily true. It is quite possible for national welfare to improve simultaneously with a deterioration in the terms of trade. What is crucial is not the price of a good exported relative to the price of a good imported. Rather, it is the *cost* of the good exported, that is, the sum of the factor prices, relative to the *price* of the good imported. Thus, since the price of copper declined from $1.10 per pound in 1975 to $0.76 per pound in 1985, the commodity terms of trade for copper exporters have, assuming stable import prices, deteriorated by over 25 percent. But if the *cost* of manufacturing that copper has fallen from, say, $1.00 to $0.50 per pound, the profit or foreign exchange a LDC would earn from the sale of the same amount of copper would be much higher in 1985 than it was a decade earlier ($0.10 per pound in 1975; $0.26 per pound in 1985). It is obvious that a LDC could import more goods in 1985 than in 1975 even with deteriorating terms of trade. This is just what has happened in much of the Third World. Because of improvements in transportation and in the introduction of newer production techniques, usually through the MNCs, the cost of producing such goods as cocoa, sugar, rubber, and many other primary products has dramatically declined (Bauer, 1972, p. 241; Haberler, 1968, p. 329; Lewis, 1965, pp. 1–16; Vernon, 1977, pp. 2–3). Since the same line of reasoning applies to wage rates, deteriorating terms of trade are also consistent with rising real wages. The key fact is that nearly *everyone* pays less for food, shelter, *and* clothing today than he or she did in, say, 1900. This is because the economic pie has been increasing more rapidly than population. True, the improvement has tended to be less rapid for the LDCs than the MDCs. But, of course, that is what is meant by the term *less developed country.*

Moreover, the thesis is based on the assumption that LDCs are solely exporters of primary products while developed countries are solely exporters of manufactured goods. This may have been largely true in the first half of the century but certainly no longer holds. Singapore, Hong Kong, Taiwan, South Korea, and Brazil have all become major exporters of electronic equipment such as TVs and radios. And automobile production has recently been increasing at a yearly rate of 14 percent in Brazil and nearly 10 percent in Mexico, compared with only 4.4 percent in the United States and 3.4 percent in Britain. The Philippines, South Korea, and Malaysia are quietly becoming major producers of automobiles (Godsell, 1988; Kimball, 1980; Lall, 1983; Samuels, 1990, p. 6; Spanier, 1981, p. 372). In fact, as Leff has observed (1983, p. 246), "Multinational corporations with 'sourcing' subsidiaries located in the Third World have had a large role in this expansion of manufactured exports from developing countries." Conversely, MDCs like the United States are major exporters of agricultural products or, in the case of Canada, major exporters of raw materials.

Finally, even if the Prebisch–Singer thesis were logically valid, it is difficult to see how it could account for the poverty of the poorest of the LDCs. They have so little trade with other countries that changes in the terms of trade, regardless of direction, would have a negligible impact.

Given the statistical and theoretical problems of the Prebisch–Singer thesis, one would not expect it to explain the data. It does not. As Table 7-1 shows, the commodity terms of trade for the LDCs improved by 23 percent during the period 1937–1959. As for the post-1959 period (Table 7-2), the terms of trade for both Latin American exports as a whole and Latin American exports of primary products were stable up to 1970. They showed significant fluctuations during the 1970s and early 1980s, due no doubt to the oil crisis. But overall the data show no indication of systematic, long-term deterioration. This is especially the case in view of the fact that the data have not been adjusted for quality changes and other biases (Cole, 1986, pp. 13–14).

Despite its shortcomings, the Prebisch–Singer thesis is regarded by many as true. This is tragic, since if trade with the MDCs is harmful to the LDCs as the thesis suggests, it follows that the LDCs would be better off severing their ties with the MDCs. The Prebisch–Singer thesis thus leads logically to a policy of protectionism and economic autarky. But protectionism most harms the countries practicing it. Withdrawing from the world market means that a country must produce what it needs within its own borders. This in turn means that the country must divert factors to use in the production of goods that were previously imported. But since the only reason these goods were not produced domestically in the first place is because they could be purchased more cheaply from abroad, the factors are diverted from areas where they were used more productively into areas where they are utilized less productively. The basic problem is that "the use of protection to promote substi-

TABLE 7-1.   Terms of Trade, 1937–1959 (1937 = 100)

Year	Underdeveloped Countries	Latin America
1937	100	100
1948	108	123
1951	160	138
1954	128	139
1957	127	128
1959	123	110

Source: Cole, 1986, p. 33. Reprinted by permission of *Journal of Economic Growth.*

TABLE 7-2.   Terms of Trade for Latin America, 1959–
1983 (1970 = 100)

Year	Total	Non-oil	Primary Products
1959	102	—	108
1960	102	—	106
1961	100	—	101
1962	94	—	98
1963	95	—	105
1964	97	—	109
1965	93	—	105
1966	95	—	105
1967	93	—	98
1968	95	—	98
1969	96	—	102
1970	100	100	100
1971	97	—	90
1972	100	—	93
1973	113	—	124
1974	131	—	130
1975	114	82	95
1976	119	—	105
1977	126	98	117
1978	113	—	98
1979	117	82	100
1980	121	—	98
1981	110	66	88
1982	101	—	80
1983	94	—	88

Source: Cole, 1986, p. 33. Reprinted by permission of *Journal of Economic Growth.*

tution of local for foreign production does nothing to reduce the comparative disadvantage of local as contrasted with foreign entrepreneurship" (H. Johnson, 1968, pp. 371–375). For example, since it is often the case, especially in the LDCs, that the domestic market for a good is too small to permit the exploitation of economies of scale, the costs of production are inordinately high.

Thus, although protection may artificially stimulate industrialization, industrialization should not be confused with development. It usually correlates with development because on the free market new technologies are introduced only when they reduce costs by increasing output per unit of input. Such is not the case with protectionism. Since what has occurred is a shifting of resources from more to less productive uses, the result is that everyone, except perhaps the domestic producers of the good, is less well off. Moreover, a policy of protectionism or import substitution requires a great deal of governmental interference. And as the domestic economy becomes politicized, effort is diverted from the production of wealth to its transfer. The reduction in output means that the country is now poorer than it otherwise would have been.

This argument is consistent with the data. Figures 7-3 and 7-4 show that those

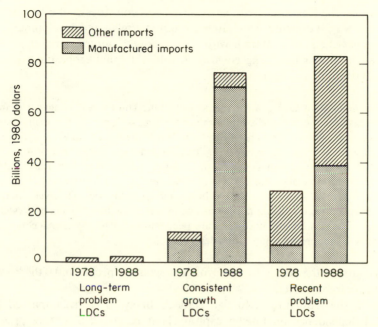

FIGURE 7-3. U.S. imports from LDCs. From USAID, 1989, p. 76. Reprinted by permission.

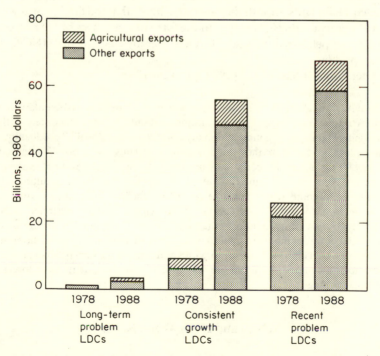

FIGURE 7-4. U.S. exports to LDCs. From USAID, 1989, p. 76. Reprinted by permission.

LDCs having the least trade with such developed countries as the United States have had the most difficulty generating economic growth and development, while those that have had the most trade with the developed countries have also been the most successful at stimulating consistent, self-sustaining economic growth. As Bauer has pointed out (1981, p. 70),

> Far from the West having caused the poverty in the Third World, contact with the West has been the principal agent of material progress there. The materially more advanced societies and regions of the Third World are those with which the West established the most numerous, diversified and extensive contacts: the cash-crop producing areas and entrepot ports of South-East Asia, West Africa and Latin America; the mineral producing areas of Africa and the Middle East; and cities and ports throughout Asia, Africa, the Caribbean and Latin America. The level of material achievement usually diminishes as one moves away from the foci of Western impact. The poorest and most backward people have few or no external contacts; witness the aborigines, pygmies and desert people.

This, of course, is the exact reverse of what one would expect to find if the Prebisch–Singer thesis were correct.

Finally, the reduction in foreign trade is likely to be accompanied by an increased dependence on foreign capital. That is, goods that were previously obtained via imports must now be produced locally. If the country is not able to do this on its own, it must entice foreign firms to construct plants in its country. But this *must* mean a misallocation of resources, since otherwise the MNC would have constructed such plants prior to the tariff. It is likely that the foreign firm will now demand a "compensating advantage" in the form of guarantees by the host country to keep out competitors, domestic or foreign, thereby enabling the MNC to obtain monopoly profits.

As Peter Drucker has written (1974, pp. 128–129):

> The multinational's capacity to allocate production across national boundary lines and according to the logic of the world market should . . . be a major ally of the developing countries. The more rationally and the more "globally" production is being allocated, the more they stand to gain. . . . Thus, the most advantageous strategy for the developing countries would seem to be to replace—or at least supplement—the policy of "domestic content" by a policy that uses the multinationals' integrating ability to develop large production facilities with access to markets in the developed world. . . . As Taiwan and Singapore have demonstrated, it can make much more sense to become the most efficient large supplier worldwide of one model or one component than to be a high-cost small producer of the entire product or line. This would create more jobs and provide the final product at lower prices to the country's own consumers. And it would result in large foreign-exchange earnings.

MNCs and High Wage Rates

It is true that in the LDCs the wage rates paid by the MNCs tend to be higher than those of domestic firms. This, argue critics of the MNCs, widens the income gap between the elite and masses, thereby creating polarization and social conflict between economic classes in the LDCs (Akinsanya, 1989, p. 58; Nafziger, 1984, p. 242).

In contrast with the terms-of-trade critique, which maintains that MNCs exploit workers by holding prices and wages down, this argument criticizes the MNCs for paying above domestic market levels. However, so long as the higher incomes of the MNC employees are a result of wealth creation rather than redistribution of existing wealth, the presence of the MNC, *even by the logic of the critique*, constitutes a welfare gain for the domestic economy: some are made better off while no one is made worse off. It is hard to understand why anyone would oppose such a phenomenon except on the grounds of envy.

Of course the process does not stop there. The higher income of those working for the MNC increases their purchasing power, which thereby generates additional demand for goods and services. Many of these can be supplied, or can *only* be supplied, locally. This additional local demand therefore opens up wealth opportunities for other segments of the population. This is precisely what Krauss meant by the transfer of prosperity. The creation of new wealth sets in motion a self-sustaining process by which additional wealth is created and *diffused* throughout the society. The MNCs play a vital role in this process. To focus solely on its initial phase is to misrepresent entirely the nature of the market process.

MNCs and Local Businesses

Another criticism is that MNCs are so large and powerful that local firms cannot compete and are either driven out of business or bought out by the MNCs (Akinsanya, 1989, p. 55; Barnet and Muller, 1974, p. 139; I. Frank, 1981, pp. 43–44; Hymer, 1970, pp. 444–45). This, it is alleged, not only results in foreign-owned monopolies but also impedes or prevents economic growth in the LDCs by retarding the acquisition of entrepreneurial and other skills needed for self-sustaining economic growth.

It is true that local businesses are sometimes "smothered" by the entry of a MNC. But the conclusions usually drawn from this do not follow. If a foreign-owned enterprise is able to offer enough to buy out a locally owned firm, *both parties* must believe that the MNC is able to utilize those assets more productively than the local firm. If this is correct, then resources are transferred from those using them less productively to those who are able to use them more productively. This is clearly a benefit to the local economy. The same is no less true for local firms driven into bankruptcy. For the government to stimulate local businesses by protecting them from competition rewards inefficiency and harms local consumers who must pay higher prices, either directly or indirectly in the form of subsidies, for the products they buy.

Moreover, insulating inefficient firms from competition is hardly the way to foster entrepreneurial and other business skills. As already mentioned, far from inhibiting the development of local entrepreneurship, it is precisely through the foreign-owned firm that such skills are best developed. Frank (pp. 87–88) has noted that the data show that a "substantial majority of managerial positions in subsidiaries are held by nationals." This is because "it is very costly to transport and maintain foreign managers and their families. Moreover, foreign assignments may take an executive out of the mainstream of career development." Where "indigenous personnel are not experienced enough to run the operation," the MNCs will have no choice but to send in foreign executives at least on a temporary basis. Frank quotes one executive as saying: "When we send in a foreign manager, we hope he will do himself out of a job."

Finally, it is not true that local businesses cannot compete with MNCs. Local businesses often have advantages such as a better knowledge of the market or lower overhead costs that will enable them to be quite competitive. Ghanaian economist George Ayittey has observed (1988b) that "many native [African] businessmen, despite their lack of capital and managerial skills, competed successfully with European firms." But even where the MNC does achieve a monopoly by buying up or bankrupting local firms, this may still not harm the local consumers. Not only do excessive profits correct themselves by attracting new entrants, domestic or foreign, but

> while direct investment may gobble up competitors and exploit its monopolistic advantages, its main impact is in widening the area of competition. Domestic markets are protected, if not by tariffs, at least by distance, ignorance, lethargy. The small, inefficient domestic producer is typically more of a monopolist than the large, monopolistically competitive wide-ranging firm. Such a domestic market thrives on high prices and low volume. . . . The cost advantages of the intruder are so great, even when its conduct is not aggressively competitive, that prices are reduced, volumes expanded, and the monopolistic phenomenon extends the area of competition.   (Kindleberger, 1979, p. 104)

In brief, the presence of the MNC increases rather than reduces competition and the efficient utilization of local resources. It also stimulates rather than retards the acquisition of entrepreneurial and other business skills by the indigenous population.

MNCs and Local Capital

Yet another criticism is that much of the capital used by the MNCs is obtained locally, thereby providing little if any additional capital. In fact, since much of the profit obtained by the MNC is taken out of the country, the result is that the MNCs actually drain the LDCs of their wealth. Barnet and Muller, for example, contend (1974, p. 135) that the activity of the multinationals is little more than

> a process of wealth depletion which has resulted inevitably in lower consumption for the local population. The net outflow of finance capital from the underdeveloped societies weakened their capacity to develop the knowledge to produce wealth, and thus further decreased their bargaining power.

This, like many of the other criticisms of the MNCs, misunderstands the nature of the economic process. First, it should be noted that the inhospitable environment, especially the ever-present possibility of nationalization by the LDC governments, deters the inflow of capital from abroad. One estimate has placed the uncompensated losses from expropriation at $6 billion in the postwar period (Schmidt, 1983, p. 276). Obviously, MNCs do not like to have their assets nationalized; their losses are significantly reduced if the expropriated factory was built with funds borrowed locally.

Second, and more importantly, the real issue is not whether the capital used by the MNCs was imported from abroad or borrowed locally. The real issue is whether it is efficiently used. As Bauer and Yamey have noted (1957, p. 114), often one of the essential problems in the LDCs is not the shortage of capital but the inefficiency with which a large part of the available capital is used. If foreign investors borrow capital locally, they believe that they are able to use that capital more productively than local borrowers. Once again, if they are correct the result is an expansion of local output and a rising local standard of living. If they are wrong their firms go bankrupt and the capital is again available to local borrowers. As Glade has observed (1987, p. 1900), the common complaint that "in some given period the outward flow of interest and profit exceeds the current inward capital flows," like the related criticism that "a portion of the interest or profits eventually remitted to the home office constitutes a foreign exchange 'drain' for which no offsetting initial inflow of capital was ever received," simply ignores "what exactly is done with the capital in between inflow and outflow: that is, the use of investment to expand productive capacity, with a possible saving on imports or an increase in exports."

Finally, far from squeezing out local investors, the use of local capital by the MNCs has actually had the opposite effect. This is so for two reasons. The increased demand for local capital causes interest rates to rise. This in turn stimulates increased local saving. And second, once the profitability of an investment has been demonstrated and the environment has been shown to be relatively safe for saving and investment, additional entrepreneurs in need of additional capital will be attracted. As a result, not only will foreign capital begin to flow into the country, but capital flight, which plagues so many LDCs, would cease to be a problem (Bauer and Yamey, 1957, pp. 133–134; Glade, 1987, pp. 1900–1901; Krauss, 1984, p. 129).

MNCs and Sovereignty

According to many of their critics, perhaps the most serious problem with the MNCs is that they undermine national sovereignty. Akinsanya (1989, p. 58) says that "MNCs are beyond national control; they constitute *imperium in imperio* and thus undermine the territorial nation state." Hymer (1970, pp. 446–447) referred to the "great disparity between the bargaining power of the corporation and the bargaining power of the government." He believed that one of the most "serious problems" of the MNCs is that "they reduce the ability of the government to control the economy."

First of all, it is doubtful that MNCs have seriously undermined the sovereignty of the nation-state. Much, of course, depends on the bargaining positions of the two parties, and that will vary from case to case. However, the scenario commonly used to demonstrate the inferior bargaining position of the state vis-à-vis the MNC is that of a single state with few or even no options and a MNC with numerous options. Thus the MNC is presented as being in a position to present the state with a take-it-or-leave-it proposition (see, e.g., Hymer, 1970, p. 447). But this is hardly the typical situation. There are now approximately 170 sovereign nations; the number of MNCs has been placed at 10,000 (Hughes, 1991, p. 362). If anything, the bargaining strength would seem to lie with the nation-state rather than the MNC.

But more importantly, one must ask just what is wrong with undermining the ability of the government to control the economy? Government control of the economy is probably the principal obstacle to economic development in today's world. Therefore, as Krauss has put it (1984, p. 129), "to the extent that the multinationals help control governments by inducing competition between them, they render the public a valuable service." Probably the only reason this is not more widely recognized is the common failure to distinguish between the freedom of a nation-state and the freedom of its people. There is no necessary connection between the two, as the situation in Africa should make evident. As Ayittey has made clear, the political independence of black Africa went hand in hand with the subjection of large numbers of black Africans. As the countries of Africa became free, many of the new leaders used their new-found freedom to enslave their subjects (see Ayittey, 1985, 1987a).

On this issue, one can only hope that the critics are correct.

Government and the Multinational

A method often used by critics to illustrate the economic power of the MNCs is to compare their gross incomes with the GNPs of various countries. One recent list (Kegley, Wittkopf, and Rawls, 1984, pp. 275–277) shows that the gross sales of British Petroleum are equal to the GNP of Algeria; that the income of Volvo is about the same size as the GNP of Bangladesh, and that Standard Oil's income is roughly equal to the size of the economy of Malaysia. But just what do these figures mean?

PepsiCo operates in well over 100 countries. Does it really make any sense to compare the total value of all economic activity inside one country with the gross sales from a single, often very narrow, type of activity, say, the production of one brand of soft drink in a multitude of countries scattered around the world? Comparing the GNP of a country with the gross income of a MNC makes about as much sense as comparing apples with kangaroos. The two are so different that any comparison is meaningless.

The point of such comparisons is to show that the MNCs are too powerful; that they have become so large that governments can no longer control them. Ranis, for example, refers (1976, p. 106) to the "undoubtedly correct accusation that the MNC . . . has unprecedented power, unchallenged by either the LDC governments or Developed Country governments." And Hymer (1970, p. 448) has bluntly stated that "in a word, the multinational corporation reveals the power of size and the danger of leaving it uncontrolled." This argument clearly assumes that, *regardless of the nature of the institution,* size confers power. It is also based on the subsidiary assumptions that the market is not an effective mechanism for regulating the activities of the MNC, and that to keep them in check, governments must become even more powerful. None of these assumptions hold.

MNCs and Size

First, the prevalent view of the multinational as a giant monster corporation is not borne out by the data. According to a recent U.N. report (see *The Economist,* 1988, p. 73), only 600 companies have annual sales in excess of $1 billion and half of all multinationals are in fact small to medium-sized operations. Twenty-three percent of all Japanese MNCs employ fewer than 300 people; nearly 80 percent of all British multinationals have fewer than 500 employees.

MNCs and Power

Second, governments are centers of power. Many obtain labor services through conscription; all obtain revenue through taxation. Firms, however, are purely *voluntary* institutions. They can neither conscript nor tax. They can merely offer their goods and services for sale. This applies not just to consumers but to laborers and factor suppliers as well. Any firm that fails to produce what consumers want to buy at prices they are willing to pay will lose its customers to other firms. Any firm trying to underpay its employees or factor suppliers will lose them to other firms. The MNC is nothing more than a firm. The fact that it does business in more than one country does not alter the nature of the process. It is a mistake to assume that *on the free market* ownership confers power. It is not the owners but the consumers, by their buying and abstention from buying, who really control the activities of the firm.

A common criticism of MNCs is that their often close relationship with the governments of the world does, in fact, enable them to acquire monopolistic positions by influencing governments to pass laws or adopt policies insulating them from competition. They are then able to exploit workers by paying below-free-market wages and consumers by charging above-free-market prices.

There is a good deal of truth to this charge. The relationship between governments and MNCs is a complicated one. And these relationships may alter the very nature of the MNC investment by changing it from a positive to a zero-sum operation. First, a MNC may attempt to pressure the host government in order to receive special privileges, such as tax exemptions and subsidies, or licensing restrictions and tariffs, thereby protecting it from competition. It may do this either through lobbying, bribery, or veiled threats to locate elsewhere. This should hardly be surprising. Contrary to the usual Chamber of Commerce rhetoric regarding the glories of free enterprise, businesses are not particularly fond of competition. Far from favoring open entry, businesses have often been at the forefront of attempts to get the government to "rationalize" the economy through the imposition of regulations restricting entry and thus competition (see, e.g., Kolko, 1977; Radosh and Rothbard, 1972). This does not change merely because a firm crosses a political boundary.

But there is no reason that such questionable practices have to originate with the MNC. It would be surprising if there were not at least some highly placed host-country government officials who have used their positions to obtain special advantages for themselves, that is, to extort MNCs for their own benefits.

There is a variety of questionable payments. Two types of payments originating from the MNC are intended to influence public officials in the host county: "grease" and bribery. Grease is so-named because its purpose is to lubricate, or facilitate, certain government activities. Grease payments normally go to low-level government employees and are typically small bribes—gratuities—intended to get the government employee either to perform his or her duties or at least to perform them expeditiously. These duties include obtaining work permits, visas, licenses, customs clearances, police protection, hotel accommodations, appointments with public officials, and a host of other services. But grease may also be used to get local officials to look the other way, to shirk their duties, or to ignore certain regulations, thereby enabling the MNC to conduct certain types of illegal business operations or at least to conduct them at a lower cost. Examples include payments by the MNC to allow it to evade customs duties or to circumvent various tariff restrictions on imports. Gladwin and Walter (1980, p. 299) reported that while grease accounts for about 95 percent of all questionable payments made by the MNCs, the dollar amount is probably less than 25 percent of the total.

Bribery is the payment of large sums of money, or their equivalent, to high-ranking government officials. The purpose is to obtain benefits that lower level officials are not in a position to grant. These include such things as the acquisition of contracts, tax concessions, import as well as export exemptions, and changes in the laws and policies of the host country (Gladwin and Walter, 1980, p. 299). While cash is the most common form of payment, other forms are not unheard of. Examples might include a gift of a Mercedes Benz, jobs for the official's relatives or friends, or free vacations on the Riviera.

Finally, there is blackmail or extortion, where the questionable practice originates at the receiving end. Blackmail would include such things as threats to renege on existing or potential contracts, to nationalize or expropriate the company, or even to harm or kill MNC officials, if the demands are not met (Gladwin and Walter, p. 300).

Since both bribery and extortion are illegal, it is probably impossible to determine just how common such practices are. However, available information suggests that they are fairly common. Investigations of MNC activities in such countries as the United States, Canada, Venezuela, Spain, Germany, Switzerland, Greece, Iran, and Egypt have resulted in massive revelations about the illegal activities of the MNCs. They have led to the arrest and trial of former Japanese Prime Minister Kakuei Tanaka, the resignation of Giovanni Leone, President of Italy, and the overthrow of the head of Honduras, General Oswaldo Lopez Arella. They have also resulted in the demotion or dismissal of over a hundred corporate officials as well as the suicide of a few top executives such as Eli Black, Chairman of the Board of United Brands (Gladwin and Walter, p. 297). A 1974 U.N. report indicated that "more than 100 United States MNCs have engaged in these practices [large-scale bribery such as the paying of large commissions or giving gifts to government leaders or their families] to the tune of millions of dollars a year" (Feld, 1980, p. 32). And investigations by the U.S. Securities and Exchange Commission disclosed that American-based MNCs had made in excess of $1 billion in "questionable payments" (Gladwin and Walter, 1980, pp. 297,299). As investigations in other countries show, such activities are not limited to MNCs based in the United States (Feld, p. 32).

There is also clear evidence that government officials have used their positions to extract benefits for themselves from the MNCs. Consequences for refusing to pay range from outright expropriation to physical harm and even death. For example, Ashland Oil was forced to pay $190,000 to two government officials in Gabon to satisfy "two outstanding obligations" of highly questionable validity. Haitian government officials attempted to extort $250,000 from Translinear, Inc. following the firm's $3 million investment in a port facility there. When the firm refused, the project was terminated. And Gulf Oil was forced to pay $4 million to the Democratic Republican Party of South Korea. The party's finance chairman, S. K. Kim, subjected Gulf's Chairman Bob Dorsey to "severe personal abuse" and, according to Dorsey, "left little to the imagination if the company would choose to turn its back on this request" (Gladwin and Walter, 1980, p. 300). On a far less dramatic scale, grease payments may often be more in the nature of extortion than bribery. Most low-level government officials in the Third World are badly paid. The expectation is that they will use their positions to augment their income. Thus, bribes are often a sine qua non to get them to perform their duties. Although it is difficult to prove, the same is probably true of many tariffs, licensing restrictions, and other interferences with the market process: they are created to elicit bribes for their circumvention.

Not surprisingly, studies by, for example, Freedom House, show that bribes and extortion payments are concentrated in those countries with the most centralized and authoritarian political structures.

> In "less free" settings MNEs [multinational enterprises] confront governments that hold essentially unlimited power. Civil servants are vested with discretionary authority to grant or withhold permits for almost any kind of commercial activity. Those at the seat of power see themselves as dispensers of privileges and exceptions, and the ordinary workings of political processes or free market cannot be relied upon to safeguard legitimate business interests. Constantly threatened with governmental interference in business affairs or afraid of worse things to come, MNEs are moved to dispense "good will" or yield to extortion to protect themselves. And on top of this are the inevitable grease or whitemail payments, based on political and social connections necessary to obtain favorable treatment. (Gladwin and Walter, 1980, p. 308)

What can be said of these questionable practices? Where the economy is rigidly controlled and changes in government personnel or policies can mean the difference between continued operation and bankruptcy or even expropriation, access to those determining policy is merely prudent business practice. Further, by facilitating the flow of resources, such practices can serve to stimulate economic growth and development. However, when access is used to go beyond this and enters the realm of extracting such special privileges as tariffs or licensing restrictions, it impedes rather than facilitates the operation of the free market and therefore becomes an obstacle to economic development.

There is also a more subtle, and for that reason a more pernicious, method by which MNCs manage to use the political process to secure huge profits at the expense of the LDCs. Many MNCs have, for example, become ardent proponents of foreign aid. This is because much of foreign aid is "tied," which means that the recipient LDC must use the money to purchase products from companies in the donor country. This enables the MNCs to raise their prices for recipient country purchasers well above market prices. Markups of 30 percent are common and even 50 percent markups are not unheard of (Hancock, 1989, p. 162). But not only are products overpriced, they are often of poor quality or simply unsuited to the needs of the recipient country. For example, Great Britain extended nearly 2 million pounds in aid to Zambia to improve its transportation system. Since the aid was tied, Zambia had to use it to purchase 50 buses from British manufacturers. British Leyland provided the chassis parts and Willowbrook International supplied the bodies. Within a few months the bodywork had deteriorated beyond repair, and shortly after that the same thing happened with the chassis. While the two English companies benefited handsomely, the losers were the taxpayers in both England, who paid for the aid, and Zambia, who had to pay for expensive maintenance and repairs in a futile attempt to keep the buses going (Hancock, p. 164). Similarly, a 10 million pound subsidy was extended to Egypt by the British aid agencies to help out Rolls-Royce. Rolls-Royce was eventually paid 28 million pounds to supply Egypt with gas turbines for generating electricity. The turbines have proven very expensive to operate and, according to one commentator (Hancock, p. 163), "represent a real and on-going burden to Egypt." Cheaper and more appropriate alternatives were available but were not even considered by the aid authorities. This is hardly surprising, since the proposal originated with Rolls-Royce.

These examples could be multiplied many times. They certainly help to explain the animosity so many in the LDCs have toward MNCs. What needs to be pointed out, however, is that the only reason MNCs have been able to get away with providing such shoddy products and services is that the nature of the foreign aid process systematically excludes any direct connection between the company and the "customer," and such a connection is necessary to keep the firm responsive to the needs of its clients. The projects are worked out between the aid agencies in the donor countries, the rulers in the recipient counties, and the MNCs. The "official" beneficiaries in the recipient countries are seldom even consulted on the projects, nor are those footing much of the bill for the projects: the taxpayers in the donor countries. There can be no doubt about the response of the citizens of Peru if asked if they would voluntarily pay for the construction of a road, if they knew that the policy of the contractors was, when meeting an obstacle such as a river, simply to stop at one side and begin again on the other (Hancock, p. 148). And how many Ghanaians would have voluntarily supported the construction of a mango-canning plant whose capacity exceeds the entire world trade in mangoes (Ayittey, 1987c, p. 212)?

The coalition of the MNC, the LDC governments, and the aid agencies in the developed countries enables all three to benefit. The MNCs are able to make huge profits at little risk, since they are paid by the taxpayers in both the LDCs and the donor countries; the elites in the LDCs benefit, since the normal "leakage" (official jargon for theft by high-level government officials) tends to run at between 10 and 20 percent of the total aid package (Hancock, 1989, pp. 174–183); and the aid agency officials in the donor countries benefit, since the more aid they dispense, the faster they are promoted. Ironically, the only losers, it seems, are the official beneficiaries in the LDCs, that is, the customers of the MNCs, and the tax-paying citizens in the developed countries who shoulder a large part of the cost.

Finally, there is the relationship between the MNC and the government of the home country. Harry Magdoff, for example, has stated (1976, p. 207) that "the pervasive military presence of the United States around the globe, the strength of this military power, and the design of the imperial world order under U.S. leadership" have benefited the MNCs by opening "doors in advanced as well as underdeveloped countries" and by inspiring "confidence in foreign investors—most especially, of course, in U.S. business interests—about the security of their overseas investments." There is more than a kernel of truth in this statement. In a very famous comment, Major General Smedley Butler of the U.S. Marine Corps said in 1931:

> I helped make Mexico safe for American oil interests in 1914. I helped make Haiti and Cuba a decent place for the National Bank boys to collect revenue in. I helped purify Nicaragua for the international banking house of Brown Brothers.... I brought light to the Dominican Republic for American sugar interests in 1916. I helped make Honduras "right" for American fruit companies in 1903. Looking back on it I might have given Al Capone a few hints.   (Richman, 1982, p. 21)

More recently, the interventions by the Central Intelligence Agency (CIA) or the American military have benefited U.S. MNCs. In 1954, for example, the CIA engineered the overthrow of the recently elected government of Jacobo Arbenz Guzman in Guatemala, who had expropriated 160,000 acres of land belonging to United Fruit. Arbenz was replaced by Colonel Castillo Armas, who quickly restored the land to United Fruit. Interestingly, Allen Dulles, the head of the CIA, was a former president of United Fruit; his brother, Secretary of State John Foster Dulles, was not only a stockholder in the company but his law firm had handled United Fruit's legal affairs. And the Assistant Secretary of State, John Moors Cabot, was also a major stockholder (LaFeber, 1989, pp. 517–520; Swomley, 1970, pp 153–157).

The 1965 intervention in the Dominican Republic bears striking similarities to that in Guatemala. A new constitution prohibited large land holdings, required landowners to sell all land in excess of the legal maximum, and restricted the amount of land foreigners could acquire. In May 1965, the Organization of American States (OAS), an inter-American security association, sent a 23,000-man military force into the Dominican Republic. The force was dominated by the United

States and was ordered in at the insistence of United States President Lyndon Johnson with the objective of removing President Juan Bosch, one of the principal architects of the constitution. It is probably more than a coincidence that several of Johnson's closest advisers had significant economic interests in the Dominican Republic. These included Abe Fortas, who had been on the board of directors of Sucrest, a large sugar refinery heavily dependent on sugar from the Dominican Republic; Adolf Berle, formerly Chairman of the Board of Sucrest; Ellsworth Bunker, former President of the National Sugar Refining Corporation, and "molasses magnate" J. M. Kaplan (Swomley, pp. 157–165).

But undoubtedly the best known story is the ITT-CIA role in undermining the government of Dr. Salvador Allende in Chile in the early 1970s. Allende, a self-proclaimed Marxist who made no secret of his intentions to nationalize Chilteco, a subsidiary of ITT, was the favorite to win the November 1970 presidential election. John McCone, a director of ITT and a former director of the CIA who was still a consultant to that agency, expressed his concern about Allende to the then head of the CIA, Richard Helms, and later to the Special Assistant to the President for National Security Affairs, Henry Kissinger. What followed was a systematic and massive attempt first to prevent the election of Allende and, when that failed, to undermine Allende's presidency by generating economic chaos. In its report on its investigation of the affair, the U.S. Senate acknowledged that the "company's concern was perfectly understandable," as was "its desire to communicate that concern to the appropriate officials of the U.S. Government and to seek their judgment as to how the United States would view the possible eventuality of a seizure of company property without adequate compensation." But, it continued, "what is not to be condoned is that the highest officials of the ITT sought to engage the CIA in a plan covertly to manipulate the outcome of the Chilean presidential election. In so doing the company overstepped the line of acceptable corporate behavior" (U.S. Senate, 1979, p. 242). These strictures seem reasonable. For, as the Senate report later notes, morality aside, such activities "are incompatible with the long-term existence of multinational corporations," since "no sovereign nation would be willing to accept the specter of foreign intervention" in any dispute between a MNC and the host government "as the price of permitting foreign corporations to invest in its territory" (p. 242).[2]

Home government interventions on behalf of MNCs are the exception rather than the rule. Numerous companies have been expropriated by many different countries. The vast majority have not precipitated such intervention (Spanier, 1981, pp. 411–412). Intervention has occurred only when additional special considerations have been present. That is, it has occurred only when, to cite the two most common examples, the nationalized company has had major stockholders in key positions in the home country government or when nationalization has been, accurately or not, perceived by the intervening government as part of a "communist takeover," or "a threat to national security." This is not meant to justify the interventions, merely to point out that they have been the exception rather than the rule and have occurred only when factors other than simple nationalization have been present.

MNCs are commonly criticized for exploitation of, and retarding development in, the LDCs. Much of this criticism is misdirected and stems from a misunderstanding of the nature of the free-market process. But part of it is legitimate. One must then ask: How is it that a voluntary organization such as the MNC is able to engage in exploitation? The answer is that too often it is able to acquire what may be termed second-hand power. While it has no intrinsic power, it quite often is able to obtain power from government in the home and/or host countries. It is then able to use this power to exclude competitors, obtain subsidies, hold down wages, charge exorbitant prices, and foist its products on people who neither need nor want them.

MNCs and the Market

The answer to this problem, however, lies not in additional government regulation. It lies rather in the complete separation of the economy and the government, in the creation of a wall of separation between the two, in both the LDCs and the MDCs. The data show, in fact, that the notion of consumer sovereignty, so derided by critics of the MNC, is an effective method of regulating the multinationals. "As one reads Hobson's *Imperialism*, published in 1902, or Lenin's book by the same name," wrote Vernon (1977, p. 99), "a striking aspect of both works is the archaic nature of their illustrations, the repeated references to cases that no longer exist." Today, foreign-owned companies in nearly every area mentioned by Lenin and Hobson—mining, agriculture, banking, railroads, textiles, and utilities (see, e.g., Hobson, 1954, pp. 226–227, 240, 247–249)—are, notes Vernon, gone, having been pushed out by local competitors.

For example, in the approximately quarter century of Fulgencio Batista's rule in Cuba (1933–1944, 1952–1959), a period of friendly relations between the United States and Cuba, the share of Cuba's industry owned by U.S.-based MNCs fell from 65 to 40 percent. The reason, according to Vernon, was the learning and adoption of the technology by native Cubans (1977, pp. 99–100). This was not an isolated occurrence, in terms of geography, sector, or time. As the U.N. Center on Transnational Corporations has noted (1985, p. 64),

> the complete hegemony of the transnational corporations in developing country minerals that prevailed until about 1960 had been reduced by 1980 to a situation where the corporations have ceded a large part of their ownership positions to other agents, and where their financial contributions towards expansion constituted only a minor proportion of the total.

Perhaps surprisingly, trends in the manufacturing area parallel those in the primary goods sector. Between 1968 and 1974, Vernon notes, U.S. multinationals sold 717, or more than 10 percent, of their 6,500 foreign-based subsidiaries (1977, p. 100).

What perhaps is even more important is the *growth* in the Third World manufacturing sector, something that, according to Lenin, Hobson, and the dependency theorists, could not happen. Figure 7-5 shows that between 1963 and 1985

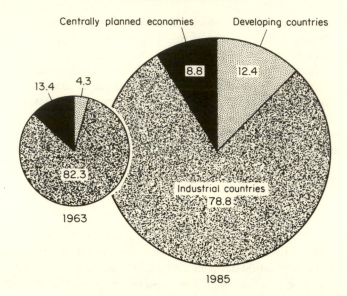

FIGURE 7-5. World exports of manufacturers, 1963–1985 (percentage shares). From World Bank, *World Development Report 1987,* Fig. 8.3, p. 147. Copyright © 1987 by The International Bank for Reconstruction and Development/The World Bank. Reprinted by permission of Oxford University Press, Inc.

the percentage of world exports supplied by the LDCs increased from 4.3 to 12.4. Figure 7-6 shows that in every category of manufactured goods, LDC exports are growing at a faster rate than those from the MDCs. It ought to be pointed out, however, that some of this industrialization was a result of attempts by MNCs to circumvent LDC tariffs and non-tariff barriers (NTBs). Such "tariff jumping" artificially stimulates industrialization. It therefore entails some factor distortion and

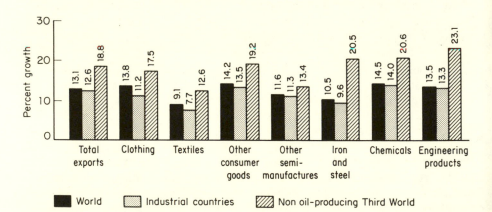

FIGURE 7-6. Comparative growth in export rates by category of exports and commodity, 1973–1982. From Jones, 1988, p. 207. Copyright © 1988 by Walter S. Jones. Reprinted by permission of Harper Collins Publishers.

thus exaggerates the amount of LDC industrialization that would have occurred in a free market. But it should also be noted that tariffs and NTBs imposed by the developed countries constitute a serious impediment to Third World industrialization. Estimates are that the cost to the Third World of MDC trade restrictions is "worth several billion dollars a year" (World Bank, 1987, p. 148). Restrictions on the exports of carbon steel, for example, reduced South Korean sales to the United States by $207 million, or by nearly 25 percent, although sales of carbon steel to other countries did increase as a result (World Bank, 1987, p. 148). Significantly, since developed nations typically allow primary products to be imported duty free, not only do MDC trade policies impede Third World industrialization, they also hamper attempts at economic diversification.

While the international picture has changed drastically during the twentieth century—while MNCs no longer dominate sectors such as the mineral extraction industries, having been pushed out by a variety of market and government actions—this still leaves open the question of whether the market is sufficient to control the MNC. Table 7-3 strongly suggests that this is the case. In every instance, the reasons given by U.S. parent companies for establishing overseas subsidiaries was to deal with local competitive threats.

> The decision to set up manufacturing facilities abroad has commonly been triggered by the perception of a threat to an established export market. . . . In the case of nine petrochemicals, for example, the original producers did not set up a plant outside their domestic market without first being threatened by the appearance of some uncontrolled competitor. More generally, unlicensed imitators or parallel innovators have commonly provided the immediate threat that has led to the initial overseas investment. . . . The decisions of innovators to try to prolong their hold on overseas markets by direct investment has induced not only their rivals but also their suppliers to take similar action. (Vernon, 1979, pp. 111–113)

Looked at from the other end, the data likewise suggest that the market is an effective means to regulate the MNC. Standard Oil was able to obtain a large share of the domestic U.S. market in the late nineteenth century only by reducing prices from $0.26 to $0.08 per gallon of kerosene. Yet despite the price cuts, its market share began to decline, and well before the court ordered Standard Oil's dissolution in 1911, it declined rapidly. There have also been repeated attempts by producers to control prices through voluntary cartellization. Yet none lasted more than a very short time, due to "cheating" by cartel members and the actions of independents, leading the American Petroleum Institute in the early 1930s to plead for government-imposed mandatory controls to hold prices up. The numerous attempts to establish international oil cartels met with the same fate. The first such attempt, the Achnacarry Agreement of 1928, lasted only a few months. It is doubtful that even OPEC (Organization of Petroleum Exporting Countries), the best-known oil cartel, had any significant impact on oil prices. It was founded in 1959, fully 14 years before the first oil "price shock," and has had virtually no impact on prices since the late 1970s. OPEC's "control" of oil prices during this brief period was more apparent than real. U.S. oil production peaked in the early 1970s and was declining by 1973, creating an oil shortage. Oil prices began to rise as early as February 1971,

TABLE 7-3. Characteristics of Foreign Manufacturing Plants Established Before 1900 by Specified U.S. Parents

U.S. Parent	Principal Products	Location of Foreign Plants	Substantial U.S. Exports Prior to Foreign Investment?	Asserted Reasons for Foreign Investment
Colt	Firearms	Great Britain	Yes	Local competitive threat
Singer	Sewing machines	Great Britain/ Austria/ Canada	Yes	Local competitive threat, lower costs
ITT	Communications	Great Britain/ Belgium/ Germany/ Austria/ France/ Italy/ Russia/ Japan	Yes	Local competitive threat, lower costs
General Electric and its predecessors	Electrical products and equipment	Great Britain/ France/ Germany/ Canada	Yes	Local competitive threat, lower costs, national pressures
Westinghouse Air Brake	Air brakes and signal equipment	Great Britain/ France/ Germany/ Russia	Yes	Local competitive threat, lower costs, national pressures
Westinghouse Electric	Electrical products and equipment	Great/ Britain/ France/ Russia	Yes	Local competitive threat, lower costs
Eastman Kodak	Photographic goods	Great Britain	Yes	Local competitive threat, lower costs
United Shoe Machinery	Shoe machinery	Great Britain/ France/ Germany/ Switzerland	Yes	Not determined
Parke, Davis	Pharmaceuticals	Canada	Yes	Lower costs
American Radiator and Standard Sanitary's predecessor	Radiators	France	Yes	Lower costs, larger demand

Source: Table from Sovereignty at Bay: The Multinational Spread of U.S. Enterprises by Raymond Vernon, copyright © 1971 by Basic Books, Inc. Reprinted by permission of Basic Books, a division of Harper Collins Publishers, Inc.

more than two years before the October 1973 price shock. While OPEC may have had an impact on the timing of the price increases, it probably had little influence on its ultimate height (Osterfeld, 1987b). As Paul MacAvoy has put it, OPEC "never really controlled the world crude oil market. Rather, market forces were the dominant factor all along" (1985, p. 3). As conditions changed, the pre-1973 government-regulated prices were far too low to be maintained much longer. And the 1973 price controls only played into the hands of OPEC by reducing oil production in the United States.

Further, while admittedly somewhat speculative "due to the poor quality of much of the data on direct investment," a 1985 International Monetary Fund study of rates of return on foreign direct investment in LDCs between 1974 and 1982 do show that average rates of return (1) are not "excessive," ranging between a low of just under 10 percent in 1980 and 1982 to a high of just under 13 percent in 1974, and (2) are positively correlated with annual rates of growth of LDC economies (IMF, 1985, pp. 38–39).

Finally, a look at the *Fortune* 500, practically all of which are multinationals, clearly illustrates the tenuous hold of even the largest corporations. Over the past several years, the number of corporations on the *Fortune* 500 list that are losing money has averaged over 50 per year, or more than 10 percent of the list. Some, such as the Dallas-based steel company LTV, acknowledged bankruptcy by filing for Chapter 11. And the turnover rate is also high, with about 44 companies displaced from the list each year.

The simple fact is that it is neither necessary nor desirable for governments to regulate the activities of the MNC. The free market is a much more effective and less costly method of regulation. It is also far more conducive to the maintenance of a free and prosperous society than reliance on ever larger and more powerful governments. Similarly, while one can sympathize with the expropriated MNC, military intervention and other types of home government pressure are unacceptable. The free market means that individuals must shoulder the risks of their own decisions. This should apply to both the economic and the political realms. Moreover, nationalizations are self-defeating, at least in the long run. If LDCs truly desire foreign investment, they will have to provide a secure environment. They must provide an environment for investments in which there is little or no fear of expropriation. In such an environment, the MNCs will be able to live up to their potential as engines for development.

Notes

1. Much has been made of the MNCs' use of internal transfer pricing to drain the LDCs of their wealth (e.g., Brandt et al., 1980, pp. 188–189). What is uniformly ignored is the use of transfer pricing as a method of investing in the LDCs. As Schmidt has noted (1983, p. 274), "research in the area fails to point in any particular direction."

2. For a very different assessment of ITT's activities see Krauss, 1984, pp. 133–134.

8

Migration

Migration is the second way by which the "transfer of prosperity" can take place. While capital flows from areas where the capital/labor ratio is high, and thus returns to capital are low, to where the capital/labor ratio is low, and thus returns on it are higher, labor does the reverse. It flows from areas where the returns to labor are relatively low to areas where the returns are higher. More precisely, migration will occur as long as an individual's *expected income*, that is, the nominal wage $\times$ the probability of finding employment in the "foreign" area (minus the cost of immigration, monetary and psychic) exceeds that person's average *actual income* in the "domestic" area (Nafziger, 1984, p. 238; Todaro, 1976, p. 372).

Assuming a world without trade and migration barriers, this process of capital and labor migration would cease once the returns to both were equalized. Wage rates are higher in the area the worker migrates to than in the area he or she emigrates from because, given the capital/labor ratios, one's marginal contribution to the productive process is higher in the former than the latter. Thus the equalization of returns would imply that factors have been allocated to their most valued productive point. However, due to the constant change in such conditions as birth rates, the rate of technological advancement, and so on, full equilibrium could never be achieved in the real world. Thus one can speak only of a continuing tendency toward equilibrium.

Migration barriers prevent workers in areas where there is a relative oversupply of labor, and thus where wage rates are low, from moving to areas where labor is relatively scarce, and thus where wage rates are higher. If workers do have the option of emigrating from areas with low wage rates but they choose to remain where they are, then "wage rates are equalized internationally only if we incorporate such psychic factors into the wage rate" (Rothbard, 1970b, pp. 40–41). A far more common situation, however, is that citizens in overpopulated areas do not move abroad because the government of other countries will not admit them. Of course it is only high-wage areas that have to worry about immigration; in low-wage areas the incentive is to emigrate. Since immigration will, other things remaining equal, tend to reduce the amount of invested capital per head and thus lower wage rates, immigration barriers confer a gain on domestic workers *at the expense* of foreign workers (Mises, 1985, pp. 138–139; Rothbard, 1970b, p. 40).

However, the disparity in the capital/labor ratio between the domestic market and foreign countries will encourage domestic capitalists to invest in countries where wage rates are low. A reduction in the capital/labor disparity will tend to bring about an equalization of returns to capital and, in the process, a partial equalization of wage rates. Complete equalization will not be attained because of the disparity in such things as transportation costs, proximity to major markets, and differences in resource endowments between the two areas. Thus the restrictions imposed by government will cause a distortion in the location of the capital investment. This is not without its consequences. The effects of immigration restrictions

> are just the same as those of the protective tariff. In one part of the world comparatively favorable opportunities of production are not utilized, while in another part of the world less favorable opportunities for production are being exploited. Looked at from the standpoint of humanity, the result is a lowering of the productivity of human labor, a reduction in the supply of goods at the disposal of mankind. (Mises, 1985, pp. 138–139)

Put differently, the equalization of returns to capital and labor solely through the movement of capital will result in the most efficient utilization of resources *given government restrictions on the movement of labor*. There can be no doubt that this will be less efficient than equalization of returns brought about through the unimpeded movement of both capital *and* labor, that is, *in the absence of government restrictions* (Mises, 1985, p. 139). The question for those living in the country imposing immigration restrictions is whether they, in their capacity as workers, will gain more from the restrictions than they will lose in their capacity as consumers from the reduction in world output resulting from the economic distortions brought about by those restrictions. There are good reasons to believe that this is *not* the case.

The Impact on Employment

Probably the most commonly heard argument is that of job displacement—that immigrants take jobs held by natives. Immigration, it is argued, increases unemployment among natives.

For example, Stacy and Lutton (1985, p. 336) contend that the "real" unemployment rate in the United States—the official rate plus the number of discouraged workers who have given up looking for jobs—has been 15 percent for the past decade. The "reason it has remained at historically high levels for so long" they conclude, is that "half of the new jobs created in the past decade have been taken by aliens."[1] Huddle (in Stacy and Lutton, pp. 336–337) argues that if undocumented workers in the United States could be removed, "we find that all male youths and minority youths, aged 16–24, could, in principle, have been removed from the rolls of the unemployed . . . and that adds up to one million U.S. workers who have been displaced." And former U.S. Secretary of Labor Ray Marshall (in Stacy and Lutton, p. 337) says that if all illegal workers were removed from the work force, the unemployment rate in the United States would drop by approximately one-half.

The argument that immigrants create unemployment among natives is based on the assumption that the number of jobs is fixed. This is certainly not the case. Not only do immigrants work; they also consume. And this consumption generates increased demand for labor and therefore additional jobs. A moment's reflection should make this evident. People work in order to consume. The supply of one good is therefore a demand for other goods (B. Anderson, 1979, pp. 383–400; Hazlitt, 1959, pp. 32–43). Consequently, not only is there a much greater demand for jobs in a larger society than a smaller one, there are also many more jobs available. In short, the argument that the immigrants create unemployment is fundamentally flawed. The number of jobs available varies with the size of the market. And the size of the market is largely determined by the size of the population. The larger the population, the greater the number of jobs, both demanded and supplied; the smaller the population, the fewer the jobs.

Some object to this on the ground that the immigrants send their earnings back home. But this does not alter the situation. The fact remains: the supply of labor is simultaneously a demand for goods and services. Assume that a Mexican youth, Pedro, immigrates to the United States to earn money to take care of Maria, his elderly mother living in Guadalajara. Pedro gets a job washing cars in Laredo, Texas. After a month's work Pedro has saved up $100, which he dutifully sends to Maria. What is Maria going to do with the dollars? She must first exchange them for pesos. This means that she must find someone who has pesos and is in need of dollars. The only reason someone would wish to exchange pesos for dollars is that that individual intends to buy in the United States. And those purchases generate jobs *there*. Thus, regardless of whether Pedro spends the money he earns on himself or sends it to his mother, his supply of labor creates a demand for goods and therefore additional labor in the United States. Although the type and location of the jobs may change, the number of jobs available for Americans is unaffected by the level of immigration.

In an expanding economy the number of jobs increases. Immigrants (1) tend to be young, strong, and better educated and more ambitious than their fellow countrymen who do not migrate (Chiswick, 1982a, p. 121; Lipton, 1980, pp. 7–8; Simon, 1982, p. 321; 1986b, p. 13; Todaro, 1976, pp. 369–370), and (2) have historically had higher saving rates than natives (Bauer and Yamey, 1957, pp. 107–109; Chiswick, 1982b, p. 296; Sowell, 1981b, p. 136; 1983, pp. 43, 47). One thus would expect to find that immigrants actually stimulate economic growth and therefore create additional jobs. This is what one does find. For example, numerous studies show that, with the exception of refugees, in nearly every time period and location immigrants, on arrival, earn less than the average for native workers. But within a relatively short time, about three decades, immigrant family earnings reach or exceed those of the average native family (Chiswick, 1982a, p. 121; 1982b, p. 305; Simon, 1986b, p. 13; Sowell, 1981b, 1983). Immigrants, for example, are more likely than natives to open their own businesses. A recent study (Simon 1986b, pp. 11–12) has shown that the number of jobs created by immigrants exceeded the number of immigrants by about 30 percent. Put differently, rather than destroying jobs, each immigrant creates about 1.3 additional jobs.

In fact, one of the oft-cited problems of immigration is precisely that the able-bodied young men emigrate, leaving in the village only the unambitious, the very young, the very old, and the women, whose job it is to care for the young and the old. In places such as East Africa, for example, well over one-half of all adult males have emigrated (Boserup, 1981, p. 149). The result of this substantial contraction in the labor force is that jobs are destroyed as local capital emigrates in search of better employment elsewhere. Whether labor emigration results in economic deterioration depends largely on how much the emigres remit to their villages. So much was remitted to Toishan in the Kwantung Province in southern China in the late nineteenth century that it became one of the most prosperous areas in China (Sowell, 1983, p. 47). Studies of Mexican and Pakistani migrants indicate that they send home more than 50 percent of their earnings (Lipton, 1980, p. 11). And studies of the migration of workers from Southern and Eastern Europe to the industrialized nations of Western Europe in the post-World War II period show that remittances have been of "substantial magnitudes" and of "major economic importance" (I. Hume, 1976, pp. 500–501). This may not be representative of all migrant groups, however. Studies of émigrés from India, Thailand, and Malawi indicate that their remittances are of little significance. Moreover, remittances tend to go to the better-off, thereby increasing the income inequality within the villages (Hill, 1986, p. 125; Lipton, 1980, p. 11–13).

One objection to this is that even if immigrants do create additional jobs, the jobs do not benefit natives, since the immigrants prefer to hire and buy from those of their own ethnic origin. Stacy and Lutton (1980, p. 338) state that it is seldom the case that Americans benefit from new jobs created by immigrants because "aliens with their own businesses prefer to hire other aliens. What is happening is that alien enclaves are being built in metropolitan areas across the United States. These areas act as magnets for more aliens. Local retail and service jobs are then filled by aliens to the exclusion of American citizens."

Several points are worthy of note. First, the argument that immigration does not create *additional* jobs for the native population is far different from the argument that immigration takes these jobs away from the natives. Second, to the extent that, say, Chinese-Americans hire and buy only from other Chinese-Americans, the enclave is self-contained. There is no contact between it and the surrounding economy. If that is the case, then the immigrants can neither create nor destroy jobs for the natives. And if immigrants have no impact on natives, why is there a problem? Further, to say merely that immigrants prefer to hire other immigrants begs the question of why. One reason is cultural affinity. A Japanese or Jewish immigrant may desire to work for a Japanese or Jewish businessperson because working for someone who shares the same cultural and ethnic traditions, and who speaks the same language, would greatly ease the difficulty and trauma of the immigration experience. Another is that a store owned and operated by a member of a particular ethnic group is far more likely to know of and to cater to the special preferences of that group. For example, one is more likely to find kosher food in Jewish-owned groceries and sushi in Japanese-owned groceries than in groceries owned and operated by natives. Further, one cannot ignore the hostility, ranging from insults and threats to job discrimination, beatings, and even lynchings, that natives have commonly inflicted on immigrants (Bauer and Yamey, 1983, p. 125; Sowell, 1981b, pp.

138–140; 1981c, pp. 60–61; 1983, pp. 221–249). It is hardly a coincidence that "not a Chinaman's chance" is a phrase used to describe hopeless odds. It originated in the late nineteenth century because of the brutal treatment of the Chinese immigrants on the West Coast of the United States (Sowell, 1981b, p. 138). Such treatment creates significant incentives for self-employment, working for others of the same ethnic background, and the formation of ethnic enclaves. There is also a tendency for the enclaves to wither over time as the immigrants become more acclimated to the native culture. Finally, a reason immigrants would prefer to hire other immigrants is that, as already noted, immigrants are usually not only hard working but willing to work for less than the natives. It is precisely for this reason that native businesspeople also often prefer to hire immigrants. All that this objection really amounts to is that, other things being equal, additional job seekers will mean lower wage rates. But requiring employers to hire members of a particular group, that is, natives, when there are others available who are not only equally or even more productive and willing to work for less means that labor is being utilized inefficiently, and thus that aggregate output is less than it would otherwise be. At any rate, this is not an argument against immigration; it is an argument against additional people, foreign or domestic (Rothbard, 1970b, p. 41).

But aren't the high unemployment rates in so many urban areas in the Third World a result of rural-urban migration? And doesn't this therefore refute the argument that immigrants create rather than destroy jobs? I do not think that this is the case. The foregoing assumed, for purposes of analysis, an environment in which government economic intervention was absent. But most Third World governments intervene extensively. In contrast to the MDCs, where legally mandated minimum wages are well below the average per capita income, frequently in the LDCs the income of workers paid the minimum wage is "several times the per capita GNP" (Nafziger, 1984, p. 242). Minimum wage laws in the LDCs are restricted to a small part of the work force. They generally apply to government employees, businesses employing more than, say, 25 workers, and a few other occupations in which union pressure or political lobbying has been especially effective. Another common feature of economic life in the LDCs is licensing restrictions. Licensing restrictions are really *functional* immigration laws; they prevent individuals from immigrating to higher paying occupations. Significantly, minimum wage and licensing laws are usually restricted to the modern, or urban, sector.

Moreover, it is a common practice that public goods such as housing, transportation, sewerage, fuel, and food are heavily subsidized in urban areas. This, of course, artificially reduces the cost of living in urban areas. Conversely, since the rural sector is heavily taxed to provide for these amenities, the cost of rural living is artificially increased. The result is to encourage migration from rural to urban areas. Even if the prospect of landing a job in the city is low, the significant disparity in *real* incomes between the rural and urban sectors will still make it quite rational to take the chance. It is important to realize that it is not immigration itself that is responsible for the high unemployment rates in LDC urban areas. It is government intervention, in particular the above-market income levels of urban dwellers compared with the below-market income levels of rural workers. It is the distortions caused by the intervention of government that induce, or "trap," people to act in ways that differ markedly from the way they would act if prices, including those for labor, were permitted to reflect actual economic conditions.

The Impact on Income

Another common charge is that immigrants reduce natives' incomes. This charge is false, for both the short- and the long-run. Immigration may indeed reduce wage rates, but this would be the case only for particular occupations or in particular places and for the short run. Both economic theory and empirical data indicate that immigrants increase not only their own standard of living but that of the natives as well. To understand this, it is best to follow the process through its logical phases.

As individuals migrate from areas where wage rates are low to areas where wage rates are higher, the immediate impact is an alteration of the capital/labor ratios in both areas. In the former, labor becomes more scarce, causing wage rates to rise. In the latter, it becomes more abundant, causing wage rates to fall. This process would cease, of course, once wage rates in the two areas became equal. Thus, the wage rates of the immigrants are now higher, as are the wages of those remaining in the "sending" community, whereas the wage rates for the natives in the "receiving" community are now lower. However, the *aggregate income* of the natives—wages plus returns to capital—is higher. This is because aggregate output has increased and because the capital dilution caused by immigration has made capital relatively more scarce, thereby increasing the returns to capital.[2] Conversely, both aggregate income and returns to capital are reduced in the sending community.

The increase in the returns to capital in the receiving community immediately creates an incentive for increased domestic saving and importation of foreign capital. The additional capital causes the marginal productivity of labor to rise. This increases aggregate output still more. By shifting the capital/labor ratio in favor of labor, it increases the returns to labor relative to capital. Thus the original decline in wage rates is short-lived and more than made up for by the subsequent rise in labor's share of the increased aggregate output. In the sending community, however, the reduction in returns to capital discourages investment and encourages capital flight. This process will cease when the returns to capital between the sending and receiving communities are equalized. It is obvious that this will be reached at a point where wages in the sending country are higher than they were before the original emigration began.

In brief, while wage rates may fall in the receiving community in the short run, in the long run, as Chiswick has pointed out (1982b, pp. 291–293)

emigration has the favorable effects of raising the level of and narrowing the inequality of income. For those accustomed to thinking in terms of "zero sum games," in which one party must lose if another party gains, the implication of the two-factor, two-country model . . . would appear inconsistent. How can each of the three major groups in the international migration model gain? The gains arise from the movement of some workers from where they are less productive to where they are more productive. Because factors of production are not perfect substitutes

for each other, marginal products change as factors move; this results in the gains
to both the native population of the receiving country and the remaining population of the sending country.

One can, following Chiswick (1982b, pp. 299–300), become a bit more discrim-
inating by dividing labor into two groups: skilled and unskilled. If the bulk of the
immigrants are skilled workers, the initial impact will be to reduce wage rates for
native skilled workers relative to unskilled workers. The reverse is the case if the
bulk of the immigrants are unskilled workers. But again, since capital will be
attracted to those areas where wages are low relative to the groups' productivity, the
capital/labor ratio between the two labor groups will reassert itself. Thus the decline
in wages for either group will tend to be of a short term duration. Moreover,
attempts to artificially raise the income of low-wage workers by restricting the entry
of unskilled laborers are generally not very successful, since they stimulate employers to substitute capital for labor, that is, to increase mechanization and automation
(Chiswick, 1982b, p. 300).

Another argument, found especially in the developed countries, is that immigrants pay a disproportionately small share of their income in taxes and receive a
disproportionately large share of public benefits. Thus residents of the receiving
communities are thought to have their incomes reduced through the transfer of
wealth from the resident taxpayers to the immigrant tax consumers (Stacy and Lutton, 1980, pp. 339–340).

This argument is not compelling. First, migrants seldom become public
charges. On the contrary, they are typically young, single, male adults. Studies of
the United States, Canada, Great Britain, and Israel confirm that immigrants find
jobs very rapidly, usually within three months of migrating (see, e.g., Simon, 1982,
pp. 321–322). The result is that immigrants pay taxes at the same rate as natives
but need, and consume, far less in government benefits. For example, studies of
immigrants in the United States show that there is a considerable disparity between
the government benefits received by immigrants and the taxes paid by them. During the first five years, immigrants paid, on average, $1,354 per year more in taxes
then they received in benefits. This disparity appears to hold quite steady, with
immigrants paying $1,592 per year more in taxes than they receive in government
benefits for the period 16 to 25 years after immigration (Simon, 1986b, p. 13, 1990,
pp. 264–276). Precisely because their "illegal" status makes it more difficult for
such individuals to receive government benefits, the situation with illegal immigrants is even more favorable for natives. In terms of government services received
compared with taxes paid, conservative estimates indicate that the transfer of
income from illegal immigrants to natives is at least $99 million and could be as
much as $213 million per year. As Weintraub and Cardenas have concluded,
"Despite our biasing the costs upward and the revenues downward, tax revenues
from undocumented aliens clearly exceed the costs to provide services to them" (in
Simon, 1986b, pp. 13–14).

Moreover, this flow of transfers does not appear to be reversed in the immigrants' later years. As already noted, immigrants or their offspring tend to reach or,
in most cases, exceed the average native per capita income within a few decades.

The result is that they continue to more than pay their way. "When the immigrants get older," Simon has commented (1982, p. 322), "the immigrants' own offspring more than supply the necessary retirement transfers."

Of course, if one still believes that government revenues are transferred from natives to immigrants, the answer is straightforward: either privatize these services or have the government charge user fees high enough to cover their full cost. That would eliminate any income-transfer effect, regardless of direction.

The Impact on Productivity

There are additional reasons to believe that freedom of movement will lead to increased aggregate output and higher incomes not only for the world but for the receiving country as well. As shown in Chapter 5, higher population densities are positively correlated with rapid economic growth. This is so for a number of reasons. Higher density areas (1) expand the size of the market, thereby deepening the division of labor, facilitating specialization, and permitting the utilization of economies of scale; (2) have better communications and transportation networks, which not only facilitate the allocation of resources and the transfer of technology but also stimulate the diffusion of skills; and (3) facilitate the exchange of ideas, thereby stimulating the advance of knowledge and technology. All of these increase productivity.

Studies confirm the relationship between worker productivity and population density. As Simon (1982, pp. 327) comments,

> It surely should have been all the easier 10,000 years ago than now to find important improvements because so much still lay undiscovered. Progress was surely agonizingly slow in prehistory, however. Whereas we develop new materials . . . almost every day, it was centuries or thousands of years between the discovery and use of, say, copper and iron. It makes sense that, if there had been a larger population then, the pace of increase in technological practice would have been faster.

Even excluding the impact of education, studies of both the United States and Europe during the twentieth century show, for example, productivity increasing at a rate of about 1 to 1.5 percent per year as population densities rise (Simon, 1982, p. 328).

Simon has summarized the evidence (1982, p. 329): "Taken altogether, the evidence seems irresistible that the more people, the more technological advance and productivity increase, other things being equal. And immigrants are people."

Conclusions

Migration is a complicated phenomenon. Much, perhaps most, of it is rural-rural; a considerable part of rural-urban migration is circular or temporary. And much of it is for noneconomic reasons. These include (1) physical factors such as preferences in climate or scenery; (2) cultural factors such as the preference for the excitement and vitality of the city over the boredom and drudgery of village life; (3) social factors such as the desire of migrants to break away from village traditions or parental constraints (Hill, 1986, pp. 122–134; Todaro, 1976, p. 369).

It should be pointed out, however, that these noneconomic reasons usually have significant economic consequences. For example, individuals who migrate to the city to be free from parental constraints or to participate in the excitement of city life actually pay for that independence or that participation by receiving less income than they otherwise could have obtained had they either not migrated or migrated to a different location. Similarly, individuals who prefer to live in other locations but remain in their present ones because they are receiving a higher income than they could get elsewhere, or because, even though wages may be higher elsewhere, the chances of obtaining jobs there are remote, are paying for the size or certainty of their present income by forgoing their preferences to live in other locations. Thus, such noneconomic factors invariably entail "psychic utilities," which enable the economist to integrate them into an analysis of migration. For example, an individual who migrates to the city to participate in the excitement of city life but, in short order, returns to the village is, in effect, saying that he or she miscalculated the size of the psychic returns. Either the returns were less than anticipated or the cost was higher than expected. Put differently, individuals will migrate when they believe that the economic or money income plus the psychic income derived from noneconomic factors elsewhere exceeds the money income plus the psychic income in their present location. The psychic income is, of course, subjective and therefore difficult if not impossible to measure or to compare interpersonally. But, as is well known, the *value or utility* one attaches to money income is *equally subjective*.

Returning to more familiar economic grounds, migration brings about a more efficient allocation of the world's resources and facilitates the flow of ideas, thereby stimulating the diffusion of knowledge and skills and the development of new technology. All of these work to increase the productivity of labor, expand world output, and raise the standard of living of practically all individuals. Immigration is an important element in the transfer of prosperity. It helps to set in motion a self-sustaining process by which additional wealth is created and diffused throughout the society.

The empirical data confirm this. In addition to the studies already cited, one should note that the United States, whose standard of living is the envy of the world, is literally a nation of immigrants. This is hardly an isolated case. As Bauer and Yamey (1957, pp. 106–107) have pointed out:

> The important part in economic development played by foreigners is indeed a striking feature in economic history generally; often it has been very large in relation to the small numbers involved. Obvious examples include the role of the Huguenots in the development of British and German industry, and, more recently, of German refugee businessmen in various part of the world. . . . [T]he work of immigrant Chinese in South-east Asia, of Indians in East Africa, of Lebanese and Chinese in the West Indies, and of Lebanese and other Levantines in West Africa has done much to further the growth of the exchange sector of backward economies and to promote their economic growth generally.

Notes

1. That the height of the wage might have something to do with this does not seem to have occurred to them. The literature on this is extensive. But see, for example, Brozen, 1974; M. Friedman, 1981, pp. 226–228; Hazlitt, 1969, pp. 93–97; Peterson, 1957, on the effects of the minimum wage.

2. This will also benefit native workers who participate in pension plans and insurance programs.

9

Corruption

Revelations about Somoza in Nicaragua, Duvalier in Haiti, and especially Marcos in the Philippines have generated numerous commentaries about corruption in the Third World. These commentaries have generally been long on righteous indignation but short on detached analysis. Corruption clearly has a pejorative connotation. As David Bayley has noted (1966, p. 719), most observers "uncritically assume that the presence of corruption is an important hindrance to economic growth and progressive social change."

Where this assumption is not made, where it is recognized that corruption may at times have beneficial consequences, usually what follows is little more than a laundry list of activities showing those having beneficial and those having detrimental results. Seldom is any attempt made to ascertain why certain corrupt acts may have beneficial consequences, while others are clearly harmful. For instance, Marcos's massive embezzlement of funds from the Philippine state treasury is a case of corruption that clearly hurt society. However, a Peruvian street vendor's bribing of a low-level government official to obtain a license to sell his wares makes a positive contribution to society.

A set of general principles can be established to decide what separates corrupt but beneficial activities from those that are corrupt and perverse. In this way the Marcoses, Duvaliers, and Noriegas of this world can be distinguished from the humble street vendors both in the effect of their corruption on the economy and society as a whole, and in the morality of their actions. This chapter shows that certain kinds of so-called corruption are a direct response to government intervention that restricts freedom and socially beneficial exchange. And, because these actions effectively offset government encroachment on freedom, they move the economy closer to a free market and therefore have a positive effect on economic growth and development.

Corruption Defined

Numerous attempts have been made to define corruption. None has met with general acceptance. Perhaps a fruitful approach would be to begin with what political corruption is not. Generally speaking, a "good citizen" is one who obeys the laws and policies of the government; a "good public official" is one who implements the laws and policies of the government as opposed to his or her own personal interests. Hence the term *public servant*. Political corruption can be defined in terms of the obverse of these. There are two distinct categories of corruption: one involves private individuals and the other involves public officials. Any satisfactory definition of corruption must take this into account. For if offering a bribe is corrupt, then accepting a bribe must be equally corrupt. While these categories are closely related they are not necessarily identical. A public official who embezzles department funds would be corrupt regardless of whether there was any involvement by a private individual. Similarly, a private individual who offered a bribe would be corrupt even if the offer were rejected by the public official.

It follows that any satisfactory definition of corruption must be double-pronged, including within its purview those inside as well as those outside government. Political corruption may be defined as follows:

> 1. Activities by individuals outside government that bestow benefits on a public official in an attempt to induce that official to permit them to (a) evade existing laws or policies and/or (b) obtain a change in the laws or policies, either enactment or repeal, which would transfer wealth from others (society) to themselves.
>
> 2. Activities of those inside government to obtain benefits for themselves, families, and friends by using their positions (a) to solicit or accept benefits from private individuals in exchange for the bestowal of direct and immediate benefits on those individuals, (b) to enact or repeal laws or policies the immediate effect of which would be to directly benefit themselves, and/or (c) to benefit themselves via the diversion of public money into their own pockets, that is, embezzlement.

This definition may seem overly cumbersome, and some explanation is in order. Although corruption is generally viewed as both immoral and illegal, the definition has carefully avoided references to either. "Immoral" can and does have a variety of meanings. What is immoral for some may not be for others. This is especially true when dealing with different cultures and traditions. If corruption is defined so as to require moral censure, then the crossing of cultural boundaries would almost immediately ensnare one in a hopeless web of ad hoc rationalizations to explain why public officials who accept bribes or engage in nepotism are corrupt, and thus subject to censure, in some societies but not in others. Since the focus of this chapter is to examine the economic effects of corruption, its morality, while an important issue, is not a relevant consideration here.

The Ambiguity of Laws

Legality has the merit of precision. But this precision is purchased at a heavy price. For if corruption is defined solely in terms of legality, then that individual or group in control of government and thus able to make the laws and policies for the society would be able to grant itself the legal right to engage in activities that are commonly regarded as corrupt. But because these activities would be "legal," they would fall outside the parameters established by the definition. For example, the ruler or law-maker could simply rule that the entire wealth of the country belonged to him. As long as the official legal canons were observed, such an act of expropriation, though probably unanimously regarded as corrupt, would not be so according to the legal definition.

This type of legal expropriation is quite common. Graft is seldom as blatant or crass as that of, say, the nineteenth-century Argentinian dictator Rosas, who alleg-edly seized the fortunes of his enemies and distributed them to his friends and sup-porters saying, "This belongs to you" (see Andreski, 1966, p. 130). Today expro-priation is more commonly accomplished by legal subterfuge. Examples of such actions span the globe and the decades. In Mexico following the 1910 Revolution the government began implementing a series of reforms that entailed the nation-alization of all basic industries and the "reapportionment" of the land into collec-tive units (Andreski, 1966, pp. 219–223; West and Augelli, 1976, p. 297). In the Soviet Union, for example, the November 1917 "Declaration of the Rights of the Toiling and Exploited People" abolished all private land holdings. In June 1918, the Fourth All-Russian Congress of the Soviets nationalized all industry (Tread-gold, 1964, pp. 150–151, 162–165). In Nazi Germany the Nuremberg Laws of 1935, and the thirteen supplementary decrees, reduced Jews from the status of cit-izen to "subject," permitting the wholesale expropriation of their property and eventually, their extermination (Arendt, 1971, pp. 288–289; Shirer, 1965, p. 323). In 1951, less than two years after Mao Tse-tung's rise to power in China, the hold-ings of landlords were ruthlessly expropriated under the Agrarian Reform Act of 1950. According to the new law, "war criminals, traitors, bureaucratic capitalists, and counter-revolutionaries" had their property confiscated and were subject to punishment ranging from three years in prison to death. As Michael and Taylor note (1965, p. 458), these classifications were vague enough to be "applied to any-one who stood in the way of the regime." In Cuba all estates of more than 400 hec-tares (988 acres) were "socialized," that is, confiscated by the state. The program began in May 1959, only five months after Castro attained power. In 1963, all estates of more than 63 hectares were confiscated (Rydenfelt, 1983, pp. 124–125). In 1967 the government of Tanzania, under the authority of the Arusha Declara-tion, "socialized" all industries and financial establishments. Practically all agri-cultural land was appropriated by the state in order to establish "efficient collec-tives" known as *ujamaa* villages. About 90 percent of the country's peasants, or about 13 million of its 19 million people, were herded onto the collectives. To pre-vent the peasants from trying to leave the *ujamaas*, the government burned their old homes (Rydenfelt, pp. 117–118). The overseas Chinese have long been subject to legal discrimination throughout many areas of Asia, the Pacific, and the Amer-ican West. They have been the victims of laws forbidding them to own particular types of property, excluding them from numerous occupations, preventing them from voting, and barring them from schools, all of which severely restricted their economic opportunities. They have often been the victims of mob violence and looting, which usually occurred with either the approval or even the encouragement of the local authorities (Sowell, 1983, pp. 21–50). In 1942, shortly after the Japanese attack on Pearl Harbor, about 150,000 Japanese Americans living on the West Coast of the United States were rounded up and placed in internment camps in isolated areas. The financial losses alone suffered by these Japanese Americans have been estimated as about $400 million in 1942 prices (Sowell, 1981b, pp. 171–172). And, since the British victory in the Boer War in 1902, white supremacy has been the cornerstone of legal policy in the overwhelmingly black country of South Africa. One of the first such laws was the Mines and Works Act of 1911, which reserved all skilled work for whites (Sowell, 1983, p. 112).

Graft can also take place by less direct legal means, such as granting monopolistic positions to businesses that happen to be owned by the ruling elite, and by enacting subsidies, tariff barriers, and licensing restrictions. All of these practices were common in the Philippines under Marcos (Manning, 1986; Overholt, 1986; Sacerdoti, 1983; University of the Philippines, 1984). Another means for obtaining wealth, used extensively by African governments but not confined to that continent, is to establish government marketing boards as the sole purchaser of agricultural produce from local farmers. By purchasing produce at artificially low prices and then selling it at world market levels, the boards are legal vehicles for channeling large sums of money into the pockets of the rulers. These practices have already been discussed in Chapter 3. A method used in Cuba after Castro's seizure of power in 1959 is for the government to establish maximum prices that are well below a product's cost of production, thereby driving firms into bankruptcy. The government then assumes operation of the business (Fleming, 1966, p. 17). While probably everyone would regard at least some of the foregoing actions as corrupt, all would be excluded by a definition of corruption solely in terms of legality.

Opportunity Costs and the Value of Government Services

Another way of viewing the problem is to define corruption quantitatively, that is, in terms of its returns. Those in charge of government "may make use of their powers to increase their own income above and beyond that which is necessary to provide the government services which justify the existence of government." Corruption exists when the ruler takes "for himself an income which is larger than the opportunity cost for his services" (Tullock, 1974, p. 69). This approach is misdirected.

The implicit analogy between government and the market does not hold. The size of the returns could be an accurate measurement of corruption only if one could determine the value of economic output, since the monetary units do have some meaning. This meaning, however, derives from the ability to calculate the opportunity costs of the factors of production, and opportunity costs can only be determined where there are alternative possibilities for employment. (This is the case in a market economy when entrepreneurs bid for factors.) One of the distinguishing characteristics of government is precisely the absence of alternatives in the economic sense. There may be elections but there can be only one government at any given time. Elections, coups, and wars may replace a particular regime with a new one, but the new regime becomes the new sole supplier of government services. Those dissatisfied with government services cannot turn to other suppliers, as can those dissatisfied with the services they receive in private enterprises.

This creates an insurmountable obstacle in ascertaining the value of government services. Such value cannot be measured by the proceeds from total sales, because government does not usually sell its services and even if it did, its monopolistic position would seriously distort its price. Similarly, it cannot be determined by summing the value of component factors, since values are determined by opportunity costs that, in the absence of alternatives, cannot be ascertained. The solution to this approach would require not merely the existence of competitive political parties, which are generally confined to the industrialized West, but the existence of "competitive government," which is a contradiction in terms. Thus the absence of a competitive market in the government arena, that is, the absence of alternative, coexisting suppliers, makes the measurement of government "output" impossible.

These difficulties in defining corruption can be avoided by viewing it as an activity rather than something characterized by its morality, legality, or the size of its returns.

The Taxonomy

It is now beyond dispute that the free market is an indispensable agent for economic development. Official statistics clearly show that the standard of living of the average citizen in the more market-oriented countries and areas such as the United States, Western Europe, South Korea, or Hong Kong is considerably higher than the standard of living of the average citizen in the Soviet Union, Eastern Europe, North Korea, or China. And, as was pointed out in Chapter 1, the actual differences are probably greater than official statistics indicate. It is certainly noteworthy that the introduction of interventionist or socialist measures has invariably been followed by dramatic economic deterioration (Rydenfelt, 1983).

As a first step toward the construction of a taxonomy, one can imagine a spectrum characterized at one pole by the unrestricted right of exchange, that is, the voluntary transfer of ownership titles, and at the other end by the complete absence of legally permissible exchange. Ownership can be defined as the right to dispose freely of what one has obtained through work, voluntary exchange, or as a gift.[1]

Assume that Jones the farmer has an excess of wheat but needs size-12 shoes. Also assume that Smith the cobbler has size-12 shoes but needs ten pounds of wheat. There is obviously room here for mutually beneficial exchange between Jones and Smith and there is little doubt that, given freedom of exchange, the transaction would occur. What is noteworthy is that while the exchange may not have increased physical output, it nevertheless produced a redistribution of that output, the result of which benefited both Smith and Jones while harming no one. But this is true of any voluntary exchange, for anyone believing that he or she will not benefit can reject the proffered exchange. Thus, any voluntary exchange must be perceived as mutually beneficial by all parties—it is Pareto-optimal. And if economic development is viewed as not simply the expansion of physical output but the increase in utility or *desired* output, then the transaction between Jones and Smith is, as is any voluntary transaction, a contribution to economic development. That is, regardless of its impact on physical output, voluntary exchange is productive exchange.

On the other hand, if all property is "owned" by the ruler—either a single individual or a group—then no exchange is legally permissible without the ruler's advance permission or, more accurately, direction. Hence the exchange between Jones and Smith could not be consummated without the consent of the ruler, which may or may not be forthcoming. In any society beyond the most rudimentary levels of specialization, the exchanges routinely transacted number in the millions each day. Were the advance permission of the ruler required, it is obvious that, even under the best of circumstances and with the best of intentions, there would be no way for the ruler, even if it were a group using high-speed computers, to stay abreast. Thus, unless the requests for all transactions were perfunctorily granted, which would constitute an abdication of authority by the ruler and a return to de facto private property and free trade, the inevitable result of the need to secure the ruler's permission would be that innumerable possibilities for gains from trade would go unrealized or be seriously delayed. Put differently, transaction costs in such a situation would be enormous and the result, even assuming no impact on physical output, would be a significant loss in social utility.

Moreover, there can be little doubt that restrictions on free exchange do adversely affect physical output. As noted in Chapter 2, the free market works spontaneously, as it were, to produce precisely those things consumers most desire. In the process, it allocates factors to their most productive point relative to the priorities that consumers have established by their buying and abstention from buying. The dilemma, in fact contradiction, of the centrally planned economy is obvious. Where there is no voluntary buying and selling there is no market; and where there is no market there is no economic information on which to construct the plan. Thus, because of the impossibility of economic calculation, a centrally planned economy would entail massive inefficiencies and distortions resulting in a significant reduction in physical output. It follows that the more numerous the economic restrictions the less efficiently the economy can function; and the less efficiently it functions the smaller the output, both in physical and value terms.

Thus, free exchange produces economic development in two distinct ways: (1) by expanding physical output and (2) by increasing the value of that output. The further one moves down the spectrum from free exchange to the absence of exchange, the more both aspects of economic development are adversely affected. It follows that those corrupt acts that move the economy in a free-market direction are economically beneficial; those that inhibit the operation of the market are economically detrimental. The former may be termed *expansive* corruption, since it expands opportunities for socially beneficial exchange. It entails increased competition and market flexibility. The result is that the quantity of goods produced expands and their quality improves. It is, in short, characterized by productive investment, that is, the expansion of the overall wealth of the society. The latter may be labeled *restrictive* corruption, since its principal effect is to constrict opportunities for socially beneficial exchange. It entails reduced competition and increased market rigidities. The quantity of the goods produced therefore declines and their quality deteriorates. It is characterized by what may be termed parasitic investment—investment of time and resources into activities that transfer wealth from its owners to others. Restrictive corruption is also an immoral act because it constitutes an assault on the property of others as well as their right to engage in voluntary activities.

This rather simple taxonomy requires amplification. The definition of corruption distinguished between the activities of private and public individuals, or those outside government and those inside government. This results in two categories: (1) public-sector corruption, in which corrupt activities are carried on solely by public officials, acting alone or in cooperation with other officials, and (2) dual-sector corruption, which entails the cooperation of individuals from both sectors. Since corruption was defined in terms of influencing government policies, purely private-sector activities, including those that are illegal or immoral, nevertheless fall outside the parameters of the definition.

Public-Sector Corruption

This type, in which public officials use their positions to channel benefits to themselves, can be divided into legal and illegal activities.

Illegal activities include embezzlement or the "straightforward transfer of funds from the state treasury to the private accounts of the principal members of the ruling clique" (Andreski, 1966, p. 65). This profiteering approach to government, the notion that government is simply a vehicle for plunder, is quite common, especially in the Third World. "Kleptocracy, or rule by thieves," is the apt term coined by Andreski for this phenomenon (p. 62). Marcos's fortune has been placed at nearly $10 billion; the estimated worth of Zaire's Mobutu is $5 billion; the Shah of Iran's fortune was placed at $20 billion, and the Sultan of Brunei is commonly thought to be the wealthiest man in the world with an estimated worth of $30 billion (Ayittey, 1987c, pp. 213–218). It is common knowledge that these fortunes were acquired all or in large part from embezzlement or other illegal activities. Mobutu, for example, is widely suspected of having embezzled at least $1 billion and placed it in Swiss bank accounts (*Time*, 1984, p. 28). The illegal activities of Marcos likewise netted him millions if not billions of dollars (Manning, 1986; Overholt, 1986; Sacerdoti, 1983; University of the Philippines, 1984). Haiti's former rulers, Papa Doc and Baby Doc Duvalier, acquired their fortunes in large part by hiring private gangs of terrorists to extort the citizenry. Argentina's Peron and Venezuela's Perez Jiminez were able to place $700 million and $400 million, respectively, in foreign bank accounts, most of which was the product of straightforward embezzlement. And the former head of the Dominican Republic, Raphael Trujillo, managed to acquire a fortune in excess of $1 billion dollars, despite ruling one of the smallest and poorest states in the world (Andreski, 1966, pp. 65–66).

Another example of illegal corruption is the very common practice by customs officials of using their positions to obtain goods and/or money from importers in return for allowing the importers' goods, even those legally permissible, into the country. Importers refusing to pay often have their goods "lost" or damaged. This is an example of restrictive corruption: instead of using their positions to circumvent legal obstacles to trade such as tariffs or exchange controls, the officials use them to establish additional but extralegal obstacles, thereby restricting opportunities for exchange. Payment is therefore not a case of voluntary exchange but extortion, or what some have termed "coerced exchange." The result is the transfer of wealth from importers to officials.

It is easily shown that society is hurt by such activities. Importers have three options: they can (1) try to get the authorities to put an end to the extortion, (2) pay the extortion bribe, or (3) cease importing into that country. The legal option is almost bound to fail. Salaries for minor officials are often so low that such behavior is implicitly condoned by their superiors as a necessary means for augmenting their income. Moreover, higher officials also benefit, since money flows into their pockets in exchange for their acquiescence (Andreski, pp. 63–64). Payment of the extortion bribe raises the cost of doing business in the country and therefore the prices that importers must charge the local consumers. Ceasing importing reduces the quantity of goods available in local markets, thereby causing shortages or price rises. Either way, society is harmed as wealth is transferred from the importers to the corrupt officials. The final result is that importation is discouraged, the amount of goods available in the local markets is reduced, and prices rise.

In contrast to the first type of public-sector corruption, which consists of illegal activities by public officials, the second type consists of the legal use of their positions by public officials to benefit themselves directly. This consists largely of enacting or decreeing laws or implementing policies that, either directly or indirectly, transfer wealth from its owners to the ruling elite. This method is more prevalent under democracies, even "imperfectly functioning parliamentary regimes," while straightforward embezzlement is probably more common in outright dictatorships, although the correspondence is far from perfect (Andreski, 1966, pp. 65–66). Reference has already been made much earlier in the chapter to the widespread use of such legal subterfuges. The point is that expropriations are expropriations. Their economic impact is identical regardless of whether they are carried out through outright seizures or are undertaken under the guise of legality.

By severing the connection between work and wealth, expropriation undermines the incentive to produce. Moreover, it diverts investment in time, effort, and money away from activities that expand the production of wealth and into those activities that merely transfer wealth, that is, into "rent-seeking" activities. The result is that the production of wealth is impeded.

What is most significant about public-sector corruption is that it consists solely of wealth transfers. By placing obstacles in the way of socially beneficial exchange, it retards the production of wealth. Thus, public-sector corruption, whether legal or illegal, is entirely restrictive corruption, that is, it always hampers the functioning of the free market, reduces growth, and restricts freedom.

Dual-Sector Corruption

This type, characterized by the cooperation of individuals from both the public and private sectors, consists primarily of bribes. There are two points to be made at the outset. First, it makes no difference whether the transaction is initiated by private individuals or public officials. The result is the same: a mutually beneficial exchange is consummated. Second, since a bribe is a mutually beneficial transaction, it must be clearly distinguished from such activities as extortion, in which one party is paid for not harming the person or property of the other, and theft, in which property is transferred from its owner to others without the owner's consent.

Dual-sector corruption can be subdivided into three types: (1) bureaucrat bribing, (2) judge bribing, and (3) politician bribing.

Bureaucrat Bribing

The bureaucrat is responsible for executing the laws and policies of the regime. The opportunities for bureaucrat bribing are directly related to the scope of the government's activities. Since such government policies as price controls, licensing restrictions, immigration controls, tariffs, and the like place obstacles in the way of socially beneficial exchange, they present clear opportunities for expansive corruption. Evading price controls or tariffs by bribing bureaucrats to permit smuggling or black marketeering, or evading licensing restrictions or immigration/emigration controls by bribing bureaucrats to ignore illegal entry into an occupation or into or out of the country, are obvious cases in point.

An examination of the effects of corruption on the allocation of licenses, a common practice, will make this clear. Licenses can be granted in two different forms: (1) the government can establish a price for licenses and sell them to whomever is willing to pay, and (2) the government can restrict access to the field by allowing only a limited number of licenses to be issued. Assume, in the former case, that the government charges $1,000 for a license. If a corrupt bureaucrat charged $1,000 for either a counterfeit license or for permission to enter the occupation without a license, it would be immaterial to the individual, other things being equal, whether he paid the bribe or purchased a government license. By reducing his charge to $900 the bureaucrat could tip the scales in his favor. The result is a benefit to society. Paying the bribe rather than purchasing the license has reduced the individual's cost of doing business by $100. The reduced cost facilitates entrance into the field, thereby introducing an element of competition into an otherwise monopolistic situation. The resulting lower prices and increased efficiency serve to *reduce the economic harm to society* caused by the establishment of the licensing restrictions.

If, however, the number of licenses, and therefore the number of operators in a field, were strictly fixed by the government, the bureaucrat could not simply sell additional licenses or permit individuals to enter the field informally. If, however, the number of available licenses were less than the demand for them, he would be in a position to accept bribes or receive kickbacks from those desiring licenses. It is not uncommon, as an Indian investigatory committee put it, for "each license [to] fetch anything between one hundred per cent to five hundred per cent of its face value" (its governmentally decreed price) (in Bayley, 1966, p. 723). Granting licenses to those offering the highest bribes, and then pocketing the difference between the bribe and the official price of the license, not only benefits the bureaucrat but, more importantly, ensures that the licenses are allocated efficiently, since those able to offer the highest bribes are the most efficient firms. The result, once again, is that the corruption serves to reduce the harm of the government policy.

In short, these bribes are the grease that keeps the wheels of the economy running. Without them, more producers would enjoy monopolies. The bribes increase competition and thereby expand the choices available to consumers, reduce prices, and, just as importantly, create new jobs in businesses that, if licensing restrictions were met, would not exist.

The strikingly different results from price controls on food, imposed in Brazil and Chile in the 1960s, provide a graphic illustration of the beneficial effects of corrupt activities of the sort discussed here. "In Chile the bureaucracy acted loyally to maintain price controls." Food shortages and inflation quickly followed. "In Brazil, however, the bureaucracy's ineffectiveness sabotaged the enforcement of price controls, and prices received by producers were allowed to rise." The result was increased food supplies and very little inflation (Leff, 1964, pp. 11–12).

Other examples include the following:

• Official channels in China, the former Soviet Union, and other socialist countries are so inefficient and unreliable that state enterprises routinely purchase materials on the black market to meet their quotas. Estimates indicate that less than one-half of all production passes through official production channels (Grossman, 1972, pp. 25–40; H. Smith, 1984, pp. 30–67, 106–134; Zafanolli, 1985, pp. 718–719).

• Even with the post-Mao reforms there is little in the way of a labor market in China. Children usually inherit their parents' jobs and remain in a particular enterprise for life. Since they usually can be neither penalized nor rewarded according to their individual job performances, they have little incentive to work. To meet production quotas managers therefore hire peasants, usually the poorest of the poor in China. Since the practice is illegal, the workers can be released when the quota is reached. Wage payments are hidden by clever bookkeeping. The size of this temporary work force is thought to be 25 to 50 percent of China's entire industrial labor force (Zafanolli, 1985, pp. 726–728).

• Because little in China can be done without the approval of the appropriate bureaucrat or Communist Party cadre, an individual who does not have personal contacts can hire the services of the "compradores" who will negotiate a deal on his behalf. These agents ordinarily receive a commission equal to 2 percent of the value of the deal. They can arrange anything from reassigning one's household registration from peasant to worker—thereby permitting one to move from the village to a town, where wages are higher and job prospects are better—to escaping from China itself. Payment for the latter service is higher, apparently because part of it goes to secure the cooperation of the border patrols (Mosher, 1983a, pp. 83–85; Zafanolli, 1985).

• In India individuals often pay the appropriate officials in order to secure positions as telephone operators. The reason is that the telephone system is so bad that businessmen will pay operators large sums to make sure that their calls are given priority. If the payments are high enough, businessmen can even conduct business when all telephone lines are out of order, since the most competent operators cultivate contacts with telegraph operators and radio stations for use in just such emergencies (Rashid, 1981, pp. 453–456).

• The scores of monopolistic marketing boards across Africa often pay farmers less than half the market value of their produce. In Mali, for instance, the official price of rice is 40 percent below its cost of production. The only way agricultural production can continue is for farmers either to pay off public officials so they can sell their produce privately or to smuggle it out of the country to sell where prices are higher (Bezineau, 1989; Jackson and Park, 1986, pp. 126–129; Osterfeld, 1985).

• In Eritrea, which was sealed off by the Ethiopian army to starve the rebels there into submission, food could only enter the province illegally. Had it not been for the much-maligned "food profiteers," death tolls from the 1985 famine would have been considerably higher (Suau, 1985, pp. 391–400).

• Licensing restrictions are pervasive throughout Central and South America. In Peru, where it may take as long as six years and cost as much as several years' average income to secure a license, probably more than 50 percent of all businesses operate illegally. In Lima alone, 95 percent of all public transportation is operated "informally" (Bonnet, 1988, p. 49; de Soto, 1989; Vargas Llosa, 1987).

• India's confiscatory tax rates have resulted in an underground economy that in 1985 was estimated to be at least one-half the size of its official economy (Ohri, 1987, p. 49). Imagine India's poverty if the bureaucracy were able to stifle all of this illegal activity.

These examples, which could be multiplied many times over, are all instances of corrupt behavior resulting in a far more efficient allocation of factors, human and material, than could ever have occurred if government policies were strictly followed. Moreover, such cases are neither unique to the Third World nor limited to the modern age. According to John Nef (in Leff, 1964, p. 12),

> the honesty and efficiency of the French bureaucracy were in great measure responsible for the stifling of economic innovation and progress during the 18th century. By way of contrast, the laxity of the British administration permitted the subversion of Colbertism, and allowed the new economic processes and activities to flourish. [In all of these cases] we see the success of entrepreneurs and corrupted officials in producing a more effective policy than the government.

Not all bureaucratic corruption is expansive, however. Some is clearly restrictive. This would be the case if the local police or other public officials were bribed to ignore such things as theft, private-sector extortions, or murder. Local police accepting bribes to allow a theft ring to operate in their jurisdiction is a case of restrictive corruption. The exchange benefits the police and the ring, but it is not socially beneficial. The reason is clear. Expansive corruption is beneficial because it helps to create an "enabling environment," which enables or allows development to occur. Such an environment is nearly identical to the classical liberal society based on the legal protection of person and property. In such a society individuals would have the right to engage in any *noninvasive* activities they desired, that is, in any activities that did not entail the use of force, fraud, or the threat of force against others. Without such an environment "foreign capital will stay away, domestic capital will either leave the country or go into short-term speculative rather than long-term productive investments." The result is that the country "will continue travelling down the road to further decline" (Richardson and Ahmed, 1987, p. 37). The evidence regarding the use of capital, domestic and foreign, confirms this analysis (see Ayittey, 1986a; Eberstadt, 1985a, p. 28; Nye, 1967, pp. 421–422).

By undermining the security of both person and property, the theft ring makes normal business practices riskier and more costly, thereby placing obstacles in the way of development. The obvious result is to reduce or restrict opportunities for productive exchange, as businesspersons are forced to either take their business elsewhere or purchase insurance to cover their losses, thus increasing their costs of doing business. Either way, economic development is impeded or even reversed.

There is a technical but very important point to be discussed. It may seem that the example of the theft ring contradicts the claim that no exchange is socially harmful. But this is based on a misinterpretation. The claim was that no voluntary exchange was socially harmful. Such coerced exchanges as extortion and theft were specifically excluded. The transaction can be viewed in one of two ways. (1) It involved not just the ring and the police but also the property owners. Since they were unwitting and unwilling participants, the exchange is coercive. (2) The transaction can be divided into two distinct exchanges, one voluntary, the other coercive. The exchange between the police and the ring may be voluntary but its effects are socially neutral: no one is either benefited or harmed, since nothing is actually exchanged. Rather than an exchange, it may therefore be more appropriate to view the transaction as an agreement to violate the property rights of others. It is the subsequent theft, that is, the coerced exchange between the property owners and the ring, that is harmful. It is true that the thefts may not have occurred without the complicity of the police. But this only makes the police partners in the crime, not beneficiaries of a voluntary exchange. Either way, the socially damaging exchange is coercive. It is a predatory act that transfers wealth from its rightful owners to others. And such transfers, as we have seen, restrict opportunities for voluntary exchange and productive investment.

Bureaucrat bribing can be either expansive or restrictive. But since the opportunities for expansive corruption are positively correlated with the scope of the government's activities, and since the latter are typically quite large throughout the Third World, it is likely that bureaucrat bribing is, on balance, a contribution to Third World development.

Judge Bribing

Bribing judges has been roundly condemned by most, if not all, commentators on the subject. According to its critics, it permits wealthy lawbreakers to buy their way out of punishment, it violates the principle of the rule of law, and it demoralizes and alienates the citizenry (Nye, 1967, p. 423; Tullock, 1974, p. 69). In fact, judge

bribing does not differ in any relevant respect from bureaucrat bribing. Judge bribing would be economically beneficial when used to circumvent punishments from
violating laws prohibiting the nonviolent or noninvasive use of one's property.
Thus, bribing a judge to obtain a favorable ruling in cases pertaining to offenses
such as smuggling, entering an occupation without a license, black marketeering,
violating price controls, or bribing public officials to receive exemptions from such
laws—what Murray Rothbard (1970b, pp. 57–58) called "defensive bribing"—
would all fall into the category of expansive corruption. To the extent that such acts
become known, they could actually stimulate development by rendering person
and property more secure. Even if society becomes demoralized or disillusioned by
such corruption, the effects may not be an impediment to development, as many
have claimed, for cynicism may well "act as a solvent on traditional inhibitions"
and lead to "increased self-seeking in the rest of the society," in which case "economic development may be furthered" (Leff, 1964, p. 12).

However, judge bribing in cases of murder, rape, and theft is both immoral and
economically detrimental. By placing the person and property of individuals in
jeopardy, it would render the society less secure. To the extent that it is successful,
it would undermine the enabling environment, and thus impede development.
Judge bribing of this type would therefore fall into the category of restrictive corruption.

Politician Bribing

The politician is the one who creates the laws and policies of the society. Bribing
politicians to obtain laws that are beneficial to oneself or one's group is nothing new
and doubtless takes place in every society. The question is: What are its effects? Is
the practice socially beneficial or harmful?

It is certainly possible for a law or policy benefiting an individual or group to
also benefit society at large. Laws against murder, theft, pollution, and the like are
cases in point. It is also possible for both particular individuals or groups and society
to benefit by the repeal of a law or policy. Price controls and licensing restrictions
are examples. The difficulty is that the confluence of individual and public benefits
does not usually provide a sufficient motive for action. In fact, the opposite is more
often the case. The repeal of a tariff, for example, will benefit society by lowering
prices. But even though the aggregate benefits may be quite large, they are diffused
throughout society. They may therefore amount to only a few dollars per individual. Consequently, the average individual will have little or no incentive to work
for the repeal, since the cost to her or him of such work will far exceed the benefits
received. On the other hand, since the benefits of the tariff are concentrated on those
few engaged in the industry covered by the tariff, they can be considerable for each
individual or firm. The beneficiaries of the tariff therefore have a strong incentive
to work for its retention. Given the asymmetry between the costs and benefits of
the tariff, it is obvious that the tariff is likely to be retained, even though society is
harmed (Olson, 1977, 1982).

The point is important. Individuals or groups are far more likely to be actively
engaged in influencing politicians when their interests conflict with what is socially
beneficial than when they converge. If so, then those laws and policies that benefit

particular groups of individuals while harming society will be the ones most likely to be implemented. It follows, therefore, that since bribery is one means of influencing politicians, it is likely to be overwhelmingly, if not solely, restrictive.

This raises a very important issue. Tullock (1974, pp. 67–70) noted that wealth transfers "appear to be intrinsic to all forms of government." But, at least in terms of their volume, they appear to be especially characteristic of modern democracies, where well in excess of half of all budgets involve what can easily be termed wealth transfers. Tullock referred to these activities as "very similar to corruption." But according to the above definition, such transfers *are* corruption. In fact, they are identical, in all relevant aspects, to the agreement between the police and the theft ring: one party, the politicians, enact a law that transfers wealth from a second party, the owners of the wealth, to a third party, the beneficiaries, in return for which the politicians receive from the beneficiaries blandishment in the form of money, political support, or both. If this is so, then corruption is far more common in Western democracies than is commonly thought. The primary difference between the Western democracies and the rest of the world is not so much the magnitude of corruption as the means by which it is undertaken.

In summary, public-sector corruption is solely parasitic or restrictive; dual-sector bureaucratic and judicial corruption can be either restrictive or expansive, but public-sector political corruption is predominantly, if not solely, restrictive. Purely private-sector corruption is, by definition, an empty category.

Conclusions

This chapter distinguished between two fundamentally different types of corruption: restrictive corruption that reduces opportunities for socially beneficial exchange, thereby retarding economic growth, and expansive corruption which, by increasing the opportunities for socially productive exchange, is economically beneficial.

It needs to be stressed, however, that corruption is beneficial only in context. By placing obstacles in the way of socially beneficial exchange, intervention is economically harmful. Evading laws and policies that are economically detrimental is referred to here as expansive corruption. Consequently, expansive corruption is beneficial relative to the situation: it helps to undo the harm created by intervention. In a purely noninterventionist society, therefore, expansive corruption could not exist, since there would be no obstacles in the way of socially productive exchange. It follows that expansive corruption is positively correlated with restrictive corruption. Since restrictive corruption places obstacles in the way of socially productive exchange, it generates incentives for evasion, that is, for expansive corruption. There is also a positive correlation between corruption and the scope of government activities: the more interventionist the government, the greater the corruption. Though obviously scanty, the empirical data do seem to confirm this. There is an abundance of evidence to show that the amount of corruption found in such quasi-totalitarian societies as the Soviet Union, Eastern Europe, and the Peoples' Republic of China was enormous (Dallago, 1991; Grossman, 1972; Mosher,

1983a, Chapters 1–3; Simis, 1982; H. Smith, 1984, Chapters 1, 3). Simis (1982, p. 39), for example, referred to the Soviet Union, where the state attempted to exercise universal control, as a universally corrupt society. Moreover, if wealth transfers are, in fact, corrupt, then it is clear that the amount of corruption in the Western democracies has increased dramatically as the scope of government activities there has expanded. In short, corruption is hardly restricted to the Third World.

The relevant distinction is not between developed and undeveloped societies, but between limited and unlimited states. The more unlimited the state—the larger the scope of its activities—the greater the incidence of corruption, both restrictive and expansive.

The policy implications are clear. Those concerned about corruption and/or economic development should focus their attention on reducing the scope of government activities. Such an effort would reduce both types of corruption. Restrictive corruption would be reduced because, as government activities became more restricted, there would be fewer opportunities for using it as a vehicle for transferring wealth and thus less time, money, and effort would be invested in such attempts. Since expansive corruption is positively correlated with restrictive corruption, the former would decline with the latter. Moreover, there would be less need to engage in such activities as the government restrictions on the free market that prompt them are reduced.

Note

1. It is true that the thief does exert effort or work in the process of his theft. But this does not constitute a legitimate transfer of ownership because it violates the logically prior right of the current owner to freely dispose of his property. See Nozick, 1974, pp. 150–231.

IV

CONCLUSION: THE ENABLING ENVIRONMENT

10

Property, Law, and Development

Government intervention, under the best of circumstances, has retarded economic growth, restricted economic development, and often resulted in famine, starvation, and serious malnutrition. While sometimes providing gains for the poor in the short run, it has placed them in a situation where, in the long run, they are poorer than they would have been in the absence of the intervention. Political control over all or a large part of an economy generates an almost irresistible temptation for political elites to use that control to benefit themselves. Thus, government intervention seldom takes place for the best of intentions. More commonly, intervention in the form of licensing restrictions, tariffs, and marketing boards has been used by local elites to enrich themselves at the expense of the poor and to insulate their own positions in the socioeconomic hierarchy from competition from potential economic rivals. The result has been the creation of a caste structure characterized by a permanent ruling elite and an equally permanent poverty-stricken underclass. It has also been used by the elites to persecute and even to exterminate their political enemies by, for example, the deliberate creation and perpetuation of famine.

What is sorely needed is the creation of a wall of separation between the political and economic spheres. Restricting government activity to the enforcement of laws protecting the person and property of individuals, to the creation of an enabling environment, would not only eliminate those obstacles to economic growth, it would simultaneously eliminate the ability of political elites to manipulate markets for their own personal benefits. Such a wall of separation would therefore go a long way toward ensuring not only economic growth—the quantitative increase in economic output—but also economic development—improvement in the quality and variety of goods and services that are widely available in a society.

The strategy for achieving such an environment is double-pronged. It requires, first and foremost, a policy of *privatization*: the elimination of as much government activity as possible. And second, it requires *decentralization*: the handling of all remaining government activity as locally as possible.

Property and Privatization

Property

It is difficult to overestimate the importance of a system of private property for economic growth and development.

> Without well-defined property rights, all activity and interchange is difficult. When neither exclusivity nor the right to transfer resources exists, the means for determining relative values and for maximizing economic benefits are lacking. On the other hand, the more secure are property rights, the less costly will be transactions, and the greater will be the interest in discovering and taking advantage of existing opportunities.   (de Soto, 1988, p. 25)

"Economic exchanges have become so much a part of our everyday routine," James Buchanan has observed (1975, pp. 17–18), "that we often overlook the bases upon which such institutions rest." One can, for example, stand in a checkout line of a modern grocery store and consummate a hundred or more transactions in a matter of a minute or two. Although this is taken for granted, it is possible only because there are well-defined property rights. I recognize the vendor's ownership right to the merchandise in his store and therefore my obligation not to take any of it without the owner's consent. The owner, in turn, recognizes my right to my wallet and cannot compel me to purchase anything from the store that I do not want to buy or at a price that I do not wish to pay.

But, asks Buchanan, what if ownership rights are unclear? What if I do not recognize the property rights of the vendor to the merchandise in the store?

> I am reluctant to pay, despite the fact that my evaluation may exceed the money price asked. On the other hand, the nominal possessor of the goods is unwilling to meet my demands without a price. . . . Ordinary exchange, which seemed so simple and straightforward in the first example, is made extremely difficult here because the parties do not agree on the 'law of property' in being, which means that they are uncertain as to what action the state might take in any dispute.   (Buchanan, 1975, pp. 17–18)

Not only is mutually beneficial exchange rendered exceedingly difficult, the uncertainty regarding the rightful owner makes it highly unlikely that the vendor would undertake capital investments to increase the productivity and thus the value of the property.

This is clearly borne out in empirical work on the informal economy in Peru by de Soto (1988, p. 25):

> The function of property rights is to encourage those who hold them to add value to them by innovating, investing, or combining them productively. All of our empirical research regarding property demonstrates incontrovertibly that the lack of secure property rights enormously reduces the productivity of the majority of Peruvians. Not having legal recognition of their possessions causes people in infor-

mal settlements to limit their investment in them. Through a sample of 38 settlements, it was determined that, on average, the value of their investment increased 9 times once people had title to their land.

Law

A necessary condition for economic growth is the ability of human beings to interact efficiently. This, it is clear, cannot occur in the absence of a well-defined system of property rights. By property is meant not simply material objects but what Hayek has termed (1969, p. 167) a "protected domain" into which others are prohibited from encroaching. Thus the law specifies a domain that belongs to or is owned by the individual. This domain includes not only material objects but the very person of the individual. It follows that the restraints that the law of the enabling environment, or what de Soto terms "facilitative law," impose on us are negative. They are not designed to achieve any *particular* concrete purpose such as a correct distribution of wealth or a just price for a particular good or service. Their function is to establish an environment within which human interaction may take place, although it does not command individuals to interact. Consequently, the law does not direct individual activity in any particular direction or toward any particular goal. Such law merely tells us what we may not do, thereby leaving individuals free to select and pursue their own particular goals or cultivate their own individually selected projects. It is in this sense that such law may be termed "purpose-independent" (Hayek, 1969, pp. 160–177; 1973, p. 50; 1988, p. 31).

By proscribing encroachment on the protected domains of others, by prohibiting such things as murder, theft, rape, and the like, facilitative, or purpose-independent law, enables individuals to enter into voluntary, and mutually advantageous, contractual commitments with others. These commitments introduce an important element of certainty or regularity into human intercourse. And it is this regularity, the negative expectation that individuals will not interfere with one's protected domain coupled with the positive expectation that individuals will do certain things because they have voluntarily committed themselves to do them, that not only permits individuals to select and pursue *their own* projects or goals, but also, by greatly reducing the risk or cost of interaction, makes possible the emergence of an extended and complex network of human intercourse.

To the extent that there are benefits to an extended and complex order that small and less complicated orders cannot provide, benefits such as specialization, economies of scale, sophisticated transportation and communications networks, and the like, such an order greatly enhances the probability that these individual pursuits will be successful. That is, facilitative, or purpose-independent, law provides a framework that not only enables individuals who may not have any interests in common to cooperate with one another in the pursuit of their own particular goals, but also permits literally millions of individuals who do not even know of one another's existences to interact peacefully and to each other's benefit.[1]

In contrast to purpose-independent law is what may be termed purpose-directed legislation, the attempt to use legislation to achieve certain specific goals.

Rather than being content with general principles to guide behavior, purpose-directed legislation must empcwer government officials to examine each case on its own merits. These officials must have full knowledge of all the particulars in each and every case to be in a position both to ascertain whether a given action, or price, is congruent with the goal and to know that the commands they issue move the community closer to that goal. It is precisely because attainment of the goal cannot be ensured without endowing certain government officials with the *discretionary* use of force that goal-directed legislation is, in a fundamental sense, *lawless*. The officials cannot be limited by a higher law, or by abstract rules or norms. If the goal is to be achieved, they must possess the discretionary power to issue different decrees for different locations as well as to issue additional decrees in order to adjust these policies to changing circumstances. Thus, the achievement of particular goals requires the use of discretionary power by individuals. It is incompatible with adherence to general or abstract rules that are applicable to all members of the community. Since a rule of law is intended to let individuals know when the state will act and when it will not, it is incompatible with legislation designed to achieve particular concrete goals or ends.

The legal uncertainty created by purpose-directed legislation constitutes a serious impediment to economic growth. First, when the status of property is uncertain, when individuals are never sure whether their property will be seized by the state, they are reluctant to increase the value of their possessions through investment. And even if they were inclined to invest, they are unlikely to obtain access to credit. Significantly, legal uncertainty regarding property rights seriously impedes the emergence of the extended order, since it limits the scope of exchange to those whom the trader can trust, that is, to those whom the trader personally knows (Landa, 1988, pp. 97–99). As a result of the size limitations imposed by uncertainty, "it is virtually impossible to achieve economies of scale" (de Soto, 1988, p. 27). Second, the uncertainty resulting from the discretionary authority of government officials necessitates the diversion of effort from the economic function of production to the political function of influencing the decision-making process. It is only by attaining such influence that one is in a position to ensure that one's property is protected. Since the crying need in the LDCs is for increased production, the diversion of vast amounts of time and resources into acquiring political influence constitutes pure social waste. Such efforts would simply not occur in a liberal social order because government would not be invested with the authority to transfer wealth.

> A legal system that does not guarantee the fundamental rights of property, contract, legal process, and commercial organization to the majority of its citizens cannot maximize incentives to innovate, invest, and produce. At the same time the legal system imposes excessive charges on the private sector through red tape and regulation, discourages private initiative, and increases the costs of goods produced. In this setting the traditional prescriptions of structural reform are destined to fail because they do not get at the heart of the problem, which is a mercantilist structure that limits competition, functions on favoritism rather than efficiency and represses entrepreneurship.   (de Soto, 1988, p. 43)

Legal certainty regarding property rights can only be achieved through a policy of full-scale privatization, that is, the complete withdrawal of government from the economic sphere and the corresponding specification, as completely as possible, of property rights law to ensure that externalities are internalized. The latter is nothing more than a logical corollary of the former—without such specification there is uncertainty as to where one's protected domain ends and another's begins.

Law and Power

Some analysts, Marxists for example, have argued that *any* system of laws institutionalizes the interests or preferences of the dominant group or class in the society. This is what Marx and Engels meant when they wrote that "the executive of the modern state is but a committee for handling the affairs of the whole bourgeoisie" ([1848] 1968, p. 5). And Marxists such as C. B. Macpherson (1962) interpret philosophers like Thomas Hobbes and John Locke as spokesmen for the emerging bourgeois class. The notion that there could be a political or economic system that was not, to use Marx's term, "antagonistic" ([1859] 1970, p. 21), that is, that did not operate to the benefit of one particular class such as the bourgeoisie or capitalists and at the expense of another class such as the proletariat or laborers,[2] was regarded as nothing more than ideological special pleading, or a "political illusion" designed to veil the fact of exploitation (Marx and Engels [1848], 1968, p. 6). The possibility that a system could be anything other than zero-sum was entirely foreign to Marx.

Marx and Engels summed up the essence of the bourgeois mode of production, that is, capitalism, in terms of "that single, unconscionable freedom, Free Trade" ([1848] 1968, p. 6). This would seem to proscribe government interference with the economy. Yet, curiously, Marx and Engels drew the opposite conclusion: "The necessary consequence of this [free competition] was political centralization" ([1848] 1968, p. 10). Since competition forced the capitalists to reduce their prices, free competition squeezed profits. The only way the *existing* bourgeoisie could maintain their positions at the top of the social pyramid was by using the state to hold wages down and prices up.

While Marx's analysis may have a good deal of historical validity, it is obvious that it contains a fundamental conceptual flaw. There is little reason to dispute the fact that the emerging bourgeois class used the state for its own advantage. Recognition of this was hardly new with Marx. It can be traced back at least to Adam Smith's *Wealth of Nations* in 1776. However, it makes no sense to regard an economic system based on "free trade, free selling and buying" (Marx and Engels, [1848] 1968, p. 30) as one with an economic system in which the government rigidly controls all trade, all selling, and all buying. Smith made precisely this distinction. He critiqued the network of government restrictions (the mercantilist system) on the grounds that its only beneficiaries were the "rich and powerful" ([1776] 1937, p. 609) and advocated its replacement by "the system of natural liberty," that is, free-market capitalism. The former he viewed as a zero-sum system; the latter as positive-sum. Marx, on the other hand, officially defined the bourgeois system in terms of free trade yet devoted nearly his entire analysis to critiquing the way the bourgeoisie had used the state to regulate the economy for their own benefit. He did not recognize the absolutely fundamental distinction between capitalism and mercantilism. In fact, while Marx attempted to provide a complete taxonomy of economic systems and toyed with no fewer than nine distinct modes, including such obscurities as the Slavonic and Germanic, and eventually settled on five or six, depending on when he was writing, mercantilism was never even considered by Marx.

It is significant that Marx did *not* argue that since the desire of capitalists is to make profit, and to make it in the easiest and least risky way possible, and since laissez-faire capitalism holds out the possibility not only of great profits but also of heavy losses, the capitalists would attempt to eliminate the risks attendant to free trade and use the government to regulate the market. This would guarantee their profits and institutionalize their positions at the top of the socioeconomic hierarchy. That is, Marx did not argue that laissez-faire capitalism would be unstable and quickly evolve into mercantilism. This he was unable to do, since he would then have to explain why the capitalist class opposed capitalism. And his answer would have to be that it did not operate to the specific benefit of the capitalist class but rather to the benefit of everyone in general, and the poor in particular. He would then have to acknowledge that there was no such thing as economic power and therefore that the only way any individual or group could maintain its position in the open market was by providing goods and services that people wanted to buy at prices that they were able to pay; and the only way capitalists could attract and keep the workers they needed was by paying them wages high enough to prevent them from taking their services elsewhere. To acknowledge this would be to admit that the liberal-capitalist order was a positive-sum system; that everyone, and not merely the capitalists, benefited. Rather, Marx's implicit assumption was that capitalism and mercantilism were synonymous; that there was no reason to distinguish between the two. Only by blurring the distinction between capitalism and mercantilism was Marx able to depict the capitalist process as zero-sum.

It is incorrect to argue that any set of laws must reflect the interests of whatever group happens to be dominant in society. There is at least one system of law, that of the liberal order, that works to benefit every group or class. In fact, it is precisely for this reason that the proponents of the liberal order have had so much difficulty in implementing liberal legal principles. Those groups that have obtained government privileges such as subsidies, licensing restrictions, tariffs, and legal monopolies, that is, usually Adam Smith's "rich and powerful," have opposed losing these privileges and have therefore vigorously fought any attempt to implement the liberal order (M. Friedman, 1989, pp. 98–104).

Privatization

It has been argued that the creation of an enabling environment—the existence of a wall of separation between government and the economy—is a necessary condition for economic growth and development. One of the more effective strategies to achieve this goal is privatization.

Privatization is intended to reduce the role of government in the economy by increasing the private sector's role in the provision of goods and services. The rationale is derived from the assumption that "alternative forms of property ownership give rise to different economic incentives and, subsequently, different economic results" (Hanke, 1987b, p. 48. Also see De Alessi, 1987; Waters, 1987). When property is privately owned, the owners bear the costs and reap the benefits of their activities and decisions. If their enterprises are able to provide goods and services that consumers want to buy at costs that are below existing market prices, they earn profits, and the value of their assets increases. If their enterprises are unable to do this, they suffer losses and the value of their assets declines. Thus, the incentives of private ownership generate economic efficiency (Hanke, 1986, p. 9; 1987b, pp. 48–49).

Conversely, the nominal owners of public enterprises are the taxpayers. They, however, can neither buy nor sell their assets. Moreover, while it is true that by increasing the economic efficiency of public enterprises the taxpayer-owners might benefit in the form of tax reductions, this benefit, when dispersed among the millions of taxpayers, would be quite small. The costs involved in acquiring these benefits, including the costs of obtaining the necessary information, monitoring the activities of public employees, and organizing effective political organizations in order to bring the requisite pressure to bear on the relevant political officials who in turn are able to exert sufficient pressure on the public employees to force them to modify their behavior, would be extraordinarily high. Consequently, resources end up being allocated by people who do not own them and who neither reap the benefits nor suffer the losses from their decisions and activities. The result is that there is little incentive for the managers or employees of a public enterprise to serve either the consumers or the taxpayer-owners in an economically efficient way.

Insulated from the threat of competition and assured that economic losses will be covered by increased government funding, public employees are free to shirk as well as to direct their attention not to the satisfaction of consumer desires but to the acquisition of various perquisites. Both increase costs (Hanke, 1986, pp. 10–11; 1987b, p. 49; 1987c, p. 2). To ameliorate some of the more blatant abuses, public officials must impose an extensive network of rules and regulations. Again, the incentives generated by these rules are significant. Employees are rewarded—promoted—for following the rules, not for serving the consuming public. And hemmed in by restrictions, the public enterprise cannot, even if it wanted to, adapt efficiently to changes in consumer desires, advances in production technologies, and the like. The conclusion is that the very nature of public enterprises renders them inefficient mechanisms for the satisfaction of consumer demands, and therefore social liabilities whose functions could be far more efficiently performed by private enterprises. This was clearly demonstrated in a recent and exhaustive study of the American school system (Chubb and Moe, 1990). Public and private enterprises, says Hanke (1987b, pp. 49–50),

> are similar in that they must both plan. Public planning is, however, fundamentally different from private planning. Public plans are developed by public managers and employees who neither bear the costs of their mistakes nor legally capture benefits

generated by foresight. Moreover, public plans are developed by people who do not have to answer to any of the owners. As long as the planning and procedures are followed, a public plan is considered a good plan. Private planning is quite a different story. Private plans attempt to anticipate consumer demands and production costs correctly because the present value of the private enterprise depends on correct anticipation of demands and costs. Needless to say, private planners ultimately have to answer to the owners of private enterprises, who keep a watchful eye on the value of the enterprises that they own.

The bulk of the empirical evidence supports the theory. Hanke refers to the "bureaucratic rule of two," which is that the operating costs of public enterprises are about twice those of private firms providing the same or comparable goods and services (Hanke, 1987b, pp. 50–51). Numerous other empirical studies indicate that privatization has resulted not only in significant savings but in improved service as well (see, e.g., Cervero, 1985; Fitzgerald, 1980; Fixler and Poole, 1987; Hanke, 1986, 1987d; Martin, 1986; Moore, 1987; Walters, 1987).

There are, however, some important anomalies. In a number of cases, the expected benefits of privatization have not materialized. In fact some studies show that "even in those countries where the total net performance has been negative, there are some state enterprises with positive profit performance." Consequently, it has been concluded (Haile-Mariam and Mengistu, 1988, p. 1574), "it is therefore impossible to say that public enterprises are universally profitable or universally unprofitable."

Of course human society is immensely complex and one would hardly expect to find universally constant empirical results. Nor, as far as I am aware, has any proponent of privatization ever made such a claim. Privatizers have tried to account for these anomalies in several ways.

First, they have pointed out that cost-accounting procedures used by public agencies are often quite different from those employed by private firms, with the result that "the costs of state service provisions are often greatly understated" (Poole, 1987, p. 37). For example, government agencies will often quote the price of a good or service as if it were the cost, "ignoring the fact that the firm must price to cover all of its costs while the government is generally subsidized" (Poole, 1987, p. 37). Thus, an agency's share of the government's overhead costs is often ignored or incompletely accounted for, its share of such things as pension programs and other retirement costs is traditionally omitted, and usually no allowance is made for capital depreciation costs (Fitzgerald, 1987, pp. 226–228; Poole, 1987, pp. 37–38). In addition, government agencies have adjusted private bids upward while intentionally and grossly underestimating its own costs. Sometimes these adjustments were even made after the bidding process was closed (Fitzgerald, p. 227).

Second, privatizers have emphasized that to avoid abuses, the privatization process must be handled properly. Given

the vagaries of human nature, the contracting out of public services harbors its share of potential abuses. It goes without saying that proper steps must be taken and care exercised to protect the public from possible abuses of a contractor system as well as to insure that terms of the contract are fulfilled.   (Fitzgerald, 1980, p. 82)

Fitzgerald went on to say that the best means of accomplishing this is to maintain a system of "open, competitive bidding and tightly written, closely monitored contracts." Where these criteria are absent, it is hardly surprising to find that the results of privatization are less than satisfactory.

This leads to the third response. The principal reason for the inefficiency of government agencies stems from the monopoly status they typically enjoy. The goal of privatization is to induce efficiency by replacing these public monopolies with private competition. What is really crucial is not the formal, legal status of the supplier, it is not whether it is public or private, but whether entry into the field is open, that is, whether the field is characterized by competition or monopoly. Transforming a public monopoly into a private monopoly is merely a change in form, not in substance. It will do little or nothing to ensure that the public is served either more efficiently or responsively. Similarly, transferring public-owned factories or agencies to the private sphere will mean little if the private sphere is saddled with government restrictions such as price controls, minimum wage laws, ceilings on interest rates, and the like (Berg, 1987, p. 26–27; McPherson, 1987, p. 19). In either case the results of privatization are likely to be unsatisfactory. In the former, the private monopolies will find themselves in positions where they are free to exploit rather than compelled to serve the public; in the latter, the operators in the newly privatized field will find themselves unable to charge prices high enough to cover costs. Nor will they possess the flexibility to make the adjustments necessary to provide the goods and services to the public. Consequently, the private operators will suffer losses, the experiment will be declared a failure, and the government will be forced to resume provision of the services.

But privatizers have made it quite clear that they do not regard such privatization as genuine. Firms that are technically private but either enjoy government-sanctioned monopoly status or are subject to extensive government restrictions are not regarded as genuinely private. Similarly, public agencies that must operate purely on their own, without government subsidies and in an environment that does not prohibit entry by private firms, are not regarded as genuinely public. This point is particularly important. Too often, and this is especially true of the Third World, countries are "less characterized by the separation of political and economic decisions than by their merger" (Tanoira, 1987, p. 54). De Soto and Tanoira have compared existing Third World economies to European mercantilism of the fifteenth and sixteenth centuries. Given the merger between government and the economy, the question "public or private," Tanoira notes, has little meaning. "In mercantile societies privatization might mean no more than an expansion of not-so-private enterprise, or an expansion of government by another name" (pp. 55–56). Perhaps, he adds, "if the world provided a clear comparison between an unprotected public enterprise and its protected private counterpart, the public enterprise might be found to be more productive and profitable." If privatization is to work, he says, "first we've got to privatize the private sector" (pp. 54–57).

While these considerations may account for the anomalies regarding the performance of private and public enterprises, they do raise a serious question. Privatization has become associated with contracting out. But contracting out, say its proponents, will function properly only as long as the "proper steps" are taken—

the bidding is free and open, the contracts are awarded fairly, there is no revolving door between private firms and the government agencies, and the private performance is closely monitored by the appropriate government officials to ensure compliance with the terms of the contract.

How realistic is it to think that the process will actually work this way for any period of time? There is a contradiction, or at least a tension, in the logic of contracting out. For the program to work, government officials must take the proper steps. But if government officials could be relied on to take the proper steps, there would be little need to contract out in the first place. What reason is there to believe that the bidding process will continue to remain open or that the programs will be tightly monitored by the government and that private firms not living up to their contractual obligations will be dismissed? Don't both history and logic suggest that it is far more likely that a close relationship will develop between the private firms and the monitoring government officials?

Contracting out may be, as many of its proponents maintain, only partial privatization. The problem is that the term *privatization* has rapidly become a synonym for contracting out. But contracting out can easily become a trap. While reducing government expenditures in the short run, it may well increase them in the long run, especially if the contractors are able to use their close relations with the government agencies to obtain de facto monopoly status. Certainly the network of government-created and -protected private monopolies extending from Asia to Latin America (de Soto, 1989; University of the Philippines, 1984, pp. 72–110) does not give one confidence that the process would remain competitive. Moreover, contrary to the intentions of the privatizers, contracting out not only does not reduce government economic responsibility, it actually expands it. "As professionals who have worked with governments at all levels in their privatization efforts, it is our view," write Miller and Steinberg in a revealing passage (1986, p. 25), "that public agencies [must] retain both decision making and ultimate responsibility for public services."

What is needed is not a policy of contracting out, in which the government retains its responsibility and thus involvement in the economic arena, but a policy of genuine privatization in which government is relieved of its responsibility for, and thus its interference in, the economic affairs of its citizens. While there may be times when contracting out is a useful policy, it must be stressed that it is not what is meant here by privatization.

Government and the Provision of Essential Services

Many critics of privatization believe that government has a responsibility to provide certain functions and that "privatization signals a diminished commitment to include the poor in the national household" (Starr, 1987, p. 135). The "difficulty of privatizing some public goods," Starr continues, "is that public administration is essential to their character," and the very appearance of buying and selling undermines the claim" (p. 133). (Also see Page, 1990.)

Aside from the fact that the equation of government with altruistic and impartial activity on behalf of the entire community is precisely what ought to be called into question, the deeper issue is: How can the government best realize its public responsibilities? There is no doubt that there would not be famines in Africa if the governments there did not intervene so heavily in the agricultural sector. If one feels that the government has a responsibility to ensure that its citizens are well fed, then it follows that the best way for it to fulfill this responsibility is by refraining from intervening in the agricultural sector. Several empirical studies have disclosed that delays for new drug approval by the Food and Drug Administration (FDA) have saved between 5,000 and 10,000 lives per decade. However, these delays have caused 21,000 to 120,000 additional deaths during the same time period. On balance, therefore, the FDA regulations have resulted in between 4 and 12 deaths for every life saved (D. Friedman, 1973, pp. 123–125; Gieringer, 1985; Kinsky, 1974). Thus if one feels that the government has a responsibility for seeing to it that people receive adequate health care, perhaps the best way for it to fulfill this responsibility, especially in light of what was said earlier in this chapter about bureaucratic incentives, would be for the government to terminate much, perhaps even all, of its activity in this area.

There is also considerable empirical evidence that the poor would be better off in the absence of the plethora of government programs ostensibly designed to help them (Brozen, 1966; Gwartney and McCaleb, 1985; Murray, 1984; Osterfeld, 1980). Yale Brozen (in De Alessi, 1987, p. 24) has estimated that current income in the United States would be at least 25 percent higher in the absence of postwar poverty programs and sundry government regulatory activities. And Hutt (1971, p. 38) has concluded, because of the retarding effect of government regulation on economic growth and the regressive nature of many taxes, that in countries like the United States and Great Britain "it is difficult to believe that the poorest classes are not the net losers [of government income transfer programs] by a formidable amount." It seems likely that the amount would be considerably higher in far more politicized Third World countries. For example, de Soto has found (1988, p. 17) that, "because of the labyrinth of rules and regulations" in Peru,

> it is virtually impossible for poor people to comply with all of the requirements to live and work legally. And even for those who are able to do so, the costs of remaining legal are overwhelming.

To follow all of the steps required to obtain legal title to a piece of land, he found, took an average of seven years. It took street vendors an average of nearly ten years to meet all bureaucratic requirements. Moreover, it took 289 days and $1,231, or 32 times the minimum wage, even for college students used to dealing with paperwork and bureaucracy, to legally establish a small garment factory consisting of just two sewing machines (1988, pp. 22–23). The result is a sort of legal apartheid in which the poor are systematically excluded from the legal or formal sector. This drastically reduces aggregate production and, by shielding the wealthy from competition, channels much of what is produced into their pockets. Again, if one believes that the government has a responsibility to care for the poor, the evidence suggests that the best way for it to fulfill this function is to repeal many, and perhaps even all, of its poverty programs and other regulations on economic activity and rely on the market.

In brief, rather than protecting the public from abuse, the government is more often than not the *source* of abuse.

Other Objections to Privatization

What is called for is a massive reduction in governmental or mercantilist restrictions on market processes and the establishment of a clear rule of law in which property rights are fully specified and protected. Such an environment would stimulate economic development in several ways. Security of property would encourage savings and investment, both domestic and foreign. As de Soto asks (1988, p. 24), "How much investment would have taken place in the Western world without well-defined and secure property rights and court systems to protect them?" Security of property would significantly reduce transaction costs by reducing the risks and difficulties inherent in long-term investment projects, credit transactions, and the like. The reduction in transaction costs would increase productivity by extending the scope of the market, thereby intensifying specialization and the division of labor and permitting the realization of economies of scale. Security in property would unleash the native entrepreneurial energy that is now smothered by the welter of government controls. The reduction in government functions would permit a corresponding reduction in taxes. This would stimulate productive behavior by allowing individuals to retain a much larger portion of their income.

State-owned enterprises, or SOEs, came to dominate the manufacturing sector in many Third World countries during the 1960s and 1970s, in many cases totaling more than 50 percent of the industrial assets. In Bangladesh the figure reached 85 percent in the 1970s (Young, 1987, p. 196). SOEs have operated in practically every nook and cranny of both the agricultural and industrial sectors. They produce cement in Algeria; they make gasohol and operate geothermal steam wells in Kenya; they produce steel and electricity in Brazil, and oil and fertilizer in India; they operate textile, jute, and paper mills in Bangladesh, as well as banks, newspapers, and magazines; and they have produced rice, flour, and cotton in Pakistan. In the Philippines, SOEs have produced such things as bananas, coconuts, and sugar. In Argentina the state has operated travel agencies, ceramics factories, and pipe-manufacturing firms. SOEs in Nigeria operate in the brewing, hotel, and appliance industries; in Rwanda they make everything from banana wine to paste; in Mozambique they operate in the construction and building materials industries. In nearly all countries SOEs have responsibility for operating the telephones, radio stations, and other means of communication; they own and operate both airports and airlines, provide buses, and other forms of transportation; produce gas and electricity; operate banks and dispense credit; run schools and build roads. This list covers just a few of their activities. In many if not most cases the SOEs have monopoly status; and yet in nearly all cases they operate with substantial losses (see Berg, 1987; Fitzgerald, 1980, pp. 261–274; Krauss, 1984, pp. 168–169; Young, 1987). Since this means that individuals and private-sector firms must pay higher taxes to cover these losses, the former are left with less spendable income whereas the latter must charge higher prices for their goods and services. The obvious result is the retardation of economic growth.

Governments have no business producing steel, running beauty parlors, or repairing televisions. Invariably, their performances in such areas have been quite poor. From the point of view of stimulating economic growth and development, the clear policy implication is for the state to divest itself of all state-owned enterprises. One objection to this is that, at least in the Third World,

> state ownership and control often involves projects with large capital outlays which may not be profitable. Such projects, therefore, may not appeal to the private investor. However, such industries which may provide vital products and services, including steel plants, fertilizer factories and manufacturing plants, may have to be established by the government with no regard to their profitability. Such state enterprises were established with a conscious choice for security and self-reliance over profit, and the desire to control the "commanding heights" of the economy. (Haile-Mariam and Mengistu, 1988, p. 1569)

There are two serious difficulties with this argument. First, provided the market is free, if returns are not high enough to cover costs there is in the eyes of consumers a more important use for the resources elsewhere. Consequently, when the government acts "with no regard to . . . profitability," when it overrides the decisions of the consumers as manifested in the marketplace, it *reduces* social utility. If, however, the market does fail to respond to the demand for certain vital products and services, if there is market failure, one must ask why. The usual answer is that the market is unable to supply public goods, that is, goods that cannot be broken down into marginal units and therefore cannot be supplied individually. In fact, as an increasing number of studies have shown (Cheung, 1988; Coase, 1988; Demsetz, 1988; Goldin, 1972; Osterfeld, 1986, pp. 273–375), very few goods or services are *inherently* "public," and those that are can often still be provided efficiently on the market through tying arrangements or the development of other exclusion technologies. While lighthouses are a public good, port space is not. Lighthouses can be financed by making lighthouse fees into part of general port fees (Coase, 1988). The problem is that by prohibiting ownership of certain goods such as, say, forests or rivers, or permitting ownership only under very restricted conditions, as is the case with rent controls, *the law transforms these goods and services into collective goods.*

The consequences of this transformation are well known and have been abundantly documented. Rent controls prevent apartment owners from being able to receive the full value for their apartments, with a consequent decline in the value of the property, a corresponding reduction in the maintenance of the building, and a shifting of investment from housing to other areas. The result is a reduction in both the quantity and quality of housing units. "The effect of rent control," Waters has pointed out (1987, p. 105), "is a partial transfer of property rights from the owners of the buildings to the present group of tenants—with slums being the ultimate result." Similarly, price controls or other government regulations that interfere with the market process often make it impossible for the market to respond to consumer demand. Put differently, what is commonly referred to as market failure is actually government failure. What is required is an institutional setting that encourages the property owner to respond to market demand. And this is precisely what a system of private property does. By establishing the owner as the residual claimant, private property ensures that the owner not only enjoys whatever profits remain after expenses, but is equally liable for any accompanying losses. This provides the owner with a powerful incentive to see that the property is employed in its most productive uses. Thus, what is called for is not increased government interference with the economy but rather the full articulation of private property. "The beneficial results of competition and price signals," Waters notes (1987, p. 103), "cannot be achieved unless ownership rights are established."

What needs to be stressed is that a defense of property rights is not a defense of the position of the existing wealthy. In fact, insofar as their wealth was a product, solely or in part, of government privileges such as licenses, tariffs, subsidies, and the like, the adoption of a fully specified and protected system of private property would actually *undermine* the position of the existing wealthy. This is so because government restrictions on the peaceful use of one's property constitute a violation of the property owner's rights. Thus a system of universal private property rights is incompatible with tariffs, subsidies, and other government restrictions, and their elimination would terminate the upward transfer of wealth through the government.

Another common objection to divestiture of SOEs is that regardless of its desirability, it is not feasible because of insufficient private capital. "To whom would these state enterprises be sold?," ask Haile-Mariam and Mengistu (1988, p. 1583).

> They would probably have to be sold to foreign interests, because the private indigenous sector does not have the capital and is not sufficiently organized to secure funds from local banks who demand unreasonable collateral and charge exorbitantly high interest rates. Would not the sale of these enterprises to private foreign buyers conjure up the fear of neo-colonial domination?

This raises a number of interesting questions. On the issue of the availability of private capital it must be borne in mind that the state has no resources it does not first take from its citizens in the form of taxes. It is simply disingenuous, therefore, to argue that the state must build and maintain such enterprises because of the lack of private capital. The causal relationship is actually the reverse: if there is a shortage of private indigenous capital it is because so much of it has been seized by the government in order to stimulate industrialization. But, because these factories were artificially stimulated by the government, they usually turn out to be little more than white elephants, with little demand for their products. The capital is there. The problem is that government interference with the market process resulted in its employment in projects that constitute a serious drain on the resources of the country.

A related objection is that even if there is enough capital in general, it is too diffused. It is not concentrated enough to allow any single individual to purchase the SOE. This can be overcome in at least two ways. First, an SOE does not have to be sold as a single unit. If, for example, the state operated several steel mills, there is no reason why they would all have to be sold to a single purchaser. In fact, it would probably be better to sell them independently to different individuals or groups, since that would facilitate competition. And second, even if capital is diffused, there is no reason why a SOE could not be sold in public offerings to a broad base of small, individual shareholders (Hanke, 1987e, p. 215).

There is also the serious matter of capital flight. But capital flight occurs only because of the uncertainty surrounding property rights. Once investors became convinced that their property was secure and would not be seized by the state, not only would capital flight come to a grinding halt, but foreign capital would begin to flow in.

But, according to Haile-Mariam and Mengistu, foreign ownership is bad because it is a symbol of "neo-colonial domination." Is it not possible to turn this logic on its head? As long as the government doesn't get involved, a company can earn profit only by providing consumers with what they desire to buy at prices they are prepared to pay. Thus the only way a company can make money on the free market is by serving the public. The question then becomes, What is wrong with foreign ownership? Whoever owns the company, whether a local businessman or a foreigner, can earn money only by working for, by serving, the indigenous population. *Rather than the owner's controlling them, they are controlling him.*

However, even if the prospect of foreign ownership proved to be an emotional stumbling block, it need not be fatal. A simple resolution to the problem is apparent: prohibit foreign ownership of privatized SOEs, at least for the time being, while simultaneously encouraging domestic competition by the repeal of government obstacles to market entry. In terms of economic development, this is clearly a second-best solution. Politically, however, it may be the most practical (Hanke, 1987a).

This is not to suggest that divestiture is simple or that care need not be exercised in the process. It is only to indicate that the most common objections to divestiture are manageable, that divestiture is feasible.

Getting the Enabling Environment

In terms of priorities, a movement toward an enabling environment ought to focus primary attention on abolishing those programs that impose the largest immediate loss on the poor. These would include such things as marketing boards, licensing restrictions, tariffs, price controls, and minimum wage laws. The abolition of these programs would have two major benefits. First, it would spur economic development by removing numerous impediments to productive economic activity, especially for the poor. And second, it would permit a reduction in the cost of government, and therefore in taxes. Since these sorts of programs transfer wealth upward, their elimination would constitute an immediate benefit for the poor.

Of less immediate, but perhaps of greater long-run, benefit for the poor would be the removal of government from the business sector. This would entail the sale of all SOEs.

To say that a policy of government divestiture is of less immediate benefit than the reduction of government economic regulations does not mean that it should take second place in terms of implementation. On the contrary, Milton Friedman has commented (1989, p. 101) in regard to the effort to "educate the public about tariffs in general [and] about the virtues of free trade as a general policy," that economists "have been trying it for two centuries without notable success." While arguing that such efforts ought not to be abandoned, he acknowledges that they are not enough. Friedman counsels "keeping options open for times of crisis" (1989, p. 102). If, for example, an SOE has become a particularly significant liability for an LDC government, and if enough interest and financing can be found or generated in the private sector, then one ought to take advantage of the opportunity and attempt to arrange for its sale. Of course it is vitally important that the project be handled carefully, since a success in one case would ease the way for additional sales, while the reverse is equally true.

Unemployment is a ticklish problem in practically any sale of an SOE, but especially in the LDCs, since they are so often characterized by bloated bureaucracies. In Ghana, for example, fully 20 percent of the public-sector work force was declared redundant by the Secretary of Finance. The Ghana state shipping line has so many redundant staff that since 1981 no fewer than 254 employees have been paid just to stay home (Ayittey, 1987c, p. 211). The elimination of these redundant employees would permit a major reduction in the operating costs of the newly privatized firm. However, the political cost of the resulting unemployment is likely to be unacceptable to the government. There are a variety of ways this problem can be dealt with and in the process used to reduce some of the fears of privatization. The contract negotiated between the government and the private purchasers could stipulate that the newly privatized firm give first preference in hiring to the government employees of the SOE. Since it would be impossible for the firm to retain all of the redundant workers and still manage to make a profit or even, perhaps, stay in business, a method by which privatization is phased in could be worked out. For example, the government might agree to *temporarily* reassign the redundant workers to other government enterprises with the stipulation that the firm would agree to a temporary freeze on outside hiring, thereby giving the former SOE employees first preference when any vacancies arise from normal attrition. Other possibilities to reduce the impact of unemployment could no doubt be worked out (Poole, 1987, pp. 38–40).

Of course, as privatization made headway, stimulating economic growth and thus the demand for labor in the private sector, layoffs from privatizing the remaining SOEs would become a progressively smaller and more easily manageable problem. Similarly, *if* the government is the necessary provider of roads and other public goods, the expanding economy would increase the tax base, thereby making government financing less difficult.

In addition to public education and taking advantage of crisis situations, a third strategy would be to "make your own breaks." This has been employed in Latin American countries, Peru in particular, with notable results. Since government regulations make it far too costly, in both time and money, for any but the already wealthy to obtain legally either land to live on or licenses to operate small businesses, citizens in Peru have more and more resorted to what de Soto calls "invasions." Invasions are a form of organized, massive civil disobedience. Their success depends on the participation of a fairly large number of citizens, a "critical mass" as de Soto refers to them, in order to dissuade public officials from opposing them, and a detailed plan so that the invaders are able to establish at least the rudiments of a settlement before the police or military forces are able to respond. The preinvasion planning meetings are held in secret to reduce the possibility that the authorities will find out and take preventive measures. During the meetings a place, usually unoccupied government land, and a date, usually a holiday, are chosen. Both choices are designed to reduce the likelihood of resistance. The invasion begins in the early morning so that by evening the boundaries of the settlement have been demarcated, plots have been apportioned to the invading families, and dwellings, constructed from rush matting and poles, have been erected. Such things as temporary communal kitchens and day-care centers are also organized to free the adults so they can carry out their assigned duties during the early days of the invasion. It is also standard practice for the invaders to have arranged with informal minibus operators to provide transportation and informal street vendors to supply food, clothing, and even building materials. Committees are also organized to defend the settlement, repel eviction attempts, and maintain order within the community (de Soto, 1989, pp. 19–23).

An invasion deliberately places the government in a difficult position. It has to either allow it to proceed, in effect recognizing the invaders' ownership of the land, or try to evict the invaders forcibly. As more and more invasions have occurred, it has become increasingly costly for the government to suppress all of them. The cost is not only monetary but also political, since the eviction attempts often result in violence and bloodshed, making the police look like bullies.

The longer the invaders remain, the less likely it is that the authorities will take action to evict them. Thus, the longer they remain, the stronger their claim to the land. Often the invaders negotiate with the government to begin the process by which they will receive official legal entitlement. Thus, instead of obtaining legal title to property and then taking possession of it, invasions work in reverse: occupation comes first, leading eventually to legal ownership.

Invasions, as de Soto demonstrates in detail (1989, pp. 59–127), can also be extended to commercial occupations such as vending and transportation. Much like the experience in the United States with Prohibition during the 1920s and the current "War on Drugs," or like the existence of the second economy in the Soviet Union and the Eastern bloc nations, as more and more people enter various occupations informally, it becomes increasingly difficult, as well as prohibitively expensive, for any government to suppress these illegal activities. Eventually the government may simply be compelled, as it was in the 1930s with Prohibition, to cease trying to regulate the sale of land and controlling occupational entry.

Three methods for moving society in the direction of an enabling environment have been advanced: public education, taking advantage of crises, and manipulating the environment or "making your own breaks." The latter is by far the most daring and aggressive. However, it seems unlikely than any strategy by itself can achieve complete success. Fortunately, there is no reason that all three cannot be utilized in tandem.

Maintaining the Enabling Environment

Even if one could get government to withdraw from the economy, is it realistic to believe that it would *remain* uninvolved? After all, both history and theory indicate that there is a tendency for the state to grow. It has been known for a long time that when benefits are concentrated on a small group but the costs are widely dispersed, the beneficiaries of the proposed programs will act vigorously to secure their implementation while the opponents will remain largely inactive, thereby all but ensuring passage (Meltzer, 1976; Olson, 1977, 1982). This is usually the case with various labor and business groups. For example, sweater manufacturers threatened by foreign competition can protect themselves by lobbying for a tariff raising the costs of foreign sweaters. This will increase the cost of sweaters for domestic consumers. People buy only one or two sweaters a year, however, while the industry sells millions, and thus the tariff would cost each domestic consumer only a few dollars but would be worth millions of dollars to manufacturers. Consequently, those in the industry will find it in their interest to work hard for the tariff while consumers will find it not worth their while to oppose it. Given this asymmetry, it is likely that the tariff will be passed.

Is there any way to preserve the enabling environment once it has been completely or even largely attained? The price of liberty—and correlatively economic development—may be eternal vigilance. But is this too much to expect? After all, people have their own lives to run and their own individual problems to deal with. Can one realistically expect that, in addition, people will be able to find the time, and be willing to continually monitor the actions of government? As Tullock has said (1972, p. 101)

> Public problems are normally more important than private problems, but the decision by any individual on a private problem is likely to be more important than his decision on a public problem, simply because most people are not so situated that their decisions on public matters make very much difference. It is rational, therefore, for the average family to put a great deal more thought and investigation into a decision such as what car to buy than into a decision on voting for President. As far as we can tell, families, in fact, act quite rationally in this matter, and the average family devotes almost no time to becoming informed on political matters, but will carefully consider the alternatives if they are buying a car.

The job is made much easier with the appropriate institutional framework. The constitutional separation of the government from the economy could create a significant barrier to future government expansion. This is so because an act of government intervention, or reintervention, into a laissez-faire economy would constitute an important departure from the existing policy, and thus be a far more noteworthy event, than an additional act of intervention in an already highly interventionist environment. But is this enough? Given the asymmetries between the costs and benefits of intervention, as well as the rationality of political ignorance, the answer is probably no.

There are several ways to increase the barriers to special interest legislation. Probably the easiest and most effective would be through a constitutional amendment specifically prohibiting the passage of tariffs, subsidies, and licensing restrictions as well as any other form of special interest legislation. This might not be nearly as difficult to achieve as it might appear. For reasons explained above, the asymmetry between costs and benefits inherent in any debate regarding any *particular* tariff or subsidy makes its passage by the legislature almost a certainty. However, changing the level of debate to the passage of tariffs, subsidies, or other forms of special interest legislation *in the abstract* quite literally removes that asymmetry. Individuals tend to lose as much by all of the privileges granted to other groups as they gain by the privileges granted to their group. Thus, when one considers in addition the reduction in productivity caused by the government's interference, as well as the costs of administering these programs, there is a clear net loss not only to society but to nearly every individual as well. It would therefore be in practically everyone's interest to oppose special interest legislation in the abstract. This makes it likely that a constitutional amendment prohibiting such policies would receive widespread support.

Of course, constitutions are not always honored. However, a clear violation of the fundamental law of the land is more likely to arouse the ire of citizens than violation of an ordinary piece of legislation. For example, the United States has protected those liberties spelled out in the Bill of Rights far better than those not so clearly enumerated. Thus a constitutional provision outlawing special interest legislation would change its status. In passing special interest legislation the legislature would no longer be merely enacting a law; it would be violating the Constitution. This would be more likely to arouse not only the attention but also the widespread opposition of the people.

Constitutional provisions might be utilized to prevent other types of legislative or executive interference in the economy. For example, a constitutional provision establishing a maximum rate of taxation coupled with a provision limiting the increase in the supply of money to 2 or 3 percent a year would prevent government officials from, in effect, buying political support by dispensing benefits to special groups of voters and paying for such benefits by printing money, thereby passing on the cost to the citizens in general in the form of higher prices. Such a provision is likely to receive widespread support for the same reason that the tariff provision would.

There are many other possibilities by which the scope of legislation, as well as executive decrees, could be effectively restricted. A constitutional provision might, for example, stipulate that passage of a bill required the support of two-thirds of the legislature. Another possibility would be to state that the national legislature could meet only at the request of a majority of state or local governments. Or the Constitution might require that any legislation passed at the national level be ratified by a majority or even two-thirds of the local government units. And constitutional amendments might be made to require the support of, say, 75 percent, or even the unanimous support, of local governments.

But if the law-making power of the national assembly is so restricted, wouldn't this provide minorities with veto power, thereby enabling them to frustrate the wishes of the majority? The answer is no. To understand this, we need to examine the second component of the enabling environment, decentralization.

Decentralization

It is important to recognize that the difference between government at the national level and government at the local level is not just a difference in degree; it is a difference in kind.

Democracy, Responsiveness, and Efficiency

In contrast to the competitive economic sphere, where adjustments are *marginal*, that is, each individual is able to evaluate each transaction separately, adjustments in the political sphere are *holistic*. *All* individuals residing within the jurisdiction of the same political unit *must* deal with the same agent, namely the government. A very important but too often overlooked issue is not so much *how* decisions are made or even who is consulted in the decision-making process, but the *scope* of the decision, once made. The democratic process must ultimately result in the selection of one alternative from an indeterminate number of possible alternatives and adopt it in the name of, and impose it upon, the entire society. Whether that alternative reflects the interests of an intense minority, an intense majority, or even an apathetic majority is immaterial. Those whose preferences are not incorporated into government policy cannot, as is generally the case with the market, satisfy their preferences by taking their business elsewhere. The best the losers can hope for is to exercise enough influence to get the policy changed. But this only means that the old losers are now winners and the old winners now losers. It does not change the nature of the game, only the final score.

The point is not that democracy is bad but that it is a zero-sum process. As such, it is not, *by itself*, a particularly good instrument for keeping government limited. It places tremendous power in the hands of the winners, which creates a very strong incentive for them to utilize that power to enact special programs to benefit themselves at the expense of the losers.

If the focus is shifted from the type of government, democracy or dictatorship, to the scope of its jurisdiction, very different consequences emerge. Government, according to Max Weber's classic definition, is that agency which exercises a monopoly over the (legitimate) use of force in society. However, the number of government units must increase in direct proportion to the degree to which the units are localized. Other things being equal, the more government units there are, the easier it would be to transfer loyalties. This means that the more local the government unit, the more closely the institutional political arrangement will resemble that of the positive-sum process of the competitive market: those who dislike the services they are receiving from one government are able to "vote with their feet" by moving to another area and joining another community. Conversely, those governments that alienate their citizens (their customers) by charging high prices (taxes), providing shoddy services, or violating peoples' rights, would soon find themselves with very few customers. In short, each "consumer-voter," to use Tiebout's term, would select that community that comes closest to satisfying his or her "total preference pattern." The greater the number of communities, that is, the larger each individual's choice set, the higher the level of satisfaction (Tiebout, 1956, p. 419).

Of course, cost considerations are by no means limited to monetary costs. There are often tremendous emotional and psychological costs involved in decisions to emigrate. And in selecting a community one invariably chooses a package or bundle of services, economic and noneconomic. It is most unlikely that one would agree with everything in the bundle. Thus, political decentralization can never be expected to operate with the efficiency of the economic market. However, since the bundles at the local level would be much smaller than at the national level, people would have to put up with much less of what they don't like. Decentralization is not a political panacea:

> It is easy to talk about the freedom of people to leave cantons whose political or economic system they do not like, and move to more congenial areas. But this will cause considerable disruption, hardship, and loss of wealth. A . . . farmer working and living on land that has been in his family for generations will not be greatly comforted by the knowledge that if he does not like the local policy . . . he can sell his farm and move. (Kendall and Louw, 1987, p. 139)

Still, while the result would never be Pareto-optimal, decentralization is the least bad realistic political alternative. And the general thesis holds. The cost of moving from, say, Rensselaer, Indiana, to Hong Kong would be much greater, monetarily and psychologically, than moving from Rensselaer to DeMotte, a distance of about 20 miles. Since the cost of emigration—monetary, psychological, and emotional—tends to be higher at the national than at the local level, one would expect its incidence to decline as the size of the government's jurisdiction expands. Emigration at the national level and especially at the international level tends to occur only under extreme circumstances. In other words, as the cost of emigration rises, the demand for it declines.

This has important consequences. First, one would expect local governments to be more responsive than state governments and the latter to be more responsive than national governments. Second, the more local the government, the *relatively* less important the type becomes. This is so because as soon as a dictator became oppressive, citizens would have an incentive to leave. Enough exits would, quite literally and peacefully, put the dictator out of business. Since emigration is much more costly under a national government, regardless of type, it would not occur as frequently, and therefore the threat of exit would be less credible (see Osterfeld, 1989a). However, since these only hold when emigration is possible, perhaps one of the primary responsibilities of the national government would be to see to it that the local governments do not obstruct the free movement of citizens and property. Emigration can, especially when used in tandem with democracy, be a very powerful tool protecting the rights of minorities while simultaneously keeping government responsive to the will of the community.

In brief, the more closely political institutions resemble the economic institutions of the market, the more responsive they will be. And the more restricted the scope of a political decision, the more localized the political unit, the more it approximates that arrangement. Since the greater the number and variety of communities the greater the likelihood that everyone, or practically everyone, can find communities following policies closely reflecting their own preferences, decentralization is able to combine the protection of minority rights with the ability of the (local) majority to implement those policies it prefers. Consequently, to the extent that legislation is needed, it should be limited largely to the local level.

Certainly one healthy consequence of such an arrangement would to depoliticize society, at both the local and the national levels. It would be depoliticized at the local level because the autonomy of the communities would allow a self-selection process to operate. People who opposed government interference could seek out communities following laissez-faire principles; those who desired a good deal of welfare measures could live in interventionist communities. Those subscribing to socialist principles could live in socialist communities. As Kendall and Louw note (1987, pp. 128–129), decentralization provides a framework within which localities adhering to very different principles "can operate comfortably side by side in one country." Decentralization would depoliticize society at the national level because, with government stripped of its ability to grant and withhold special benefits, it would make very little difference who controlled the national government.

Moreover, decentralization has the significant merit of substituting what Karl Popper has termed (1971, pp. 157–168) "piecemeal social engineering" for holistic or "utopian social engineering." The former allows for experimentation within a restricted domain. If the effects are unfortunate, the harm is confined to a relatively small group of people. If the law is not promptly repealed, citizens are in a position to avoid the harmful effects either by voting in new leaders or by emigrating. If the effects are beneficial, however, the experiment can be imitated by other local communities and thereby extended to much greater numbers of people. As P. M. Jackson has observed (1988, p. 18),

> Local government offers diversity, difference and variety in the supply of publicly provided goods and services. Expanded variety is an improvement in efficiency. Variety matches local variations in needs and preferences. Local governments can experiment and learn from variety. This is compared to the application of centrally determined rules that establish national standards and ignore local conditions.

Further, competition between communities (and their governments), which is possible only at the local level, would not only stimulate experimentation, it would also provide a market for the supply of government services. Both are absent when the decision-making takes place at the national level. As is the case in the economic sphere, competition generates efficiency; its absence breeds waste and inefficiency.

The ever-present threat of leaving would put strict limits on the ability of local governments to exploit their monopolistic positions for their own gain. Contracting out, a policy that may result in the creation of powerful vested interest groups that will actually lobby vigorously and effectively for increased government spending at the national level, can be a very efficient method for supplying services at the local level. The lobbying would no doubt occur, but it could be held in check by exits or the threat of exiting if lobbying actions pushed government costs too high. By the same logic, it would also reduce, although probably not eliminate, the transfer of wealth from taxpayers to government officials and their cronies, or what Bastiat has called (1950, pp. 10–13) "legal plunder."

How Far Should Decentralization Go?

How far should decentralization be taken? The optimal size of a government unit, suggests Tullock (1969), would be a size that provided the maximum amount of both efficiency and responsiveness, or control, at the lowest total cost. He reasons as follows. At one extreme one can envision a situation in which all government services are provided at the national level. Clearly, the larger the bundle of services and the greater the number of individuals involved in the decision-making process, the greater the costs inflicted on the voter through poor control. The costs of control decline as the size of the government unit declines. But as control over the unit increases, so do information demands on the individual. Eventually government would become so dispersed or localized that it would all but cease to exist, and each individual would be forced to make numerous decisions in areas in which he or she has little or no expertise. It is at this point, says Tullock, that the suppliers of government services become "quite uncontrolled." This is depicted by line C in Figure 10-1.

Line E is the cost that will be imposed through grouping government units in nonoptimum ways. For purposes of analysis, Tullock assumes that government is reduced in size only it if increases efficiency. Hence, "the curve falls monotonically

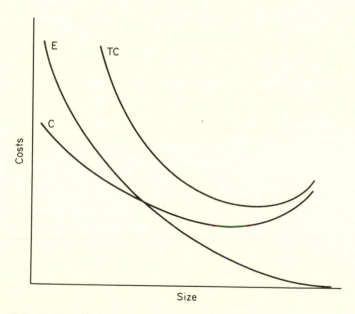

FIGURE 10-1. Optimal size of government. (See text.) From Tullock, 1969, p. 27. Reprinted by permission of Kluwer Academic Publishers.

from left to right and eventually reaches a point of zero" (Tullock, 1969, p. 28). The total cost (TC) for a government of any size is obtained by summing C and E. The optimal size of government is the lowest point on TC.

Exactly what should be decentralized and to what extent are empirical questions, and the answer will no doubt vary from community to community depending on the preferences of its members. However, given both the increased responsiveness and efficiency of local government, there seems to be no reason why practically *all* of the functions of the national government could not be better handled at the local level. The national government would have to retain responsibility for foreign policy and national defense and, as noted, it would be charged with enforcing a Bill of Rights, including the protection of the free movement of people and property between localities. A national judiciary would also have to decide cases dealing with (1) disputes arising between the communities and (2) charges by individuals that their freedom of movement, either of their person or their property, has been violated. Beyond these, there would be little that the national government should do.

One reason that it would be advantageous to err on the side of overlocalization is that history indicates quite clearly that it is much easier for several smaller government units to establish a larger government entity than for a large government to subdivide itself into smaller units. Hence a reasonable approach would be to decentralize as much and as far as possible. When and if necessary, one could always recentralize.

The point that needs to be emphasized is that the ease of exit provided by a policy of radical decentralization would not only reduce the inefficiency of government by enabling a market of sorts to exist in the provision of government services, it would also help to ensure government responsiveness to the average citizen by penalizing unresponsive governments with a loss of revenues as citizens transferred their loyalties to governments that were more responsive and efficient. By curbing the inherent tendency for government to expand, decentralization is a powerful tool for maintaining the enabling environment that is the precondition for economic growth and development.

Conclusion: Is It Feasible?

Is it at all realistic to expect that the legislative authority of national assemblies could be so drastically restricted or that national governments would surrender most of their functions either to the market or to local government units?

The argument that such proposals are impossible can mean one of two things: (1) that the proposals contain internal errors or inconsistencies that render their attainment *logically impossible*, or (2) that the proposals depart so fundamentally from the status quo as to render their attainment *politically impossible*. I am convinced that the former is not the case, that the proposals are internally consistent and therefore not logically impossible. In fact, as was noted in Chapter 2, not only did similar policies operate in medieval Europe and in nineteenth-century United States (Morley, 1959) with beneficial results, they have also been in operation for the past 700 years in Switzerland (Kendall and Louw, 1987, pp. 115–122), and have recently been proposed as a solution for South Africa's problem of racial apartheid (Kendall and Louw, 1987, pp. 113–196).

As for the latter, perhaps proposals such as those advanced here are, in fact, politically impossible. But labeling them as politically impossible means nothing more than that they depart so widely from the views that *currently* prevail that politicians would regard them as too risky to advance (Hutt, 1971).

As Mises has noted (1969b, p. 179), "trends of evolution can change, and hitherto they have almost always changed. But they changed only because they have met firm opposition. The prevailing trend toward what Hilaire Belloc called the servile state will certainly not be reversed if nobody has the courage to attack its underlying assumptions." Thus the argument that such proposals are simply too radical to be taken seriously, that they are politically impossible, is in fact a self-fulfilling prophecy: one should not waste one's time talking about such things because they are too radical to be seriously considered, but if no one talks about them they have no chance of ever being taken seriously.

One thing seems clear to me: sustained economic growth and development are possible. What is preventing them from occurring is not the depletion of resources, overpopulation, or domination by foreign-owned multinationals. The principal obstacle is an environment that penalizes individual initiative, is hostile to private ownership, discourages saving and investment, and severely restricts the operation of the free market. Accordingly, development will not occur in the absence of radical changes in the politico-legal frameworks now existing in most of the countries of the so-called Third World.

What is perhaps the most striking phenomenon of our age is precisely the speed with which the underlying dogmas of development economics, which had seemed so unassailable just 10 or 15 years ago, have fallen into disrepute. And this phenomenon has occurred on both the political and academic fronts. The reforms currently under way in the Second World, from China to the former Soviet Union and Eastern Europe, as well as the economic reforms in many Third World countries following the African famine of the mid-1980s, are monumental historic events that would have been unthinkable just a few years ago. And the revival of interest, among both economists and politicians, in the market as an indispensable coordinating process for any society above the most primitive level is certainly encouraging.

The assumptions and principles of development economics that have dominated both thought and action for the past half century have become increasingly discredited. The time is right for a paradigm shift. What was politically impossible yesterday may well be politically practical—even inevitable—tomorrow.

Notes

1. The possibility of what Hayek was to call "the spontaneous" or "the extended order" was clearly recognized over two centuries ago by Adam Smith. In his *Theory of Moral Sentiments*, which he published in 1759, Smith wrote (1969, p. 124) that man,

who can subsist only in society, was fitted by nature to that situation for which he was made. All the members of human society stand in need of each other's assistance, and are likewise exposed to mutual injuries. Where the necessary assistance is reciprocally afforded from love, from gratitude, from friendship, and esteem, the society flourishes and is happy. All the different members of it are bound together by the agreeable bands of love and affection, and are, as it were, drawn to one common centre of mutual good offices.

But though the necessary assistance should not be afforded from such generous and disinterested motives, though among the different members of the society there should be no mutual love and affection, the society, though less happy and agreeable, will not necessarily be dissolved. Society may subsist among different men, as among different merchants, from a sense of its utility, without any mutual love or affection; and though no man in it should owe any obligation, or be bound in gratitude to any other, it may still be upheld by a mercenary exchange of good offices according to an agreed valuation.

Society, however, cannot subsist among those who are at all times ready to hurt and injure one another. The moment injury begins, the moment that mutual resentment and animosity take place, all the bands of it are broken asunder, and the different members of which it consisted are, as it were, dissipated and scattered abroad by the violence and opposition of their discordant affections. . . . Beneficence, therefore, is less essential to the existence of society than justice. Society may subsist, though not in the most comfortable state, without beneficence; but the prevalence of injustice must utterly destroy it.

2. Marx and Engels' use of the term *laborers* or *laboring class* was a masterstroke of propaganda, for it clearly insinuates that only the members of this group actually perform productive work and therefore that the bourgeoisie or capitalists are nothing more than unproductive leeches, living off the work of the laborers. Of course, as Smith made very clear in *The Wealth of Nations*, many *were* leeches, having obtained monopoly positions from the state. But it is certainly quite arbitrary to define productive labor solely in terms of *physical* work.

REFERENCES

Adelman, Kenneth. (1990). "Is the Soviet Threat Over?" *The Intercollegiate Review* (Spring): 3–12.

Akinsanya, Adeoye. (1989). "Multinationals in a Changing Environment." In Herbert Levine (ed.), *World Politics Debated*. New York: McGraw-Hill: 54–59.

Aliber, Robert. (1970). "A Theory of Direct Foreign Investment." In Charles Kindleberger (ed.), *The International Corporation*. Cambridge, Mass.: MIT Press: 17–34.

Anderson, Benjamin. (1979). *Economics and the Public Welfare*. Indianapolis: Liberty Press.

Anderson, Gary. (1988). "Profits from Power: The Soviet Economy as a Mercantilist State." *The Freeman* (December): 483–491.

Anderson, Gary, McCormick, Robert, and Tollison, Robert. (1983). "The Economic Organization of the English East India Company." *Journal of Economic Behavior and Organization* (Vol. 4): 221–238.

Andreski, Stanislav. (1966). *Parasitism and Subversion*. New York: Pantheon.

Arendt, Hanna. (1971). *The Origins of Totalitarianism*. New York: Meridian.

Armentano, D. T. (1972). *The Myths of Antitrust*. New Rochelle, N.Y.: Arlington House.

Armey, Dick. (1990). "Moscow on the Mississippi: America's Soviet-Style Farm Policy." *Policy Review* (Winter): 24–29.

Ashton, T. S. (1965). "The Standard of Life of the Workers in England, 1790–1830." In F. A. Hayek (ed.), *Capitalism and the Historians*. Chicago: University of Chicago Press: 123–155.

Atlas, Terry. (1984). "UN Tries to Defuse Population Bomb." *The Chicago Tribune* (August 12): Sect. 1, p. 5.

Avery, Dennis. (1987). "Can U.S. Farmers Compete in the World?" Address before the Institute of Cooperative Leadership, Colombia, Mo. (June 3).

Avery, Dennis. (1989). "The Green Revolution Is Our Real Food Security." Testimony before the Subcommittee on Wheat, Soybeans, and Feed Grains of the House Committee on Agriculture (September 26).

Avery, Dennis. (1990). "Will Rising Global Demand By-Pass the U.S. Farmer?" Address before the Chicago Agricultural Economics Club, Chicago, Ill. (March 20).

Ayittey, George. (1984). "Truth in Lending to Third World Governments." *The Wall Street Journal* (October 11): 32.

Ayittey, George. (1985). "A Double Standard in Black and White." *The Wall Street Journal* (July 22).

Ayittey, George. (1986a). "Africa's Agricultural Disaster: Governments and Elites Are to Blame." *Journal of Economic Growth* (Vol. 1, No. 3): 3–17.

Ayittey, George. (1986b). "The Real Foreign Debt Problem." *The Wall Street Journal* (April 8): 30–31.

Ayittey, George. (1986c). "Third World 'Kleptocrats' Play U.S. for a Sucker." *Press-Enterprise* (March 12): 8–9.

Ayittey, George. (1987a). "African Freedom of Speech." *Index on Censorship* (January): 16–18.

Ayittey, George. (1987b). "Democracy, African-Style." *The Globe and Mail* (October 6): A7.

Ayittey, George. (1987c). "Economic Atrophy in Black Africa." *Cato Journal* (Spring/Summer): 195–222.

Ayittey, George. (1987d). "Muzzled Media Is the Norm in Black Africa." *The Globe and Mail* (March 30): A7.

Ayittey, George. (1988a). "Africa Doesn't Need More Foreign Aid; It Needs Less." *The Hartford Courant* (August 4): B-12.

Ayittey, George. (1988b). "Who Ruined Africa? Don't Blame the Colonialists." *Herald Examiner* (September 9).

Ayres, Robert. (1983). *Banking on the Poor*. Cambridge, Mass.: MIT Press.

Bandow, Doug. (1985). "The U.S. Role in Promoting Third World Development." In Doug Bandow (ed.), *U.S. Aid to the Developing World*. Washington, D.C.: Heritage Foundation: vii–xxxii.

Bandow, Doug. (1988). "Foreign Aid: The Oxymoron of the 1980s." *Business and Society Review* (Fall): 35–39.

Bandow, Doug. (1989). "What's Still Wrong with the World Bank?" *Orbis* (Winter): 73–89.

Banks, Arthur. (1988). *Political Handbook of the World 1988*. New York: CSP.

Barnet, Richard, and Muller, Ronald. (1974). *Global Reach*. New York: Simon and Schuster.

Barnett, Harold J. (1982). "Scarcity and Growth Revisited." In V. Kerry Smith (ed.), *Scarcity and Growth Reconsidered*. Washington, D.C.: Resources for the Future: 163–217.

Barnett, Harold J., van Muiswinkel, Gerald, Shechter, Mordecai, and Myers, John. (1984) "Global Trends in Non-Fuel Minerals." In Herman Simon and Julian Kahn (eds.), *The Resourceful Earth*. New York: Basil Blackwell: 316–338.

Bartlett, Bruce. (1986a). "The Effect of Implicit Taxes on Development." *Journal of Economic Growth* (Vol. 1, Second Quarter): 20–27.

Bartlett, Bruce. (1986b). "Supply-Side Sparkplug: The Case for Tax Cuts in the Third World." *Policy Review* (Summer): 42–47.

Bartlett, Sarah. (1989). "A Vicious Circle Keeps Latin America in Debt." In Christian Soe (ed.), *Comparative Politics 89/90*. Guilford, Conn.: Dushkin: 206-207.

Bastiat, Frederic. ([1850] 1972). *The Law*. Irvington-on-Hudson, N.Y.: FEE.

Bauer, Peter. (1972). *Dissent on Development*. Cambridge, Mass.: Harvard University Press.

Bauer, Peter. (1978). "Western Guilt and Third World Poverty." In Karl Brunner (ed.), *The First World and the Third World*. Rochester, N.Y.: University of Rochester Policy Center: 149–168.

Bauer, Peter. (1981). *Equality, the Third World, and Economic Delusion*. Cambridge, Mass.: Harvard University Press.

Bauer, Peter. (1984). *Reality and Rhetoric*. Cambridge, Mass.: Harvard University Press.

Bauer, Peter. (1986). Paper on "Are World Population Trends a Problem?" In Ben Wattenberg and Karl Zinsmeister (eds.), *Are World Population Trends a Problem?* Washington, D.C.: American Enterprise Institute: 19–24.

Bauer, Peter. (1987). "Creating the Third World: Foreign Aid and Its Offspring." *Journal of Economic Growth* (Second Quarter): 11–22.

Bauer, Peter. (1989). "Accounts Receivable." In Herbert Levine (ed.), *World Politics Debated*. New York: McGraw-Hill: 57–63.

Bauer, Peter, and Yamey, Basil. (1957). *The Economics of Under-Developed Countries*. Chicago: University of Chicago Press.

Bauer, Peter, and Yamey, Basil. (1980). "East-West/North-South, Peace and Prosperity?" *Commentary* (September): 57–63.

Bauer, Peter, and Basil, Yamey. (1983). "Foreign Aid: What is at Stake?" In Scott Thompson (ed.), *The Third World*. San Francisco: ICS: 115–135.

Bauer, Peter, and Yamey, Basil. (1985). "Foreign Aid: Rewarding Impoverishment?" *Commentary* (September): 38–40.

Bayley, David. (1966). "The Effects of Corruption in a Developing Nation." *Western Political Quarterly* (December): 719–732.

Beckerman, Wilfred. (1975). *Two Cheers for the Affluent Society*. New York: St. Martin's Press.

Beckmann, Petr. (1984). "Solar Energy and Other 'Alternative' Energy Sources." In Julian Simon and Herman Kahn (eds.), *The Resourceful Earth*. New York: Basil Blackwell: 415–427.

Benedict, Burton. (1970). "Population Regulation in Primitive Societies." In Anthony Allison (ed.), *Population Control*. Hammondsworth, England: Penguin: 165–180.

Berg, Elliot. (1987). "The Role of Divestiture in Economic Growth." In Steve Hanke (ed.), *Privatization and Development*. San Francisco: International Center for Economic Growth: 23–32.

Berry, Sara. (1977). "Economic Change in Contemporary Africa." In Phyllis Martin and Patrick O'Meara (eds.), *Africa*. Bloomington, Ind.: Indiana University Press: 268–277.

Bezineau, Marie-Claire. (1989). "Les Clandestins du Desert" ["The Smugglers of the Desert"]. *L'Hebdo* (December 28): 38–39.

Bonnet, Nicole. (1988). "Even Central Bankers Do It." *World Press Review* (November): 49.

Boserup, Ester. (1981). *Population and Technological Change*. Chicago: University of Chicago Press.

Bovard, James. (1984). "Free Food Bankrupts Foreign Farmers." *The Wall Street Journal* (July 2): 18.

Bovard, James. (1987). "The World Bank's Structural Adjustment Loans." *Journal of Economic Growth* (Vol. 2, No. 3): 14–22.

Bovard, James. (1988). "The World Bank vs. the World's Poor." *The Freeman* (May): 184–187.

Bovard, James. (1989). "Food Aid Is Harmful." In Janelle Rohr (ed.), *The Third World*. San Diego: Greenhaven Press: 127–131.

Brass, W. (1970). "The Growth of World Population." In Anthony Allison (ed.), *Population Control*. Middlesex, England: Penguin: 131–151.

Brandt, Willy, et al. (1980). *North-South: A Program for Survival*. Cambridge, Mass.: MIT Press.

Brandt, Willy, et al. (1983). *Common Crisis North-South: Co-Operation for World Development*. Cambridge, Mass.: MIT Press.

Brooke, James. (1987). "Nigeria Pushes Agriculture with Aim of Self-Sufficiency." *The Indianapolis Star* (February 18): 51.

Brown, Lester, and Wolf, Christopher. (1986). "Reversing Africa's Decline." In Lester Brown et al. (eds.), *State of the World 1986*. New York: Norton: 177–194.

Brown, Lester, et al. (1989). "World At Risk." In Lester Brown et al. (eds.), *State of the World 1989*. New York: Norton: 3–20.

Brown, William. (1984). "The Outlook for Future Petroleum Supplies." In Julian Simon and Herman Kahn (eds.), *The Resourceful Earth*. New York: Basil Blackwell: 361–386.

Brozen, Yale. (1966). "Welfare without the Welfare State." *The Freeman* (December): 40–52.

Brozen, Yale. (1974). "Wage Rates, Minimum Wage Laws, and Unemployment." In Tibor Machan (ed.), *The Libertarian Alternative*. Chicago: Nelson-Hall: 386–399.

Brzezinski, Zbigniew. (1989). *The Grand Failure*. New York: Charles Scribner's.

Buchanan, James. (1975). *The Limits of Liberty*. Chicago: University of Chicago Press.

Bukro, Casey. (1987). "Population Bomb Ticks More Loudly Than Ever." *The Chicago Tribune* (February 8): Section 2, pp. 1, 8.

Caldwell, John. (1976). "Toward a Restatement of Demographic Transition Theory." *Population and Development Review* (September-December): 321–366.

Calhoun, John C. (1953). *Disquisition on Government.* Indianapolis: Bobbs-Merrill.

Carr-Saunders, A. M. (1973). "World Population." In Edward Pohlman (ed.), *Population: A Clash of Prophets.* New York: Mentor: 2–3.

Casson, Mark. (1987). "General Theories of Multinational Enterprise: Their Relevance to Business History." In Peter Hertner and Jeoffrey Jones (eds.), *Multinationals: Theory and History.* Aldershot, England: Glower: 42–63.

Central Intelligence Agency. (1989). *The World Fact Book.* Washington, D.C.: Government Printing Office.

Cervero, Robert. (1985). "Deregulating Urban Transportation." *Cato Journal* (Spring/Summer): 219–238.

Chapman, Stephen. (1986). "The Futility of Aid to Africa." *The Chicago Tribune* (June 8): Section 5, p. 3.

Cheung, Steven. (1988). "The Fable of the Bees: An Economic Investigation." In Tyler Cowen (ed.), *The Theory of Market Failure.* Fairfax, Va.: George Mason University Press: 279–304.

Chichilnisky, Graciela. (1982). *Basic Needs and the North/South Debate.* New York: Institute for World Order.

Chiswick, Barry. (1982a). "The Economic Progress of Immigrants: Some Apparently Universal Patterns." In Barry Chiswick (ed.), *The Gateway.* Washington, D.C.: American Enterprise Institute: 119–158.

Chiswick, Barry. (1982b). "The Impact of Immigration on the Level and Distribution of Economic Well-Being." In Barry Chiswick (ed.), *The Gateway.* Washington, D.C.: American Enterprise Institute: 289–313.

Chodorov, Frank. (1980). *Fugitive Essays.* Indianapolis: Liberty Press.

Chubb, John, and Moe, Terry. (1990). *Politics, Markets and America's Schools.* Washington, D.C.: Brookings Institution.

Clark, Colin. (1970). "The Economic and Social Implications of Population Control." In Anthony Allison (ed.), *Population Control.* Hammondsworth, England: Penguin: 222–237.

Clark, Gracia. (1988). "Price Control of Local Foodstuffs in Kumasi, Ghana, 1979." In Gracia Clark (ed.), *Traders versus the State.* Boulder, Colo.: Westview: 57–80.

Coale, Ansley. (1964). "The History of the Human Population." *Scientific American* (September): 41–51.

Coase, Ronald. (1952). "The Nature of the Firm." In G. Stigler and K. Bouldin (eds.), *Readings in Price Theory.* Chicago: Richard D. Irwin: 331–351.

Coase, Ronald. (1988). "The Lighthouse in Economics." In Tyler Cowen (ed.), *The Theory of Market Failure.* Fairfax, Va.: George Mason University Press: 255–277.

Cole, Julio. (1986). "The False Promise of Protectionism for Latin America." *Journal of Economic Growth* (Fourth Quarter): 28–37.

Collins, Lynn. (1982). "World Population." In John Ross (ed.), *International Encyclopedia of Population.* New York. Free Press: 679–681.

Commoner, Barry. (1976). *The Poverty of Power.* New York: Knopf.

Cook, Earl. (1976). "Limits to the Exploitation of Nonrenewable Resources." *Science* (February): 677–682.

Cox, Robert. (1979). "Labor and the Multinationals." In George Modelski (ed.), *Transnational Corporations and World Order.* San Francisco: W. H. Freeman: 414–429.

Dallago, Bruno. (1991). "The 'Second Economy': A Mechanism for the Functioning of Society in Eastern Europe." *In Depth* (Spring): 76–113.

Daly, Herman. (1974). "The Economics of the Steady-State." *American Economic Review* (May): 15–21.

Daly, Herman. (1979). "Entropy, Growth and the Political Economy of Scarcity." In V. Kerry Smith (ed.), *Scarcity and Growth Reconsidered.* Washington D.C.: Resources for the Future: 67–94.

De Alessi, Louis. (1987). "Property Rights and Privatization." In Steve Hanke (ed.), *Privatization and Development.* San Francisco: International Center for Economic Growth: 24–35.

Demsetz, Harold. (1988). "The Private Production of Public Goods." In Tyler Cowen (ed.), *The Theory of Market Failure.* Fairfax, Va.: George Mason University Press: 111–126.

Deudney, Daniel, and Flavin, Christopher. (1985). "Shapes of a Renewable Society." In Robert Jackson (ed.), *Global Issues 85/86.* Guilford, Conn.: Dushkin: 118–123.

Dickinson, H. D. (1933). "Price Formation in a Socialist Community." *Economic Journal* (June): 237–250.

Downs, Anthony. (1967). *Inside Bureaucracy.* Boston: Little, Brown.

Drucker, Peter. (1974). "Multinationals and Developing Countries." *Foreign Affairs* (October): 121–134.

Easterlin, Richard. (1968). *Population, Labor Force, and Long Swings in Economic Growth.* New York: Columbia University Press.

Easterlin, Richard, and Crimmins, Eileen. (1985). *The Fertility Revolution.* Chicago: University of Chicago Press.

Eberstadt, Nick. (1985a). "Famine, Development and Foreign Aid." *Commentary* (March): 25–31.

Eberstadt, Nick. (1985b). "The Perversion of Foreign Aid." *Commentary* (June): 19–33.

Eberstadt, Nick. (1987). "Health Nutrition and Literacy Under Communism." *Journal of Economic Growth* (Second Quarter): 11–22.

Eberstadt, Nick. (1988). *The Poverty of Communism.* New Brunswick, N.J.: Transaction.

Economic Report of the President. (February 1991). Washington, D.C.: Government Printing Office.

The Economist. (1984). "Beggaring the Poor." (February 18): 15–16.

The Economist. (1985). "In Praise of Peasants." (February 2): 86–87.

The Economist. (1988). "Come Back Multinationals." (November 26): 73.

Ehrlich, Paul. (1968). *The Population Bomb.* New York: Ballantine.

Ehrlich, Paul. (1969). "Eco-Catastrophe." *Ramparts* (September): 24–27.

Ehrlich, Paul. (1973). "*Playboy* Interview: 1970." In Edward Pohlman (ed.), *Population: A Clash of Prophets.* New York: Mentor: 13–28.

Ellis, Gene. (1980). "Land Tenancy Reform in Ethiopia: A Retrospective Analysis." *Economic Development and Cultural Change* (April): 523–545.

Engels, Frederick. (1972). *Socialism: Utopian and Scientific.* New York: International Publishers.

Erickson, Edward, and Sumner, Daniel. (1984). "The U.N. and Economic Development." In Burton Yale Pines (ed.), *A World without a U.N.* Washington, D.C.: The Heritage Foundation: 1–22.

Evenson, Robert. (1981). "Benefits and Obstacles to Appropriate Agricultural Technology." *Annals of the Academy of Political and Social Science* (November): 54–67.

Farbman, Michael. (1923). *Bolshevism in Retreat.* London: Collins.

Fauriol, Georges. (1984). "The U.N. and Economic Development." In Burton Yale Pines (ed.), *A World without a U.N.* Washington, D.C.: The Heritage Foundation: 73–92.

Feld, Werner. (1980). *Multinational Corporations and U.N. Politics*. New York: Pergamon Press.

Fenwick, Millicent. (1987). "African Famine." *Journal of Economic Growth* (Vol. 2, No. 4): 10–12.

Fields, Gary. (1962). "Growth and Distribution in the Market Economies of East Asia." *World Politics* (October): 150–160.

Fitzgerald, Randall. (1980). *When Government Goes Private*. New York: Universe Books.

Fixler, Philip, and Poole, Robert. (1987). "Status of State and Local Privatization." In Steve Hanke (ed.), *Prospects for Privatization*. New York: Academy of Political Science: 164–178.

Fleming, Harold. (1966). *States, Contracts and Progress*. New York: Oceana.

Frank, Isaiah. (1981). *Foreign Enterprises in Developing Countries*. Baltimore: Johns Hopkins.

Frank, Odile, and McNicoll, Geoffrey. (1987). "An Interpretation of Fertility and Population Policy in Kenya." *Population and Development Review* (June): 209–243.

Freedman, Ronald. (1968). "Fertility." *The International Encyclopedia of the Social Sciences*, Vol. 5. New York: Macmillan: 371–382.

Freedman, Ronald, and Berelson, Bernard. (1974). "The Human Population." *Scientific American* (September): 31–39.

Friedman, David. (1973). *The Machinery of Freedom*. New York: Harper and Row.

Friedman, Milton. (1958). "Foreign Economic Aid: Means and Objectives." *The Yale Review* (June): 500–516.

Friedman, Milton. (1981). *Free to Choose*. New York: Avon.

Friedman, Milton. (1989). "Economists and Economic Policy." In H. B. McCulloch (ed.), *Political Ideologies and Political Philosophies*. Toronto: Wall and Thompson: 98–104.

Georgescu-Roegen, Nicholas. (1971). *The Entropy Law and the Economic Process*. Cambridge, Mass.: University of Harvard Press.

Georgescu-Roegen, Nicholas. (1977). "The Steady State and Ecological Salvation." *Bio-Science* (April): 266–270.

Gerster, George. (1986). "Tsetse—the Deadly Fly." *National Geographic* (December): 814–833.

Gieringer, Dale. (1985). "The Safety of New Drug Approval." *Cato Journal* (Spring/Summer): 177–201.

Glade, William. (1987). "Multinationals and the Third World." *Journal of Economic Issues* (December): 1889–1920.

Gladwin, Thomas, and Walter, Ingo. (1980). *Multinationals under Fire*. New York: John Wiley.

Godsell, Geoffrey. (1988). "Tomorrow's Big Powers: 'Confucian Work Ethic' Thrusts Small Nations into Big League." In Chau T. Phan (ed.), *World Politics 80/91*. Guilford, Conn.: Dushkin: 161–164.

Goeller, H. E. and Weinberg, Alvin M. (1976). "The Age of Substitutability." *Science* (February): 683–699.

Goldin, Kenneth. (1972). "Equal Access vs. Selective Access: A Critique of Public Goods Theory." *Public Choice* (Spring): 53–71.

Goldman, Marshall. (1983). *USSR in Crisis*. New York: Norton.

Goode, William. (1964). *The Family*. Englewood Cliffs, N.J.: Prentice-Hall.

Gow, David, and Morse, Elliot. (1988). "The Notorious Nine: Critical Problems in Project Implementation. *World Development* (Vol. 16, No. 12): 1399–1418.

Greer, Thomas. (1987). *A Brief History of the Western World*. San Francisco: Harcourt, Brace, Jovanovich.

Gripp, Richard. (1973). *The Political System of Communism*. New York: Harper and Row.

Grossman, Gregory. (1972). "The Second Economy of the USSR." *Problems of Communism* (September-October): 25–40.

Gutmann, Peter. (1977). "The Subterranean Economy." *Financial Analysts Journal* (November-December): 26–27, 34.

Gwartney, James, and McCaleb, Thomas. (1985). "Have Antipoverty Programs Increased Poverty?" *Cato Journal* (Spring/Summer): 1–16.

Haberler, Gottfried. (1968). "Terms of Trade and Economic Development." In James Theberge (ed.), *Economics of Trade and Development*. New York: John Wiley: 323–343.

Haile-Mariam, Yacob, and Mengistu, Berhanu. (1988). "Public Enterprises and the Privatization Thesis in the Third World." *Third World Quarterly* (October): 1565–1587.

Hajnal, J. (1965). "European Marriage Patterns." In D. V. Glass and D. E. C. Eversley (eds.), *Population in History*. London: Edward Arnold: 101–143.

Hancock, Graham. (1989). *The Lords of Poverty*. New York: Atlantic Monthly Press.

Hanke, Steve. (1986). *Privatization: Theory, Evidence, and Implementation*. Washington, D.C.: Ludwig von Mises Institute.

Hanke, Steve. (1987a). "Introduction." In Steve Hanke (ed.), *Privatization and Development*. San Francisco: International Center for Economic Growth: 3–5.

Hanke, Steve. (1987b). "The Necessity of Property Rights." In Steve Hanke (ed.), *Privatization and Development*. San Francisco: International Center for Economic Growth: 47–51.

Hanke, Steve. (1987c). "Privatization versus Nationalization." In Steve Hanke (ed.), *Prospects for Privatization*. New York: Academy of Political Science: 1–3.

Hanke, Steve. (1987d). "Successful Privatization Strategies." In Steve Hanke (ed.), *Privatization and Development*. San Francisco: International Center for Economic Growth: 77–86.

Hanke, Steve. (1987e). "Toward a People's Capitalism." In Steve Hanke (ed.), *Privatization and Development*. San Francisco: International Center for Economic Growth: 213–221.

ul Haq, Muhub. (1983). "A Lingering Look at the Old Economic Order." In Herbert Levine (ed.), *World Politics Debated*. New York: McGraw-Hill.

Harris, Nigel. (1987). *The End of the Third World*. New York: Meredith Press.

Harrison, Lawrence. (1985). *Underdevelopment Is a State of Mind*. Lanham, Md.: Center for International Affairs and University Press of America.

Harrison, Lawrence. (1986). "Latin American Culture Caused the Latin American Mess." *The Washington Post National Weekly Edition* (July 14): 23–24.

Harrod, Roy. (1963). *International Economics*. Chicago: University of Chicago Press.

Hart, Gary. (1986). "Foreign Aid Can Reduce Africa's Poverty." In Janelle Rohr (ed.), *Problems of Africa*. St. Paul, Minn.: Greenhaven Press: 47–50.

Hayek, F. A. (1932). *Prices and Production*. London: George Routledge.

Hayek, F. A. (1933). *Monetary Theory of the Trade Cycle*. London: J. Cape.

Hayek, F. A. (1960). *The Constitution of Liberty*. Chicago: Henry Regnery.

Hayek, F. A. (1969). *Studies in Philosophy, Politics and Economics*. New York: Simon and Schuster.

Hayek, F. A. (1972). *Individualism and Economic Order*. Chicago: Henry Regnery.

Hayek, F. A. (1973). *Law, Legislation, and Liberty*. Vol. 1, *Rules and Order*. Chicago: University of Chicago Press.

Hayek, F. A. (1975). "The Present State of the Debate." in F. A. Hayek (ed.), *Collectivist Economic Planning*. New York: Augustus Kelley: 201–243.

Hayek, F. A. (1979). *The Counter-Revolution of Science*. Indianapolis: Liberty Press.

Hayek, F. A. (1988). *The Fatal Conceit*. Chicago: University of Chicago Press.

Hazlitt, Henry. (1959). *The Failure of the "New Economics"*. Princeton, N.J.: Van Nostrand.

Hazlitt, Henry. (1969). *Economics in One Lesson*. New York: Macfadden-Bartell.

Heilbroner, Robert. (1989). "The Triumph of Capitalism." *The New Yorker* (January 23): 98–109.

Heller, Mikhail, and Nekrich, Aleksandr. (1986). *Utopia in Power: The History of the Soviet Union from 1917 to the Present*. New York: Summit Books.

Henkin, Louis. (1979). *How Nations Behave*. New York: Columbia University Press.

Henkin, Louis, Pugh, Richard, Schachter, Oscar, and Smit, Hans. (1980). *International Law*. St. Paul, Minn.: West Publishing.

Heritage Foundation. (1984). *How the U.N. Spends Its $1 Billion from U.S. Taxpayers*. Washington, D.C.: Heritage Foundation.

Hewitt, Jenni. (1985). "The Population Bomb Ticks On." In Robert Jackson (ed.), *Global Issues 85/86*. Guilford, Conn.: Dushkin Press: 24–26.

Higgott, Richard. (1986). "Africa and the New International Division of Labor." In John Ravenhill (ed.), *Africa in Economic Crisis*. New York: Columbia University Press: 286–308.

Hill, Polly. (1963). *The Migrant Cocoa Farmers of Southern Ghana*. Cambridge, Mass.: Cambridge University Press.

Hill, Polly. (1986). *Development Economics on Trial*. New York: Cambridge University Press, 1986.

Hobson, J. A. (1954). *Imperialism*. London: George Allen and Unwin.

Hodgkinson, Edith. (1987). "Economy." *Africa South of the Sahara 1988*. London: Europa Publishing Limited.

Hopper, David. (1976). "The Development of Agriculture in Developing Countries." *Scientific American* (September): 132–144.

Hughes, Barry. (1991). *Continuity and Change in World Politics*. Englewood Cliffs, N.J.: Prentice-Hall.

Hume, David. ([1777] 1966). *Enquiries Concerning Human Understanding and Concerning the Principles of Morals*. Oxford: Clarendon Press.

Hume, Ian. (1976). "Some Economic Aspects of Labour Migration in Europe since the Second World War." In Ansley Coale (ed.), *Economic Factors in Population Growth*. New York: John Wiley: 491–509.

Hutt, William. (1971). *Politically Impossible . . . ?* London: The Institute of Economic Affairs.

Hymer, Stephen. (1970). "The Efficiency (Contradictions) of Multinational Corporations." *American Economic Review* (May): 441–448.

Insell, Barbara. (1985). "A World Awash in Grain." *Foreign Affairs* (Spring): 892–911.

International Monetary Fund. (1985). *Foreign Private Investment in Developing Countries*. Washington, D.C.: International Monetary Fund.

Irwin, Michael. (1990a). "Banking on Poverty: An Insider's Look at the World Bank." *Cato Institute Foreign Policy Briefing*, Washington, D.C., September 20.

Irwin, Michael. (1990b). "Why I've Had It with the World Bank." *The Wall Street Journal* (March 20): A10.

Jackson, P. M. (1988). "Local Government as Efficient Government." *Economic Affairs* (October/November): 17–18,44.

Jackson, Tony, and Park, Paula. (1986). "Africans Themselves Cause Famine." In Janelle Rohr (ed.), *Problems of Africa*. St. Paul, Minn.: Greenhaven Press: 126–129.

Johl, S. S. (1975). "Gains of the Green Revolution: How Have They Have Been Shared in Punjab?" *Journal of Development Studies* (April): 178–189.

Johnson, D. Gale. (1984). "World Food and Agriculture." In Julian Simon and Herman Kahn (eds.), *The Resourceful Earth*. New York, Basil Blackwell: 67–112.

Johnson, D. Gale. (1987). "Is Population Growth the Dominant Force in Development?" *Cato Journal* (Spring/Summer): 187–193.

Johnson, Harry. (1968). "Tariffs and Economic Development: Some Theoretical Issues." In James Theberge (ed.), *Economics of Trade and Development*. New York: John Wiley: 351–375.

Jones, Walter, 1988. *The Logic of International Relations*. Glenview, Ill.: Scott Foresman and Company.

Johnson, Thomas. (1975). "Poor Administration Is Snarling Huge Ethiopian Land Reform." *The New York Times* (April 3): 6.

Kahn, Herman, Brown, William, and Martel, Leon. (1976). *The Next 200 Years*. New York: William Morrow.

Kaplan, Robert. (1985). "Ethiopian Exodus." *New Republic* (January 21): 20–22.

Kaysen, Carl. (1972). "The Computer that Printed Out W*O*L*F*." *Foreign Affairs* (July): 660–668.

Kegley, Charles, Wittkopf, Eugene, and Rawls, Lucia. (1984). "The Multinational Corporation: Curse or Cure?" In Charles Kegley and Eugene Wittkopf (eds.), *The Global Agenda*. New York: Random House: 272–285.

Kendall, Frances, and Louw, Leon. (1987). *After Apartheid: The Solution for South Africa*. San Francisco: ISC Press.

Keyes, Alan. (1986). "Ethiopia: The UN's Role." Statement by the Assistant Secretary for International Organization Affairs before the Subcommittee on African Affairs of the Senate Foreign Relations Committee, Washington D.C., U.S. Department of State, Current Policy No. 803 (March 16).

Kimball, John. (1980). "The Trade Debate: Patterns of U.S. Trade." In Chau T. Phan (ed.), *World Politics 80/81*. Guilford, Conn.: Dushkin: 104–113.

Kindleberger, Charles. (1979). "The Monopolistic Theory of Direct Foreign Investment." In George Modelski (ed.), *Transnational Corporations and World Order*. San Francisco: W. H. Freeman: 91–107.

Kinsky, Lynn. (1974). "The FDA and Drug Research." In Tibor Machan (ed.), *The Libertarian Alternative*. Chicago: Nelson-Hall: 177–192.

Kirzner, Israel. (1973). *Competition and Entrepreneurship*. Chicago: University of Chicago Press.

Kolko, Gabriel. (1977). *The Triumph of Conservatism*. New York: The Free Press.

Krauss, Melvyn. (1984). *Development without Aid*. New York: McGraw-Hill.

Kurian, George Thomas. (1984). *The New Book of World Rankings*. New York: Facts-on-File.

Kuznets, Simon. (1967). "Population and Economic Growth." *Proceedings of the American Philosophical Society* (June): 170–193.

LaFeber, Walter. (1989). *The American Age*. New York: Norton.

Lal, Deepak. (1987). "Markets, Mandarins and Mathematicians." *Cato Journal* (Spring/Summer): 43–70.

Lal, Deepak. (1989). "Population and Long Run Economic Growth in India." *Economic Affairs* (June/July): 19–22.

Lall, Sanjay. (1983). "The Rise of Multinationals from the Third World." *Third World Quarterly* (July): 618–626.

Lamb, David. (1983). *The Africans*. New York: Vintage.

Landa, Janet. (1988). "Underground Economies: Generic or *Sui Generis*?" In Jerry Jenkins (ed.), *Beyond the Informal Sector*. San Francisco: ICS Press: 75–103.

Landes, David. (1969). *The Unbound Prometheus*. New York: Cambridge University Press.

Langé, Oscar. (1972). "On the Economic Theory of Socialism." In Alec Nove and D. M. Nuti (eds.), *Socialist Economics*. Hammondsworth, England: Penguin: 92–110.

Lappe, Frances, Collins, Joseph, and Kinley, David. (1981). *Aid as Obstacle*. San Francisco: Institute for Food and Development Policy.

Lavoie, Don. (1985). *National Economic Planning: What is Left?* Cambridge, Mass.: Ballinger.

Lawton, Lancelot. (1927). *The Russian Revolution*. London: Macmillan.

Lawton, Lancelot. (1932). *An Economic History of Soviet Russia*, 2 vols. London: Macmillan.

Leff, Nathaniel. (1964). "Economic Development through Bureaucratic Corruption." *The American Behavioral Scientist* (November): 8–14.

Leff, Nathaniel. (1983). "Beyond the New International Economic Order." In Scott Thompson (ed.), *The Third World*. San Francisco: ICS: 239–266.

Legum, Colin. (1975). *Ethiopia: The Fall of Haile Selassie's Empire*. New York: Africana Publishing.

Lewis, Arthur. (1965). "A Review of Economic Development." *American Economic Review* (May): 1–16.

Lichenstein, Charles, Dewey, Thomas E. L., Pilon, Juliana, and Merkle, Melanie. (1986). *The United Nations: Its Problems and What to Do about Them*. Washington, D.C.: Heritage Foundation.

Liebenow, Gus. (1986). *African Politics: Crises and Challenges*. Bloomington, Ind.: Indiana University Press.

Lipton, Michael. (1980). "Migration from Rural Areas of Poor Countries: The Impact on Rural Productivity and Income Distribution." *World Development* (Vol. 8): 1–24.

Louw, Leon. (1985). "A Critical Review of Prevailing Energy Predictions and Policies." Address to the Thirteenth Annual AIESEC Economic Congress on "Energy: A Factor in Economic Development."

MacAvoy, Paul. (1985). "The Punishing Cost of Fixing Oil Prices." *The New York Times* (December 29): Business Section, p. 3.

McCulloch, Rachel. (1981). "Technology Transfer to Developing Countries: Implications of International Regulation." *Annals of the American Academy of Political and Social Science* (November): 110–122.

McEvedy, Colin, and Jones, Richard. (1978). *Atlas of World Population History*. Hammondsworth, England: Penguin.

McLaughlin, Loretta. (1982). "Earth Headed for the Breaking Point." *Chicago Tribune* (September 19): Sect. 2, pp. 1–2.

McLean, Murdith. (1985). "Liberation Theology and Third World Development." In Walter Block and Donald Shaw (eds.), *Theology, Third World Development and Economic Justice*. Vancouver: Fraser Institute: 39–42.

McNamara, Robert. (1984). "Time Bomb or Myth: The Population Problem." *Foreign Affairs* (Summer): 1107–1131.

McNicoll, Geoffrey. (1982). "Population and Development." In John Ross (ed.), *International Encyclopedia of Population*. New York: Free Press: 519–525.

Macpherson, C. B. (1962). *The Political Theory of Possessive Individualism*. Oxford: Clarendon Press.

McPherson, Peter. (1987). "The Promise of Privatization." in Steve Hanke (ed.), *Privatization and Development*. San Francisco: International Center for Economic Growth: 17–20.

Macrae, Norman. (1975). "Survey: America's Third Century." *The Economist* (October 25): Special Supplement.

Magdoff, Harry. (1968). *The Age of Imperialism*. New York: Modern Reader.

Magdoff, Harry. (1976). "The Multinational Corporation and Development—A Contradiction?" In David Apter and Louis Goodman (eds.), *The Multinational Corporation and Social Change*. New York: Praeger: 200–222.

Maltsev, Yuri. (1990). "The Soviet Medical Nightmare." *The Free Market* (August): 1, 3–5.

Manhard, Philip. (1981). "The United States and Micronesia." *The Journal of Social, Political and Economic Studies* (Summer): 207–214.

Manley, Michael. (1984). "We are Told . . . We Must Have More of the Disease." In Christian Soe (ed.), *Comparative Politics 84/85*. Guilford, Conn.: Dushkin: 248–251.

Manning, Robert. (1986). "The Philippines in Crisis." *Foreign Affairs* (November): 1137–1167.

Martin, Neil. (1986). "When Public Services Go Private." *World* (May-June): 26–34.

Marsden, Keith. (1986). "Links between Taxes and Economic Growth: Some Empirical Evidence." *Journal of Economic Growth* (Fourth Quarter): 3–16.

Marx, Karl. ([1867] 1906). *Capital*. New York: Modern Library.

Marx, Karl. ([1859] 1970). *A Contribution to the Critique of Political Economy*. Moscow: Progress Publishers.

Marx, Karl. ([1875] 1972). *Critique of the Gotha Programme*. Peking: Foreign Language Press.

Marx, Karl, and Engels, Friedrich. ([1848] 1968). *The Communist Manifesto*. New York: Monthly Review Press.

Mazrui, Ali. (1967). *Toward a Pax Africana*. Chicago: University of Chicago Press.

Meadows, Donella, Meadows, Dennis, Randers Jorgen, and Behrens III, William. (1972). *The Limits to Growth*. New York: Universe Books.

Meigs, A. James. (1984). "Regulatory Aspects of the World Debt Problem." *Cato Journal* (Spring/Summer): 105–124.

Meltzer, Alan. (1976). *Why Government Grows*. Los Angeles: International Institute for Economic Research.

Merrick, Thomas. (1986). *World Population in Transition*. Washington, D.C.: Population Reference Bureau.

Michael, Franz, and Taylor, George. (1965). *The Far East in the Modern World*. New York: Holt, Rinehart and Winston.

Miller, Robert, and Steinberg, Harold. (1986). "The Age of Privatization." *World* (May-June): 24–25.

Mises, Ludwig von. ([1933] 1962). *The Ultimate Foundation of Economic Science*. New York: Van Nostrand.

Mises, Ludwig von. ([1949] 1966). *Human Action*. Chicago: Henry Regnery.

Mises, Ludwig von. ([1944] 1969a). *Bureaucracy*. New Rochelle, N.Y.: Arlington House.

Mises, Ludwig von. ([1952] 1969b). *Planning for Freedom*. South Holland, Ill.: Libertarian Press.

Mises, Ludwig von. ([1922] 1969c). *Socialism*. London: J. Cape.

Mises, Ludwig von. ([1912] 1971). *Theory of Money and Credit*. Irvington-on-Hudson, N.Y.: Foundation For Economic Education.

Mises, Ludwig von. ([1920] 1975). "Economic Calculation in the Socialist Commonwealth." In F.A. Hayek (ed.), *Collectivist Economic Planning*. Clifton, N.J.: Augustus Kelley: 87–130.

Mises, Ludwig von. (1979). *Economic Policy*. South Bend, Ind.: Regnery.

Mises, Ludwig von. ([1933] 1981). *Epistemological Problems of Economics*. New York: New York University Press.

Mises, Ludwig von. ([1919] 1983). *Nation, State and Economy*. New York: New York University Press.

Mises, Ludwig von. ([1927] 1985). *Liberalism*. Irvington-on-Hudson, N.Y: Foundation for Economic Education and Cobden Press.

Moore, Stephen. (1987). "Contracting Out: A Painless Alternative to the Budget Cutter's Knife." In Steve Hanke (ed.), *Prospects for Privatization*. New York: Academy of Political Science: 60–73.

Morgenstern, Oskar. (1979). *National Income Statistics*. San Francisco: Cato Institute.

Morrisson, Christian, and Schneider, Hartmut. (1987). "Economic Policy and Agricultural Performance in Low-Income Countries." *The OECD Observer* (April/May): 4–6.

Morley, Felix. (1959). *Freedom and Federalism*. Chicago: Gateway.

Mosher, Stephen. (1983a). *Broken Earth*. New York: Free Press.

Mosher, Stephen. (1983b). "Why Are Baby Girls Being Killed in China?" *The Wall Street Journal* (July 25): 11.

Muller, Ronald. (1979). "Poverty Is the Product." In George Modelski (ed.), *Transnational Corporations and World Order*. San Francisco, W. H. Freeman: 245–262.

Murray, Charles. (1984). *Losing Ground*. New York: Basic Books.

Mussa, Michael. (1984). "U.S. Macroeconomic Policy and the World Debt Problem." *Cato Journal* (Spring/Summer): 81–96.

Nafziger, Wayne. (1984). *The Economics of Developing Countries*. Belmont, Calif.: Wadsworth.

Niskanen, William. (1973). *Bureaucracy: Servant or Master?* London: Institute of Economic Affairs.

Nordhaus, William. (1974). "Resources as Constraint on Growth?" *American Economic Review* (May): 22–26.

Novak, Michael. (1982). "Why Latin America Is Poor." *The Atlantic Monthly* (March): 66–75.

Nozick, Robert. (1974). *Anarchy, State and Utopia*. New York: Basic Books.

Nutter, Warren. (1983). *Political Economy and Freedom*. Indianapolis: Liberty Press.

Nye, Joseph. (1967). "Corruption and Political Development: A Cost-Benefit Analysis." *The American Political Science Review* (June): 417–427.

O'Connor, James. (1974). *The Corporations and the State*. New York: Harper.

Ohri, Raijni Bonnie. (1987). "The Free Market Works in India." *The Journal of Economic Growth* (Vol. 2, No. 2): 40–46.

Olson, Mancur. (1977). *The Logic of Collective Action*. Cambridge, Mass.: Harvard University Press.

Olson, Mancur. (1982). *The Rise and Decline of Nations*. New Haven, Conn.: Yale University Press.

Olson, Mancur. (1987). "Diseconomies of Scale and Development." *Cato Journal* (Spring/Summer): 77–97.

Opel, John. (1987). "Technology and the Wealth of Nations." *Society* (September/October): 51–54.

Oppenheimer, Franz. ([1914] 1975). *The State*. New York: Free Life.

Osterfeld, David. (1980). "Government, the Market and the Poor." *The Freeman* (November): 643–659.

Osterfeld, David. (1984). "The Increasing Abundance of Resources." *The Freeman* (June): 360–377.

Osterfeld, David. (1985). "Famine in Africa." *Journal of Social, Political and Economic Studies* (Fall): 259–274.

Osterfeld, David. (1986). *Freedom, Society and the State*. San Francisco: Cobden Press.

Osterfeld, David. (1987a). "Finally, Good News from Africa." *Seymour* (Indiana) *Tribune* (September 24).

Osterfeld, David. (1987b). "Voluntary and Coercive Cartels: The Case of Oil." *The Freeman* (November): 415–425.

Osterfeld, David. (1988a). "Africa and the Difference Between Growing Food and Eating It." *The Freeman* (May): 190–197.

Osterfeld, David. (1988b). "Caste and Class: The Rothbardian View of Governments and Markets." In Walter Block and Llewellyn Rockwell (eds.), *Man, Economy and Liberty*. Auburn. Ala.: Mises Institute: 283–328.

Osterfeld, David. (1988c). "Taxation, Elites and Poverty in the 'Third World'." Paper presented at the Mises Institute Conference on "Taxation: An Austrian Viewpoint," Washington, D.C. (April).

Osterfeld, David. (1989a). "Radical Federalism: Responsiveness, Conflict and Efficiency." In Geoffrey Brennan and Loren Lomasky (eds.), *Politics and Process: New Essays in Democratic Thought*. New York. Cambridge University Press: 149–173.

Osterfeld, David. (1989b). "Resource Depletion and Third World Development: Is the West Guilty?" *Economic Affairs* (June/July): 11–14.

Osterfeld, David. (1989c). "The Three Worlds of Economic Growth and Development." *The Mid-Atlantic Journal of Business* (Febuary): 29–44.

Ottoway, David. (1985). "Foreign Aid Largely a Failure, U.S. Report Says." *The Washington Post* (February 21): A5.

Ovchinnikov, Yuri. (1985). "Seeds of Plenty: The Promise of Biotechnology." In Robert Jackson (ed.), *Global Issues 85/86*. Guilford, Conn.: Dushkin: 110–112.

Overholt, William. (1986). "The Rise and Fall of Ferdinand Marcos." *Asian Survey* (November): 1137–1163.

Pack, Howard. (1981). "Appropriate Industrial Technology: Benefits and Obstacles." *The Annals of the American Academy of Political and Social Science* (November): 27–40.

Page, Clarence. (1990). "Can We Rent a Social Conscience?" *Chicago Tibune* (March 11): Sect. 4, p. 3.

Palmberg, Mai. (1986). "Colonialism Made Africa Poor and Dependent." In Janelle Rohr (ed.), *Problems of Africa*. St. Paul, Minn.: Greenhaven: 17–23.

Palmer, R. R., and Colton, Joel. (1978). *A History of the Modern World to 1815*. New York: Alfred Knopf.

Palmer, Tom. (1990). "Why Socialism Collapsed in Eastern Europe." *Cato Policy Report* (September/October): 6–7,13.

Park, Charles. (1968). *Affluence in Jeopardy*. San Francisco: Freeman, Cooper.

Perlman, Lewis. (1976). *The Global Mind*. New York: Mason/Charter.

Peterson, John. (1957). "Employment Effects of Minimum Wages, 1938–1950." *Journal of Political Economy* (October): 412–430.

Phaup, Dwight E., and Lewis, Bradley. (1985). "Winners and Losers: Differentiating between High-Growth and Low-Growth LDCs." In Doug Bandow (ed.), *U.S. Aid to the Developing World*. Washington D.C.: Heritage Foundation: 75–92.

Pohlman, Edward. (1973). "A Chorus of Concern." In Edward Pohlman (ed.), *Population: A Clash of Prophets*. New York: Mentor: 8–11.

Polanyi, Michael. (1960). "Towards a Theory of Conspicuous Production." *Soviet Survey* (October-December): 90–110.

Polgar, Steven. (1972). "Population History and Population Policies from an Anthropological Perspective." *Current Anthropology* (April): 203–213.

Poole, Robert. (1987). "The Political Obstacles to Privatization." In Steve Hanke (ed.), *Privatization and Development*. San Francisco: International Center for Economic Growth: 33–46.

Popkin, Samuel. (1979). *The Rational Peasant*. Berkeley, Calif.: University of California Press.

Popper, Karl. (1971). *The Open Society and Its Enemies*. Vol. 1, *The Spell of Plato*. Princeton, N.J.: Princeton University Press.

Pray, Carl. (1981). "The Green Revolution: A Case Study in Transfer of Technology." *Annals of the American Academy of Political and Social Science* (November): 68–80.

Prychitko, David. (1987), "Modernizing Markets in Post-Mao China." *Journal of Economic Growth* (Vol. 2, No. 3): 31–42.

Rabushka, Alvin. (1987a). *The New China: Comparative Economic Development in Mainland China, Taiwan and Hong Kong*. Boulder, Colo.: Westview Press.

Rabushka, Alvin. (1987b). "Taxation, Economic Growth and Liberty." *Cato Journal* (Spring/Summer): 121–148.

Radosh, Ronald, and Rothbard, Murray (eds.). (1992). *A New History of Leviathan*. New York: E. P. Dutton.

Ranis, Gustav. (1976). "The Multinational Corporation as an Instrument of Development." In David Apter and Louis Goodman (eds.), *The Multinational Corporation and Social Change*. New York: Praeger: 96–117.

Ranis, Gustav. (1981). "Technology Choice and the Distribution of Income." *Annals of the American Academy of Political and Social Science* (November): 41–53.

Rashid, Salim. (1981). "Public Utilities in Egalitarian LCDs: The Role of Bribery in Achieving Pareto Efficiency." *Kyklos* (Vol. 34): 448–460.

Ray, G. F. (1987). "The Decline of Primary Producer Power." *National Institute Economic Review* (August): 40–45.

Ravenhill, John. (1986). "Collective Self-Reliance or Collective Self-Delusion: Is the Lagos Plan a Viable Alternative?" In John Ravenhill (ed.), *Africa in Economic Crisis*. New York: Columbia: 85–107.

Revelle, Roger. (1976). "The Resources Available for Agriculture." *Scientific American* (September): 164–179.

Revelle, Roger. (1984). "The World Supply of Agricultural Land." In Julian Simon and Herman Kahn (eds.), *The Resourceful Earth*. New York: Basil Blackwell: 184–201.

Richardson, Richard, and Ahmed, Osman. (1987). "Challenge for Africa's Private Sector." *Challenge* (January/February): 16–25.

Richman, Sheldon. (1981). "War Communism to NEP: The Road from Serfdom." *The Journal of Libertarian Studies* (Winter): 89–98.

Richman, Sheldon. (1982). "Multinationals: Peacemakers or Exploiters?" *Reason* (December): 18–22.

Ridker, Ronald, and Cecelski, Elizabeth. (1982). "Resources and Population." In John Ross (ed.), *International Encyclopedia of Population*. New York: Free Press: 590–600.

Ritter, Malcom. (1984). "Biotechnology Breaking the 'Species Barrier'." *Chicago Tribune* (August 5): Section 6, pp. 1–2.

Roberts, Paul Craig. (1971). *Alienation and the Soviet Economy*. Albuquerque, N.M.: University of New Mexico Press.

Roberts, Paul Craig. (1985). "Does Third World Aid Do More Harm Than Good?" *Business Week* (April 8): 22.

Roberts, Paul Craig, and LaFollette, Karen. (1990). *Meltdown: Inside the Soviet Economy*. Washington, D.C.: Cato Institute.

Roberts, Paul Craig, and Stephenson, Matthew. (1973). *Marx's Theory of Exchange, Alienation and Crisis*. Stanford, Calif.: Hoover Institution Press.

Rosenberg, Nathan, and Birdzell, L. F. (1986). *How the West Grew Rich*. New York: Basic.

Rothbard, Murray. (1951). "Praxeology: Reply to Mr. Schuller." *American Economic Review* (December): 943–946.

Rothbard, Murray. (1956). "Toward a Reconstruction of Utility and Welfare Economics." In Mary Sennholz (ed.), *On Freedom and Free Enterprise*. Princeton, N.J.: Van Nostrand: 67–102.

Rothbard, Murray. (1963). *America's Great Depression*. Princeton, N.J.: Van Nostrand.

Rothbard, Murray. (1970a). *Man, Economy and State*. Los Angeles: Nash.

Rothbard, Murray. (1970b). *Power and Market*. Menlo Park, Calif.: Institute for Humane Studies.

Rothbard, Murray. (1973). "Praxeology as the Method of Economics." In Maurice Natanson (ed.), *Phenomenology and the Social Sciences*. Evanston, Ill.: Northwestern University Press: Vol. II, pp. 311–339.

Rydenfelt, Sven. (1983). *A Pattern for Failure*. New York: Harcourt, Brace, Jovanovich.

Sacerdoti, Guy. (1983). "Favouritism Still in Favor." *Far Eastern Economic Review* (June 30): 50–51.

Samuels, Barbara. (1990). *Managing Risk in Developing Countries*. Princeton, N.J.: Princeton University Press.

Schmidt, Wilson. (1983). "The Role of Private Capital in Developing the Third World." In Scott Thompson (ed.), *The Third World*. San Francisco: ICS: 267–283.

Schultz, Paul. (1976). "Determinants of Fertility: A Micro-economic Model of Choice." In Ansley Coale (ed.), *Economic Factors in Population Growth*. New York: John Wiley: 89–124.

Schumpeter, Joseph. (1954). *A History of Economic Analysis*. New York: Oxford University Press.

Scully, Gerald. (1988). "Liberty and Economic Progress." *Journal of Economic Growth* (November): 3–9.

Sennholz, Hans. (1984). *The Underground Economy*. Auburn, Ala.: The Ludwig von Mises Institute.

Shepard, Jack. (1975). *The Politics of Starvation*. New York: Carnegie Endowment for International Peace.

Shipler, David. (1989). *Russia*. New York: Penguin.

Shirer, William. (1965). *The Rise and Fall of the Third Reich*. Greenwich, Conn.: Fawcett.

Simis, Konstantin. (1982). *USSR: The Corrupt Society*. New York: Simon and Schuster.

Simon, Julian. (1981a). "Global Confusion, 1980: A Hard Look at the *Global 2000 Report*." *The Public Interest* (Winter): 3–20.

Simon, Julian. (1981b). *The Ultimate Resource*. Princeton, N.J.: Princeton University Press.

Simon, Julian. (1982). "The Overall Effect of Immigrants on Native' Incomes." In Barry Chiswick (ed.), *The Gateway*. Washington D.C.: American Enterprise Institute: 314–348.

Simon, Julian, and Kahn, Herman. (1984). "Introduction." In Julian Simon and Herman Kahn (eds.), *The Resourceful Earth*. New York: Basil Blackwell: 1–49.

Simon, Julian. (1986a). *Theory of Population and Economic Growth*. New York: Basil Blackwell.

Simon, Julian. (1986b). "What about Immigration?" *The Freeman* (January): 8–16.

Simon, Julian. (1990). *Population Matters*. New Brunswick, N.J.: Transaction.

Sinclair, Ward. (1986). "The World Isn't Dying for American Farm Products Anymore." *The Washington Post National Weekly Edition* (January 13): 23–26.

Singer, S. F. (1973). "Is There an Optimum Level of Population?" In Edward Pohlman (ed.), *Population: A Clash of Prophets*. New York: Mentor: 201–203.

Smiley, Xan. (1982). "Misunderstanding Africa." *The Atlantic Monthly* (September): 70–79.

Smith, Adam. ([1776] 1937). *The Wealth of Nations*. New York: Modern Library.

Smith, Adam. ([1759] 1969). *The Theory of Moral Sentiments*. New Rochelle, N.Y.: Arlington House.

Smith, Hedrick. (1984). *The Russians*. New York: Ballantine.

Solow, Robert. (1974). "The Economics of Resources or the Resources of Economics." *American Economic Review* (May): 1–14.

Solzhenitsyn, Aleksandr. (1973). *The Gulag Archipelago*. New York: Harper and Row.

de Soto, Hernando. (1988). "Constraints on People: The Origins of Underground Economies and Limits to Their Growth." In Jerry Jenkins (ed.), *Beyond the Informal Sector*. San Francisco: ICS Press: 15–47.

de Soto, Hernando. (1989). *The Other Path*. New York: Harper and Row.

Sowell, Thomas. (1980). *Knowledge and Decisions*. New York: Basic Books.

Sowell, Thomas. (1981a). "Culture—Not Discrimination— Decides Who Gets Ahead." *U.S. News and World Report* (October 12): 74–75.

Sowell, Thomas. (1981b). *Ethnic America*. New York: Basic Books.

Sowell, Thomas. (1981c). *Markets and Minorities*. New York: Basic Books.

Sowell, Thomas. (1983). *The Economics and Politics of Race*. New York: William Morrow.

Spanier, John. (1981). *Games Nations Play*. New York: Holt, Rinehart and Winston.

Spero, Joan Edleman. (1984). "Managing the Multinational Corporation." In Stephen Speigel (ed.), *At Issue: Politics in the World Arena*. New York: St. Martin's: 463–489.

Spero, Joan Edleman. (1985). *The Politics of International Economic Relations*. New York: St. Martin's.

Stacy, Palmer, and Lutton, Wayne. (1985). "The U.S. Immigration Crisis." *Journal of Social, Political and Economic Studies* (Fall): 333–350.

Starr, Paul. (1987). "The Limits of Privatization." In Steve Hanke (ed.), *Prospects for Privatization*. New York: Academy of Political Science: 124–137.

Steele, David Ramsay. (1981). "The Failure of Bolshevism and Its Aftermath." *The Journal of Libertarian Studies* (Winter): 99–111.

Suau, Anthony. (1985). "Region in Rebellion: Eritrea." *National Geographic* (September): 394–405.

Swomley, John. (1970). *American Empire*. New York: MacMillan.

Talmon, J. L. (1970). *The Origins of Totalitarian Democracy*. New York: Norton.

Tanoira, Manuel. (1987). "Privatization as Politics." In Steve Hanke (ed.), *Privatization and Development*. San Francisco: International Center for Economic Growth: 53–64.

Tendler, Judith. (1977). *Inside Foreign Aid*. Baltimore: Johns Hopkins University Press.

Thompson, Scott. (1983). "The Third World Reconsidered." In Scott Thompson (ed.), *The Third World*. San Francisco: ICS Press: 3–17.

Thompson, W. S., and Lewis, D. T. (1965). *Population Problems*. New York: McGraw-Hill.

Tiebout, Charles. (1956). "A Pure Theory of Local Expenditures." *The Journal of Political Economy* (October): 416–424.

Tierney, John. (1990). "Betting the Planet." *New York Times Magazine* (December 2): 52–53, 74–81.

Time. (1984). "A Continent Gone Wrong." (January 16): 26–39.

Todaro, Michael. (1976). "Rural-Urban Migration: Unemployment and Job Probabilities: Recent Theoretical and Empirical Research." In Ansley Coale (ed.), *Economic Factors in Population Growth*. New York: John Wiley: 367–385.

Todaro, Michael. (1981). *Economic Development in the Third World*. New York: Longman.

Treadgold, Donald. (1964). *Twentieth Century Russia*. Chicago: Rand-McNally.

Tullock, Gordon. (1969). "Federalism: Problems of Scale." *Public Choice* (Spring): 19–29.

Tullock, Gordon. (1972). *Toward a Mathematics of Politics*. Ann Arbor, Mich.: University of Michigan Press.

Tullock, Gordon. (1974). "Corruption and Anarchy." In Gordon Tullock (ed.), *Further Explorations in the Theory of Anarchy*. Blacksburg, Va.: University Publications: 65–70.

Tullock, Gordon. (1987). *Autocracy*. Boston: Kluwer.

United Nations. (1979). "Report of the Group of Eminent Persons to Study the Impact of Multinational Corporations on Development and on International Relations." In George Modelski (ed.), *Transnational Corporations and World Order*, San Francisco: W. H. Freeman: 309–32.

United Nations. (1981). *World Statistics in Brief*. New York: United Nations.

U.N. Center on Transnational Corporations. (1985). *Trends and Issues in Foreign Direct Investment and Related Flows*. New York: United Nations.

U.N. Food and Agriculture Organization. (1977). *The Fourth World Food Survey*. Rome: United Nations.

U.S. Agency for International Development. (1989). *Development and the National Interest*. Washington, D.C.: Government Printing Office.

U.S. Bureau of the Census. (1975). *Historical Statistics of the U.S.: Colonial Times to 1970*. Washington D.C.: Government Printing Office.

U.S. Bureau of Mines. (1975, 1980, 1985). *Mineral Facts and Problems*. Washington, D.C.: Government Printing Office.

U.S. Council on Environmental Quality. (1982). *The Global 2000 Report to the President*. New York: Penguin.

U.S. Department of Agriculture. (1987). *Agricultural Statistics*. Washington, D.C.: Government Printing Office.

U.S. Department of Commerce. (Various years). *Statistical Abstract of the United States*. Washington, D.C.: Government Printing Office.

U.S. Department of Energy. (1983). *Annual Energy Review*. Washington D.C.: Government Printing Office.

U.S. Department of the Interior. (1988). *Mineral Yearbook*. Vol. 1, *Metals and Minerals*. Washington D.C.: Government Printing Office.

U.S. Department of State. (1984). *Food Production: The Success of the International Agricultural Research Centers*. (January 4).

U.S. Department of State. (1985). *Potential for Expanding World Food Production by Region and Country*. (October 15).

U.S. National Resources Committee. (1973). "Report of the Committee on Population Problems." In Edward Pohlman (ed.), *Population: A Clash of Prophets*. New York: Mentor: 7–8.

U.S. News and World Report. (1986). "China Now, Ten Years after Mao." (September 8): 26–32.

U.S. News and World Report. (1990). "Death of a Nation." (November 10): 34–39.

U.S. Senate, Subcommittee on Internal Security. (1977). *The Human Cost of Communism in China*. Washington, D.C.: ACU Education and Research Institute.

U.S. Senate, Subcommittee on Multinational Corporations. (1979). "The International Telephone and Telegraph Company and Chile, 1970–71." In George Modelski (ed.), *Transnational Corporations and World Order*, San Francisco: W. H. Freeman: 226–244.

University of the Philippines, School of Economics. (1984). *The Philippine Economic Crisis: A Workshop Report*. Manila, mimeo (June).

Utt, Ronald, and Orzechowski, William. (1985). "International Perspectives on Economic Growth." *Cato Policy Report* (July/August): 1, 11–15.

Van Buren, Abigail. (1989). "Too Many Competing for Limited Resources." *Rensselaer (Indiana) Republican* (May 16): 3.

Vargas Llosa, Mario. (1987). "In Defense of the Black Market." *New York Times Magazine* (February 22): 28–30, 42–47.

Vaughan, James. (1977). "Social and Political Organization in Traditional Societies." In Phyllis Martin and Patrick O'Meara (eds.), *Africa*. Bloomington, Ind.: Indiana University Press: 169–188.

Vaughn, Karen. (1980). "Economic Calculation under Socialism: The Austrian Contribution." *Economic Inquiry* (October): 535–554.

Vernon, Raymond. (1977). *Storm over the Multinationals*. Cambridge, Mass.: Harvard University Press.

Vernon, Raymond. (1979). "The Product Cycle Model." In George Modelski (ed.), *Transnational Corporations and World Order*. San Francisco: W. H. Freeman: 108–117.

Villegas, Bernando. (1986). "The Philippines in 1985." *Asian Survey* (February): 127–140.

Vorontsov, Yuli. (1986). "Western Capitalism Has Prevented Africa's Development." In Janelle Rohr (ed.), *Problems of Africa*. St. Paul, Minn.: Greenhaven: 72–77.

Walters, A. A. (1987). "Ownership and Efficiency in Urban Buses." In Steve Hanke (ed.), *Prospects for Privatization,* New York: Academy of Political Science: 83–92.

Waters, Alan. (1987). "Economic Growth and the Property Rights Regime." *Cato Journal* (Spring/Summer): 99–115.

Watson, Richard, and Smith, Philip. (1973). "The Limit: 500 Million." In Edward Pohlman (ed.), *Population: A Clash of Prophets*. New York: Mentor: 193–200.

Wattenberg, Ben. (1984). *The Good News Is That the Bad News Is Wrong*. New York: Simon and Schuster.

Wattenberg, Ben, and Zinsmeister, Karl (eds.). (1986). *Are World Population Trends a Problem?* Washington, D.C.: American Enterprise Institute.

Weigel, Dale. (1988). "Investment in the LDCs: The Debate Continues." *Columbia Journal of World Business* (Spring): 5–9.

West, Robert, and Augelli, John. (1976). *Middle America*. Englewood Cliffs, N.J.: Prentice-Hall.

Whitehead, John C. (1987). "Third World Dilemma: More Debt or More Equity?" Address to the Council on Foreign Relations, New York City. Washington, D.C.: Department of State (October 21).

Williams, Walter. (1977). *Youth and Minority Unemployment*. Stanford, Calif.: Hoover Institution Press.

Williamson, Oliver. (1981). "The Modern Corporation: Origins, Evolution and Attributes." *Journal of Economic Literature* (December): 1537–1568.

Wise, John. (1984). "The Future of Food from the Sea." In Julian Simon and Herman Kahn (eds.), *The Resourceful Earth*. New York: Basil Blackwell: 113–127.

Wolf, Edward. (1986). *Beyond the Green Revolution: New Approaches for Third World Agriculture*. Washington, D.C.: Worldwatch.

World Bank. (Various years). *World Development Report*. New York: Oxford University Press.

World Resources Institute. (1986). *World Resources 1986*. New York: Basic Books.

World Resources Institute. (1987). *World Resources 1987*. New York: Basic Books.

Young, Peter. (1987). "Privatization around the World." In Steve Hanke (ed.), *Prospects for Privatization*. New York: Academy of Political Science: 190–206.

Zafanolli, Wojtek. (1985). "A Brief Outline of China's Second Economy." *Asian Survey* (July): 715–736.

Zinsmeister, Karl. (1987). "Free Markets and Population: Turning Problems into Assets." *Journal of Economic Growth* (First Quarter): 18–25.

Zinsmeister, Karl. (1988). "All the Hungry People." *Reason* (June): 22–30.

Index